Design for All
The Best Path Forward

Dr. Arvid E. Osterberg

Culicidae Architectural Press
an imprint of Culicidae Press
PO Box 5069
Madison, WI 53705-5069
culicidaearchitecturalpress.com
editor@culicidaepress.com

DESIGN FOR ALL — THE BEST PATH FORWARD
Copyright © 2025 by Dr. Arvid E. Osterberg.
All rights reserved.
No part of this book may be reproduced in any form by electronic or mechanized means (including photocopying, recording, or information storage and retrieval) without written permission, except in the case of brief quotations embodied in critical articles and reviews.

ISBN: 978-1-68315-138-8

Our books may be purchased in bulk for promotional, educational or business use. Please contact your local bookseller or the Culicidae Press Sales Department at +1-352-215-7558 or email sales@culicidaepress.com

culicidaepress.bsky.social
facebook.com/culicidaepress
threads.net/@culicidaepress
x.com/culicidaepress
instagram.com/culicidaepress

Editors
Arvid Osterberg and Mikesch Muecke
(editing of previous editions of *Access for Everyone* by Donna J. Kain, Christianna I. White, Misty L. Holmes, and TaeJung Kim

Illustrations
Savannah Cirksena
(based on previous illustrations in *Access for Everyone* by Steven J. Wailes, John Den Boer, and TaeJung Kim

Design, Cover Design, and Layout
Arvid Osterberg and Mikesch Muecke

Technical Review
Arvid Osterberg

Acknowledgements
My sincere appreciation goes to Culicidae Press and Mikesch Muecke, who's dedication to the project and patience to work with me through hundreds of edits and revisions has been remarkable. My thanks also to Savannah Cirksena for redrawing and adding color and life to the illustrations based on those in previous editions of *Access for Everyone*. I thank Christopher Ahoy, former Associate Vice-President for Facilities, and Dean Morton, former University Architect, for their dedication of support to the earlier editions. I also thank the students who assisted in the production earlier editions of *Access for Everyone*, including Donna Kain, Deborah Huelsbergen, Tom Elder, Venina Tandela, Eric Anderson, and Xiaomu Yang and to many faculty and staff at ISU for their support and encouragement, especially Dan Sloan University Architect, and Wes Gee, Architect, both at Facilities, Planning and Management. And finally I sincerely thank my wife Gayle for her consistent and unwavering support as I struggled through multiple drafts and revisions of the manuscript.

Dedication
Design for All is dedicated to all those (young, old, timid, and bold) who struggle to safely navigate buildings and sites.

Table of Contents

Acknowledgements — 2
Dedication — 2
About this Publication — 5
Preface — 7
Introduction — 8

Section 1.
Accessible Routes and Spaces — 19

- RR Reach Ranges — 21
- PA Parking — 26
- CR Curb Ramps — 36
- RT Routes & Spaces — 44
- RP Ramps — 65
- EN Entrances — 72
- DR Doors — 76
- EL Elevators — 93
- PL Platform Lifts — 106
- ST Stairs — 110

Section 2.
Alarms, Safety Areas, and Signs — 119

- AL Alarms — 120
- EG Egress — 122
- AR Areas of Refuge — 125
- SN Signs — 129

Section 3.
Restrooms and Bathrooms — 139

- TS Toilet Stalls — 150
- UR Urinals — 159
- FX Fixtures — 160
- SS Shower Stalls — 167
- SE Tub/Shower Seats — 173
- BT Bathtubs — 175
- GB Grab Bars — 179

Section 4.
Equipment, Tables, and Seating — 183

- DF Drinking Fountains — 184
- PT Public Telephones — 187
- TA Tables & Seating — 191
- VS Vending/Self-serve — 196

Section 5.
Specific Use Areas — 203

- HP Historic Preservation — 204
- WA Work Areas — 208
- AA Assembly Areas — 210
- LB Libraries — 216
- RS Restaurants — 219
- BU Businesses — 222
- DS Dressing Rooms — 228
- TL Transient Lodging — 230
- DU Dwelling Units — 235
- Wheelchair Accessible Units — 237
- MC Medical Care — 241
- KT Kitchens — 244
- SG Storage — 247
- AB ABA Requirements — 249

Websites — 251
List of Figures — 252
Index — 256

(previous editions of ***Access for Everyone*** reviewed by Donna J. Kain, Steven J. Wailes, and Eric Vermeer)

About this Publication

Design for All – The Best Path Forward is a user friendly guide intended for planning and design professionals, building code officials, educators, and individuals interested in providing designs that work well for all people. The book was written to help everyone who advocates accommodating the needs of all people to the maximum extent possible in designing, constructing, and maintaining safe and accessible buildings and sites. The author presents safety and accessibility issues and solutions in a format that is easy to understand, quick to grasp, and accurate.

Whether you are a design professional evaluating accessibility for a multi-million dollar project, a small business owner remodeling a store or office, or a citizen advocating increasing accessibility, *Design for All* is a resource companion to existing standards and technical materials.

Included are references to the Americans with Disabilities Act Accessibility Standards (the ADA Standards). However, conceiving and creating accessible environments involves more than just meeting minimum accessibility requirements. Therefore, *Design for All* also includes hundreds of the author's recommendations that go beyond minimum standards for constructing environments that work well for all people, regardless of variations in ability. Minimum requirements and recommendations are in the form of clear directives that are supplemented by realistic illustrations, and informative photographs.

The Evolution of *Design for All*

Design for All represents a culmination of thinking about accessibility issues that have evolved over the author's 50 plus year career as an architect, researcher, and university professor.

As an undergraduate student in the mid 1960s he was discouraged to see wood ramps added to service entrances of classroom buildings to achieve wheelchair access.

As a professor at Iowa State University (ISU) he conducted research and developed courses emphasizing better designs for older people and those with physical and cognitive limitations.

As an advocate for innovative design solutions on campus he completed accessibility reviews with recommendations for hundreds of capital projects, including new buildings, additions, remodeling, and site improvements.

In the early 1990s, after the ADA was signed into law, the author co-directed and managed Iowa State University's (ISU) campus wide ADA assessment. The comprehensive assessment including parking lots, exterior and interior routes, entrances, doors, restrooms, classrooms, lecture halls, and other spaces to identify features and details that complied with the ADA Standards, and those that did not. Teams of students with clipboards and tape measures canvased the campus with a small print version of the 1994 ADA Standards in their back pockets. The assessment took several years as the campus was analyzed in detail, including more than 85 major buildings, sites, and university housing.

To enhance the assessment the author began rewriting the standards 'in plain simple language' and redrawing illustrations to make them clearer. With the support of ISU's Facility Planning and Management and the assistance of Donna Kain, who was completing a PhD. in Rhetoric and Communication at the time, the team extensively researched accessibility issues, government documents and other sources to fully understand dimensional requirements, accessibility issues and the needs of users.

This resulted in the 2001 edition of *Access for Everyone*. The book was revised in 2005 and was extensively revised and expanded again in 2010. *Design for All* builds on those earlier editions of *Access for Everyone*.

Important Notice

Design for All provides basic information about building and site accessibility. The author and contributors have made every effort to accurately represent the most current requirements of (the ADA Standards) and to provide references to them for your convenience. However, the information in *Design for All* is not a legal interpretation of any government statute or requirement and the most current governmental ADA publications should be consulted and used in conjunction with ***Design for All*** to ensure accurate interpretation of the ADA Standards.

For additional information and technical assistance, contact the Access Board, the Department of Justice (DOJ), and other government agencies. See References. Also consult state and local building and life safety codes, ordinances, and laws that affect the design, construction, and alterations of buildings and sites.

Individual pages of ***Design for All*** may be photocopied for private use. No part of this document may be reproduced for sale or other commercial purposes without written permission.

Preface

Design for All is thoughtful design that takes into consideration the needs of all users. It results in building and site features that are uncomplicated, intuitive, and easy-to-use. This includes routes and spaces that are simple-to-navigate, well maintained, and free of hazards. It also includes having items within reach range that easy-to-grasp. Thoughtful design features often go unnoticed, but they stand the test of time and make life easier for all of us.

Design for All is design for everyone, including those with mobility restrictions, visual limitations, auditory limitations, cognitive issues, chronic pain, muscular and/or nervous system problems, balance problems, and other issues. People often experience multiple issues that combine to make navigating the environment more challenging. A significant number of people have vision limitations or low vision. Vision impairments result from Cataracts, Glaucoma, Macular Degeneration, Diabetic Retinopathy, and other conditions. The number of individuals with low vision increases every year as the population continues to age.

People with low vision often have a reduced ability to perceive low contrast and some colors. They frequently have difficulty with depth perception and sensitivity to glare and shadows. A large percentage of people, including young children and older adults, typically need more and better lighting to identify and avoid hazards, and more time for their eyes to adjust when entering low light, or dark interior spaces.

Designers can respond to the needs of visually impaired individuals by providing adequate natural and artificial lighting, reducing glare and reflections, and avoiding confusing geometries and busy floor patterns. Interior spaces and lighting systems need to be designed with transition spaces in consideration of the time it takes people's vision to adapt from bright exterior spaces to dark interior spaces.

Design for All contains over 1200 references to the 2010 Americans with Disabilities Act Accessible Standards (ADASAD) requirements including:

- 700 + references to requirements that have not changed from the original ADA Accessibility Guidelines (ADAAG)
- 400 + references to 2010 ADASAD requirements that were not in the original ADAAG
- 30 + references to requirements that are more restrictive in the 2010 ADASAD than they were in the original ADAAG
- 30 + references to requirements that are less restrictive in the 2010 ADASAD than they were in the original ADAAG
- approximately 700 recommendations and recommended dimensions by Arvid Osterberg for improving accessibility and safety that are not in the ADA Standards

The publication also includes 56 photographs, 15 charts, and 183 drawings.

To assist the reader in understanding the origin of requirements and recommendations, statements throughout the book are referenced. Refer to page 15 for an explanation of the referencing system.

Introduction

Americans with Disabilities Act Overview	8
Title II Overview	8
New Construction and Alterations under Title II	9
Existing Buildings and Sites under Title II	9
Title III Overview	9
Entities Covered under Title III	9
Construction and Alterations under Title III	10
Existing Buildings under Title III	11
Americans with Disabilities Act Accessibility Standards Overview	11
Complying with ADA Standards	11
The Concept of Disability	12
Why the Emphasis on Wheelchairs?	12
Why *Design for All* is Needed	13
Why Following the ADA Standards is Not Enough	13
Better Designs Can Increase Safety and Reduce the Number of Falls	13
Other Resources	13
Note	14
Using *Design for All*	14
Finding Information	14
Using *Design for All* as a Notation System	14
Referencing Key	15
Understanding the Conventions Used in *Design for All*	15
Figures	16

Welcome to Design for All - The Best Path Forward, referred to hereafter as Design for All, the book will help you

- Understand the design needs of all people, including people with disabilities
- Understand the basic requirements of ADA Standards
- Understand recommended dimensions that are based on *Design for All* concepts
- Identify features of buildings and sites that need to be analyzed for accessibility
- Decide what actions need to be taken to make new and existing buildings and sites accessible to all people

Design for All can be used to evaluate plans, buildings, and sites to determine whether they are accessible. To provide the most current ideas and information about accessibility, the author references the Americans with Disabilities Act Standards for Accessible Design, commonly referred to as the ADA Standards. Throughout *Design for All*, references to the ADA Standards are included for your convenience.

The ADA Standards addresses buildings and sites covered under both the ADA and the Architectural Barriers Act (ABA). The specific guidelines for spaces and elements of buildings, facilities, and sites covered under the ADA and ABA are the same. However, scoping requirements for the ADA and the ABA contain some differences. *Design for All* focuses throughout on ADA scoping requirements. Scoping for the ABA is in the **Specific Use Areas** section. **See chapter AB (ABA Requirements, page 249).**

Americans with Disabilities Act Overview

The Americans with Disabilities Act (ADA) of 1990 is a civil rights law that protects people against discrimination on the basis of physical and mental disabilities. The ADA is important because approximately 20% of all American people, about 55 million of us, have some type of disability that affects daily life (U.S. Census Bureau, 2000).

The ADA mandates policies, procedures, and practices that provide equitable access for all people to jobs, buildings, services, transportation, and other aspects of everyday life. The ADA has five titles that include information pertaining to employment and the accessibility of programs, services, transportation, and buildings and sites.

Design for All specifically focuses on building and site accessibility requirements that may pertain to entities covered under Title II and Title III. The entities covered under Title II and Title III have different responsibilities for ensuring accessibility of buildings and sites. While the author provides a brief overview of Title II and Title III, you should consult Title II and Title III of the ADA, or refer to additional resources detailing these titles, to determine your status and responsibilities under the ADA.

Title II Overview

Title II of the ADA covers public entities, including state and local governments and all related activities, services, and programs. Federal entities are covered under other regulations, primarily Section 504 of the Rehabilitation Act of 1973.

Title II includes provisions that protect people with disabilities from discrimination in all public services, programs, or activities. Examples include, but are not limited to, public meetings and meeting places, voting activities and polling places, and state or local government-sponsored recreational and educational programs.

The ADA applies a standard to entities covered under Title II called program accessibility that requires programs, activities, and services to be readily accessible to and usable by individuals with disabilities. Even in areas where no individuals with disabilities currently use programs covered under Title II, the programs must meet the accessibility standard.

The most effective, long-term solutions include altering existing buildings to be accessible or designing and constructing new, accessible buildings. Improving accessibility for existing buildings and sites is on-going obligation under the ADA.

New Construction and Alterations under Title II

Buildings and sites that are designed, constructed, or altered by or for the use of public entities after January 26, 1992, must be readily accessible to and usable by people with disabilities. "Readily accessible to and usable by" under Title II means that buildings and sites must be designed, constructed, or altered in strict compliance with either the original ADAAG standards or, beginning March 15, 2012, the 2010 ADA Standards.

Once a standard is chosen, it must be used consistently for all subsequent construction, alteration, or barrier removal throughout the project. Also, all areas and elements of any additions to buildings that can be made accessible must be made accessible.

Existing Buildings and Sites under Title II

Access to and participation in programs covered by Title II cannot be denied to people with disabilities because buildings and sites are inaccessible. However, public entities are not required to make all areas in all existing buildings and sites accessible.

Program accessibility may be achieved through various methods, including moving program activities or providing services at alternate, accessible sites; providing equipment appropriate for people with disabilities; or providing personal assistance to people with disabilities.

Public entities covered under Title II are only required to remove barriers from existing buildings and sites when there is no other feasible solution for achieving program accessibility. However, Title II entities are expected to implement improvements over time and work towards having all facilities meet or exceed the ADA Standards.

Title III Overview

The provisions in Title III help to ensure that people with disabilities are able to participate in the "full and equal enjoyment of the goods, services, facilities, privileges, advantages, or accommodations" offered by places of public accommodation. People with disabilities must have equal opportunities to participate, equal opportunities to benefit, and they must receive services in the most integrated setting possible.

Entities Covered under Title III

Title III covers private entities that operate public accommodations in twelve categories (examples provided are not inclusive).

1. Places of lodging (e.g., inns, hotels, motels) except for owner-occupied establishments renting fewer than five rooms
2. Establishments serving food or drink (e.g., restaurants and bars)
3. Places of exhibition or entertainment (e.g., motion picture houses, theaters, concert halls, stadiums)
4. Places of public gathering (e.g., auditoriums, convention centers, lecture halls)
5. Sales or rental establishments (e.g., bakeries, grocery stores, hardware stores, shopping centers)
6. Service establishments (e.g., laundromats, dry-cleaners, banks, barber shops, beauty shops, travel services, shoe repair services, funeral parlors, gas stations, offices of accountants or lawyers, real estate and new home sales offices, pharmacies, insurance offices, professional offices of health care providers, hospitals)

7. Public transportation terminals, depots, or stations (not including facilities relating to air transportation)
8. Places of public display or collection (e.g., museums, libraries, galleries)
9. Places of recreation (e.g., parks, zoos, amusement parks)
10. Places of education (e.g., nursery schools, elementary, secondary, undergraduate, and postgraduate, and private schools)
11. Social service center establishments (e.g., day care centers, senior citizen centers, homeless shelters, food banks, adoption agencies)
12. Places of exercise or recreation (e.g., gymnasiums, health spas, bowling alleys, golf courses)

The goal of Title III is to ensure that people are not discriminated against with regard to accommodations, goods, and services that are part of participating in social and economic life. Title III addresses issues related to equitable provision of goods and services, which include access to the buildings and sites where goods and services are available.

Title III does not include private clubs or churches. However, when certain events that are open to the public are held in private clubs or churches, the individuals or organizations that sponsor those events are required to comply with the ADA. Therefore, groups that desire to provide access to all people should follow the ADA Standards to ensure the inclusion of people with disabilities.

Construction and Alterations under Title III
Buildings and sites that are used for public accommodation or commercial purposes must be readily accessible to and usable by people with disabilities, to the extent that it is not structurally impracticable, if they are first occupied after January 26, 1993, and the last application for a building permit or permit extension is certified as complete after January 26, 1992.

"Readily accessible to and usable by" under Title III means that buildings and sites must be designed and constructed in strict compliance with the Americans with Disabilities Act Standards for Accessible Design (ADA Standards).

"Structurally impracticable" is a very narrow standard applied in special circumstances where the covered entity can show that unique characteristics of the land used for new construction make incorporation of some accessibility features impossible. In the unusual event that structural impracticability prevents full compliance with ADA Standards, buildings and sites must meet the standards as much as possible.

Alterations to buildings and sites covered under Title III that are begun after January 26, 1992, must also meet the accessibility standards to the maximum extent that is technically feasible. Alterations include changes to buildings and sites that affect usability such as remodeling, renovation, rearrangements in structural parts, and changes or rearrangement of walls and full-height partitions.

Limitations based on "technical infeasibility" apply to situations where the nature or structure of the building or site being altered makes it infeasible to comply with all ADA Standards standards. An example might be where full compliance would require removing a load-bearing member that is part of the structural frame of a building.

Where conditions make full compliance with accessibility requirements infeasible, the altered area must be made as accessible as possible. All areas and elements of the alteration that can be made accessible must be made accessible. The cost of meeting accessibility requirements in an alteration is not considered a factor in technical infeasibility.

When alterations are made to a primary function area, which is any area used for a major activity for which the building is intended, the path of travel to that area must also be made accessible. The path of travel includes an accessible route to the altered area and restrooms, telephones, and drinking fountains serving the area. The ADA requires owners to do as much as it takes to make the path of travel as accessible as possible under the ADA Standards, spending up to 20% of the cost of the alteration to the primary function area (as determined by the Department of Justice [DOJ]).

Existing Buildings under Title III

Barriers must be removed from existing buildings and sites of entities that are covered under Title III where barrier removal is readily achievable (without significant difficulty or expense). Barrier removal that is readily achievable must be undertaken even if goods and services can be made accessible through other methods.

Improving accessibility for existing buildings and sites is on-going obligation under the ADA.

Americans with Disabilities Act Accessibility Standards Overview

Design for All focuses on the accessibility standards that apply to all buildings and sites covered under Title II and Title III.

To assist people with responsibility for ensuring the accessibility of buildings and sites, in 1991 the Architectural and Transportation Barriers Compliance Board (Access Board) and the Department of Justice (DOJ) published the *Americans with Disabilities Act Accessibility Guidelines (ADAAG)*.

The ADAAG, which provided the minimum required standards for accessibility enforced by the DOJ, was a comprehensive set of standards for making buildings and sites accessible to people who have disabilities.

A number of supplements were published since 1994 including: Chapter 10, Recreation Facilities and Play Areas; Chapter 11, Judicial, Legislative, and Regulatory Facilities; Chapter 12, Detention and Correctional Facilities; and Children's Requirements (throughout ADAAG).

The *ADAAG* was then substantially revised in 2010 to coordinate with other industry standards and codes, such as the American National Standards Institute (ANSI) Guidelines for accessibility and the International Building Code (IBC). The latest version of the standards (referred to as **ADASAD 2010** throughout *Design for All*), was formally adopted by the DOJ in 2010 and was published it in the Federal Register on September 15, 2010. In their adoption of the new standards, the DOJ changed the name from the Americans with Disabilities Act Accessibility Guidelines (ADAAG) to the Americans with Disabilities Act Standards for Accessible Design (ADASAD, typically referred to as the ADA Standards). Compliance with the 2010 ADA Standards was not required until March 15, 2012 (18 months after being published in the Federal Register). Beginning March 15, 2012, compliance with the 2010 ADA Standards was required for all new construction and alterations (for buildings and sites covered by Title II and Title III of the ADA), and barrier removal (for buildings and sites covered by Title III). In the period between September 15, 2010 and March 15, 2012, covered entities could choose between the 1991 ADAAG and the 2010 ADA Standards. Covered entitles that should have complied with the 1991 ADAAG during any new construction or alteration, but did not do so by March 15, 2012, were required to comply with the 2010 ADA Standards.

The ADA Standards provides extensive and precise information about accessibility requirements. Because of the comprehensiveness and complexity of the ADA Standards, it can be difficult to locate and understand needed information in the guidelines. Though not a substitute for ADA Standards, *Design for All* follows the ADA Standards and includes hundreds of recommendations that go beyond minimum ADA Standards requirements.

Following the recommendations in *Design for All* improves accessibility by enhancing the usability of buildings and sites for all people. Recommendations are highlighted with blue text and the Ca symbol throughout *Design for All*.

The author recommends following the 2010 ADA Standards and all additional recommendations in *Design for All* for new construction, alterations, and barrier removal.

Complying with ADA Standards

The ADA Standards primarily covers buildings and sites in the U.S. that are used by the public (customers, visitors, students, patients, employees, and others), such as schools, medical facilities, restaurants, hotels, and other public places.

All newly designed or constructed buildings and sites completed after 1992 must comply with the

ADA Standards, and although they are referred to as 'standards' they are, in fact, requirements.

The ADA Standards also covers some types of temporary housing, including hotels, motels, dormitories, and other buildings used as transient lodging. If you think you have a building or site that does not need to comply with the ADA Standards, refer to the Department of Justice Codes of Regulation Title 28 Part 36, Nondiscrimination on the Basis of Disability by Public Accommodations and in Commercial Facilities.

Existing buildings, including those that are eligible for historic preservation, must meet ADA requirements or comply with ADA barrier removal requirements. In most cases, when alterations and additions are made to existing buildings, these areas must meet the ADA Standard requirements for new construction.

The ADA Standards recognizes that meeting some requirements in existing buildings is not always structurally feasible; therefore, *Design for All* addresses exceptions and alternatives that are included in ADA Standards.

Design for All includes a chapter that addresses accessibility in buildings that are eligible for historic preservation status. **See HP Historic Preservation, page 204.** Exceptions to accessibility standards may be allowed if an official State Historic Preservation Officer or recognized Advisory Council on Historic Preservation determines that adherence to ADA Standards would threaten or destroy the historic value of the building or site. If you have questions about accessibility requirements in a historic building, contact the appropriate office in your state.

The Concept of Disability
Disability is a complicated term that means different things to different people. Disability is also a troubling term because it implies a standard of ability by which people are measured and perceived to be dis-abled.

Often, the term disability is used to identify people who are blind or deaf or who use wheelchairs and other assistive equipment to manage everyday life. It is important to note, however, that differences in ability include variations in stamina and/or cognitive and physical function that are not immediately apparent. In addition, individuals' abilities vary over their lifespan.

In a real sense, environments, services, and products can be disabling when they are unable to accommodate many different people who have a wide range of abilities and needs. The author advocates for a philosophy of 'design for all people' rather than a focus on accommodation of people's perceived disabilities.

Although many of the illustrations in *Design for All* depict people using wheelchairs, the illustrations must be viewed in the context of many different users' needs and circumstances.

Designs should work well for all people, regardless of variations in ability. This philosophy, known by many as 'universal design', is a more effective solution than design that incorporates 'special' features in buildings for people with disabilities (such as mechanical lifts and ramps). Special design features result in separate and different experiences for many people whereas universal design serves people with different needs without discrimination.

When circumstances in existing environments are such that a different type of access is needed to accommodate persons who have some types of disability, then ADA Standards requires that such access provides the same quality of experience for all people. In addition to providing information on ADA Standards requirements, *Design for All* provides recommendations (indicated with blue text and the ca symbol) for achieving the quality of accessibility suggested by universal design.

Why the Emphasis on Wheelchairs?
The purpose of much of the research that led to the development of ADA Standards has been to determine the minimum dimensional requirements for turning and maneuvering wheelchairs. During the past fifty years however, many types and variations of wheelchairs and electric carts have become commonplace. Therefore the *standard*-sized wheelchair is no longer the only type of wheeled mobility device that should be considered in determining dimensional requirements.

By following the *Design for All* **preferred** dimension and additional recommendations, you will be meeting the needs of people using various types of wheeled mobility devices.

Note: Although wheelchairs are shown in many illustrations throughout *Design for All*, keep in mind that electric carts are more common today than wheelchairs.

Design for All emphasizes the importance of design that meets the needs of all people, regardless of physical, cognitive, or cultural differences. Designers are encouraged to go beyond minimum standards to ensure that designs make it easier for everyone to park, to find your way, to enter buildings, to open doors, to move through doorways, and to use restrooms, assembly areas, and other public spaces. Thoughtful designs often goes unnoticed because they do not include specialized features or adaptations to accommodate people.

Why *Design for All* is Needed

There have always been differences in ability between people, but unfortunately the design of buildings and sites has not always accommodated those differences. All people experience varying abilities throughout their lives and many experience changes in ability from day to day, or throughout the course of a day. People may have intermittingly stiff joints, muscle aches, balance problems, or sinus congestion that can affect their ability to safely navigate buildings and sites. Therefore, it would be better to think beyond designing for wheelchair users, to thinking about designing for a diverse population.

In the 1960s design standards were created to accommodate people using wheelchairs and wooden ramps leading to the back doors and service entrances of buildings became commonplace. But despite the standards major public buildings often had no access at all. When the ADA Standards went into effect in the 1990s, thinking started to evolve beyond the idea of *barrier removal* towards *design-for-all* solutions.

Some features that were once thought to be good design are no longer considered to be. Ramps, for example, can be a form of discrimination that marginalize, stigmatize, or leave out individuals or groups of individuals. That is exactly what the ADA is intended to prevent. A long winding ramp that technically complies with the ADA Standards can be difficult to use for many people, and when wet leaves, snow, or ice cover the surface of a ramp, it becomes more difficult to use and potentially hazardous. Common-sense design solutions that don't call attention to themselves, like grade level entrances, are safer, easier to use, and easier to maintain.

Why Following the ADA Standards is Not Enough

Today there is a wide variety of mobility devices that vary tremendously in size and configuration to accommodate users. And many conditions require more maneuvering space than the ADA Standards minimum dimensions mandate. The minimum floor space requirements in the ADA Standards were based on the dimensions of a standard wheelchair, and it's 60 inch turning circle. However, today a 67 inch turning circle is the accepted standard, and an 80 inch turning circle is sometimes necessary.

Better Designs Can Increase Safety and Reduce the Number of Falls

According to the Center for Disease Control and Prevention (the CDC), falls are the number one preventable cause of death for people over 65. The annual costs of falls is at least $50 billion in medical costs, with $30,000 being the average cost of a hospital stay after a fall. The additional costs in the form of lost wages and suffering is unacceptably high and can be reduced significantly with safer design and construction. To assist the reader, the author has provided recommendations to reduce the number of falls and the injuries from falls. For additional information, see *Staying Vertical in a Hazardous World*, by Arvid Osterberg. (culicidaepress.com)

Other Resources

Design for All covers general accessibility issues for buildings, sites, and facilities covered under Titles II and III of the ADA described above. In addition, it provides information in the **Specific Use Areas** section that covers certain types of buildings, areas, rooms, and spaces that are commonly used by a variety of people.

Note
Design for All does not cover several specific types of facilities and services that are, or may be, covered by ADA Standards, including

- ecreation facilities and play areas
- judicial, legislative and regulatory facilities
- detention areas and correctional facilities
- transportation
- HUD housing
- electronic and information technology (Refer to Section 508 of the Rehabilitation Act) **See References.**

Many of the general accessibility guidelines covered in *Design for All* apply to these types of facilities and services. The Access Board provides additional, specific guidelines in the ADA Standards, in other publications, and on their website.

Every attempt has been made to include accurate references to the ADA Standards. However, if you have questions, you should refer to the ADA Standards itself or call your regional Disability and Business Technical Assistance Center at 800-949-4232 or the Access Board at 800-872-2253 for additional assistance and clarification.

Using *Design for All*
Design for All has three main uses.

- You can use *Design for All* to review preliminary, intermediate, and final building and site plans before construction begins to ensure that designs comply with accessibility requirements.

- You can use *Design for All* as a field guide for on-site inspections of new and existing buildings and sites by working through the sections and chapters in order.

- You can use *Design for All* as a reference resource for finding information about accessibility issues and ADA Standards requirements.

It is always best and most cost effective to address accessibility issues beginning in the project planning stages and continuing throughout design and construction.

Finding Information
A table of contents at the beginning of the book lists sections of the book and the chapters within each section that address specific accessibility topics. Each chapter begins with an additional table of contents that lists the individual topics it includes.

Using *Design for All* as a Notation System
Letters and numbers are used throughout *Design for All* to denote chapters, accessibility topics within chapters, and specific details about each topic.

Figure 1 on the next page shows a sample page from the chapter DR Doors.

As shown in **Figure 1**, each chapter that includes accessibility requirements is identified with a two-letter designation (e.g., **DR Doors**). Information pertaining to the topics in each chapter is organized from general to specific.

Accessibility topics are identified by a single capital letter, A through Z. In the example in **Figure 1**, the letter **K** identifies the topic "Maneuvering Spaces at Folding and Sliding Doors and at Passageways."

More specific details pertaining to topics are identified by numbers, and where necessary, small letters. For instance, **K1** identifies the requirement to "Provide space for a front approach that is..." and a. identifies the additional requirement that the space be "48in. (1220mm) minimum perpendicular to the doorway...."

When evaluating floor plans, you can use notations created from these numbers and letters to note accessibility issues directly on floor plans. For example, you could note **DRK1a** next to a pocket door where you need to make sure that 48 inches (1220 millimeters) of space is provided for a front approach to the door. If you prefer, you can list notations on a note pad or enter them into a spreadsheet on a computer.

Referencing Key

To assist the reader the author has adopted the following referencing system for the requirements and recommendations in *Design for All*.

Examples

Type 1 Reference:

E2   Ensure that the length of standard accessible parking spaces is at least 19ft. (5.80m). 🅒ₐ

The statement is in blue text and includes the 🅒ₐ symbol to indicate it is a *Design for All* recommendation written by Arvid Osterberg based on his fifty+ years of research on accessibility and safety issues.

Type 2 Reference:

N4   Identify accessible passenger loading zones with signs showing the International Symbol of Accessibility. **ADAAG: 1998 4.1** 🅒ₐ

The statement is in blue text with the 🅒ₐ symbol. It includes a reference to the 1998 ADAAG. In this case the 2010 ADA Standards does not include a requirement that was in the 1998 ADAAG. The author decided to endorse the 1998 ADAAG requirement as an *Design for All* recommendation.

Type 3 Reference:

F1   Select a lift that can accommodate people standing in the lift as well as people using wheelchairs. **ADA Standards: 2010 410 (Advisory)** 🅒ₐ

The 2010 ADA Standards lists a few items as advisory. The statement is blue with the 🅒ₐ symbol to indicate it is also a *Design for All* recommendation.

Type 4 Reference:

N3   Identify van accessible and alternate van accessible spaces with "Van Accessible" signs. **ADAAG: 1998 4.6 & ADA Standards: 2010 502**

The statement includes a reference to the 1998 ADAAG and a reference to the 2010 ADA Standards. The requirement is the same in both versions of the standards.

Type 5 Reference:

H8   Ensure that access aisles do not overlap a vehicular way. **ADA Standards: 2010 502 (New)**

The statement includes a reference to the 2010 ADA Standards, and the word "New". This indicates a requirement that is new to the 2010 ADA Standards and was not in the 1998 ADAAG.

Type 6 Reference:

A5   Ensure that at least 60% of all public entrances are accessible. If you only have one entrance, it must be accessible. If you have two entrances, both must be accessible. **ADA Standards: 2010 206 (Modified-More Restrictive)**

The statement includes a reference to the 2010 ADA Standards, and the words "Modified-More Restrictive". This indicates a requirement that has been revised and has become more restrictive in the 2010 ADA Standards. In these cases the reader should follow the 2010 ADA Standards rather than the older and Less Restrictive 1998 ADAAG. A few items that were 'reserved' and activated in the 2010 ADA Standards are referenced in this manner.

Type 7 Reference:

J1   Ensure that the maximum slope in any direction in accessible parking spaces, passenger loading areas, and access aisles does not exceed 1:48 (approx. 2%). **ADA Standards: 2010 502 (Modified-Less Restrictive)**

The statement includes a reference to the 2010 ADA Standards, and the words "Modified-Less Restrictive". This indicates a requirement that has been revised and has become Less Restrictive in the 2010 ADA Standards. Most of these cases represent more reasonable tolerances (or ranges) than were in the 1998 ADAAG.

Understanding the Conventions Used in *Design for All*

Measurements

Both U.S. and metric measurements are provided in the text. U.S. measurements are listed in the text immediately followed by metric equivalents in parentheses. Typically, inches and millimeters are used for distances between 0 and 96 inches (2440mm) and feet and meters are used for distances over 8 feet (2.49m).

For simplification, dimensions provided in the illustrations do not generally include the unit abbreviations 'in.' for inch or 'mm' for millimeter. U.S. measurements are provided in bold face type: metric conversion are provided below the U.S. measurements.

Figures

There are two types of figures in *Design for All*: illustrations and tables. Figures are always referred to in the text before they appear and figure numbers are sequential within each chapter.

Tables are labeled with the chapter abbreviation followed by a letter (e.g., PA-A, which is the first table included in the chapter PA Parking).

Illustrations are labeled with the chapter abbreviation followed by a number (e.g., DR.1 which is the first figure included in the chapter DR Doors). Typically **only**, the *Design for All* preferred dimensions are shown.

Many of the illustrations in *Design for All* include a person in a wheelchair. Sometimes, both the required and preferred dimensions for a space are shown so that you can see just how tight the minimum conditions are and how following preferred dimensions makes maneuvering wheelchairs easier. The dimensions of a single, stationary wheelchair often determine ADA Standards minimum space requirements. However, it is important to understand that many people who do not use wheelchairs also benefit from accessible spaces and fixtures.

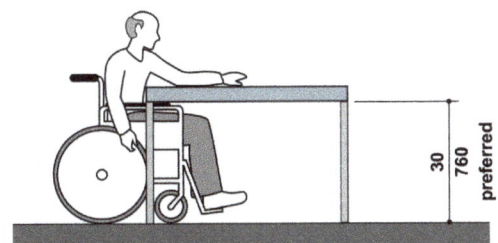

TA.2 Unobstructed legroom under a table

See Figure TA.3

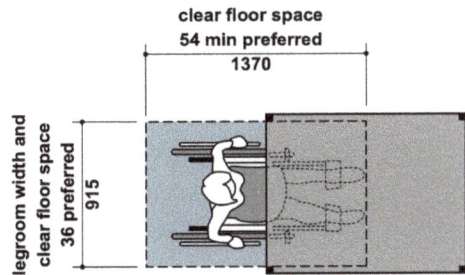

TA.3 Preferred minimum legroom width under a table

D3 Where a table is in an alcove that is 24in. (610mm) deep or deeper, or is bounded on both sides by walls or other objects, ensure that the width of the legroom measures 36in. (915mm) wide from side to side. **ADAAG: 1998 4.2 & ADA Standards: 2010 305**

D4 Ensure that legroom provides adequate toe clearance. Toe clearance
  a. includes the vertical space from the floor to 9in. (230mm) above the floor, and
  b. extends horizontally under the table at least 17in. (430mm) measured from the front edge of the table. **ADA Standards: 2010 306 (New)**
Refer to Figures RT.30 and RT.31

D5 Ensure that legroom provides adequate knee clearance. Knee clearance extends horizontally, measured from the front of the table
  a. at least 8in. (205mm) deep at a height of 27in. (685mm) above the floor, and
  b. at least 11in. (280mm) deep at a height of 9in. (230mm) above the floor. **ADA Standards: 2010 306 (New)**
Refer to Figure RT.31

D6 Legroom may extend any distance under a table and additional space for legroom is preferred. ca

D7 Only a maximum of 25in. (635mm) under a table measured from the front edge of the table can also be part of any required clear floor space. **ADA Standards: 2010 306 (New)** Ensure that the table overlaps required clear floor space no more than 25in. (635mm). **ADA Standards: 2010 306 (New)**

D8 Where the knee clearance under a table must be reduced at an angle because of angled vertical supports or other obstructions, taper the depth of the vertical knee clearance at a rate of 1in. (25mm) horizontally for each 6in. (150mm) vertical rise. **ADA Standards: 2010 306 (New)**

D9 Where people need to reach over a table to access controls or objects, ensure that the horizontal depth of the legroom is at least equal to the reach length above the table to a maximum of 25in. (635mm). **ADA Standards: 2010 306 (New)**
See RR Reach Ranges

E Benches

Accessible benches must be large enough and sturdy enough to ensure that people can transfer safely to them from a wheelchair. Accessible benches should also provide back support.

Where benches that are attached to walls are provided in dressing, fitting, shower and other rooms, consider providing grab bars on walls adjacent to the benches to assist people transferring.

E1 In rooms and areas where benches are provided, ensure that at least 5%, but not less than one, is accessible. **ADAAG: 1998 4.1 & ADA Standards: 2010 226**
Increasing the number of accessible benches to 10-20% of the total is preferred. ca

Design for All: The Best Path Forward — Dr. Arvid E. Osterberg

Figure 1 Sample Page

Chapters in Accessible Routes and Spaces

RR	Reach Ranges	21
PA	Parking	26
CR	Curb Ramps	36
RT	Routes & Spaces	44
RP	Ramps	65
EN	Entrances	72
DR	Doors	76
EL	Elevators	93
PL	Platform Lifts	106
ST	Stairs	110

Section 1. Accessible Routes and Spaces

The chapters in this section cover parking, routes to and through buildings and sites, and spaces inside buildings. All people should be able to safely and conveniently approach buildings and sites by various means of transportation. People should also be able to enter and move through corridors, passages, and spaces without encountering obstructions or barriers.

It is important to meet ADA Standards and other code requirements as well as to ensure that the overall design of routes and spaces meets the needs of the people using them. In assessing the accessibility of routes and spaces, review whether

1) accessible points of entry onto a site are connected to building entrances by accessible routes;
2) accessible routes provide direct, unobstructed, safe, and convenient means of travel to buildings and accessible areas within buildings; and
3) accessible restrooms, telephones and other commonly used spaces and equipment are located conveniently in relation to accessible routes, reception areas, and entrances.

As you use *Inclusive Design* to determine how well your building and site meets peoples' needs, examine these issues.

Traffic flow
Consider how people travel through buildings and sites. Ensure that main routes are accessible and provide additional width in busy walkways and corridors.

Slope
Wherever possible, use gently sloped walkways and plazas at the entrances of buildings and sites. When you must install ramps, use reduced slopes, rather than maximum slopes where possible.

Way-finding
Unless all areas of a building or site are accessible, provide appropriate signs and symbols to identify accessible parking, entrances, routes, and spaces. Consider color coding different areas of buildings, indicating changes in routes with different floor coverings, and installing directional kiosks with both visual and audible information.

Surfaces
Use non-slip surface materials that also reduce glare from lighting and windows.

Illumination
Provide sufficient, even levels of lighting along routes and throughout spaces. In spaces where people are permitted to adjust lighting levels, ensure that the controls are accessible.

Maintenance
Although building maintenance is not addressed by ADA Standards, your building and grounds maintenance plan should consider accessibility and safety. Ensure that routes are kept free of debris, tree branches, snow and ice, furnishings, and other obstructions; that lighting is maintained at consistent levels; and that care of ground and floor surfaces includes removing any slippery, uneven, or damaged areas.

Measuring Slopes

Providing appropriate slopes is important because excessive slopes cause difficulty for people with disabilities. You will need to check the slopes at accessible parking spaces and passenger loading zones, at curb ramps and ramps, and along accessible routes. Traveling surfaces have two kinds of slopes, running slope (the slope that is parallel to the direction of travel) and cross slope (the slope that is perpendicular to the direction of travel). Measurements for slope requirements are provided in a ratio (e.g., 1:48) and as a percentage (e.g., 2%). The following examples discuss two methods for measuring slopes.

Example One

Determine slope by applying a level to a surface, raising the down-slope end of the level until the bubble is centered, and then measuring the vertical distance between the lifted end and the traveling surface. For example, if the end of a four-foot long level is one inch above the ground, then the slope is 1 inch in 48 inches, or 1:48 (approx. 2%).

Example Two

Electronic levels, which can be placed directly on surfaces, are often more convenient and accurate than standard levels.

Figure 1 shows two methods for determining slope.

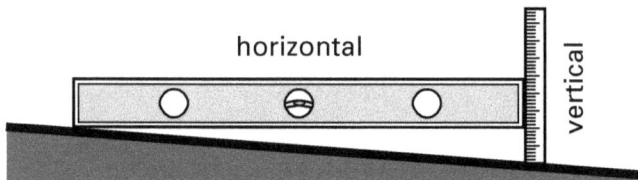

determining slope using a standard level and ruler

determining slope using an electronic level

Figure 2 How to determine slope

RR Reach Ranges

A   Controls and Objects:
    Location and Placement 21
B   Front Reach 22
C   Reduced Front Reach 22
D   Side Reach 24
E   Reduced Side Reach 24
F   Placement of Fixtures 24
G   Children's Reach Ranges 25

In buildings and sites used by the public, people are provided access to controls and objects that allow them to adjust the environment in a variety of ways (for example, opening a window or turning on a light). Unfortunately, controls and objects are often out of reach for people with disabilities, particularly for people who use wheelchairs. When controls and objects are intended to be used by the public, people with disabilities must be provided access to those controls and objects that is equivalent to the access of people without disabilities.

People must be able to find, reach, and use controls, switches, dispensers, outlets, thermostats, handles, window and window treatment controls, and other objects that are mounted along walls. People must also be able to reach and use controls on freestanding objects, such as drinking fountains and vending machines. Controls and objects must be located at heights that are appropriate for people who use wheelchairs, people of short stature, and children.

The ADA Standards requires that controls and objects be located within specified reach ranges. Reach is the distance that a person must extend his or her arm to use controls or objects. Reach depends on a number of factors including the height of the person, the height of the object, the distance of the person from an object, and the position of the person in relation to an object.

Because of the variability of these factors, ADA Standards reach ranges are expressed as the highest and lowest points of a range within which controls and objects may be located.

Minimum and maximum heights for controls and objects vary depending on whether the clear floor space in front of an object or control allows for a front or parallel approach by people using wheelchairs.

Reach ranges are often reduced by obstructions. Obstructions are objects that people need to reach over to access controls or other objects. For example, a counter below the controls of an ATM or public telephone could be an obstruction.

When planning the placement of controls and objects, consider in particular the needs of people who use wheelchairs.

The dimensions used by ADA Standards to establish reach ranges for an adult using a wheelchair are shown in figure RR.1.

See Figure RR.1

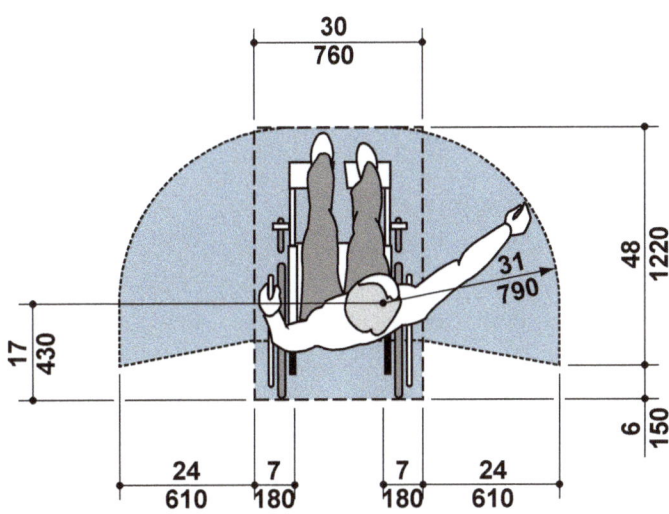

RR.1   **Dimensions used by ADA Standards in establishing reach ranges for an adult using a wheelchair**

A   Controls and Objects: Location and Placement

A consistent mounting height throughout a space helps people with visual and/or cognitive disabilities find and use controls and objects. The space in front of controls and objects should permit people to approach with minimal obstruction.

A1   Evaluate reach ranges to all controls and objects (including alarms, switches, outlets, thermostats, wall-mounted phones, coat hooks, shelves, window treatment cords) in places where people have access.

A2   Provide the minimum clear floor space in front of all controls and objects. For additional

information on minimum clear floor space, see **RT Routes and Spaces.**

A3 Locate controls and objects at least 18in. (455mm) away from inside corners of walls so that people using wheelchairs can get close enough to access them.

A4 Locate controls and objects that require manipulation (such as keypads, dials, and switches) between 36in. (915mm) minimum and 43in. (1090mm) maximum above the floor.

A5 Locate similar controls and objects at consistent heights throughout spaces.

A6 Install light switches at the same height wherever possible.

B Front Reach

Heights for a front reach apply where the clear floor space allows only a forward approach to an object by a person using a wheelchair.

Keep in mind that a forward approach (front reach) is more limited than a parallel approach (side reach).

B1 Where the forward approach (front reach) is unobstructed, locate objects no higher than 48in. (1220mm) above the floor. **ADAAG: 1998 4.2 & ADA Standards: 2010 308**
A height of 43in. (1090mm) is preferred.

See Figure RR.2

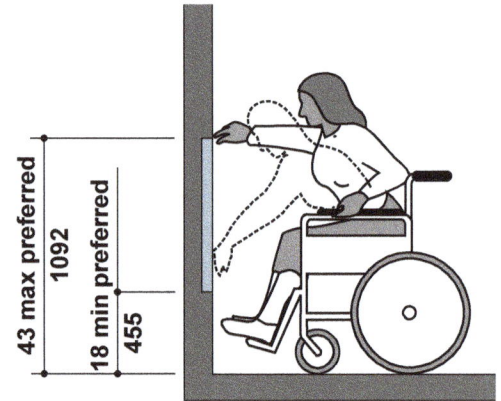

RR.2 Reach range for an unobstructed front reach

B2 Wherever possible, locate objects, switches, outlets, and controls between 36in. (915mm) and 43in. (1090mm) above the floor.

B3 Where the front reach is unobstructed, locate objects no lower than 15in. (380mm) above the floor. **ADAAG: 1998 4.2 & ADA Standards: 2010 308**
A height of 18in. (455mm) is preferred.

B4 Wherever possible, locate outlets and other objects that are normally closer to the floor at a consistent height of 18in. (455mm) above the floor measured to the centerline of the outlet or object.

C Reduced Front Reach

When people need to reach over an obstruction to access another object or control, the distance they can reach is reduced.

C1 Ensure that an obstruction below an object or control does not extend horizontally more than 25in. (635mm) into the clear floor space. **ADAAG: 1998 4.2 & ADA Standards: 2010 308**

C2 Where a front reach is over an obstruction that extends horizontally 20in. (510mm) or less into the clear floor space, locate objects no higher than 48in. (1220mm) above the floor. **ADAAG: 1998 4.2 & ADA Standards: 2010 308**
A height of 43in. (1090mm) is preferred.

See Figure RR.3

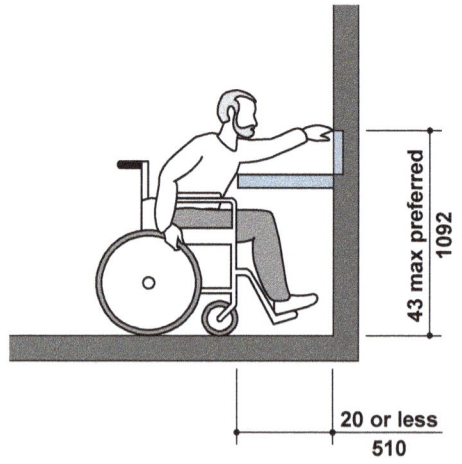

RR.3 Reach range for a front reach over a 20in. (510mm) maximum deep obstruction

Type of reach	Front reach			Side reach	
	Unobstructed	Over a shallow counter **20 in. max (510 mm)**	Over a deep counter **20 to 25 in. (510 to 635 mm)**	Unobstructed or shallow obstruction **10 in. max (255 mm)**	Over a deep obstruction **10 to 24 in. (255 to 610 mm)**
Upper (adult)	**48 in. max** (1220 mm)	**48 in. max** (1220 mm)	**44 in. max** (1120 mm)	**48 in. max** (1220 mm)	**44 in. max** (1120 mm)
	43 in. preferred (1090 mm)	**43 in. preferred** (1090 mm)	**43 in. preferred** (1090 mm)	**43 in. preferred** (1090 mm)	**43 in. preferred** (1090 mm)
Lower (adult)	**15 in. min** (380 mm)	*	*	**15 in. min** (380 mm)	*
	18 in. preferred (455 mm)	*	*	**18 in. preferred** (455 mm)	*
Upper (children age 9 to 12)	**44 in. max** (1120 mm)	*	*	**44 in. max** (1120 mm)	*
Lower (children age 9 to 12)	**16 in. min** (405 mm)	*	*	**16 in. min** (405 mm)	*
Upper (children age 5 to 8)	**40 in. max** (1015 mm)	*	*	**40 in. max** (1015 mm)	*
Upper (children age 5 to 8)	**18 in. min** (455 mm)	*	*	**18 in. min** (455 mm)	*
Upper (children age 3 to 5)	**36 in. max** (950 mm)	*	*	**36 in. max** (950 mm)	*
Upper (children age 3 to 5)	**20 in. min** (510 mm)	*	*	**20 in. min** (510 mm)	*

* not specified by ADASAD, or not applicable

RR-A   ADA Standards reach ranges for adults and children

C3 Where a front reach is over an obstruction that extends from 20in. (510mm) to a maximum of 25in. (635mm) horizontally into the clear floor space, locate objects no higher than 44in. (1120mm). **ADAAG: 1998 4.2 & ADA Standards: 2010 308**
A height of 43in. (1090mm) is preferred.
See Figure RR.4

C4 Provide clear floor space for legroom below an obstruction that is at least equal to the reach length above the obstruction. **ADAAG: 1998 4.2 & ADA Standards: 2010 308**
Example: If a 20in. (510mm) deep shelf is mounted below an ATM, the clear space below the shelf should be at least 20in. (510mm) deep.

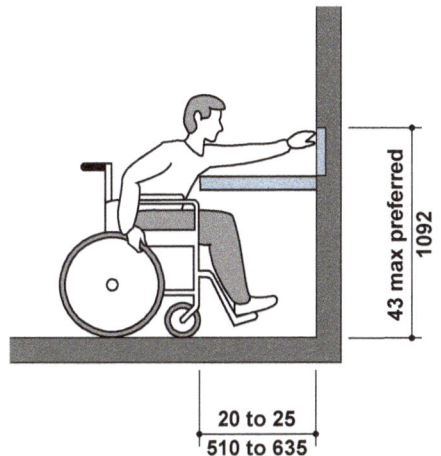

RR.4   Reach range for a front reach over an obstruction between 20in. (510mm) and 25in. (635mm) deep

See RT Routes and Spaces, RT-Q for additional information on legroom.

Design for All: The Best Path Forward — Dr. Arvid E. Osterberg

D Side Reach

Heights for a side reach apply where the clear floor space allows a parallel approach to an object by a person using a wheelchair.

D1 Wherever possible, locate controls and objects between 36in. (915mm) and 43in. (1090mm) above the floor. Ca

D2 Where the parallel approach (side reach) is unobstructed, or where the side reach is over an obstruction less than 10in. (255mm) deep, locate controls and objects no higher than 48in. (1370mm) above the floor. **ADA Standards: 2010 308 (MODIFIED-MORE RESTRICTIVE)**
A height of 43in. (1090mm) is preferred. Ca

D3 Where a parallel approach (side reach) is unobstructed, locate controls and objects no lower than 15in. (380mm) above the floor. **ADA Standards: 2010 308 (MODIFIED-MORE RESTRICTIVE)**
A height of 18in. (455mm) is preferred. Ca

D4 Wherever possible, locate outlets and other objects that are normally closer to the floor at a consistent height of 18in. (455mm) above the floor, measured to the centerline of the outlet or object. Ca

See Figure RR.5

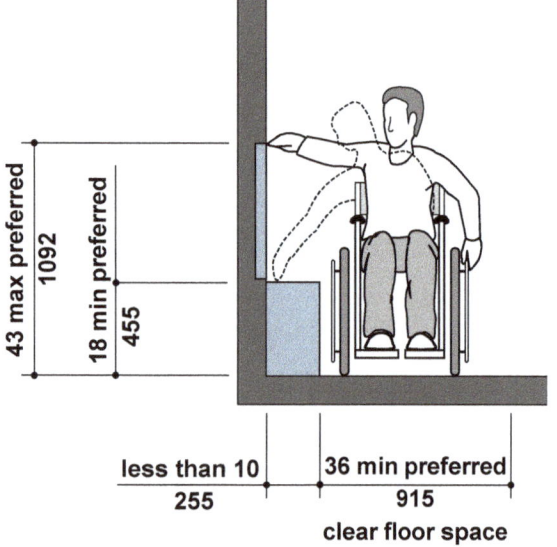

RR.5 Reach range for an unobstructed or minimally obstructed side reach

E Reduced Side Reach

When people reach over an obstruction to access another object or control, the distance they can reach is reduced.

E1 Where the side reach is over an obstruction, ensure that the obstruction is no more than 34in. (865mm) high and 24in. (610mm) deep. **ADAAG: 1998 4.2 & ADA Standards: 2010 308**

Exception: The tops of clothes washers and dryers may be 36in. (915mm) maximum above the floor. **ADA Standards: 2010 308 (NEW)**

E2 Where the side reach is over an obstruction between 10in. (255mm) and 24in. (610mm) deep, locate controls and objects no higher than 46in. (1170mm). **ADA Standards: 2010 308 (NEW)**
A height of 43in. (1090mm) is preferred. Ca

See Figure RR.6

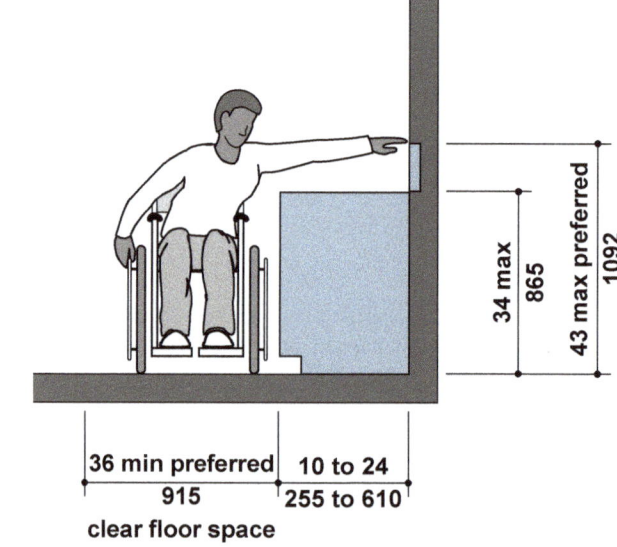

RR.6 Reach range for an obstructed side reach

F Placement of Fixture

People must be able to reach fixtures and operable parts on dispensers, vending machines, and ATMs.

F1 Locate the operable control at height of 48in (1220mm) maximum. **ADA Standards: 2010 309 (NEW)**
A height of 43in. (1090mm) is preferred. Ca

See Figure RR.7

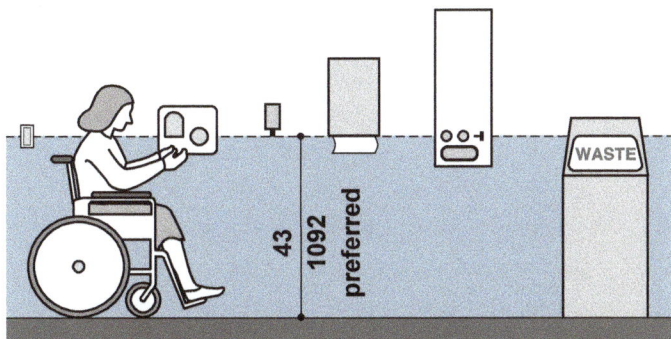

RR.7 Maximum and preferred height to operable parts of fixtures and dispensers

G Children's Reach Ranges

Where children are the primary users of a space, use the following guidelines for both front and side reaches. However, where young children use the space you may want to child proof outlets, controls, and switches.

Horizontal arrangement results in many products being out of reach

Drink dispenser in reach range; cup lids and straws out of reach

G1 For children ages 3 and 4, locate controls and objects no higher than 36in. (915mm) for a high reach and no lower than 20in. (510mm) for a low reach. **ADA Standards: 2010 308 (New)**

G2 For children ages 5 through 8, locate controls and objects no higher than 40in. (1015mm) for a high reach and no lower than 18in. (455mm) for a low reach. **ADA Standards: 2010 308 (New)**

G3 For children ages 9 through 12, locate controls and objects no higher than 44in. (1120mm) for a high reach and no lower than 16in. (405mm) for a low reach. **ADA Standards: 2010 308 (New)**
A high reach of 43in. (1090mm) is preferred. ca
A low reach of 18in. (455mm) is preferred. ca

Design for All: The Best Path Forward — Dr. Arvid E. Osterberg

PA Parking

A	Accessible Parking Spaces: Location	26
B	Accessible Parking Spaces: Number	27
C	Multiple Parking Lots	27
D	Valet parking	28
E	Standard Accessible Parking Spaces: Dimensions	29
F	Van Accessible Parking Spaces: Dimensions	29
G	Alternate Van Accessible Parking Spaces: Dimensions	30
H	Access Aisles	30
I	Passenger Loading Zones	32
J	Slope and Level Changes	33
K	Routes Connecting Accessible Parking to Entrances	33
L	Adjacent Routes and Surfaces	33
M	Marking	34
N	Signs	34
O	Parking Meters	35
P	Maintenance	35

Accessible parking involves providing wider parking spaces and access aisles as well as convenient accessible routes from parking areas to building entrances for people with disabilities.

The ADA Standards requires that you provide accessible parking spaces and access aisles for both passenger cars (standard accessible spaces) and vans (van accessible spaces). Another important aspect of accessible parking is providing adequate signs to ensure that the people who need those spaces can find and use them.

When planning and designing parking areas, consider going beyond the minimum allowable dimensions for regular (non-accessible) parking spaces. Many people who do not qualify to use accessible spaces encounter difficulties getting in and out of vehicles in narrow spaces.

Tests conducted by the Access Board showed that people who use vans with side mounted lifts or ramps need more room to conveniently exit their vehicles than is provided by standard accessible spaces. Van accessible spaces with access aisles provide enough space for most people who use side lifts.

There are additional parking requirements at facilities that provide medical care or other therapeutic services for persons with mobility impairments. **See MC Medical Care**.

A Accessible Parking Spaces: Location

Each lot or structure on a site with multiple lots or structures should include accessible parking. Exceptions to this are sometimes allowed as explained below.

A1 Wherever parking serves a specific building, locate accessible spaces on the shortest accessible route of travel from parking to an accessible entrance. **ADAAG: 1998 4.6 & ADA Standards: 2010 208**

A2 Wherever parking serves buildings that have multiple accessible entrances, disperse accessible spaces among areas adjacent to each accessible entrance. **ADAAG: 1998 4.6 & ADA Standards: 2010 208**

You may locate accessible parking spaces in different lots or structures if equal or better accessibility is provided (in terms of distance to an accessible entrance, cost, and user convenience). **See Figures PA.1, PA.2, and PA.3 for multiple parking lots.**

A3 Wherever parking does not serve a specific building, locate accessible parking on the shortest accessible route to an accessible pedestrian entrance of the parking area. **ADAAG: 1998 4.6 & ADA Standards: 2010 208**

A4 Where on-street parking is provided, consider the total amount of parking available and provide enough accessible on-street parking to comply with accessibility guidelines. Ca

A5 When providing angled on-street parking, provide adequate aisle spaces. Ca

A6 Wherever parking spaces are provided for specific purposes (such as buses, delivery trucks, and official vehicles), the spaces are not required to be accessible if an accessible passenger loading zone is provided. **ADA Standards: 2010 208** (New) See PA-I

A7 All van accessible spaces may be grouped on one level of a parking structure. **ADAAG: 1998 4.1 & ADA Standards: 2010 208**

B Accessible Parking Spaces: Number

Provide an adequate number of accessible parking spaces to accommodate the maximum number of people who might use the parking lot or structure at peak-use times.

B1 Calculate the number of required accessible parking spaces on a lot-by-lot or structure-by-structure basis for sites with multiple parking lots or structures. **ADA Standards: 2010 208** (NEW)

See Table PA-A

Total parking spaces in lot	Minimum number of accessible spaces		
	Standard	Van	Total
1 to 25	0	1	1
26 to 50	1	1	2
51 to 75	2	1	3
76 to 100	3	1	4
101 to 150	4	1	5
151 to 200	5	1	6
201 to 300	5	2	7
301 to 400	6	2	8
401 to 500	7	2	9
501 to 1000	2% of total number of spaces must be accessible		
1001+	20 spaces, plus 1 for each 100 (or fraction thereof) over 1000		

PA-A Minimum required number of accessible parking spaces

B2 Provide at least the minimum number of accessible spaces required in each parking area. **ADAAG: 1998 4.1 & ADA Standards: 2010 208**

B3 Ensure that 1 in every 6, but not less than one, accessible space is a van accessible parking space. **ADA Standards: 2010 208** (MODIFIED-MORE RESTRICTIVE)

B4 Provide additional accessible parking spaces, beyond ADA minimum requirements, where the need is great.

C Multiple Parking Lots

Where multiple parking lots serve a building, the required number of standard accessible and van accessible parking spaces must be located as close as possible to the accessible entrances.

C1 Where multiple parking lots serve a building with only one accessible entrance, locate all accessible parking spaces in the parking lot that is closest to the accessible entrance. **ADAAG: 1998 4.6 & ADA Standards: 2010 208**

See Figure PA.1

C2 Where multiple parking lots serve a building **with multiple accessible entrances**, distribute accessible parking spaces close to each accessible entrance. **ADAAG: 1998 4.6 & ADA Standards: 2010 208**

See Figure PA.2

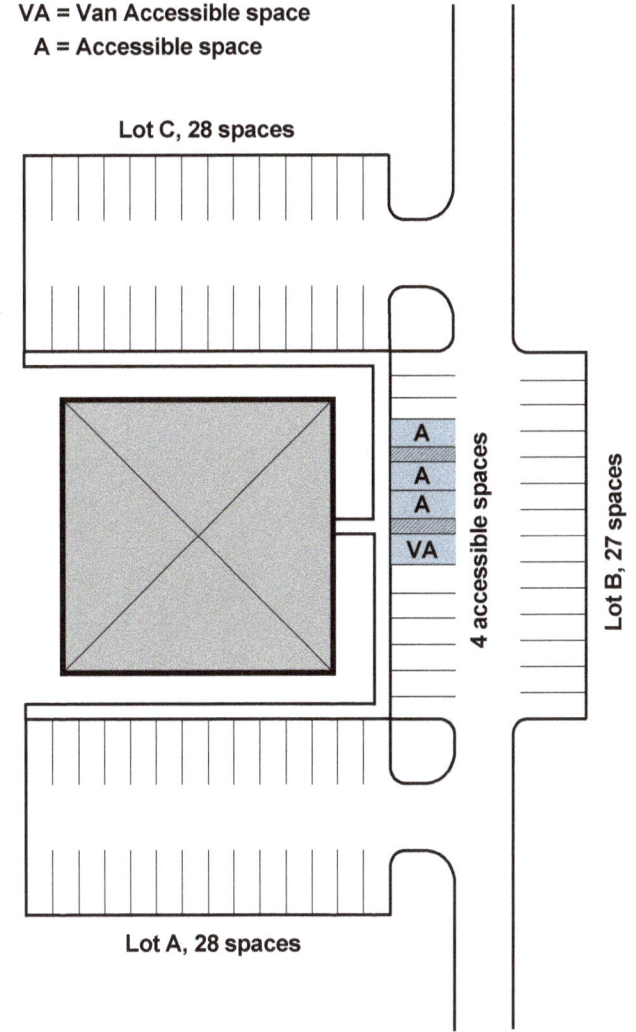

PA.1 Three parking lots serving a building *with one accessible entrance*

C3 Where multiple parking lots include a satellite lot that serves a building, locate all accessible parking spaces in the parking lots that are closest to the accessible entrances. **ADAAG: 1998 4.6 & ADA Standards: 2010 208**

See Figure PA.3

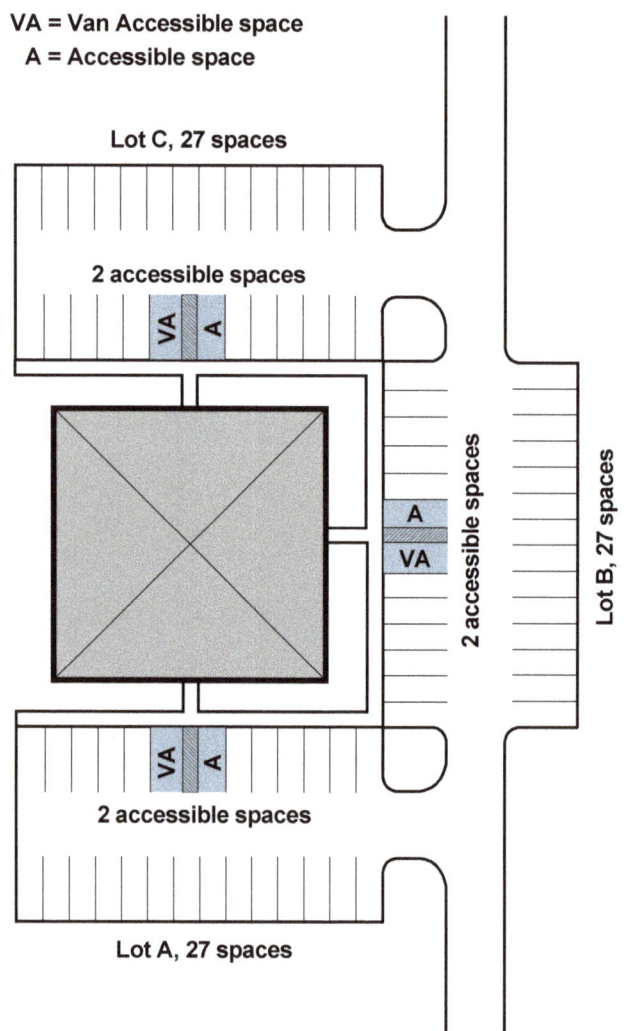

PA.2 **Three parking lots serving a building** *with three accessible entrances*

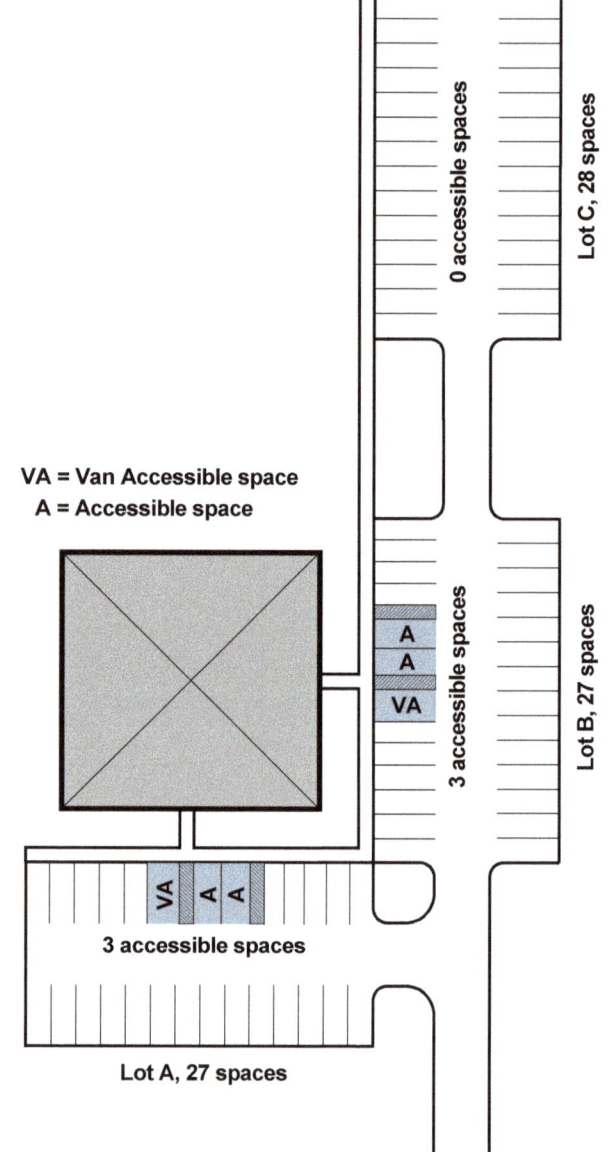

PA.3 **Three parking lots** *(including a satellite lot) serving a building*

D Valet Parking

Where valet parking is provided, it is important to plan options that accommodate all users. Persons with some disabilities have vehicles equipped with special controls that should not be operated by parking attendants.

D1 Wherever valet parking is offered, provide an accessible passenger loading zone. **ADAAG: 1998 4.1 & ADA Standards: 2010 209 See PA-I**

D2 Provide the same proportion of accessible parking in lots served by valets as in lots not served by valets. ca

Accessible Parking Spaces: Types and Dimensions

The three basic types of accessible parking spaces (standard, van accessible, and alternative van) are each defined by minimum dimension requirements.

PA-B lists the minimum required dimensions and the preferred dimensions for accessible parking spaces. It also provides dimensions for passenger loading zones.

When planning, measuring or marking adjacent parking spaces and access aisles, measure from the centerline of any marking lines to ensure that the dimension of each space complies with ADA Standards requirements.

Where parking is covered (such as in a parking structure), vertical clearance is required.

E Standard Accessible Parking Spaces: Dimensions

Standard accessible parking spaces serve passenger vehicles.

E1 Ensure that standard accessible spaces meet all of the following minimum requirements:
  a. parking space width: 8ft. (2.44m);
  b. access aisle width: 5ft. (1.53m); and
  c. vertical clearance: 6ft. 8in. (2.03m).
  ADAAG: 1998 4.4, 4.6 & ADA Standards: 2010 502

E2 Ensure that the length of standard accessible parking spaces is at least 19ft. (5.80m). **Ca**

E3 Provide access aisles on either side of an standard accessible spaces. **ADA Standards: 2010 502 (NEW)**
See Figures PA.4 and PA.5

F Van Accessible Parking Spaces: Dimensions

Van accessible parking spaces safely and comfortably accommodate vans and wheelchair lifts and other specialized equipment.

F1 Ensure that van accessible spaces meet all of the following minimum requirements:
  a. parking space width: 11ft. (3.35m);
  ADA Standards: 2010 502 (NEW)
  b. access aisle width: 5ft. (1.53m); and
  ADAAG: 1998 4.6 & ADA Standards: 2010 502
  c. vertical clearance: 8ft. 2in. (2.49m).
  ADAAG: 1998 4.6 & ADA Standards: 2010 502

F2 Ensure that the length of van accessible parking spaces is at least 19ft. (5.80m). **Ca**
Refer to Figure PA.4

F3 Provide access aisles on either side of van accessible spaces that are connected to the accessible routes. **ADA Standards: 2010 502 (NEW)**
Refer to Figure PA.4

F4 Provide access aisles on the passenger side of angled van accessible spaces. **ADA Standards: 2010 502 (NEW)**
Refer to Figure PA.5

Accessible spaces	Standard parking	Van parking	Alternate van parking	Loading zones
Space width	8 ft. (2.44 m)	11 ft. (3.35 m)	8 ft. (2.44 m)	8 ft. (2.44 m)
Access aisle width	5 ft. (1.53 m)	5 ft. (1.53 m)	8 ft. (2.44 m)	5 ft. (1.53 m) 8 ft. (2.44 m) (preferred)
Vertical clearance	6 ft. 8 in. (2.03 m)	8 ft. 2 in. (2.5 m)	8 ft. 2 in. (2.49 m)	9 ft. 6 in. (2.90 m)
Space length	19 ft. (5.80 m) or more preferred	19 ft. (5.80 m) or more preferred	19 ft. (5.80 m) or more preferred	20 ft. (6.10m)

PA-B Minimum required dimensions for accessible parking spaces

G Alternate Van Accessible Parking Spaces: Dimensions

Alternate van accessible parking spaces serve passenger vans. The difference between the van accessible and alternate van accessible is in the width of the access aisle.

Van accessible parking spaces are preferred to alternate van accessible parking spaces because the wider access aisles adjoining alternate van accessible parking spaces make it easy for unauthorized vehicles to park there.

G1 Plan, design, and construct parking lots and structures with van accessible parking spaces (rather than alternate van accessible spaces that make it easy for unauthorized vehicles to park in access aisles). ca
Refer to Figures 4 and 5

Eight-foot wide access aisles (not recommended) **invite illegal parking**

G2 Ensure that alternate van accessible spaces meet all of the following minimum requirements:
   a. parking space width: 8ft. (2.44m);
      ADAAG: 1998 4.6 & ADA Standards: 2010 502
   b. access aisle width: 8ft. (2.44m); and **ADA Standards: 2010 502 (New)**
   c. vertical clearance: 8ft. 2in. (2.49m).
      ADAAG: 1998 4.6 & ADA Standards: 2010 502

G3 Ensure that the length of alternate van accessible parking spaces is at least 19ft. (5.80m). ca
Refer to Figure PA.5

H Access Aisles

Measure the length and width of access aisles and parking spaces accurately, particularly where angled parking is provided. To ensure that angled spaces are measured correctly, measure from one side of the space perpendicular to the length of the space.

For access aisles, measure the distance from the edge of the parking space perpendicular to the length of the parking space. **Refer to PA.5**

H1 Ensure that all designated accessible parking spaces have access aisles. Two parking spaces are permitted to share the same access aisle. ca
ADAAG: 1998 4.6 & ADA Standards: 2010 502
Exception: Where van accessible spaces are angled, locate access aisles on the passenger's side only.
ADA Standards: 2010 502 (New)

H2 In existing parking lots where access aisles have not previously been provided for all accessible spaces, provide adequate access aisles when the lot is altered or re-striped. ca

H3 For standard accessible parking spaces and van accessible parking spaces, provide an access aisle that is a minimum of 5ft. (1.53m) wide.
ADA Standards: 2010 502 (Modified-Less Restrictive)

H4 For alternate van accessible parking spaces, provide an access aisle that is a minimum of 8ft. (2.44m) wide. **ADA Standards: 2010 502 (New)**

H5 Ensure that access aisles extend the full length of the parking spaces they serve. **ADA Standards: 2010 502 (New)**

H6 Ensure that the accessible parking space is flush with the access aisle. No level changes are permitted. **ADA Standards: 2010 502 (New)**

H7 Locate access aisles so they connect to accessible routes that lead to accessible building entrances. **ADAAG: 1998 4.6 & ADA Standards: 2010 502**

H8 Ensure that access aisles do not overlap a vehicular way. **ADA Standards: 2010 502 (New)**

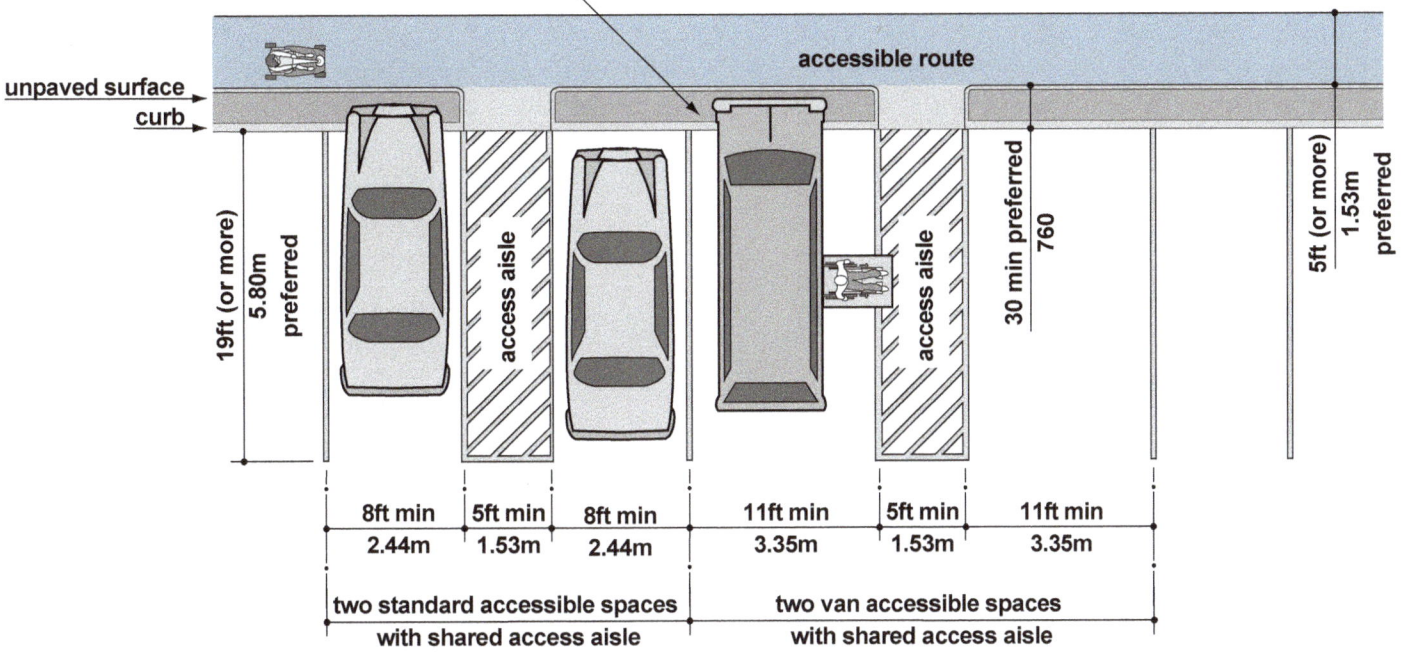

PA.4 Standard accessible and van accessible parking spaces and access aisles

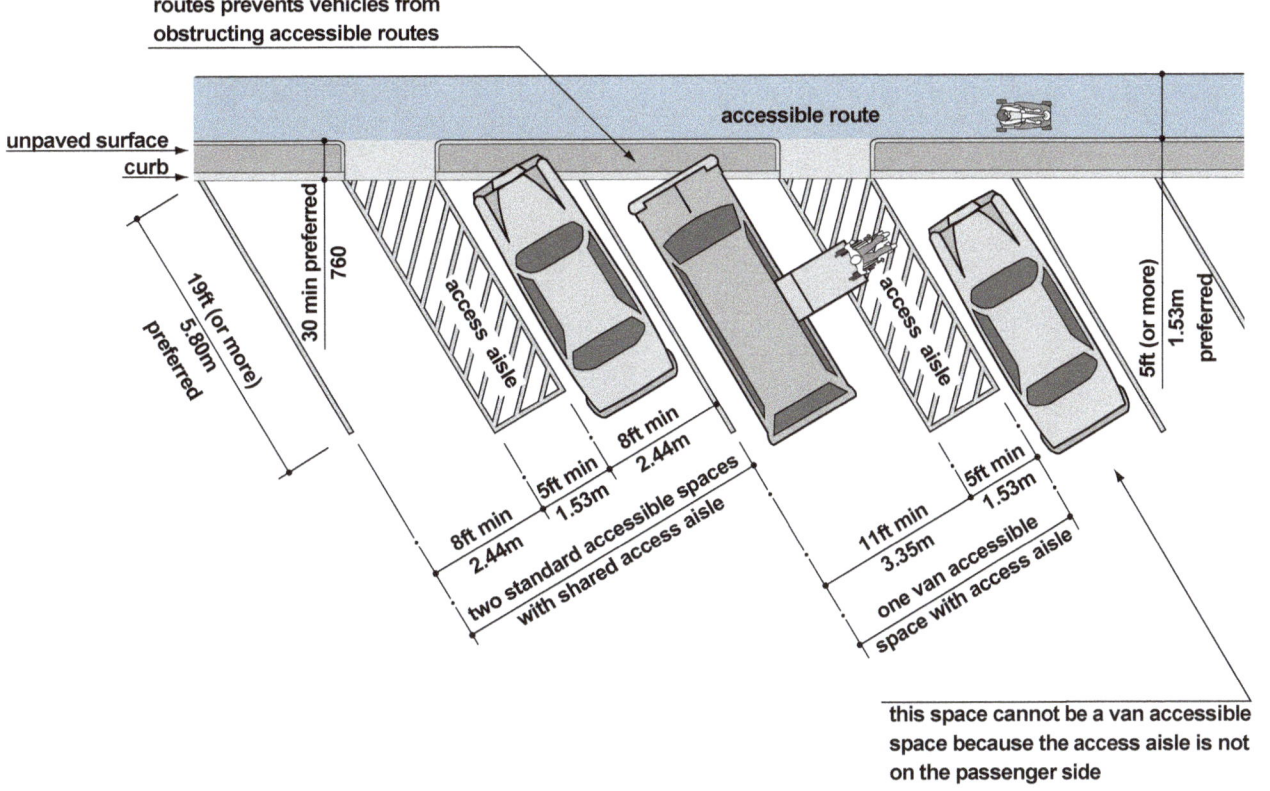

PA.5 Standard accessible and van accessible *angled* parking spaces and access aisles

Design for All: The Best Path Forward — Dr. Arvid E. Osterberg

H9 Provide non-paved surfaces between parking areas and accessible routes to prevent parked vehicles from overlapping adjacent accessible routes. Wheel stops are not recommended because they pose a tripping and falling hazard.
Refer to PA.4, PA.5, and PA.6 for designs where parked vehicles do not overlap accessible routes. ca

H10 Detectable warnings are not required where accessible parking aisles connect to adjacent sidewalks.
Refer to PA.4, PA.5, and PA.6

H11 Ensure that additional state and local *width of access aisle* requirements (if any) are followed. ca

I Passenger Loading Zones

Passenger loading zones include a vehicle pull-up area and an adjacent access aisle.

Wherever passenger loading zones are provided, they must be accessible and the areas must have appropriate markings and signs. The vertical height requirement allows for vehicles higher than typical vans, such as buses and shuttles.

Passenger loading zones are also required at bus loading areas and on-street bus stops. The requirements for bus stops and other aspects of public transportation are covered in ADAAG 1998 section 10, Transportation Facilities, and ADA Standards 2010, section 810.

I 1 Provide accessible passenger loading zones where people are routinely dropped off. ca

I 2 If passenger loading zones are not provided, then parking spaces designated for specific types of vehicles (such as buses, delivery trucks, and official vehicles) are required to be accessible. **ADA Standards: 2010 208** (New)

I 3 Provide accessible passenger loading zones at pick-up and drop-off areas in mechanical access parking structures. **ADA Standards: 2010 209** (New)

I 4 Ensure that at least one passenger loading zone in every continuous 100 linear feet (30.5m) of loading zone space is accessible. **ADA Standards: 2010 209** (New)

I 5 Provide vehicle pull-up spaces that are
   a. a minimum of 8ft. (2.44m) wide; 11ft. (3.35m) wide preferred; ca and
   b. a minimum of 20ft. (6.10m) long. **ADA Standards: 2010 503** (New)

I 6 Provide access aisles adjacent to vehicle pull-up spaces that
   a. are a minimum of 5ft. (1.53m) wide; **ADAAG: 1998 4.6 & ADA Standards: 2010 503**
      8ft. (2.44m) wide preferred; ca
   b. are at least as long as the pull-up space they serve; **ADAAG: 1998 4.6 & ADA Standards: 2010 503**
   c. are parallel to the vehicle pull-up space; **ADAAG: 1998 4.6 & ADA Standards: 2010 503**
   d. are adjacent to an accessible route; and **ADAAG: 1998 4.6 & ADA Standards: 2010 503**
   e. do not overlap a vehicular way. **ADA Standards: 2010 503** (New)

See Figure PA.6

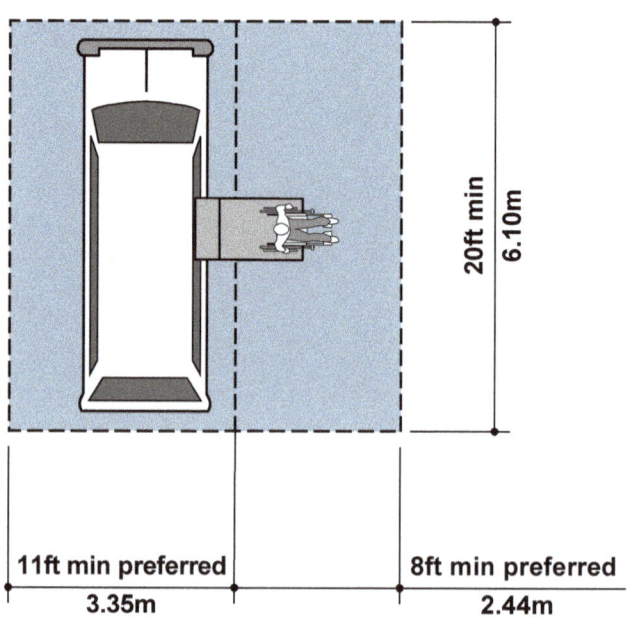

PA.6 Passenger loading zone design

I 7   Ensure that vertical clearance for passenger loading zones is at least 9ft. 6in. (2.90m) high
   a.   at the loading zone; and
   b.   along the length of at least one vehicular route connecting the accessible loading zone with a site entrance and exit. **ADAAG: 1998 4.6 & ADA Standards: 2010 503**

I 8   Ensure that the accessible vehicle pull-up space is flush with the access aisle. No level changes are permitted. **ADA Standards: 2010 503 (New)**

J   Slope and Level Changes

Accessible parking spaces, access aisles, and passenger loading zones must be level. Even moderate slopes, both running slopes and cross slopes, make usability difficult for many people.

J1   Ensure that the maximum slope in any direction in accessible parking spaces, passenger loading areas, and access aisles does not exceed 1:48 (approx. 2%). **ADA Standards: 2010 502 (Modified-Less Restrictive)**

J2   *Ensure proper slopes for drainage to prevent puddling of water in accessible parking spaces, access aisles, curb ramps, and accessible routes.* ca

J3   Eliminate level changes between parking spaces and passenger loading zones and adjacent access aisles. Curb ramps are not permitted to extend into accessible aisles and passenger loading zones. **ADAAG: 1998 4.6 & ADA Standards: 2010 502**

K   Routes Connecting Accessible Parking to Entrances

A common problem in parking lots or structures is that wheelchair users are forced to cross vehicular traffic as they travel through parking areas to reach accessible routes that lead to building entrances. Proper planning and design eliminates this problem.

K1   *Ensure that all access aisles adjacent to van accessible parking spaces connect directly to accessible routes (without having to pass through vehicular traffic areas).* ca

K2   *To the extent possible, ensure that all access aisles adjacent to any accessible parking spaces connect directly to accessible routes (without having to pass through vehicular traffic areas).* ca

K3   *To increase safety, ensure that accessible routes that cross vehicular traffic areas in parking areas are clearly marked as pedestrian crossings.* ca

K4   *Ensure that all routes connecting accessible parking to building entrances have adequate lighting.* ca

L   Adjacent Routes and Surfaces

Vehicles must not obstruct accessible routes adjacent to accessible parking spaces. Although wheel stops have been commonly used in parking areas and are not prohibited by ADA Standards, they pose a tripping hazard and we recommend that they not be installed.

Wheel stops are not necessary when parking areas and adjoining surfaces are properly planned and designed. For example, curbs and grass areas that separate parking spaces from adjacent accessible routes serve as curb stops. The front ends of vehicles that hang over grass areas do not interfere with accessible routes. **Refer to Figures PA.4, PA.5, and PA.6**

Some traveling surfaces, such as gravel, can be falling hazards. Concrete and asphalt can also be dangerous when wet or oily. Painted surfaces tend to be slick and are not recommended for traveling surfaces.

L1   Provide surfaces for parking spaces, passenger loading zones, and adjacent access aisles that are firm, stable, and slip-resistant. **ADAAG: 1998 4.5 & ADA Standards: 2010 302**

L2   Ensure that parked vehicles do not obstruct the clear width of an accessible route. **ADAAG: 1998 4.6 & ADA Standards: 2010 502**

L3 Ensure that all access routes adjacent to parking are wide enough, or separated from parking, to prevent overhanging vehicles from narrowing routes to less than 36" (915 mm). ca

L4 Provide non-paved surfaces between parking areas and accessible routes to prevent parked vehicles from overlapping adjacent accessible routes. ca

L5 Design parking areas without wheel stops to reduce tripping hazards. ca

L6 Remove wheel stops where possible to reduce tripping hazards. ca

L7 If wheel stops cannot be eliminated, ensure that they are properly positioned, anchored to the pavement, and painted a contrasting color. ca

Wheel stops (not recommended) can be tripping hazards

M Marking

The ADA Standards does not provide specific standards for pavement marking, but state and local requirements may apply.

Marking could include striping or other methods that do not interfere with accessibility. Since markings can be obscured by snow, ice, or other conditions, we recommend that you also install *No Parking* signs at access aisles where appropriate.

M1 Mark access aisles at parking spaces and passenger loading zones to deter parking in access aisles. **ADA Standards: 2010 502, 503** (New)

M2 Mark accessible parking spaces to define the width. **ADA Standards: 2010 502** (New)
Example: Outline the space, or stripe the interior of the space, with blue paint. Painting the entire space is not recommended because it may create a slipping hazard and a maintenance problem.

M3 Install *No Parking* signs and/or bollards to prevent unauthorized parking in access aisles where appropriate. ca

M4 Use slip-resistant paint for parking lot striping and other pavement markings. ca

M5 Ensure that additional state and local pavement marking placement and color requirements (if any) are followed. ca

N Signs

Clear signs that designate accessible parking are useful for all people.

N1 Clearly identify all accessible spaces, including those that are proportioned for vans, to ensure that people can easily locate accessible parking spaces. ca
See Figure PA.7

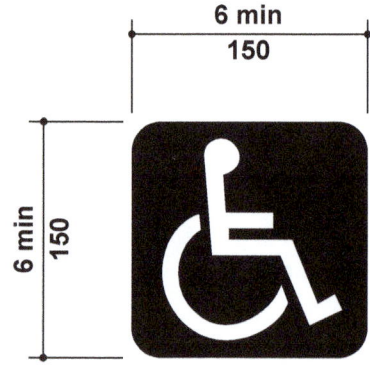

PA.7 International symbol of accessibility

N2 Designate spaces reserved for accessible parking with signs showing the International Symbol of Accessibility. **ADAAG: 1998 4.1 & ADA Standards: 2010 208, 703**

N3 Identify van accessible and alternate van accessible spaces with "Van Accessible" signs. **ADAAG: 1998 4.6 & ADA Standards: 2010 502**

N4 Identify accessible passenger loading zones with signs showing the International Symbol of Accessibility. **ADAAG: 1998 4.1**

N5 Wherever signs incorporate text with the International Symbol for Accessibility, use the word *Accessible* rather than *Handicapped* or *Disabled*.

N6 Install signs so that the bottom edge is a minimum of 60in. (1525mm) above the ground. **ADA Standards: 2010 502 (New)**
A height of 80in. (2030mm) is preferred for safety and visibility.

N7 Locate signs where they are not obscured by parked vehicles, trees, or other obstructions.

N8 Install signs that comply with all ADA Standards for color, character height, and other features.
See SN Signs.

N9 Include information on signs about fines imposed under local ordinances for illegally parking in an accessible space where appropriate.

O **Parking Meters**
Where accessible spaces are metered, people should be able to maneuver in front of parking meters and reach coin slots and operable parts.

O1 Locate meters at accessible spaces on the access aisle side of parking spaces.

O2 Place meters so that coin slots and operable parts are accessible by a parallel approach from the access aisle.

O3 Install meters so that coin slots and operable parts are a maximum height of 48in. (1220mm) from the access aisle traveling surface. **ADAAG: 1998 4.2 & ADA Standards: 2010 308**
A height of 43in. (1090mm) is preferred.

P **Maintenance**

P1 Inspect parking lot surfaces on a regularly scheduled basis to identify tripping hazards, potholes, poor drainage, and surface deterioration.

P2 Ensure that all accessible parking spaces, access aisles, curb ramps, and accessible routes are always properly maintained and are clear of leaves, seed pods, grass clippings, debris, trash, snow and ice.

Easy-to-understand sign designating accessible parking space

Design for All: The Best Path Forward — Dr. Arvid E. Osterberg

CR Curb Ramps

A Location   36
B Clear Width   36
C Landings at Curb Ramps   37
D Slope: New Construction   37
E Alterations to Existing Conditions: Slope   38
F Curb Ramps with Flared Sides   39
G Curb Ramps with Returned Curbs   39
H Built-up Curb Ramps   40
I Curb Ramps at Marked Crossings   40
J Diagonal Curb Ramps   40
K Raised Islands at Crossings   41
L Handrails   41
M Curb Ramp Surfaces   41
N Detectable Warnings   42

Ramps or curb ramps are required wherever an accessible route contains a level change greater than 0.5in. (12.7mm). Where accessible routes cross curbs, curb ramps are required to make streets and sidewalks accessible for wheelchair users and others for whom curbs are obstacles.

Curb ramps are used most often to provide transitions between sidewalks and pedestrian crossings at streets, between streets and median islands, and between parking access aisles and accessible exterior routes, though curb ramps may not extend into access aisles. Because areas that include curb ramps are complex and involve converging slopes and two or more traveling surfaces at different levels, both careful planning and careful quality control during construction are imperative.

To construct safe, accessible curb ramps, eliminate variations in running and cross slopes in all directions. Even slight variations can cause people using wheelchairs to veer off the curb ramp and can pose tripping hazards for people walking across curb ramps.

Lips, drop-offs, or other small level changes at transitions between curb ramp surfaces and adjacent surfaces create tripping hazards and can interfere with the momentum needed to travel up a curb ramp in a wheelchair, particularly if the curb ramp slope is too steep.

A curb ramp that is installed by removing a portion of an existing curb and constructing a curb ramp in that location is often called a curb cut.

The discussion of curb ramps in this chapter applies to curb ramps that are part of sites that serve buildings and facilities. The Access Board addresses curb ramps that are part of public rights of way in a separate document that is available on their website or from your regional Disability and Business Technical Assistance Center at 800-949-4232.

In the illustrations that follow curb ramps and side flares are shaded for visual clarity. However, painting those surfaces is not recommended, since painting sloped surfaces can cause slipping and falling.

A   Location

Locate curb ramps where people need to move from one surface level to another and curbs are present (e.g., at street intersections and between streets and sidewalks or parking areas).

A1 **Provide curb ramps where accessible routes cross curbs.** ADAAG: 1998 4.7 ca

A2 Locate curb ramps where they do not interfere with vehicular traffic lanes, parking spaces, or parking access aisles. **ADA Standards: 2010 406 (New)**

A3 **Locate curb ramps where they cannot be obstructed by parked vehicles.** ca

A4 **Clearly mark cross walks between curb ramps with either white parallel lines (typically used at low traffic crossings) or wide white zebra stripping (typically used at high traffic crossings).** ca

A5 **Ensure that all Federal and State Department of Transportation curb ramp and cross walk requirements (if any apply) are followed.** ca

B   Clear Width

Adequate clear width in curb ramps ensures safety and accessibility for all people.

B1 Provide a minimum clear width of 36in. (915mm) along the full length of the curb ramp, not including flared sides. **ADAAG: 1998 4.7 & ADA Standards: 2010 405**

C   Landings at Curb Ramps

Curb ramps must adjoin accessible routes. The part of the accessible route at the top of a curb ramp is considered a landing.

C1   Provide landings at the top of curb ramps that
- a. have 36in. (915mm) minimum clear floor space, 48in (1022mm) preferred, Ca and
- b. are at least as wide as the traveling surface of the curb ramp excluding flared sides.
ADA Standards: 2010 405 (New)

Exception: Where it is not possible to provide a landing at a curb ramp in an alteration, provide a curb ramp with flared sides that do not exceed a 1:12 slope. **ADA Standards: 2010 406 (New)**
A slope of 1:14 (7.1%) or less slope is preferred. Ca

C2   Where possible, provide 60in. (1525mm) by 60in. (1525mm) level landings or walking surfaces at the top and the bottom of curb ramps. Ca
See Figure CR.1

Gently sloped side flares Ca

D   Slope: New Construction

People who use wheelchairs frequently encounter difficulty traversing from curb ramps to other surfaces, particularly when the slope of side flare surfaces adjacent to the curb ramp are too steep. For an explanation of slopes and information about measuring slopes. **See Measuring Slopes, page 20.**

The combination of cross slope, running slope, and ramp run length affects the accessibility of curb ramps. Keep in mind that cross slopes greater than 1:48 (approx. 2%) cause problems for many people and interfere with wheelchair use by making it difficult for people to travel in a straight line. Excessive cross slope also causes front wheels to veer off the sides of traveling surfaces.
See Figures CR.2 and CR.3

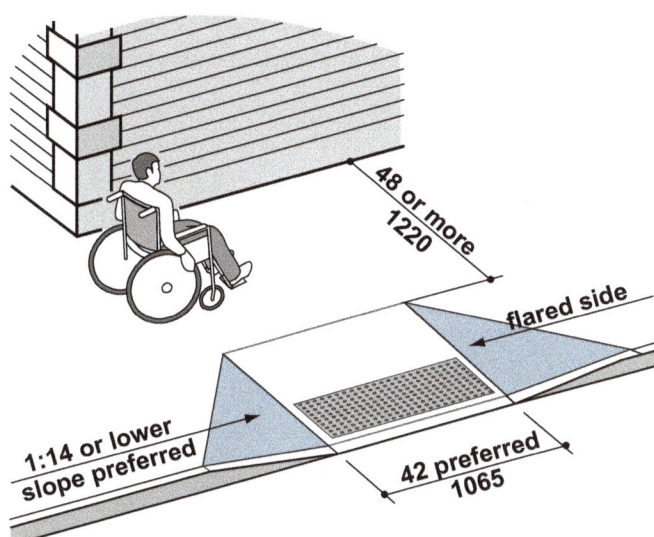

CR.1   A 48in (1220mm) wide landing at the top of a curb ramp with preferred side flares slope

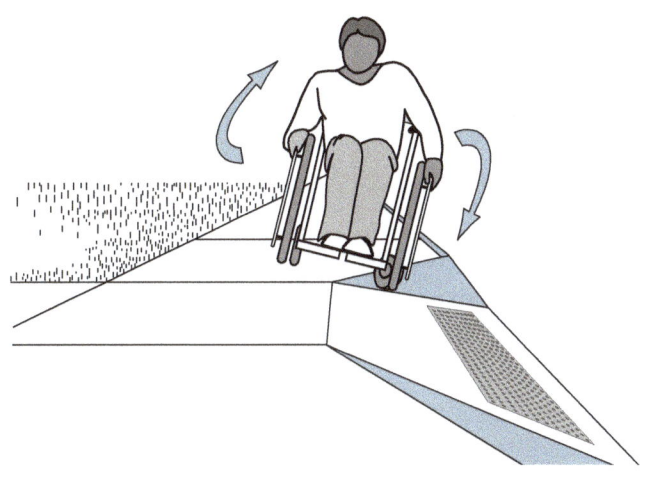

CR.2   *Hazardous* side flares at a curb ramp

Design for All: The Best Path Forward — Dr. Arvid E. Osterberg

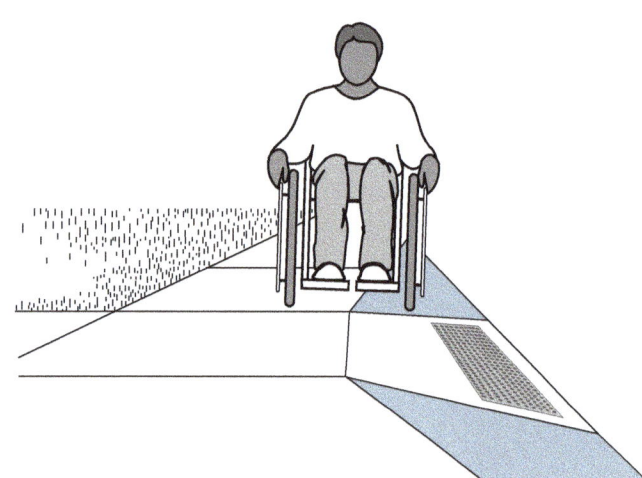

CR.3 Recommended gently sloped side flares at a curb ramp

Excessive slopes where curb ramps and streets intersect can be hazardous. This can cause pedestrians to fall, wheelchairs to lunge forward, and wheelchair toe plates to lodge against pavement surfaces.

D1 Determine the slope of curb ramps. The maximum length of a curb ramp run is determined by its slope and overall rise. **ADAAG: 1998 4.8 & ADA Standards: 2010 405**

D2 Use the least slope possible based on these guidelines:
    a. The maximum slope of the traveling surface of the curb ramp must not exceed 1:12 (8.3%). **ADAAG: 1998 4.8 & ADA Standards: 2010 405**
        A slope of 1:14 (7.1%) or less is preferred.
    b. The maximum slope of adjacent surfaces in all directions, including walks, gutters, and streets, must not exceed 1:20 (5%). **ADAAG: 1998 4.7 & ADA Standards: 2010 406**

D3 Ensure that adjacent surfaces at transitions from curb ramps to walks, gutters, and streets are at the same level.

D4 Where a curb ramp intersects a street, ensure that the sloped surfaces of the street, gutter, and curb ramp all comply with ADA Standards.

D5 To reduce slipping and falling hazards, avoid painting curb ramp surfaces. Tinting concrete, where appropriate, is preferred.
See Figures CR.4 and CR.5

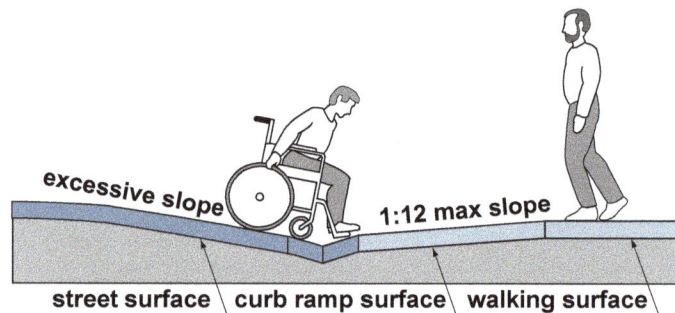

CR.4 *Excessive* slopes at street and curb ramp intersection

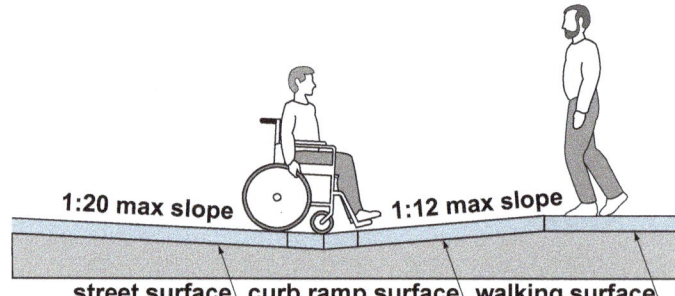

CR.5 *Maximum* slopes at a street and curb ramp intersection

D6 Design and construct curb ramps to fully comply with all slope and dimensional ADA requirements.

D7 Do not bend, warp, slope, or deviate from the ADA Standards when installing new curb ramp to fit existing conditions.

D8 Replace existing curb ramps that do not fully comply with ADA Standards.

E Alterations to Existing Conditions: Slope

Follow the guidelines for new curb ramp construction wherever possible when modifying an existing curb (by installing a curb cut) or when replacing the existing sidewalk, curb, or other traveling surface. Excessive slopes on flared sides of curb ramps result in hazardous cross slopes at intersecting sidewalks.

E1 Wherever space limitations prevent the use of a curb ramp with a maximum slope of 1:12 (8.3%), ADA Standards allows the following guidelines for slopes.

However, the author *does not recommend* using these steeper slopes due to the increased slipping and falling hazard.

- a. Maximum rise may not exceed 6in. (150mm) for 1:10 (10%) to 1:12 (8.3%) slopes.
- b. Maximum rise may not exceed 3in. (75mm) for 1:8 (12.5%) to 1:10 (10%) slopes.
- c. No slope is permitted to exceed 1:8 (12.5%). **ADAAG: 1998 4.1, 4.8 & ADA Standards: 2010 405**

E2 To reduce slipping and falling hazards, avoid painting curb ramp surfaces. Tinting concrete where appropriate is preferred. ca

E3 Ensure proper compaction of soil, aggregate, and other materials before pouring concrete curb ramps. ca

F Curb Ramps with Flared Sides

Flared sides of a curb ramp are meant to provide a smooth transition from the traveling surface into the curb ramp. But flared sides that are too steeply sloped can cause problems for people traveling across them on foot or in wheelchairs. **Refer to Figure CR.2.**

The combination of cross and running slopes must be carefully planned and constructed so that excessive slopes are avoided.

F1 If the width of the walking surface at the top of the curb ramp is **less** than 48in. (1220mm) wide, ensure that the slope of the flared sides does not exceed a maximum slope of 1:12 (8.3%). **ADAAG: 1998 4.7 & ADA Standards: 2010 406**

A slope of 1:14 (7.1%) or less steep is preferred. ca

See Figure CR.6

F2 If the width of the walking surface at the top of the curb ramp is more than 48in. (1220mm) wide, ensure that the slope of the flared sides does not exceed a maximum slope of 1:10 (10%). **ADAAG: 1998 4.7 & ADA Standards: 2010 406**

A slope of 1:14 (7.1%) or less steep is preferred. ca

Refer to Figure CR.1

F3 Measure the slope of the flared side perpendicular to the top edge of the flared side. ca

F4 Avoid painting flared side surfaces to reduce slipping and falling hazards (tinting concrete flares is preferred). ca

See Figure CR.6

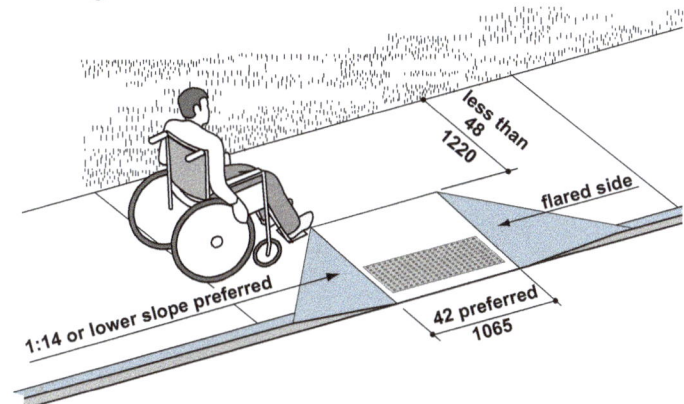

CR.6 A landing less than 48in (1220mm) wide at the top of the curb ramp with preferred slope of side flares

G Curb Ramps with Returned Curbs

The sides of returned curbs are almost vertical. Returned curbs are generally used where surfaces adjacent to the curb ramp are not part of an accessible route, and where people are not likely to walk across the curbs. For example, returned curbs are used where the curb ramp is bordered by plantings (such as grass) or another non-traveling surface.

Curb ramps with returned curbs are not covered in the 2010 ADA Standards, but the Access Board recognizes that they remain an alternative to curb ramps with flared sides in appropriate conditions.

G1 Use returned curbs only where pedestrians would not normally walk across curbs. **ADAAG: 1998 4.7 & ADA Standards: 2010 406**

See Figures CR.7 and CR.8

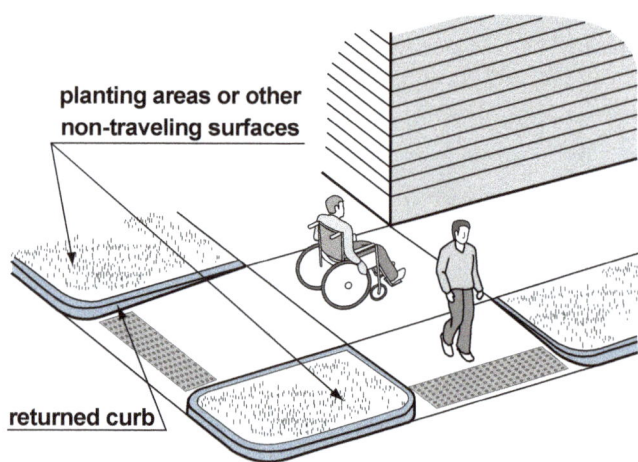

CR.7 Curb ramps with returned curbs in an urban area

CR.8 Curb ramp with returned curbs in a residential area

H Built-up Curb Ramps

The sides of built-up curb ramps, which are generally modifications to existing conditions, slope down from the curb ramp surface to a lower adjacent surface (typically a parking lot). Built-up curb ramps are not recommended in most situations because the sides often do not meet slope and edge protection requirements and can pose a tripping hazard.

H1 Ensure that built-up curb ramps comply with all the requirements of this chapter and do not project into traffic lanes or access aisles. **ADAAG: 1998 4.7** Ca

H2 Replace existing built-up curb ramps that do not comply with all requirements for new curb cuts and curb ramps. Ca

I Curb Ramps at Marked Crossings

Marked crossings are those that have been designated for pedestrians.

I 1 Completely contain curb ramps and landings (excluding any flared sides) inside the marked area at marked crossings. **ADAAG: 1998 4.7 & ADA Standards: 2010 406**

J Diagonal Curb Ramps

Diagonal curb ramps are those that are built into corners.

J1 If diagonal curb ramps have returned curbs or well-defined edges, ensure that the edges are parallel to pedestrian traffic flow. **ADAAG: 1998 4.7 & ADA Standards: 2010 406**

J2 Provide a minimum clear space of 48in. (1220mm) long in the direction of travel at the bottom of curb ramps. **ADAAG: 1998 4.7 & ADA Standards: 2010 406**

J3 Provide a 48in. (1220mm) minimum clear space between the bottom of diagonal curb ramps and the intersection of marked cross walks. **ADAAG: 1998 4.7.10 & ADA Standards: 2010 406**

See Figure CR.9

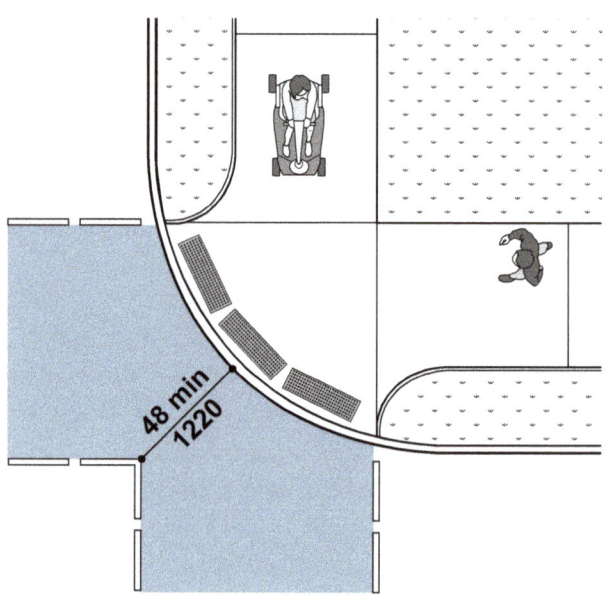

CR.9 Minimum space between a diagonal curb ramp and the intersection of a marked cross walk

J4 Wherever a diagonal curb ramp is located at a marked crossing, ensure that the clear space is contained within the marked crossing. **ADAAG: 1998 4.7 & ADA Standards: 2010 406**

J5 If a diagonal curb ramp has flared sides, ensure that there is at least 24in. (610mm) of straight curb at each side of the crossing area. **ADAAG: 1998 4.7 & ADA Standards: 2010 406**

K Raised Islands at Crossings

Raised islands at crossings must meet accessibility requirements to ensure that all people can cross intersections safely.

K1 Provide access to raised islands by
   a. cutting routes through islands level with the street, or
   b. providing a curb ramp on each side that complies with all curb ramp requirements. **ADAAG: 1998 4.7 & ADA Standards: 2010 406**

See Figures CR.10 and CR.11

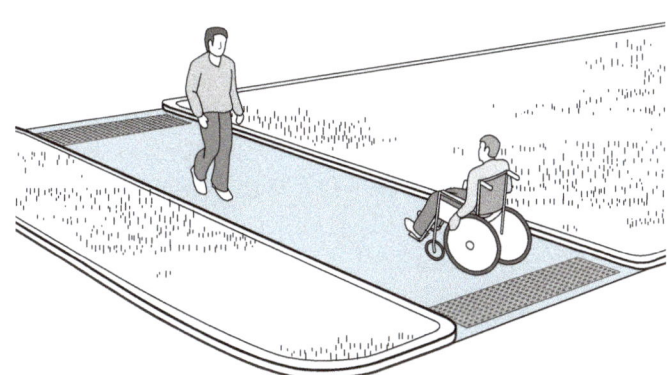

CR.10 Crossing through island *at street level*

CR.11 Crossing through island *with curb ramps*

K2 Provide a level landing a minimum of 48in. (1220mm) long by 36in. (915mm) wide in the section of the island that is between the curb ramps. **ADAAG: 1998 4.7 & ADA Standards: 2010 406**
   a. Orient the level landing so that the 48in. (1220mm) dimension corresponds with the direction of travel. **ADAAG: 1998 4.7 & ADA Standards: 2010 406**

L Handrails

Handrails are not required at curb ramps. In fact they do not improve accessibility and can, in some cases, create a barrier to accessibility.

L1 **Do not install handrails at curb ramps.** Ca

M Curb Ramp Surfaces

Curb ramp surfaces are sometimes marked with paint, which is not a good choice because paint tends to be slippery in wet conditions.

M1 Ensure that surfaces of slopes are firm, stable, and slip-resistant. **ADAAG: 1998 4.7, 4.5 & ADA Standards: 2010 406, 405, 302**

M2 **Ensure that all transitions from curb ramps to adjacent walks, gutters, or streets are flush and free of abrupt changes. ADAAG: 1998 4.7** Ca

M3 **Wherever possible, install curb ramp surface materials that contrast and stand out visually from surrounding surfaces (e.g., by tinting the concrete) and/or by installing detectable warnings that visually contrast with adjoining surfaces.** Ca

M4 **Do not paint curb ramp surfaces. Tinting concrete, where applicable, is preferred.** Ca

M5 Design and construct landings or traveling surfaces at the top and bottom of curb ramps to prevent the accumulation of water. **ADA Standards: 2010 406, 405 (New)**

N Detectable Warnings

Many people, especially people who have visual disabilities, benefit from detectable warnings. Detectable warnings signal important changes in routes at curb ramps and platform edges so people do not inadvertently enter roadways or other hazardous areas.

In the past ADAAG has required the use of truncated domes as detectable warnings at curb ramps, where pedestrian areas blend with vehicular areas, at reflecting pools, and at transportation facilities. Due to concerns about product specifications, availability of complying products, proper maintenance such as snow and ice removal, and safety concerns, the requirement for detectable warnings in most locations was suspended for several years. However, the requirement for detectable warnings remained in effect for platform edges in transportation facilities.

The 2010 ADA Standards neither extended the suspension of the requirement, nor officially added it back to the specifications. Follow the Access Board's Public Rights of Way document for scoping requirements for detectable warnings, and follow the 2010 ADA Standards for truncated dome dimensional requirements where detectable warnings are used. The Public Rights of Way document can be obtained from the Access Board website or from your regional Disability and Business Technical Assistance Center.

Specifications for truncated domes are listed below. Although a number of other detectable warnings, such as grooved or textured concrete, have been used in the past, truncated domes are the only surface that is approved as a detectable warning. Consistency in a warning surface is essential and truncated domes is the only surface that has been shown to provide a high level of detectability.

N1 **Install detectable warnings at appropriate locations where pedestrian areas and vehicular ways intersect if there is no curb, railing, or other element to demarcate the entrance into a vehicular way.** Refer to the Access Board's Public Rights of Way document. ADAAG: 1998 4.29

N2 **Detectable warnings are not required where accessible parking access aisles connect to adjacent sidewalks.** Refer to PA.4, PA.5, and PA.6

N3 Install detectable warnings as close to the edge of transit platforms as possible to alert people that the location it is not a safe place to stand. **ADA Standards: 2010 705 (NEW)**

N4 **Install detectable warnings at the edges of pools or fountains where there is no curb, railing, or other barrier to the pool or fountain edges.** ADAAG: 1998 4.29. Refer to the Access Board's Public Rights of Way document.

N5 Ensure that raised truncated domes are an integral part of the curb ramp surface. **ADAAG: 2010 302 (NEW)**

N6 Ensure that the dimensions of raised truncated domes
   a. have a bottom diameter of 0.90in. (23mm) minimum to 1.4in. (36mm) maximum; **ADA Standards: 2010 705 (MODIFIED-LESS RESTRICTIVE)**
   b. have a top diameter of 0.40in. (10mm) minimum to 0.90in. (23mm) maximum; **ADA Standards: 2010 705 (NEW)**
   c. have a height of 0.20in. (5mm); **ADAAG: 1998 4.29 & ADA Standards: 2010 705**
   d. are spaced evenly from 1.6in. (41mm) minimum to 2.4in. (61mm) maximum, measured center-to-center between adjacent domes on a square grid; **ADA Standards: 2010 705 (MODIFIED-LESS RESTRICTIVE)** and,
   e. contrast visually with adjoining surfaces (either light-on-dark or dark-on-light). **ADAAG: 1998 4.29 & ADA Standards: 2010 705**

See Figure CR.12

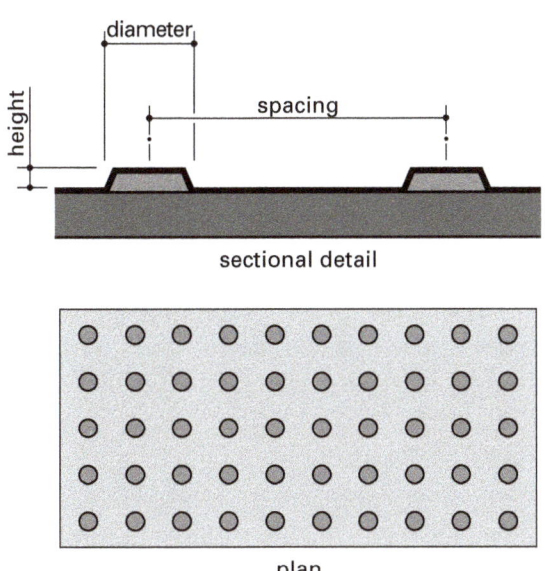

CR.12 Truncated domes

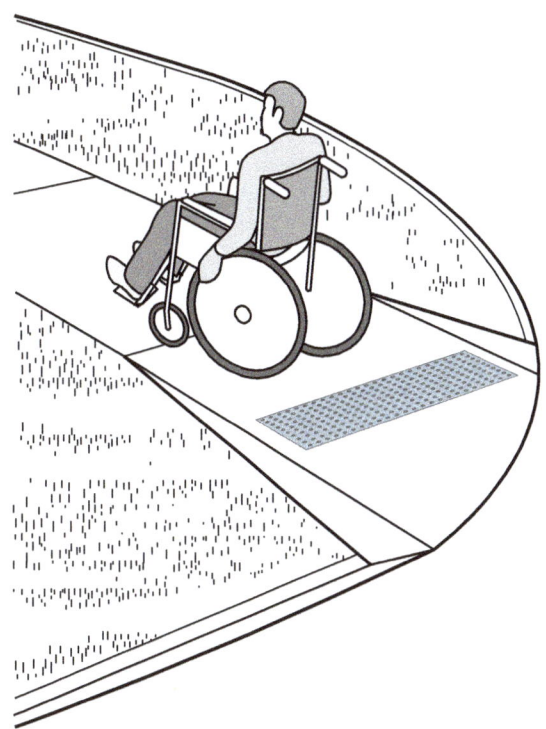

CR.13 Detectable warning perpendicular to direction of travel

Detectable warning

N7 Where truncated domes are used as a detectable warning at transit platforms, ensure that the area covered by the truncated domes is 24in. (610mm) wide and extends the full length of the platform. **ADA Standards: 2010 705 (New)**

N8 **Ensure that the truncated dome pattern has the domes in alignment (rather than a staggered arrangement). ca**

N9 **Where possible locate the detectable warning perpendicular to the direction of travel. ca**
See Figure CR.13

RT Routes & Spaces

A	Exterior Routes	44
B	Interior Routes	45
C	Alterations to Existing Conditions: Number and Location	46
D	New Construction: Vertical Access	46
E	Alterations to Existing Conditions: Vertical Access	47
F	Route Width	48
G	Route Width for Passing and Turning Around	49
H	Route Width for Turns in Routes	51
I	Slope	52
J	Level Changes	53
K	Detectable Warnings	54
L	Traveling Surfaces	55
M	Grates and Openings	55
N	Headroom	56
O	Protruding Objects	56
P	Clear Floor Space	57
Q	Legroom	59
R	Controls and Operating Mechanisms	61
S	Signs	61
T	Windows	62
U	Security Barriers and Checkpoints	63
V	Maintenance of Existing Routes	63
W	Maintenance of Interior Routes	64

Routes are the walkways, paths, corridors, passageways, and other traveling surfaces that people use to navigate buildings and sites. To be accessible, a route must, at a minimum, conform to ADA Standards requirements.

All people should be able to easily locate convenient routes. People who need routes with accessible features should be provided with equivalent or very similar experiences as people who do not need accessible features.

This chapter covers all routes, both exterior and interior. In most cases, the requirements for both exterior and interior routes are the same and, unless specifically noted, the requirements apply to both exterior and interior routes.

Important considerations for all routes include adequate route width for people using devices such as wheelchairs, crutches, and canes. This includes sample turning spaces; safe and stable traveling surfaces; and, when necessary, adequate signs along the route to indicate route locations and directions.

Obstacles (including overhead objects, freestanding objects, or objects that protrude into routes) should be carefully checked to ensure that they are not hazardous.

A route with stairs is not considered to be an accessible route. However, where stairs are provided, the stairs must meet ADA Standards requirements because the safety and usability of stairs is important for all people regardless of ability. **See ST Stairs.**

A Exterior Routes

One of the most important considerations for exterior routes is that accessible routes should coincide the routes used by most people. The best way to accomplish this is to ensure that all primary routes are accessible.

All spaces and features along accessible exterior routes must meet accessibility requirements. **See also PA Parking, EN Entrances, CR Curb Ramps, and RP Ramps.**

Locate accessible exterior routes in the same area as the general circulation path. This means that circulation paths (such as vehicular ways designed for pedestrian traffic, walks, and unpaved paths) that are designed for routine use by pedestrians must be accessible or must be close to an accessible route.

A1 Provide accessible routes from site arrival points (within the boundary of a site) to the accessible entrances of the building(s). Site arrival points include the following:
    a. public transportation,
    b. accessible parking spaces,
    c. passenger loading zones, and
    d. public streets and sidewalks. **ADAAG: 1998 4.1, 4.3 & ADA Standards: 2010 206**

Exception: If the only access route between site arrival points and the building entrance is a vehicular way that is used for pedestrian travel, then it should be marked as a pedestrian crossing. A separate accessible route is not required. ADA Standards: 2010 206 (New)

A2 Ensure that primary public routes (those that are traveled most frequently or those that provide the most direct paths to the building) are accessible. **ADAAG: 1998 4.3 & ADA Standards: 2010 206**

A3 Provide accessible routes everywhere throughout a site where possible. (Examples: college campus, business park, sports park, medical building complex, housing complex).

A4 Ensure proper compaction of soil, aggregate, and other materials before pouring concrete in accessible routes.

A5 Ensure that free standing sculptures are not collision hazards by placing sculptures out of path of travel and/or on pedestals.

A6 When sculptures are mounted on pedestals, ensure that protruding sculptural elements are not collision hazards.

A7 Ensure that the color of pedestals have contrast with the color of ground surface material.

A8 Place benches, seating, recycling bins, trash containers, signs, and other objects are out of the path of travel, so they do not result in collision hazards.

A9 Place seats and benches *in courtyards and plazas* out of the paths of travel to ensure that they are not collision hazards for people with limited vision.

A10 Ensure that benches and other objects have contrasting color to the color of ground surface material.

A11 To reduce falling risks, do not plant trees that drop nuts, cones, or fruit adjacent to (or on) routes, plazas and courtyards.

B Interior Routes

All spaces and features along accessible interior routes must meet accessibility requirements. For specific requirements pertaining to elements of interior routes, **see EN Entrances, DR Doors, EL Elevators, PL Platform Lifts, AR Areas of Rescue, and RP Ramps.**

All interior routes in all public spaces on all accessible floors should be fully accessible.

B1 Provide accessible routes that connect all accessible building entrances to all accessible spaces and features within the building. **ADAAG: 1998 4.1, 4.3 & ADA Standards: 2010 206**

B2 Ensure that all halls, corridors, aisles, skywalks, tunnels, and other spaces that are part of accessible routes are accessible. **ADAAG: 1998 4.3**

B3 Provide accessible routes to all employee work areas. Place seats and benches in courtyards and plazas, rather than in paths of travel, to ensure that they are not collision hazards for people with limited vision. **ADAAG: 1998 4.1 & ADA Standards: 2010 203**

See WA Work Areas, RS Restaurants, AA Assembly Areas, HP Historic Preservation, MC Medical Care, TL Transient Lodging, and DU Dwelling Units for additional information on routes in specific areas.

B4 Ensure that all corridor doors on all floors between various wings of a building or building complex are equipped with magnetic hold open devices (whenever possible) to make access easier for everyone.

B5 Increase visibility of interior routes and spaces by contrasting floor and wall colors.

B6 Avoid confusing flooring patterns that can be mistaken as changes in level.

B7 Specify matte finish flooring to reduce glare.

Undesirable glare and reflections

B8 To minimize glare and reflections in interior routes and hallways, provide 1) appropriate window and skylight placement, 2) appropriate lighting systems, and 4) non-glare surface materials. ca

B9 To reduce glare, avoid designs that have large glazing panels at the end of long hallways and corridors. ca

Caution 'wet floor' signs should be removed when floor is dry

B10 Install high quality flooring materials that have the appropriate amount of slip resistance. ca

C Alterations to Existing Conditions: Number and Location

All alterations and modifications of existing spaces and connecting routes should ensure accessibility for all people.

When alterations are made to a primary function area, which is any area used for a major activity for which the building is intended, the path of travel to that area must also be made accessible. The path of travel includes an accessible route to the altered area and the restrooms, telephones, and drinking fountains serving the area.

The ADA requires owners to do as much as it takes to make the path of travel to a primary function area as accessible as possible following ADA Standards, spending up to 20% of the cost of the alteration to the primary function area.

C1 In additions to buildings, follow the guidelines for new construction to the maximum extent feasible. **ADAAG: 1998 4.1, 4.3 & ADA Standards: 2010 202**

C2 In alterations that include a primary function area, ensure that the path of travel (including restrooms, drinking fountains, and telephones) is accessible to the maximum extent feasible. **ADAAG: 1998 4.1 & ADA Standards: 2010 202**

C3 When budgeting for alterations to a primary function area, allocate up to 20% of the cost of the alteration to make the path of travel to the primary function area accessible. **ADAAG: 1998 4.1 & ADA Standards: 2010 202**

Example: If your total budget for an alteration is $100,000 then you must be prepared to spend up to $20,000 of that amount to ensure that a continuous path of travel is accessible and that elements along the route (including restrooms) also are accessible.

D New Construction: Vertical Access

Accessible routes must allow travel between accessible levels of buildings (vertical access) for all people. Vertical access includes elevators, ramps, and stairs. A route that includes stairs as the only means of vertical access is not considered accessible because people who cannot use stairs would not have access. However, because people who have some types of disabilities can use stairs. Therefore, stairs and steps used by the public must meet ADA Standards requirements. **See ST Stairs.**

Platform (wheelchair) lifts are only permitted as part of an accessible route in certain, specific situations. **See PL Platform Lifts.**

The ADA Standards contains a number of exceptions to the requirements for vertical access that are addressed in this chapter and chapters pertaining to specific use areas. Exceptions related to recreation facilities, HUD housing, judicial facilities, transportation facilities, and detention areas are not included in *Design for All*.

D1 Design and construct accessible exterior routes to buildings and accessible routes within and between buildings so that they do not include stairs and steps. **ADAAG: 1998 4.3 & ADA Standards: 2010 402**

D2 In new, multi-story construction, provide accessible vertical access to all levels of the building including public mezzanines. Wherever access is provided by elevator, every full passenger elevator provided must meet the requirements in **EL Elevators**. **ADAAG: 1998 4.1 & ADA Standards: 2010 206**

Accessible vertical access is not required by ADA Standards under the following three conditions listed as exceptions. Check with local and state authorities to determine if other provisions apply.
Exception: Accessible vertical access may not be required in some buildings covered under Title III of the ADA that are less than three stories or that have less than 3000 sq. ft. (278.7 sq. m) per story. However, buildings that are less than three stories or that have less than 3000sq. ft. per story and that contain shopping centers, shopping malls, medical providers' offices, and certain other types of facilities as determined by the Attorney General must include accessible vertical access. ADAAG: 1998 4.1 & ADA Standards: 2010 206
Exception: Accessible vertical access is not required in public buildings with less than three stories where the stories above or below the accessible ground floor
 a. are not open to the general public,
 b. have a occupant load of five or fewer persons, or
 c. are less than 500sq. ft. (46.5sq. m).
 ADAAG: 1998 4.1 & ADA Standards: 2010 206

Exception: Accessible vertical access is not required to elevator pits, elevator penthouses, mechanical rooms, piping or equipment catwalks, or other equipment spaces used exclusively for maintenance or repair. ADAAG: 1998 4.1 & ADA Standards: 2010 203

D3 Wherever vertical access is provided by steps or stairs, ensure that the stairs, steps, landings, and handrails meet requirements for accessibility in **ST Stairs**. **ADAAG: 1998 4.1 & ADA Standards: 2010 504**

D4 In multi-story buildings that do not require elevators, ensure that all accessible routes on floors located above and below the accessible ground floor entrances meet all other accessibility requirements. **ADAAG: 1998 4.1 & ADA Standards: 2010 206**

E Alterations to Existing Conditions: Vertical Access

The requirements for vertical access in existing buildings are similar to those for new buildings. Platform (wheelchair) lifts are only permitted as part of an accessible route in certain, specific situations but may be used in existing buildings where elevators and/or ramps are not feasible because of site constraints. **See PL Platform Lifts.**

E1 In existing buildings without elevators, ensure that alterations to spaces and elements above or below the accessible ground floor meet all other accessibility requirements. **ADAAG: 1998 4.1** ca

E2 Provide alternate vertical access (such as a ramp or elevator) if stairs or escalators are included in a route that must be accessible. **ADAAG: 1998 4.3** ca

E3 Provide alternate vertical access (such as a ramp, elevator, or platform lift) if stairs or escalators are added through major structural modifications where no stairs previously existed.
ADAAG: 1998 4.1 & ADA Standards: 2010 206
See RT-D2 for exceptions.

F Route Width *(exterior and interior)*
Wide routes allow people to travel together and pass others more comfortably than routes that meet only minimum width requirements.

A person dressed in winter clothing, walking straight ahead with arms moving needs at least 32in. (815mm) of space to comfortably move past other people. A person using an assistive device (such as a wheelchair, scooter, walker, or crutches) needs more clear space in a route.

F1 Provide a clear route width of 36in. (915mm) minimum. **ADAAG: 1998 4.3 & ADA Standards: 2010 403**
Wider routes are preferred. ca
See Figure RT.1

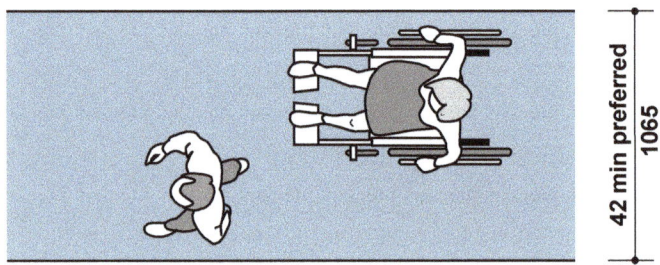

RT.1 Preferred minimum route width for a wheelchair

F2 Provide a clear route width of 48in. (1220mm) minimum to allow for a pedestrian to pass a wheelchair. ca
See Figure RT.2

RT.2 Preferred minimum route width for a pedestrian to pass a wheelchair

F3 Routes are permitted to narrow to a minimum of 32in. (815mm) wide where
  a. the reduced width occurs for no more than 24in. (610mm) in length; and
  b. repeated reductions in width are 48in. (1220mm) minimum apart. **ADAAD: 1998 4.2 & ADA Standards: 2010 403**
See Figure RT.3

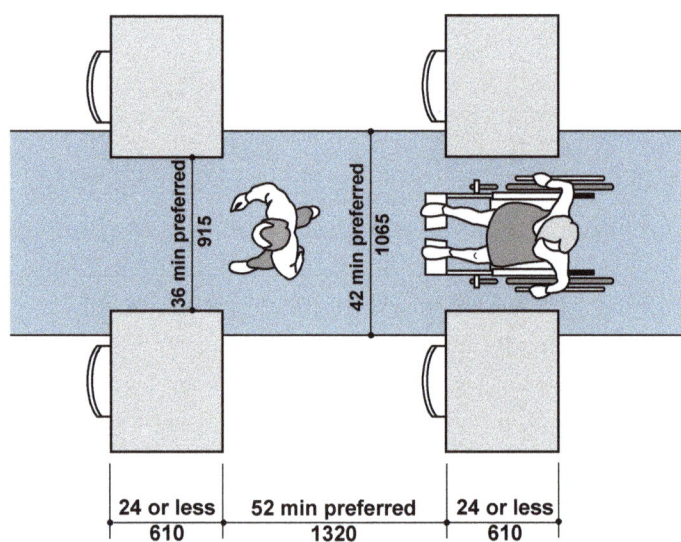

RT.3 Preferred minimum dimensions for a route with protrusions less than 24 inches in length

F4 Allow adequate width and maneuvering space at entrances and doors. **ADAAG: 1998 4.3 & ADA Standards: 2010 404 See EN Entrances and DR Doors.**

F5 To prevent parked vehicles from obstructing accessible routes, ensure that sidewalks bordering parking lots are extra wide (or install grass strips to separate parking lots from sidewalks). ca

Outdoor seating alongside accessbible route

Outdoor seating alongside accessbible route

G Route Width for Passing and Turning Around

People using wheelchairs need sufficient space to pass others and turn around. Ideally, in moderately traveled areas, routes should have a clear width of 60in. (1525mm) to accommodate passing and turning around.

The minimum space required for a person in a wheelchair to make a 180° turn is 60in. (1525mm) by 60in. (1525mm). Where two intersections meet to form an adequate sized T-shaped space, people can also maneuver for turning.

People using wheelchairs also need space along routes to pass and to allow others to pass. Where routes are 60in. (1525mm) wide or wider, people have sufficient passing space. Where routes are less than 60in. (1525mm) wide, spaces must be provided at intervals so that people can move out of the way of other traffic. Like turning space, passing space can be provided by including a 60in. (1525mm) by 60in. (1525mm) clear space. Space created by a **T**-intersection of two routes is also considered to be passing space.

The ADA Standards specifies the intervals where you must provide passing spaces along routes but does not specify intervals for turning spaces. However, required passing spaces can also serve as turning spaces.

G1 Provide routes that are at least 60in. (1525mm) wide.
  Routes wider than 60 inches are preferred
  When a route is 60in. (1525mm) wide, you do not have to provide additional space in the route for passing and turning around. **ADAAG: 1998 4.2, 4.3 & ADA Standards: 2010 403**
See Figure RT.4

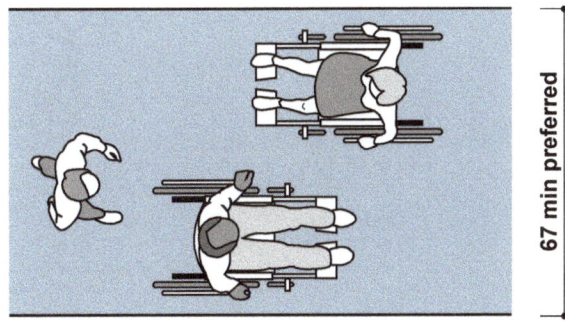

RT.4 Preferred minimum route width for two wheelchairs to pass

G2 If the route is less than 60in. (1525mm) wide, provide turning spaces at reasonable intervals that meet one of the following conditions:
  a. clear space of 60in. (1525mm) minimum in diameter.
    A space of 60in (1525mm) by 78in (1980mm) or more is preferred.
  b. **T**-shaped space formed by a 60in. (1525mm) length of a 36in. (915mm)

Design for All: The Best Path Forward — Dr. Arvid E. Osterberg

minimum width route and an adjacent, centered leg that is 24in. (610mm) deep minimum and 60in. (1525mm) wide minimum.

Additional space is preferred ⓒa ADAAG: 1998 4.2 & ADA Standards: 2010 304

See Figures RT.5, RT.6, and RT.7

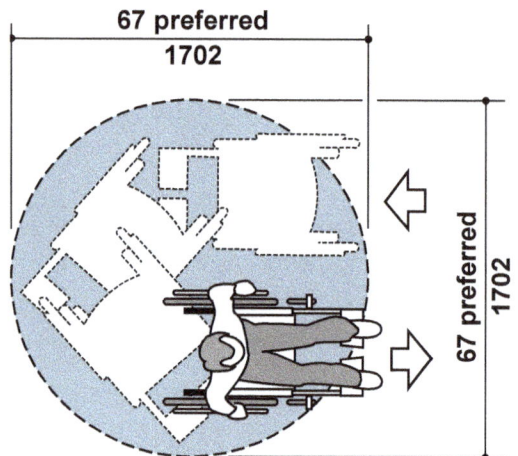

RT.5 **Preferred** minimum clear space for turning around and passing

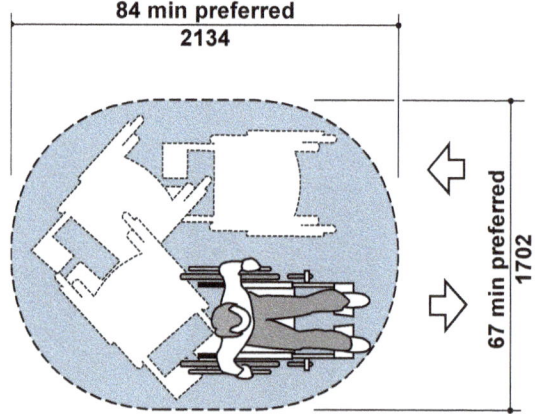

RT.6 **Preferred** minimum clear space for turning around and passing

G3 Where routes are 200ft. (60.96m) long or longer and are less than 60in. (1525mm) wide, provide passing spaces at intervals of not more than 200ft. (60.96m). **ADAAG: 1998 4.3 & ADA Standards: 2010 403**

G4 Provide passing spaces that meet one of the following conditions:
   a. clear space of 60in. (1525mm) by 60in. (1525mm) minimum.

A space of 67in (1702mm) min by 78in. (1980mm) is preferred. ⓒa

Refer to Figures RT. 5 and RT.6
   b. T-shaped spaces (such as those created by the intersection of two routes) where each leg of the T is a minimum of 36in. (915mm) wide for a minimum of 48in. (1220mm).

42in (1065mm) min wide by 52in (1320mm) is preferred ⓒa ADAAG: 1998 4.2 & ADA Standards: 2010 304, 403

See Figure RT.8

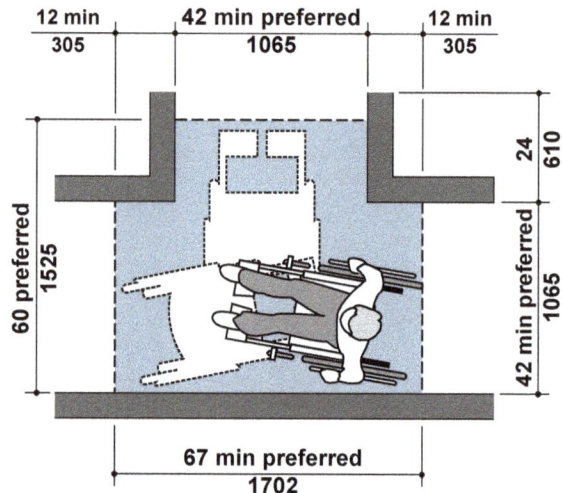

RT.7 **Preferred** minimum space at a T-shaped **intersection** for turning **around**

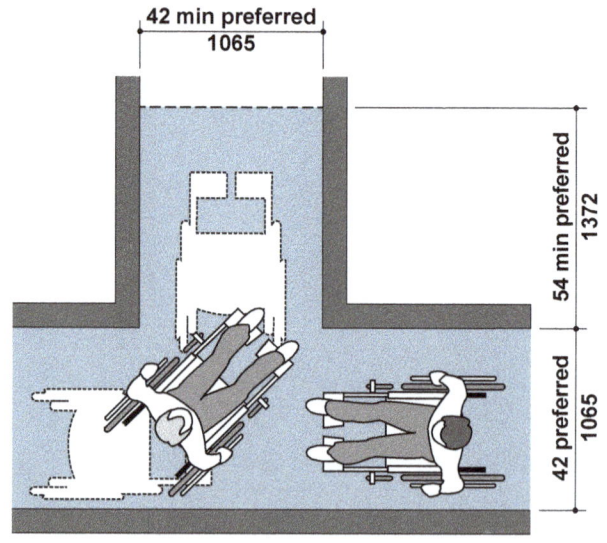

RT.8 **Preferred** minimum space at a T-shaped **intersection** for passing

G5 Ensure that 60in. (1525mm) minimum clear width is provided between display cases where turning or maneuvering is required.
   67in (1702mm) min is preferred
See Figure RT.9

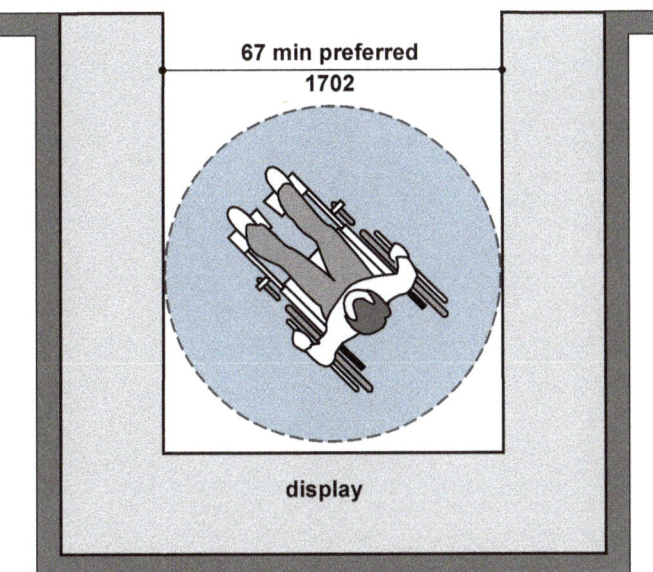

RT.9 **Preferred** minimum space needed for maneuvering between display cases in an exhibition area

H Route Width for Turns in Routes

To evaluate the accessibility of routes, measure the distance between turns and check the angle of turns in accessible routes. Examine routes to ensure that there is sufficient space for wheelchairs to turn around corners and obstructions.

H1 **For turns in routes**
   a. **provide adequate width in all routes;**
   b. **provide smooth, wide turning spaces along all routes; and**
   c. **eliminate obstructions in turning areas.**

H2 When a route contains turns around obstructions that are less than 48in. (1220mm) wide, or where the route turns around obstructions that are less than 48in. (1220mm) wide, ensure that the route meets all of the following conditions:
   a. a clear width of 48in. (1220mm) minimum at the turn;
      60in. (1525mm) min is preferred;
   b. a clear width of 42in. (1065mm) minimum

in the routes approaching and leaving the turn; **48in (1220mm) min is preferred** and

   c. a clearance of 60in. (1525mm) past any obstruction before narrowing a route to the minimum width for an unobstructed route.
   ADAAG: 1998 4.3 & ADA Standards: 2010 403

Examples: Library stacks, museum displays, and 180° turns between ramp runs are situations where the guidelines apply.
See Figures RT.10, RT.11, and RT.12

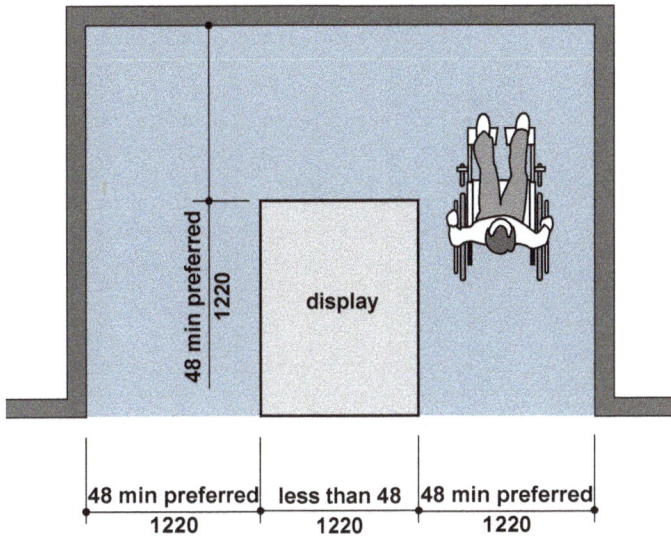

RT.10 **Preferred** minimum dimensions for maneuvering around a display case that is *less than* 48 inches wide

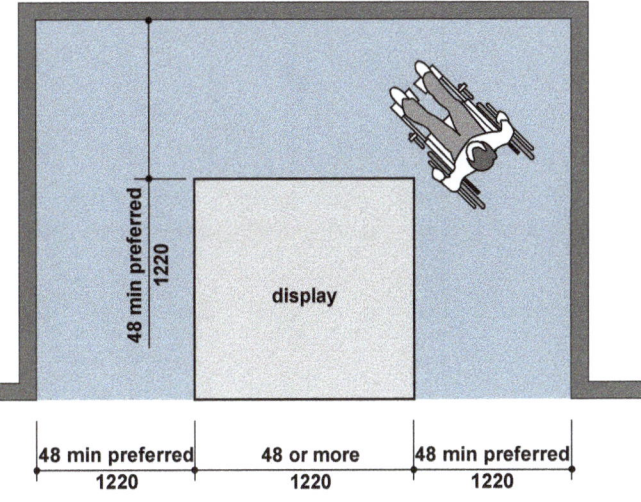

RT.11 **Preferred** minimum dimensions for maneuvering around a display case that is *more than* 48 inches wide

Design for All: The Best Path Forward — Dr. Arvid E. Osterberg

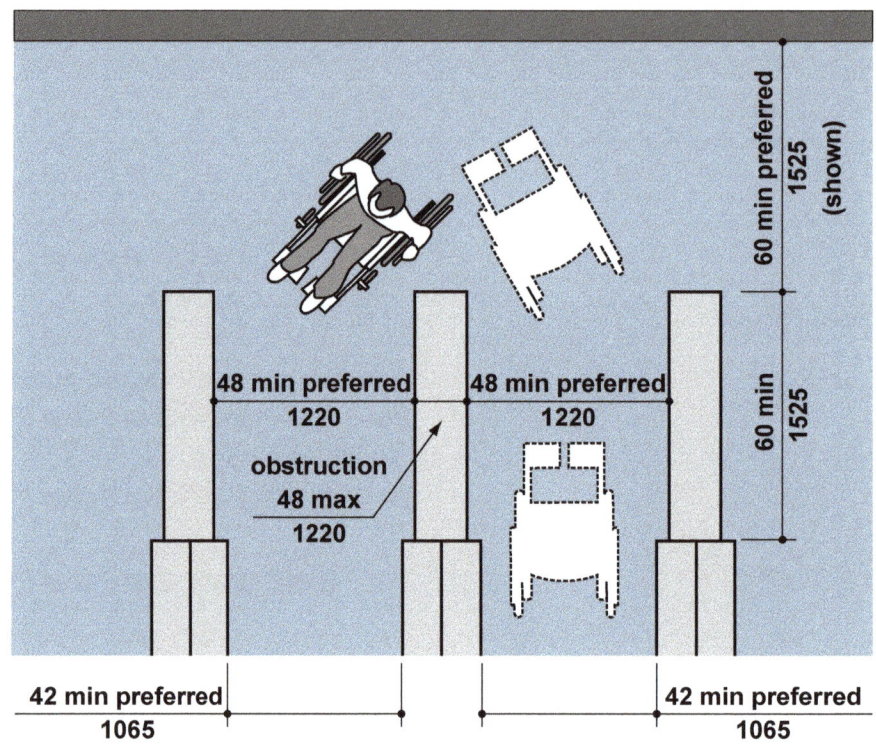

RT.12 Preferred minimum dimensions for a route with turns around obstructions (e.g. library stacks or bookstore shelves)

I   Slope

Wherever possible, keep the running slope below 1:20 (5%). When the running slope in an accessible route exceeds 1:20 (5%), the route must be considered a ramp and must meet the requirements for a ramp.

Cross slopes greater than 1:48 (approx. 2%) cause balance problems for many people and interfere with wheelchair use by causing front casters to veer and by disrupting the balance needed to move wheelchairs forward.
See Measuring Slopes, page 12 for an explanation of slopes and information about measuring slopes.
See RP Ramps and CR Curb Ramps for information about altering existing conditions where a running slope exceeds 1:20 (5%).

I 1   Determine the running slope and the cross slope of all route traveling surfaces. Ca

I 2   Ensure that running slopes do not exceed 1:20 (5%). **ADAAG: 1998 4.3 & ADA Standards: 2010 403**

I 3   Ensure that cross slopes do not exceed 1:48 (approx. 2%). **ADAAG: 1998 4.3 & ADA Standards: 2010 403**
See Figures RT.13 and RT.14

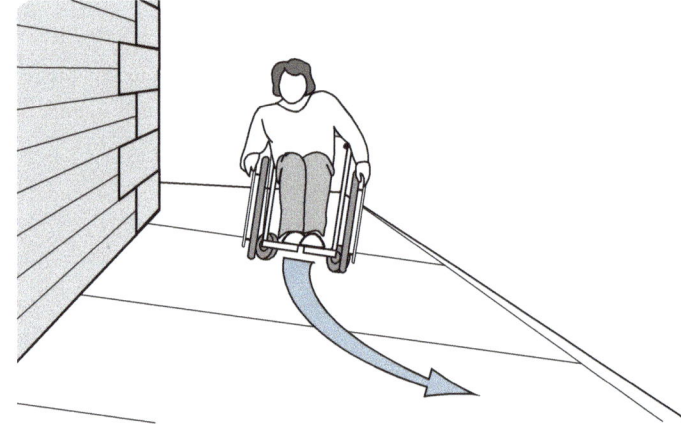

RT.13 A wheelchair user struggling to travel straight on a sidewalk with excessive cross slope

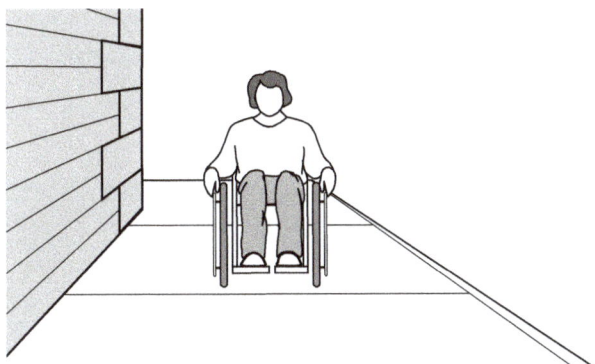

RT.14 A wheelchair user traveling straight on a sidewalk with cross slope less than 1:48 (approx. 2%)

I 4 Where handrails are provided along routes that have slopes of 1:20 or less, follow ADA Standards requirements for height, clearance, continuity, profile, and gripping surfaces. **See RP Ramps, RP-E, RP-F** ca

J Level Changes

Level changes include changes between routes and adjoining surfaces and changes within the route (such as a junction where the traveling surface changes). Level changes in routes as small as 0.25in. (6.4mm) can cause tripping hazards.

Keep adjoining surfaces flush with route edges wherever possible. Even where the difference in level between two adjoining surfaces is small, it is best to provide edge protection. If a wheelchair slips off an edge, it is difficult for the user to get the wheelchair back on the traveling surface.

J1 Do not design or construct small level changes that result in single-step conditions in any exterior or interior routes or at doorways. ca

Small level change along path

J2 Where level changes are between 0.25in. (6.4mm) and 0.5in. (12.7mm), bevel edges with a maximum slope of 1:2 (50%). ADAAG: 1998 4.5 & ADA Standards: 2010 303

J3 Plan routes with gradual slopes of less than 1:20 (5%) and with continuous, smooth surfaces to minimize the need for ramps or curb ramps. ca

Tripping hazard from uneven settling of tiles

Tripping hazard at grate

J4 When a small level change that is a tripping hazard in a route is present, paint the top and vertical edges a bright contrasting colored slip-resistant paint, and eliminate the hazard as soon as possible. ca

Design for All: The Best Path Forward — Dr. Arvid E. Osterberg

Common tripping hazard in route due to settlement of sidewalk

J5   Avoid level changes along the edges of accessible routes wherever possible. ca
See Figure RT.15

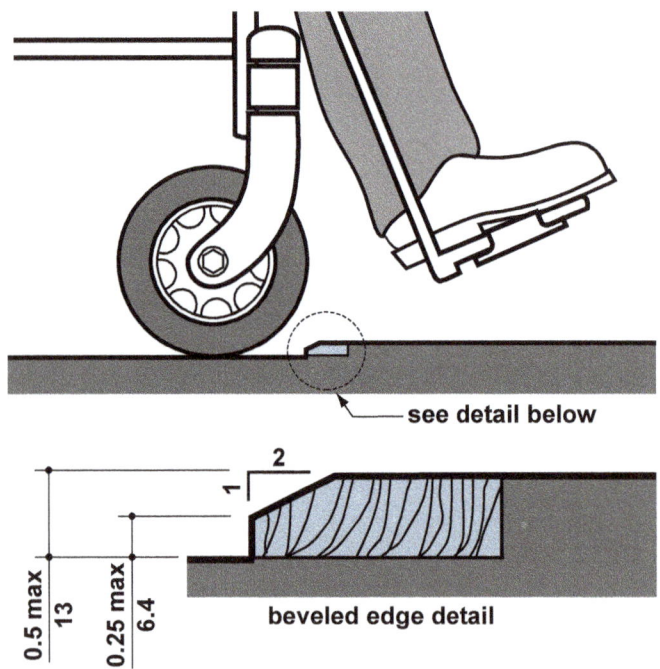

RT.15 Level change with a beveled edge

J6   Install curb ramps or ramps where level changes in routes are greater than 0.5in. (12.7mm). **ADAAG: 1998 4.5 & ADA Standards: 2010 303**   See RP Ramps and CR Curb Ramps.

J7   Provide edge protection or barriers along routes where the surfaces adjacent to the routes are 0.5in. (12.7mm) or more below the level of the routes. ca

J8   To reduce missteps, construct standard curb profiles and avoid gradual blending of curbs into flat walking surfaces. ca

Standard curb profile blending into non-standard profile; a misstep hazard

J9   To reduce trip and misstep hazards, avoid installing tapered curbs. ca

Exception: tapered curbs at curb ramps that fully comply with ADA Standards are permitted but should be painted with bright colored slip-resistant paint.

J10 Where tapered curbs exist, paint the top and vertical edges with a bright color to help alert pedestrians. ca

J11 Where tapered curbs exist (especially in unexpected locations), paint the top and vertical edges with a bright colored slip-resistant paint to help alert pedestrians of misstep hazards. ca

J12 Ensure that transitions between flooring materials, such as from tile to carpet, are not tripping hazards [the maximum vertical elevation change permitted is 0.25in. (6.4mm)]. ca

K   Detectable Warnings

Some people, especially people who have visual disabilities, need detectable warnings to identify critical changes in routes.

Detectable warnings are required as part of an accessible route in many situations, including most curb ramps, and at loading docks and boarding platforms in transit stations. For more information on detectable warnings. **See CR Curb Ramps, CR-N**

L Traveling Surfaces

Route surfaces should allow all people to safely and comfortably travel in all weather conditions. Concrete and asphalt surfaces that are too smooth can be slipping hazards, especially when they are wet or oily. Thick or loose carpet can be tripping hazards and can interfere with the mobility of wheelchairs.

L1 Provide traveling surfaces on all routes and adjacent spaces that are firm, stable, and slip-resistant. **ADAAG: 1998 4.5 & ADA Standards: 2010 302**

L2 When specifying carpeting for an interior route, choose a product with a short pile and a tight weave. Ca

L3 Ensure that all carpeting is:
    a. attached securely;
    b. un-backed or backed with firm padding;
    c. level or textured loop, level cut pile, or cut/uncut pile texture; and
    d. no more than 0.5in. (12.7mm) pile thickness. **ADAAG: 1998 4.5 & ADA Standards: 2010 302**

L4 Fasten carpet edges to floor surfaces with carpet edge trim along the entire length of all exposed carpet edges. **ADAAG: 1998 4.5 & ADA Standards: 2010 302**

L5 Bevel carpet edge trim with a slope no greater than 1:2 (50%) where the carpet trim is between 0.25in. (6.4mm) and 0.5in. (12.7mm) higher than the adjacent surface. A ramp is required for level changes over 0.5in. (12.7mm). **ADAAG: 1998 4.5 & ADA Standards: 2010 302, 303**

M Grates and Openings

Grates or other openings in the surface of a route can cause tripping, slipping, falling and other problems including catching canes and crutches and interfering with wheelchair casters.

M1 Eliminate and/or avoid installing grates or other openings in traveling surfaces wherever possible. Ca

M2 Place grates with elongated openings so that the long dimension is perpendicular to the dominant direction of travel. **ADAAG: 1998 4.5 & ADA Standards: 2010 302**
See Figure RT.16

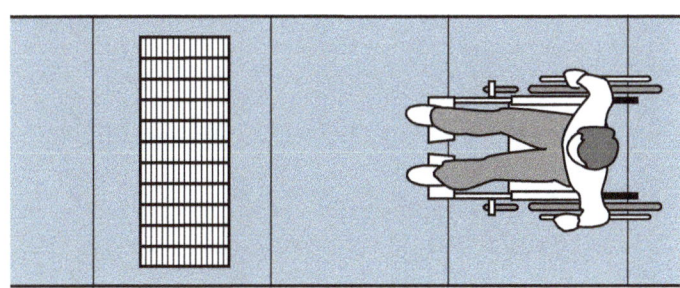

RT.16 Grate opening orientation

M3 Ensure that the width of spaces in a grate is not more than 0.5in. (12.7mm) in the dominant direction of travel. **ADAAG: 1998 4.5 & ADA Standards: 2010 302**
See Figure RT.17

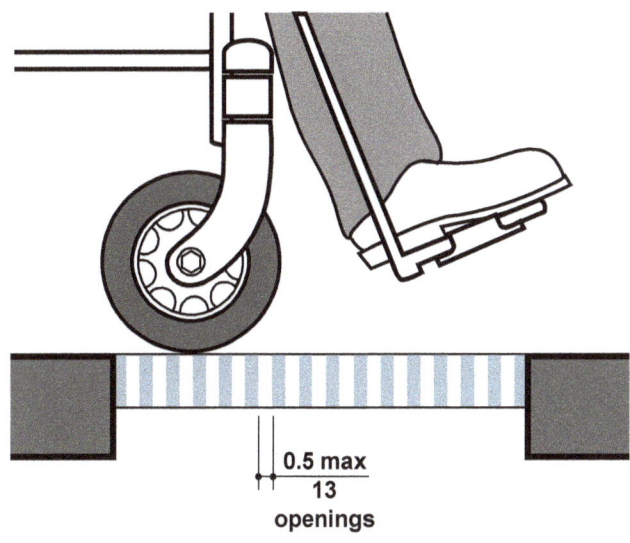

RT.17 Maximum allowable grate opening in the dominant direction of travel

N Headroom

People traveling along exterior routes need sufficient headroom to avoid injury from overhead obstacles including tree branches or overhead signs. People traveling along hallways, corridors and other interior routes also need sufficient headroom to avoid injury from overhead obstacles like overhead signs and overhead stairways. Sufficient headroom is especially important for people with visual impairments.

N1 Ensure that headroom (vertical clearance) along routes is 80in. (2030mm) minimum above the route surface. **ADAAG: 1998 4.4 & ADA Standards: 2010 307**

N2 Mount any overhanging object (such as a sign or banner) so that the lowest surface or edge is 80in. (2030mm) minimum above the route surface. **ADAAG: 1998 4.4 & ADA Standards: 2010 307**
See Figure RT.18

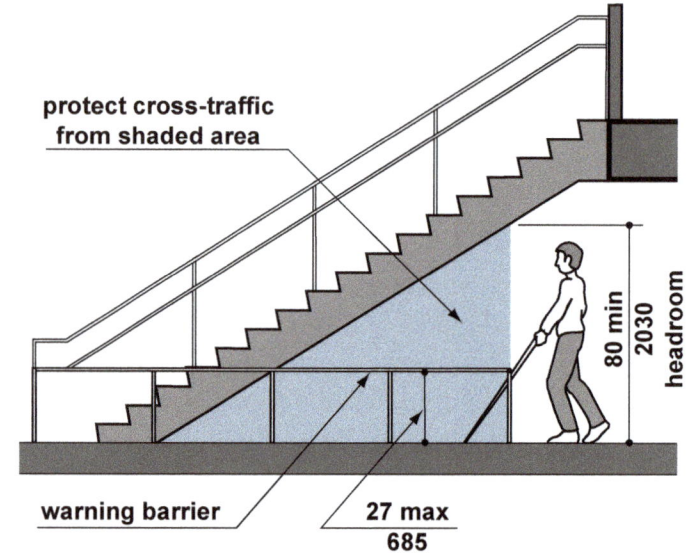

RT.19 A warning barrier used to alert people of limited headroom

O Protruding Objects

Protruding objects should be located so that people who use canes can detect them. The standard cane sweep allows detection of the leading edges of objects up to 27in. (685mm) from the traveling surface. People using canes may not detect a protruding object in time where the bottom edge is higher than 27in. (685mm). Protruding objects must not reduce the required minimum clear width in a route.

O1 Check for objects that extend into the routes, including protrusions from the walls and ceilings and freestanding objects within the routes.

O2 Remove protruding or freestanding objects that reduce the minimum accessible route width and maneuvering space.

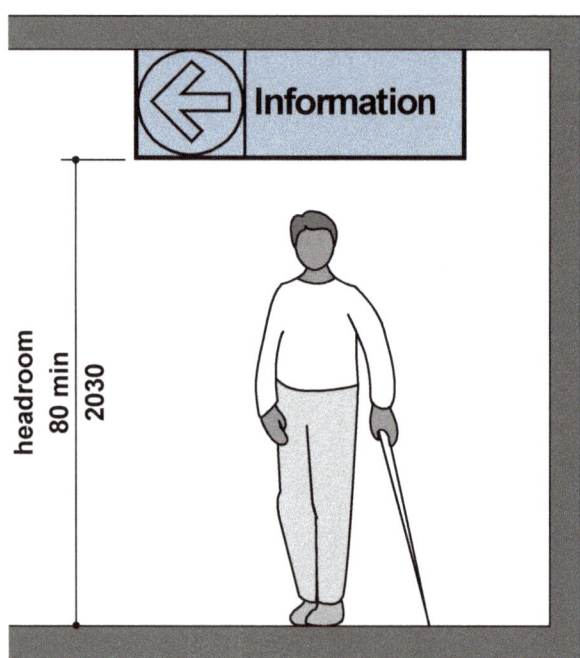

RT.18 Minimum headroom in an accessible route

N3 Install warning barriers (such as gates, rails, curbs, appropriate landscaping, or planters) between accessible routes and adjoining areas where the vertical clearance is between 27in. (685mm) and 80in. (2030mm) above the route surface. **ADAAG: 1998 4.4 & ADA Standards: 2010 307**
See Figure RT.19

O3 Ensure that where the leading edge of a protruding object is between 27in. (685mm) and 80in. (2030mm) above the route surface, the object protrudes no more than 4in. (100mm) into the route and does not extend into the required minimum clear width of the route. **ADAAG: 1998 4.4 & ADA Standards: 2010 307**
Exception: Handrails are permitted to extend into the clear width 4.5in. (115mm) maximum.
See Figure RT.20

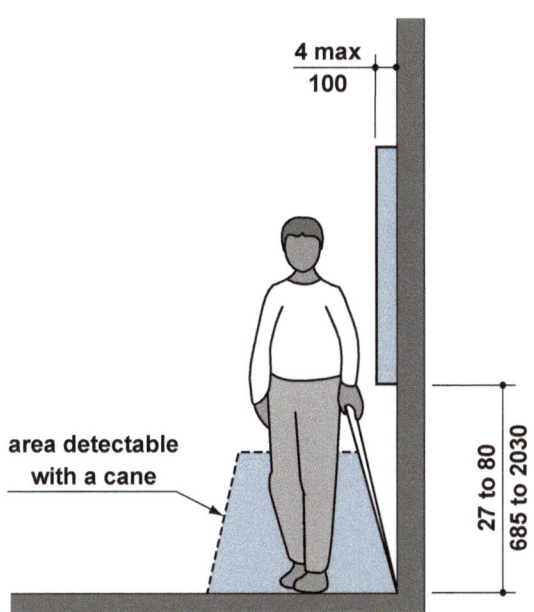

RT.20 Person using a cane to detect obstacles in a route while passing an allowable protrusion

O4 Where a sign or object is mounted on posts that are 12in. (305mm) or more apart, ensure that the lowest edge of the sign or object is
  a. 27in. (685mm) or less above the traveling surface to ensure that a person using a cane will be able to detect the object, or
  b. 80in. (2030mm) or more above the traveling surface to provide sufficient headroom. **ADAAG: 1998 4.4 & ADA Standards: 2010 307**

See Figure RT.21

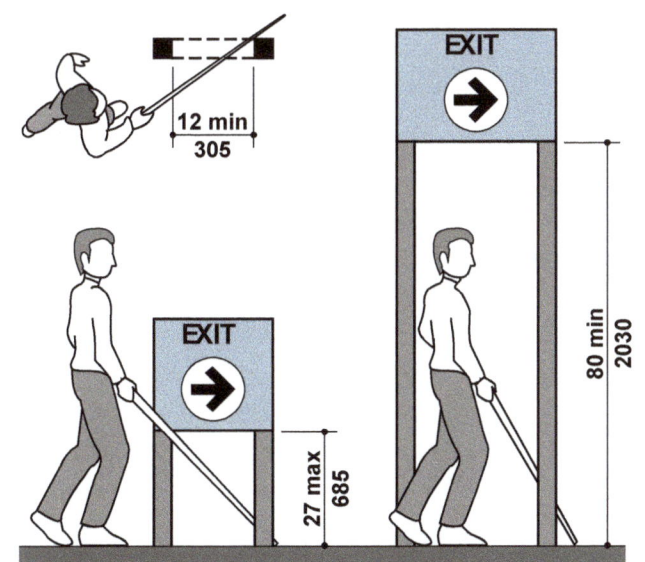

RT.21 Objects mounted between posts and required clearances

O5 Ensure that the overhang of any object mounted on a post that is between 27in. (685mm) and 80in. (2030mm) above the route surface does not exceed 12in. (305mm). **ADAAG: 1998 4.4 & ADA Standards: 2010 307**

See Figures RT.22 and RT.23

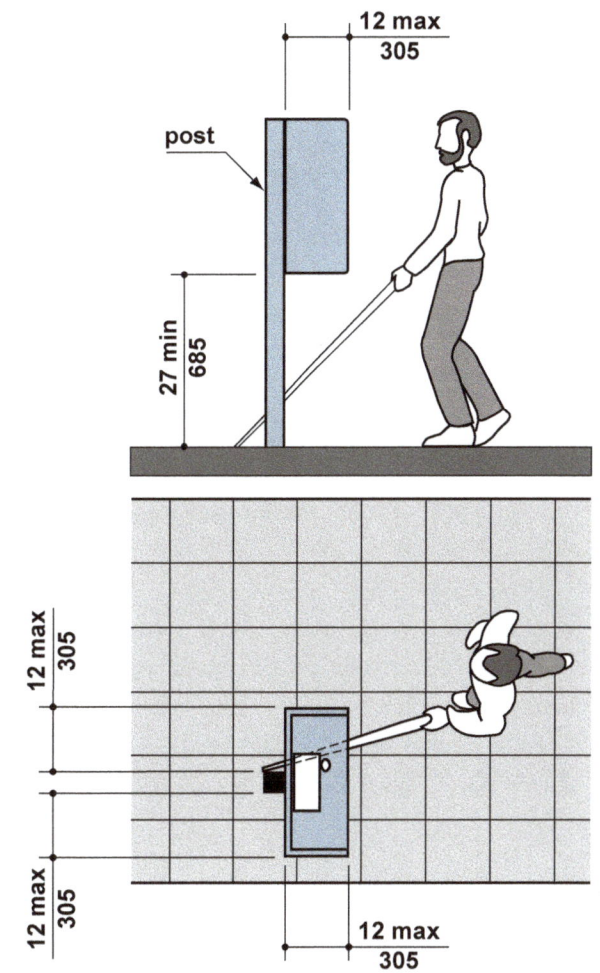

RT.22 Maximum overhangs for objects mounted on a post

P Clear Floor Space

At any place where people may stop along a route (such as at a telephone or building directory), it is important to provide enough space for others to safely and comfortably pass by.

Clear floor space is necessary for stopping, standing, and maneuvering in any accessible area.

Clear floor space is also essential in primary function areas joined by accessible interior routes in order to provide safe, comfortable use by all people.

Design for All: The Best Path Forward — Dr. Arvid E. Osterberg

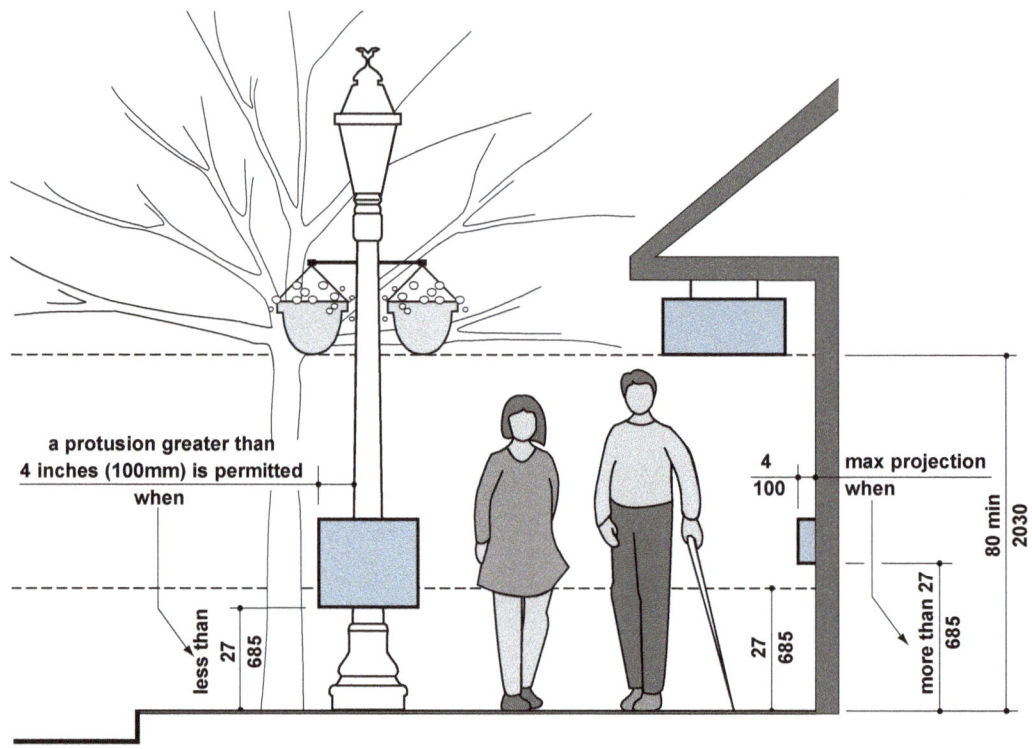

RT.23 Minimum headroom and protruding tolerances in an accessible route

P1 Provide clear floor space that is 30in. (760mm) by 48in. (1220mm) minimum to accommodate a single wheelchair.
36in (915mm) by 54in (1370mm) is preferred Ⓒa
ADAAG: 1998 4.2 & ADA Standards: 2010 305

P2 Ensure that one fully unobstructed side of the clear floor space overlaps or adjoins an accessible route or a clear floor space. **ADAAG: 1998 4.2 & ADA Standards: 2010 305**

P3 Configure clear floor space for either
  a. a forward approach where the clear floor space is open on two or more sides to an accessible route, or in an alcove 24in. (610mm) deep or less; or
  b. a parallel approach to an object where the clear floor space is open on two or more sides to an accessible route, or in an alcove 15in. (380mm) deep or less. **ADAAG: 1998 4.2 & ADA Standards: 2010 305**

See Figures RT.24 and RT.25

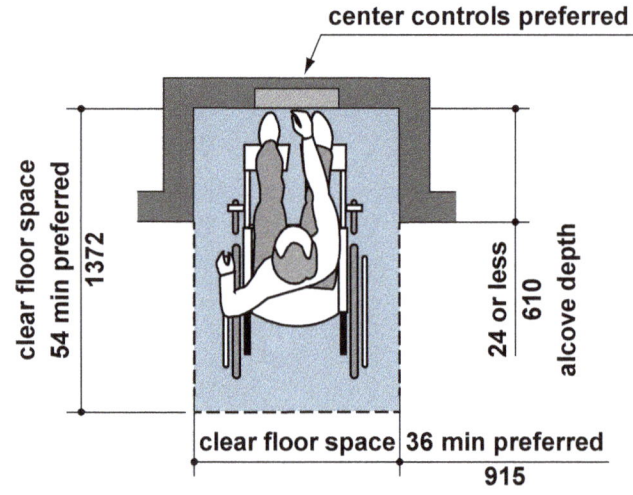

RT.24 Preferred minimum clear floor space for a forward approach (front reach) into a shallow alcove

P4 If a clear floor space is confined on all or part of three sides or is in an alcove, provide additional maneuvering spaces as follows:
  a. If a forward approach clear floor space extends more than 24in. (610mm) into an alcove, provide a 36in. (915mm) wide minimum clear floor space in the alcove.
  b. If a parallel approach clear floor space extends more than 15in. (380mm) into

an alcove, provide clear floor space in the alcove with a minimum length of 60in. (1525mm). **ADAAG: 1998 4.2 & ADA Standards: 2010 305**
See Figures RT.26 and RT.27

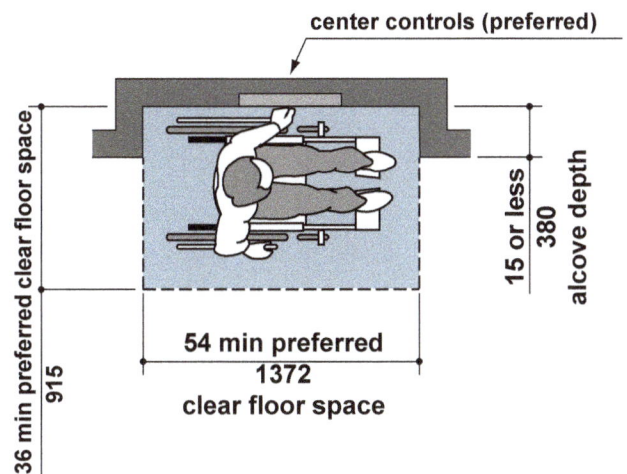

RT.25 Preferred **minimum clear floor space for a parallel approach (side reach) into a shallow alcove**

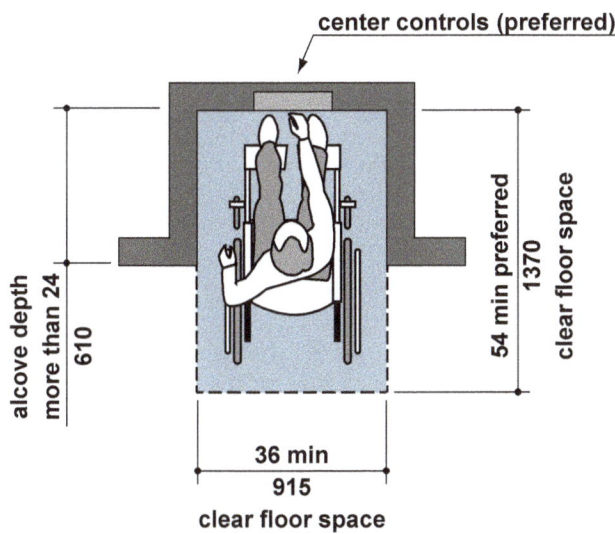

RT.26 Preferred **minimum clear floor space for a forward approach (front reach) in a deep alcove**

P5 Ensure that the slope of clear floor space does not exceed 1:48 (approx. 2%) in any direction. **ADA Standards: 2010 305 (NEW)**

P6 No level changes are permitted in clear floor spaces. **ADA Standards: 2010 305 (NEW)**

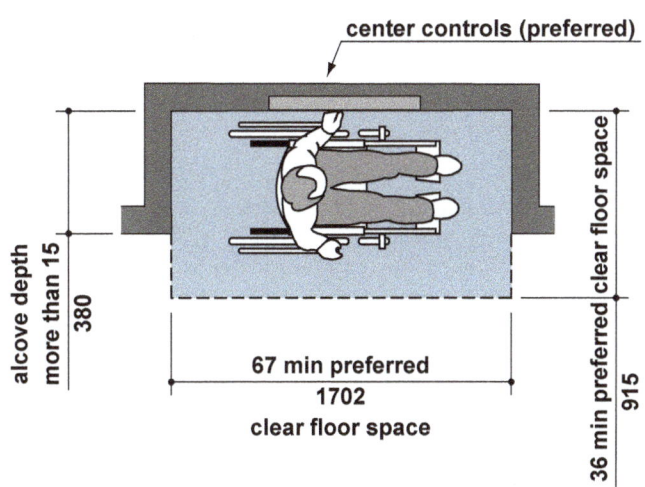

RT.27 Preferred **minimum clear floor space for a parallel approach (side reach) in a deep alcove**

Q Legroom

Legroom is space under surfaces, fixtures, and other objects. Legroom serves two important functions. First, people need legroom to sit at and comfortably use counters, fixtures, desks, tables, and other surfaces. Second, where the clear space in a route or other accessible area is limited and/or where surfaces and fixtures overlap clear floor space, people who use wheelchairs need space under obstructions for maneuvering.

Adequate legroom is a safety factor for wheelchair users who may not detect potentially dangerous conditions where they might be bruised, burned, cut, or scraped by an obstruction.

To ensure that adequate space is provided under surfaces, fixtures, and other obstructions to accommodate the height and angle of wheelchair foot and leg rests, ADA Standards divides the legroom under surfaces into toe clearance and knee clearance.

When you are determining the appropriate space for legroom, consider the space three dimensionally. The ADA Standards includes requirements for the width, height, and depth of toe clearance and knee clearance. Legroom coincides with required clear floor space where ADA Standards allows knee and toe clearance to be included as part of that space.

Design for All: The Best Path Forward — Dr. Arvid E. Osterberg

Q1 Ensure that the space provided for legroom is unobstructed.

Q2 Ensure that legroom under a surface or object is 27in. (685mm) minimum. **ADAAG: 1998 4.32 & ADA Standards: 2010 306**
A height of 30in. (760mm) is preferred.
See RT.28

RT.28 Preferred unobstructed legroom

Q3 Ensure that the legroom measures at least 30in. (760mm) from side to side. **ADAAG: 1998 4.2 & ADA Standards: 2010 306**
See Figure RT.29

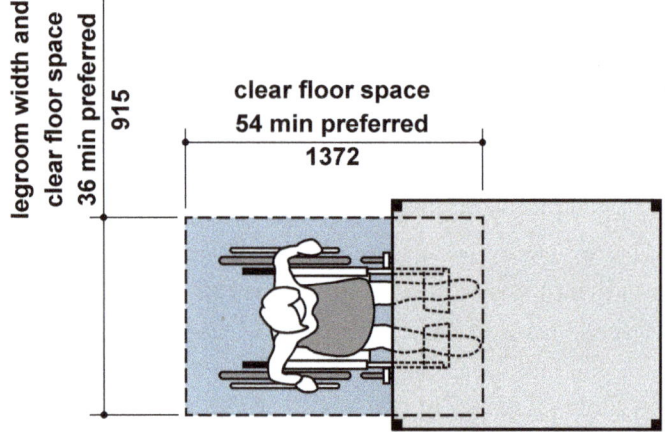

RT.29 Preferred minimum legroom width

Q4 Where an accessible surface or object is in an alcove that is 24in. (610mm) or more deep, or is bounded on both sides by walls or other objects, ensure that the width of the legroom measures 36in. (915mm) from side to side so that people using wheelchairs can maneuver more easily. **ADAAG: 1998 4.2 & ADA Standards: 2010 305**

Q5 Ensure that the legroom provides adequate toe clearance. Toe clearance

   a. includes the vertical space from the floor to 9in. (230mm) above the floor, and
   b. extends horizontally under the surface/object at least 17in. (430mm) measured from the front edge of the surface/object. **ADAAG: 1998 4.19 & ADA Standards: 2010 306**
See Figure RT.30

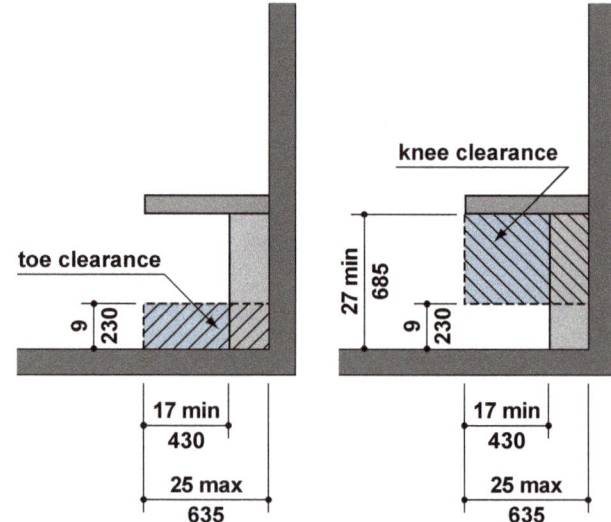

RT.30 Toe clearance and knee clearance

Q6 Ensure that the legroom provides adequate knee clearance. Knee clearance extends horizontally, measured from the front of the surface or object,
   a. at least 8in. (205mm) deep at a height of 27in. (685mm) above the floor, and
   b. at least 11in. (280mm) deep at a height of 9in. (230mm) above the floor. **ADAAG: 1998 4.19 & ADA Standards: 2010 306**

Q7 Legroom may extend any distance under a surface or object and additional space for legroom is preferred.
Refer to Figure RT.28

Q8 Ensure that the surface or object overlaps required clear floor space no more than 25in. (635mm).
Only 25in. (635mm) maximum under a surface or object measured from the front edge of the surface or object can also be part of any required clear floor space. **ADA Standards: 2010 306 (NEW)**

Q9 Where the knee clearance must be reduced at an angle because of plumbing, angled vertical supports, or other obstructions, taper the depth of the vertical knee clearance at a rate of 1in. (25mm) horizontally for each 6in. (150mm) of vertical rise. **ADA Standards: 2010 306 (New)** See Figure RT.31

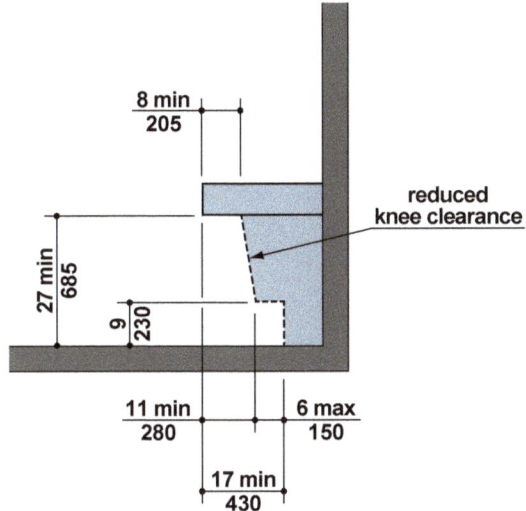

RT.31 Legroom with reduced knee clearance

Q10 Where people need to reach over a surface or object to access controls or objects, ensure that the horizontal depth of the legroom is at least equal to the reach length above the surface/object to a maximum of 25in. (635mm). **ADAAG: 1998 4.2 & ADA Standards: 2010 308 See RR Reach Ranges.**

R Controls and Operating Mechanisms

Ideally all controls and operating mechanisms (such as electrical outlets, light switches, and dispenser controls) along accessible routes and in accessible spaces should meet requirements for accessibility.

R1 Provide and mount controls and operating mechanisms in accessible spaces and along accessible routes so that all controls and mechanisms are accessible. **ADAAG: 1998 4.1 & ADA Standards: 2010 309**

R2 Provide sufficient clear floor space to allow a forward (front reach) or parallel (side reach) approach to controls, dispensers, or operating mechanisms. **ADAAG: 1998 4.27 & ADA Standards: 2010 309 See RT-P**

R3 Install all controls and operating mechanisms within ranges specified in **RR Reach Ranges. ADAAG: 1998 4.27 & ADA Standards: 2010 309**

Exception: Height requirements do not apply where the use of special equipment dictates otherwise or where electrical and communications system receptacles are not normally intended for use by building occupants. ADAAG: 1998 4.27 & ADA Standards: 2010 309

R4 Install controls and mechanisms that
   a. are operable with one hand;
   b. do not require grasping, pinching, or twisting of the wrist; and
   c. are operable with a force no greater than 5 lbs. (22.2N). **ADAAG: 1998 4.27 & ADA Standards: 2010 309**

S Signs

The information in this section applies to signs that are part of an accessible route. Additional information pertaining to signs that are required in specific locations and to signs for specific purposes is provided throughout *Design for All*.

The two main accessibility issues related to signs are 1) providing information about the accessibility of spaces and fixtures, and 2) making the information on various types of signs accessible.

Signs that identify permanent designations are used to label areas, rooms, or spaces where the designation is not likely to change over time. Signs that identify permanent designations for rooms and spaces; that direct people to permanent rooms and spaces; or that provide information about a permanent room or space must meet accessibility requirements for signs.

An accessible sign may be required to be visual, tactile, or a combination of both, depending on the purpose and location of the sign. The items below explain where accessible visual information, tactile information, and pictograms are required. For specific information about the accessibility of signs, including mounting heights, visual and tactile characters, color, size, and other features. **See SN Signs.**

Where signs are required to be both tactile and visual, you may install one sign that includes both types of information or you may install two signs, one visual and the other tactile.

S1 Install accessible visual and tactile signs where signs along exterior and interior routes are used to designate permanent spaces or features.
   a. Where pictograms are included, ensure that pictograms and text descriptors are accessible. **ADAAG: 1998 4.1 & ADA Standards: 2010 216**

Exception: Exterior signs (other than those located at the door to the space they serve) must be visually accessible but are not required to include tactile characters. ADA Standards: 2010 216 (New)

S2 Install accessible visual signs where signs are used to provide directions to, or information about, permanent interior spaces and facilities of a site. **ADAAG: 1998 4.1 & ADA Standards: 2010 216**

Exception: The following types or parts of signs are not required to be accessible:
   a. building directories and menus, **ADAAG: 1998 4.1 & ADA Standards: 2010 216**
   b. temporary signs (7 days or less), **ADAAG: 1998 4.1 & ADA Standards: 2010 216**
   c. occupant names, **ADA Standards: 2010 216 (New)**
   d. building addresses, **ADA Standards: 2010 216 (New)**
   e. company names and logos, and **ADA Standards: 2010 216 (New)**
   f. seat and row designations in assembly areas. **ADA Standards: 2010 216 (New)**

S3 Even though accessible building directories, menus and temporary signs are not required to meet accessibility requirements, make the information readily available to all people wherever possible. ca

S4 Install accessible visual directional signs indicating the location of accessible means of egress at
   a. exit passageways,
   b. exit discharge,
   c. stairways, and
   d. elevators that serve a required accessible space but are not an accessible means of egress. **ADA Standards: 2010 216 (New)**

See International Building Code (IBC): 2003 1007 for additional information.

S5 Identify exit doors with accessible visual and tactile signs at
   a. passageways,
   b. exit discharge, and
   c. stairways. **ADA Standards: 2010 216 (New)**

See IBC: 2003 1007 for additional information.

S6 In buildings where not all entrances are accessible,
   a. identify accessible entrances with accessible **visual** signs that include the International Symbol of Accessibility.
   b. direct people from inaccessible entrances to the nearest accessible entrances using accessible **visual** directional signs.
   c. locate directional signs to eliminate or at least minimize backtracking. **ADAAG: 1998 4.1 & ADA Standards: 2010 216**

T Windows

T1 In accessible rooms or spaces, where windows that are required (by state and local building and life-safety codes) to be operable, ensure that at least one window meets the ADA Standards requirements for accessible windows. **ADA Standards: 2010 229 (New)**

See DR Doors for information about windows in or adjacent to doors.

T2 Ensure that the bottom edges of all viewing windows from corridors *to interior rooms* are no more than 43in (1090mm) above the floor. ca

See Figure RT.32

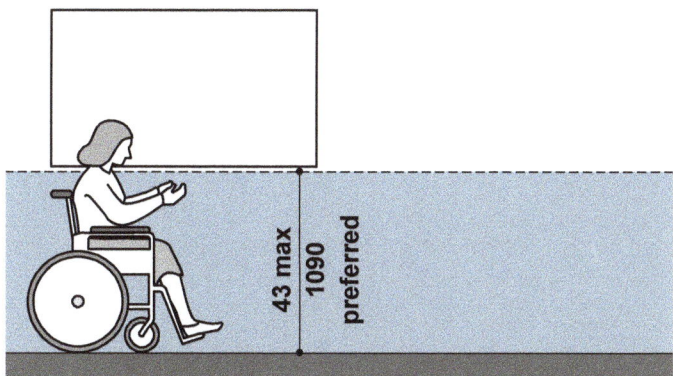

RT.32 Preferred maximum height to the bottom of corridor windows

T3 Ensure that the bottom edge of viewing windows *to the exterior* are no more than 43in (1090mm) above the floor. 🅒ⓐ

T4 Provide adequate clear floor space at accessible windows so that a person can approach and open the accessible windows. 🅒ⓐ

T5 In accessible spaces where building occupants are permitted to open and close windows, ensure that at least one window has controls and operating mechanisms that
    a. are operable with one hand;
    b. do not require tight grasping, pinching, or twisting of the wrist;
    c. are activated with a force less than or equal to 5 lbs. (22.2N); and
    d. are within the appropriate reach range. **See RR Reach Ranges. ADAAG: 1998 4.27 & ADA Standards: 2010 229, 309**

U Security Barriers and Checkpoints

Security has increasingly become a concern in public areas. Security barriers and checkpoints include such elements as gates, bollards, metal detectors, and other types of screening devices. Such devices and elements are designed to restrict access. However, areas that are used for security and that include these elements must not obstruct the accessibility of routes, spaces, or means of egress.

U1 Where bollards, checkpoints, gates, metal detectors, and other security features are installed, ensure that at least the minimum requirements for accessible routes and spaces are met. **ADA Standards: 2010 206 (NEW)**
Exception: Where security features in primary routes cannot be installed to meet minimum route requirements, provide an alternate accessible route adjacent to the primary route. ADA Standards: 2010 206 (NEW)

U2 Where security procedures are required, train staff to assist people with disabilities to travel through security elements and to find the appropriate alternate accessible routes when necessary. 🅒ⓐ

V Maintenance of Exterior Routes

V1 Frequently inspect exterior routes to: identify slip, trip, and misstep hazards, provide warnings, and eliminate hazards as soon as possible. 🅒ⓐ

V2 Paint the top and vertical edges of tripping hazards with bright colored slip-resistant paint until hazards can be eliminated. 🅒ⓐ

V3 Inspect edges of routes to ensure they are flush and level with adjacent surfaces and eliminate any hazardous drop-offs. 🅒ⓐ

V4 Identify elevated and dropped sections of concrete due to freeze-thaw cycles, settling, or tree roots, provide warnings, and grind down or replace concrete as needed. 🅒ⓐ

V5 Identify large gaps between sections of paved walking surfaces that can catch shoes, canes, and walkers and repair or replace concrete where necessary. 🅒ⓐ

V6 Seal cracks in sidewalks, between landings and sidewalks, and between driveways and sidewalks, to prevent frost heave, settling, and tripping hazards. 🅒ⓐ

V7 Identify walking surfaces with inadequate slip resistance, and those with excessive slip resistance, and replace surface materials where necessary. 🅒ⓐ

V8 Identify and eliminate signs, tree branches and other obstacles that protrude into routes from the side or above. Ca

V9 Ensure that stones, pebbles, and mulch in areas adjacent to sidewalks and parking lots are kept in place or eliminate those materials. Ca

V10 Keep exterior walking surfaces clear of obstacles including leaves, trigs, and grass clippings. Ca

V11 After ice melts off walking surfaces, sweep up remaining sand, salt, and ice melt products. Ca

V12 Direct downspouts and drainpipes to discharge water into the ground or route them underneath (rather than draining onto or over) sidewalks and plazas. Ca

W Maintenance of Interior Routes

W1 Ensure there is adequate lighting on all interior walking surfaces. Ca

W2 Ensure that interior routes are kept clear of obstacles and extension cords. Ca

W3 Keep floor surfaces free of water, grease, and other liquids. Ca

W4 Ensure that floor areas that are prone to having water on them, including building entrances, restrooms, and drinking fountains, are slip-resistant. Ca

W5 Use slip-resistant floor cleaning and sealing products. Ca

W6 Use non-skid waxes and do not over polish floors. Ca

W7 Train staff to identify and report spills, to barricade them off, and to clean up spills as soon as possible. Ca

W8 Ensure that carpeting is in good condition and is securely fastened without loose edges, holes, rips, tears, or bunching. Ca

W9 Replace loose and bunched-up carpeting that cannot be securely fastened. Ca

RP Ramps

A	All Ramps	65
B	New Construction	65
C	Alterations to Existing Conditions	66
D	Cross Slope	66
E	Traveling Surfaces	66
F	Handrails: Location and Placement	67
G	Handrails: Mounting and Profiles	68
H	Landings	69
I	Edge Protection	70

Wherever the slope of an accessible route or a portion of an accessible route exceeds a 1:20 ratio (5%), it is by definition a ramp.

A single length of a ramp is a *run*. Ramps have two kinds of slopes, *running slope* (the slope that is parallel to the direction of travel) and *cross slope* (the slope that is perpendicular to the direction of travel). The slopes and the length of a ramp determine how easy it is to use. Measurements for slopes are provided in a ratio (e.g., 1:48) and as a percentage (e.g., 2%).

A series of short ramp runs with landings is preferable to longer ramp runs even when slopes are low. Indirect ramps with lower slopes are often better solutions because people generally have less difficulty with lower inclines. Curved ramps typically have uneven surfaces that violate requirements for minimum cross slopes and pose hazards to people using wheelchairs.

A All Ramps

Buildings and sites that are designed and constructed without ramps are safer and easier to use for everyone. When ramps are necessary the least possible slope is preferred.

The 'double door' is the most common type of entrance to public buildings. However, the double door arrangement requires a person to stand in front of one door in order to pull the other door open, creating an unnecessary conflict with people exiting. (see photo) When two doors are separated with a glass panel between them, people entering are not in the way of people exiting. (see photo)

The separation of doors with panels is not appropriate for all entrances, but it works well in many situations, especially in high traffic doorways. Building entrances should be designed to be easier to use for everyone.

A1 Design accessible exterior and interior routes without ramps whenever possible. In exterior routes, choose alternatives to ramps (such as sidewalks and proper grading) to achieve gentler slopes. In interior routes, elevators are preferred wherever level changes are necessary. ca

A2 When a ramp is necessary, use the least possible slope. ca

A3 Avoid designing and constructing curved ramps. ca

A4 Where curb ramps are constructed, ensure that they comply with all ADA Standards requirements (including maximum cross slope) for ramps. ca

A5 Ensure that ramps intended to be used as *service ramps* comply with all ADA Standards ramp requirements (in reality, service ramps are often used by the public). ca

A6 Ensure that transitions between ramps, landing, and sidewalks are smooth and without tripping hazards. ca

B New Construction

The maximum length of a ramp run is determined by its running slope and overall rise. The maximum rise permitted for any single ramp run is 30in. (760mm).
ADAAG: 1998 4.8 & ADA Standards: 2010 405

B1 Determine whether ramps meet requirements for length and slope. ca
See RP-A

Slope (rise to run)	Maximum run
1:12 to 1:16	30ft. (9.14m)
1:16 to 1:20	40ft. (12m)

RP-A Maximum ramp run permitted for various slopes

B2 Ensure that the maximum running slope of any ramp run does not exceed a 1:12 ratio (8.3%). **ADAAG: 1998 4.8 & ADA Standards: 2010 405** Slopes between 1:14 (7.1%) and 1:16 (6.3%) or less steep are preferred because they reduce the likelihood of falling and because many people have difficulty with slopes of 1:12. ca

B3 Use multiple low-sloped runs between 1:14 (7.1%) and 1:16 (6.3%) or less steep with intermediate landings where the total rise of a sloped area or ramp exceeds 30in. (760mm). ca

B4 When landings are incorporated into a long, multi-run ramp, provide wheelchair resting spaces that are out of the path of travel. ca

B5 Ensure that transitions between ramps and other areas (such as sidewalks and streets) and transitions between sections of ramps are smooth and free of abrupt changes. ca

See RT Routes and Spaces, RT-I and RT-J

B6 Eliminate switches, outlets, drinking fountains, controls and other features from ramped areas of accessible routes. ca

B7 Provide handrails and landings where required. ca

See RP-E through RP-G

C Alterations to Existing Conditions

C1 To increase safety and reduce the likelihood of falls do not construct any ramp (regardless of height or length) that exceeds 1:12 (8.3 %). ca

C2 When altering existing buildings or sites, follow the requirements for ramps in new construction to the maximum extent feasible where

a. ramps are part of an accessible route to or within areas containing primary functions.
b. a stairway or escalator is planned or installed (where none previously existed), and
c. a ramp is provided as an alternative means of vertical access. **ADAAG: 1998 4.1 & ADA Standards: 2010 405**

C3 When modifying existing buildings or sites to comply with accessibility guidelines, and where the use of a 1:12 (8.3%) ramp is not feasible due to space limitations, use the following guidelines for running slopes and rises:
a. maximum rise may not exceed 6in. (150mm) for 1:10 (10%) to 1:12 (8.3%) slopes,
b. maximum rise may not exceed 3in. (75mm) for 1:8 (12.5%) to 1:10 (10%) slopes, and
c. running slope may not exceed 1:8 (12.5%). **ADAAG: 1998 4.1 & ADA Standards: 2010 405**

D Cross Slope

Cross slope is the slope that is perpendicular to the direction of travel. Excessive cross slopes make negotiating ramps and landings much more difficult for wheelchair users. Excessive cross slopes also pose hazards to wheelchair users by causing them to veer off course.

Refer to Figure RT.13 and RT.14

D1 Ensure that the maximum cross slope of a ramp or landing surface does not exceed 1:48 (approx. 2%). **ADA Standards: 2010 405 (Modified- Less Restrictive)**

E Traveling Surfaces

Smooth or slippery surfaces on ramps increase the risk of falling.

E1 Provide a minimum clear width of 36in. (915mm) along ramps. **ADAAG: 1998 4.8 & ADA Standards: 2010 405**

E2 Ensure that traveling surfaces of ramps, approaches, and landings are firm, stable, and slip-resistant. **ADAAG: 1998 4.8, 4.5 & ADA Standards: 2010 302**

E3 Design all ramps, approaches, and landings so that water will not accumulate on surfaces. **ADAAG: 1998 4.8 & ADA Standards: 2010 405**

E4 Provide edge protection where needed or required. Ca
See RP-H

F Handrails: Location and Placement

Handrails provide all people with support for ascending and descending ramps.
See RP.1

F1 Provide handrails on both sides of a ramp run where the rise exceeds 6in. (150mm). **ADAAG: 1998 4.8 & ADA Standards: 2010 405, 505**
Exception: Only one handrail is required on aisle ramps. The handrail can be at either side or within the aisle width but cannot reduce the required 36in. (915mm) clear width. ADA Standards: 2010 505 (New)

F2 Ensure that handrails are continuous along the full length of ramp runs. **ADAAG: 1998 4.8 & ADA Standards: 2010 505**
Exception: In assembly areas, handrails are not required to be continuous in ramped aisles serving seating. ADAAG: 1998 4.8 & ADA Standards: 2010 505

Providing continuous handrails along the walls of ramped aisles serving seating areas is preferred. Ca

F3 Extend handrails at least 12in. (305mm) beyond the top and bottom of ramp runs and ensure that extensions are parallel to the landing surface. **ADAAG: 4.8 & ADA Standards: 2010 505**
Exception: Handrail extensions are not required where existing conditions make it impossible to add extensions or where extensions would create a hazard. ADA Standards: 2010 505 (New)
Exception: Handrail extensions are not required at the inside turns of switch-back ramps. ADAAG: 1998 4.8 & ADA Standards: 2010 505

F4 Ensure that handrails are continuous with the handrails of adjacent ramp runs and that handrail extensions return to walls, posts, guards, or walking surfaces. **ADAAG: 1998 4.8 & ADA Standards: 2010 505**

F5 Install handrails so the top of the gripping surface is at a consistent height of 34in. (865mm) minimum to 38in. (965mm) maximum above the ramp surface. **ADAAG: 1998 4.8 & ADA Standards: 2010 505**
A top surface height of 36in. (915mm) is preferred. Ca

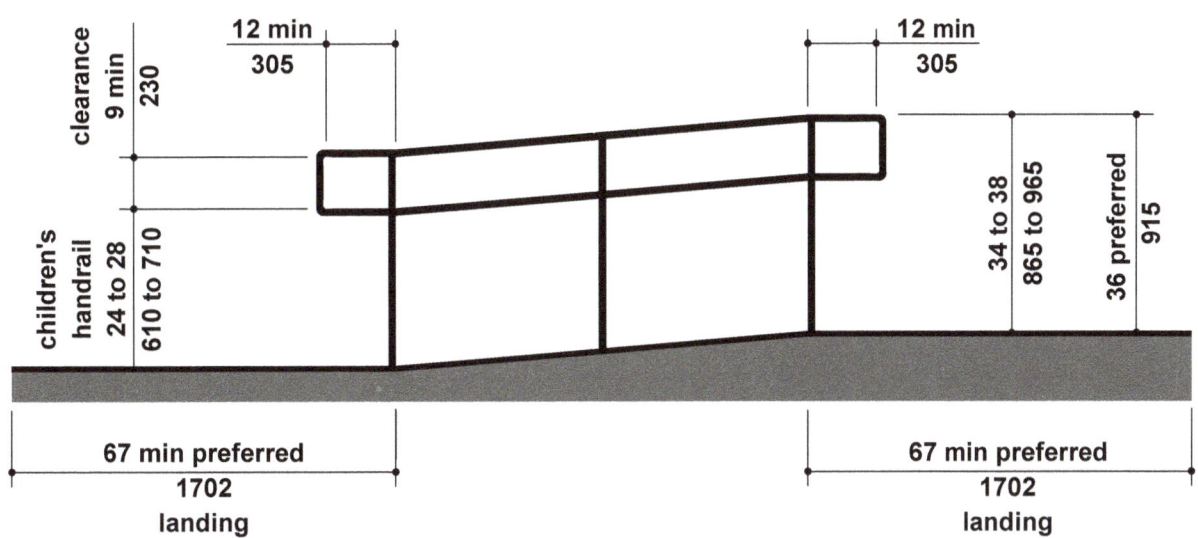

RP.1 Ramp with top and bottom landings, handrails, and handrail extensions

Design for All: The Best Path Forward — Dr. Arvid E. Osterberg

F6 Provide a second, lower set of handrails if children are primary or frequent users of the ramp.
  a. Install children's handrails so the top of the gripping surface is at a consistent height of 24in. (610mm) minimum to 28in. (710mm) maximum. **ADA Standards: 2010 505 (Advisory)**
     A top surface height of 26in. (655mm) is preferred.
  b. Ensure that there is a 9in. (230mm) minimum clear space between the children's handrail and any handrail or obstruction above it to prevent children from becoming trapped between rails. **ADA Standards: 2010 505 (Advisory)**

Note: Most building codes require 4in. (100mm) maximum between handrails to prevent entrapment. The 9in. (230mm) minimum allows the correct height for both children's and adults' handrails. Check with your state and local code authorities to determine if the 9in. (230mm) minimum also complies with entrapment prevention requirements.

Refer to RP.1

F7 Provide a minimum clear width of 36in. (915mm) measured between handrails along ramps that require handrails. **ADAAG: 1998 4.8 & ADA Standards: 2010 405**

G   Handrails: Mounting and Profiles

Properly designed and mounted handrails reduce falls and mishaps on ramps.

G1 Provide gripping surfaces on handrails that fit one of the following profiles:
  a. circular with an outside diameter of 1.25in. (32mm) to 2in. (51mm). **ADAAG: 1998 4.26 & ADA Standards: 2010 505**
  b. non-circular with a perimeter dimension of 4in. (100mm) minimum to 6.25in. (160mm) maximum and a cross-section width of 2.25in. (57mm) maximum. **ADA Standards: 2010 505 (New)**
     Circular handrail profiles are preferred.

See Figure RP.2

G2 Secure handrails so they do not rotate in their fittings. **ADAAG: 1998 4.8 & ADA Standards: 2010 505**

G3 Ensure that the surfaces of handrails and adjacent surfaces are free of abrasive or sharp elements and have rounded edges. **ADAAG: 1998 4.26 & ADA Standards: 2010 505**

G4 Provide 1.5in. (38mm) minimum clear space between handrails and walls or other objects, such as posts. **ADAAG: 1998 4.8 & ADA Standards: 2010 505**

G5 Ensure that handrails protrude from a wall no more than 4.5in. (115mm) and do not extend into the required 36in. (915mm) minimum clear width of the ramp. **ADA Standards: 2010 307, 405 (New)**

See Figure RP.2

G6 Provide a continuous gripping surface on handrails that is not obstructed by posts or other elements on the top or sides. **ADAAG 1998 4.8 & ADA Standards: 2010 505**

G7 If handrails are attached from underneath by balusters (posts) or brackets, ensure that
  a. at least 80% of the bottom of the length of the handrail is unobstructed by brackets or balusters, and
  b. all edges are rounded.

ADA Standards: 2010 505 (New)
Exception: Handrail brackets or balusters that are attached to the bottom of railings are not considered obstructions if (1) they do not obstruct more than 20% of the handrail, and (2) any horizontal projections beyond the sides of the handrail are 1.5in. (38mm) minimum below the bottom of the handrail. **ADA Standards: 2010 505 (New)**
2.5in (64mm) is preferred
Exception: The bottoms of handrails along walking surfaces with a slope of 1:20 or less (routes that are not ramps) may be obstructed along the entire length if they are used for crash rails or bumper guards. **ADA Standards: 2010 505 (New)**
Exception: A handrail must have a perimeter dimension of 4in. (102mm) minimum. For each additional 0.5in. (12.7mm) of perimeter above 4in.

(102mm), an extra 0.125in. (3.2mm) of space is allowed between the bottom of the handrail and a horizontal projection. ADA Standards: 2010 505 (NEW)

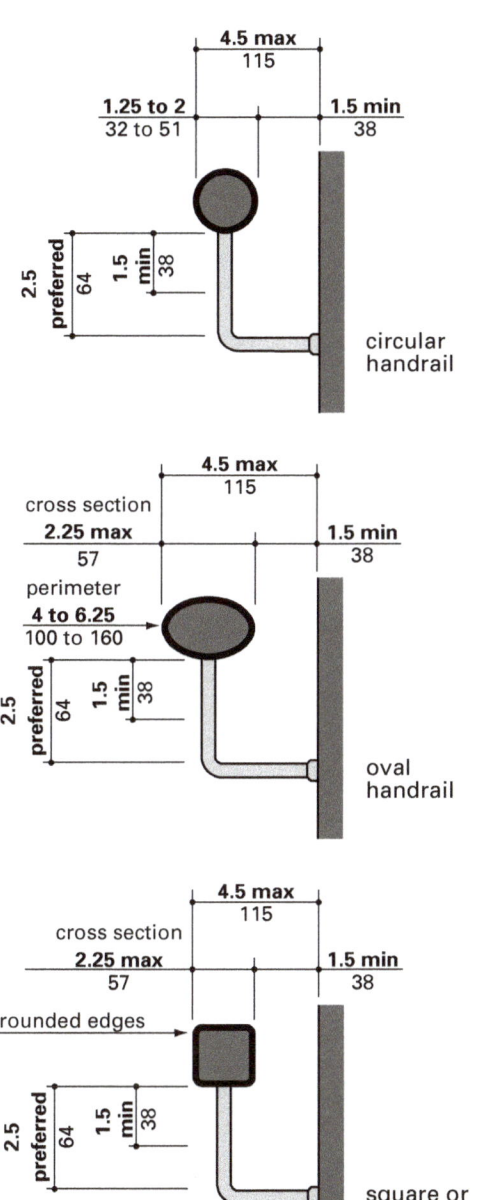

RP.2 Accessible handrail dimensions and profiles

G8 Locate handrails in recesses only if the recesses are 3in. (75mm) deep maximum and extend at least 18in. (455mm) above the top of the handrail. ADAAG: 1998 4.26
See Figure RP.3

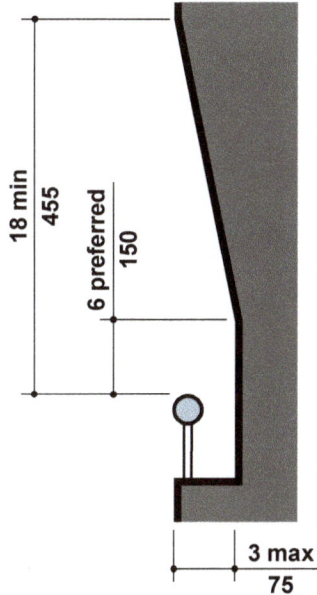

RP.3 Accessible recessed handrail profile

H Landings

No level changes or compound slopes are permitted in landings. Landings often are incorrectly constructed with slopes that are too great. Landings with excessive running and/or cross-slopes may cause wheelchair users to go off course or tip over. Entrances and doors adjacent to ramp landings can pose hazards if adequate maneuvering space and clearance for door swings are not provided.

H1 Provide landings at the top and bottom of each ramp and between ramp runs that have
    a. a minimum clear width equal to the widest part of the ramp, **ADAAG: 1998 4.8 & ADA Standards: 2010 405**
    b. a minimum clear length of 60in. (1525mm),
       67in (1702mm) min is preferred
       ADAAG: 1998 4.8 & ADA Standards: 2010 405 and
    c. a maximum slope of 1:48 (approx. 2%) in any direction **ADA Standards: 2010 405** (MODIFIED-LESS RESTRICTIVE)
See Figure RP.4

H2 Provide a minimum landing space of 60in. (1525mm) by 60in. (1525mm) where the direction of travel changes at a landing. **ADAAG: 1998 4.8 & ADA Standards: 2010 405**

Design for All: The Best Path Forward — Dr. Arvid E. Osterberg

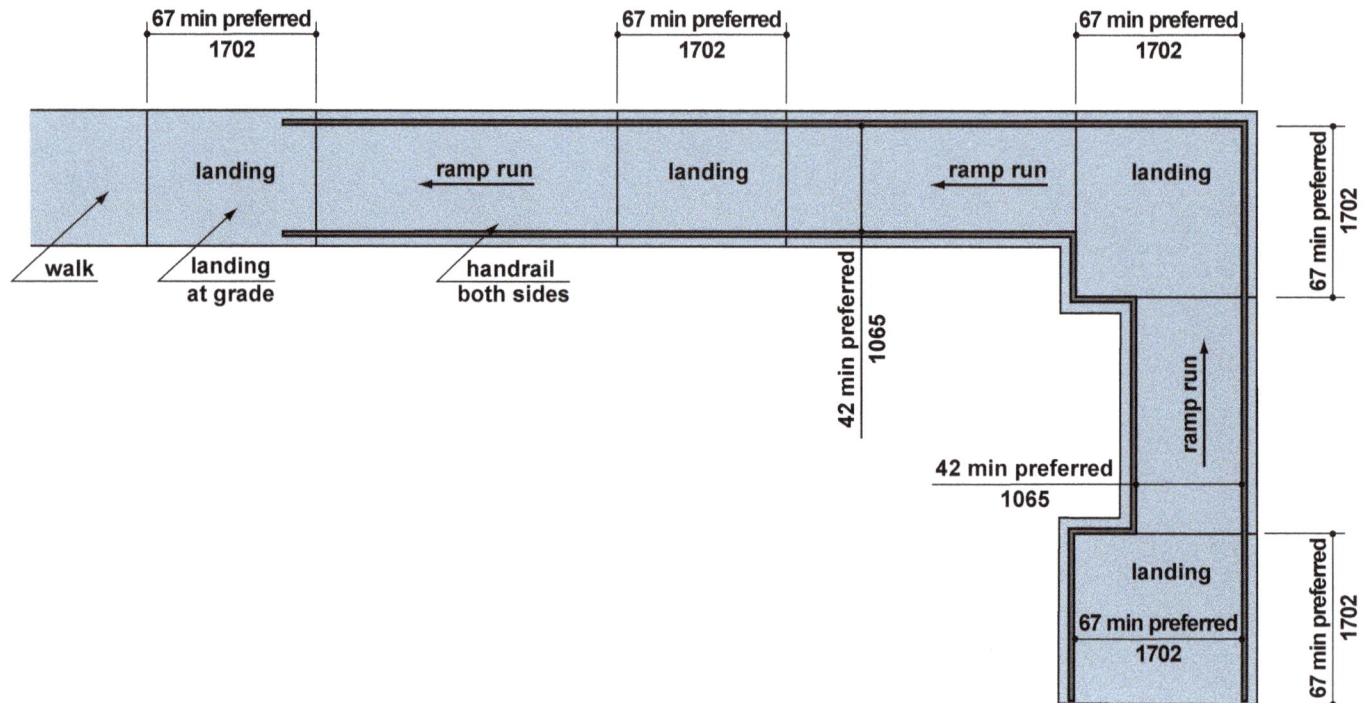

RP.4 Preferred minimum landing dimensions for a ramp

Refer to Figure RP.4

H3 Design landings and adjacent doorways to prevent open doors from obstructing the clear space of landings. ca

H4 Ensure that doors swing clear of the minimum dimensions of the landing. ca

H5 Provide adequate maneuvering space where a doorway or entrance is located adjacent to a landing. ca

H6 Provide smooth transitions between landings and ramp runs. ca

I   Edge Protection

Edge protection provides both a tactile warning of the edge of a ramp and a barrier to keep tips of canes and the casters of walkers and wheelchairs from dropping off ramp edges. Edge protection can be provided by extending the traveling surface or by installing one of several types of barriers.

I 1 Install edge protection on both sides of ramp runs and ramp landings. ca

I 2 Provide edge protection
   a. where handrails are required, or
   b. where ramps have a vertical drop-off of more than 0.5in. (12.7mm) within 10in. (255mm) horizontally of the ramp. **ADAAG: 1998 4.8 & ADA Standards: 2010 405**

I 3 Provide edge protection by extending the traveling surface of the ramp run and/or landing 12in. (305mm) minimum beyond the inside face of a handrail along the length of the ramp run and/or landing. **ADAAG: 1998 4.8 & ADA Standards: 2010 405**
See Figure RP.5

I 4 Provide edge protection by installing a barrier (such as a wall or panel) where ramps and landings have vertical side drop-offs. **ADAAG: 1998 4.8 & ADA Standards: 2010 405**
See Figure RP.6

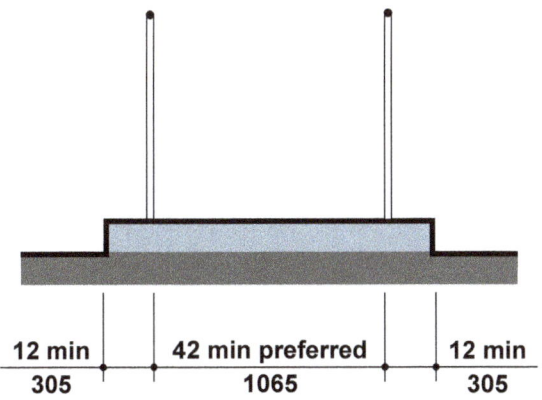

RP.5 Ramp with extended platform edge protection

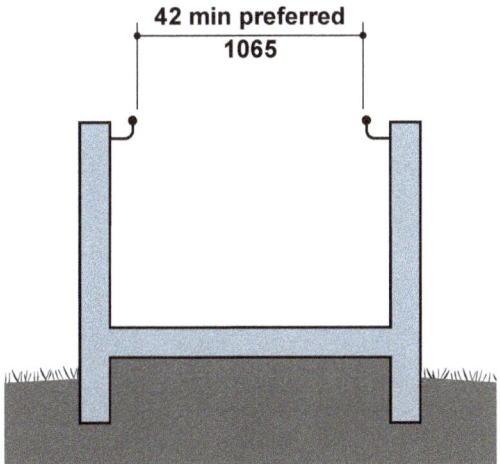

RP.6 Ramp with edge protection walls and handrails

15 Provide edge protection by installing curbs where ramps and landings have vertical side drop-offs.
   ADAAG: 1998 4.8 & ADA Standards: 2010 405
   See Figure RP.7

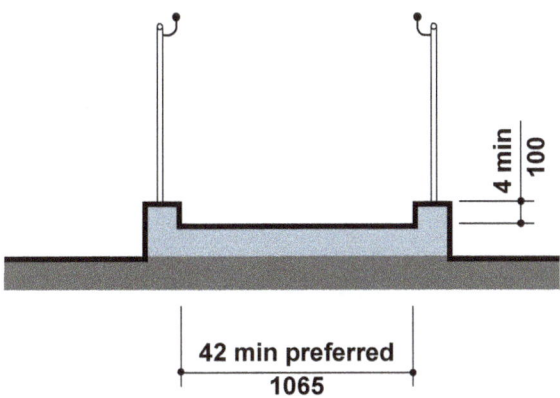

RP.7 Ramp with edge protection curbs and handrails

16 Provide edge protection by installing rails where ramps and landings have vertical side drop-offs.
   ADAAG: 1998 4.8 & ADA Standards: 2010 405
   See Figure RP.8

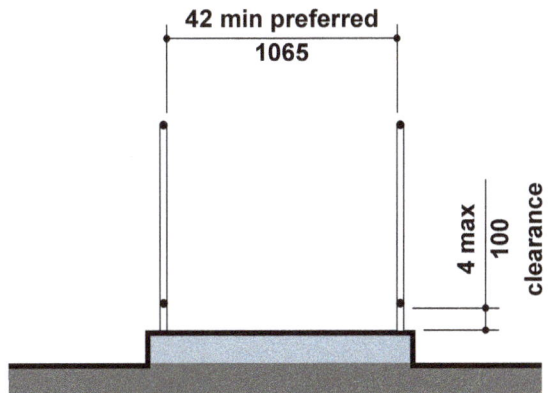

RP.8 Ramp with edge protection rails and handrails

17 Where curbs or rails are installed, ensure that the height and configuration of the barrier prevents the passage of a 4in. (100mm) diameter sphere, where any portion of the sphere is within 4in. (100mm) of the ramp or landing surface.
   ADAAG: 1998 4.8 & ADA Standards: 2010 405

EN Entrances

A   New Construction: Number and Location   72
B   Alterations to Existing Conditions:
        Number and Location   74
C   Doors and Passageways   74
D   Signs   75
E   Vestibules   75
F   Maintenance   75
G   Warnings   76

Accessible entrances serve all people, including visitors and employees. The maximum degree of accessibility is provided when all primary routes, entrances, and doors are accessible. The ADA Standards places a high priority on accessible entrances for alterations and barrier removal in existing buildings and sites. This chapter only deals with entering buildings. Routes, doors, gates, and other parts of accessible entrances must also meet accessibility requirements. **See DR Doors and RT Routes and Spaces, and see EG Egress** to determine the requirements for accessible exits and means of egress.

Standing in front of one door to open another door

A   New Construction: Number and Location

While ADA Standards requires that only some entrances meet accessibility requirements, making all entrances accessible ensures equal participation for all people. Additionally, building entrances that are equipped with automatic or power-assisted door openers are easier for everyone to use.

The 'double door' is th emost common type of entrance to public buildings. However, the double door arrangement requires a person to stand in front of one door in order to pull the door open, creating an unnecessary conflict with people exiting. When two doors are separated with a glass panel between them, people entering are not in the way of people exiting.

Separated doors can reduce congestion ca

The separation of doors with panels is not appropriate for all entrances, but it works well in many situations, especially in high-traffic doorways. Building entrances should be designed to be easier to use for everyone.

A1   Make all entrances to a building accessible where possible. ca

Appropriate placement of auto door activator ca

Poor placement of auto door activator

A2 Install high quality *automatic* door openers at accessible entrances where possible. See DR Doors, DR-T Ca

A3 Install high-quality *power-assist* door openers at accessible entrances, where appropriate Ca

See DR Doors, DR-T

A4 Place *automatic* door activators in appropriate locations that are not too close to doorways and not in the direct path of travel. Ca

A5 Ensure that at least 60% of all public entrances are accessible. If you only have one entrance, it must be accessible. If you have two entrances, both must be accessible. **ADAAG: 2010 206 (MODIFIED-MORE RESTRICTIVE)**

A6 Ensure that accessible public entrances are on accessible routes. **ADAAG: 1998 4.1 & ADA Standards: 2010 206**

A7 Provide at least one accessible entrance
   a. from an enclosed parking structure to the building if a direct pedestrian route is available, **ADAAG: 1998 4.1 & ADA Standards: 2010 206**
   b. from each tunnel or elevated walkway to the building if a direct pedestrian route is available, **ADAAG: 1998 4.1 & ADA Standards: 2010 206**
   c. at each tenant space in a building (such as individual stores in a strip shopping center), **ADA Standards: 2010 206 (NEW)**
   and
   d. at each restricted entrance (where restricted entrances are used). **ADA Standards: 2010 206 (NEW)**

The following two examples explain conditions that meet the requirements in EN-A2 and EN-A3 for the numbers must be accessible.

Example: A building has two entrances, one from the street and one from the parking garage. Both entrances must be accessible.

Example: A building has four entrances, one from the parking garage and three from the street. Two of the street level entrances must be accessible and the parking garage entrance must be accessible.

A8 Provide easy-to-use low-sloped routes and grade level entrances. Do not construct exterior stairways and/or ramps at entrance approaches whenever better alternatives, such as repositioning a building on a site, or changing grades, are possible. Ca

A9 Ensure proper compaction of soil, aggregate, and other materials before pouring concrete at entrance approaches and door landings. Ca

Grade Level Entrance Ca

Design for All: The Best Path Forward — Dr. Arvid E. Osterberg

B Alterations to Existing Conditions: Number and Location

Alterations to entrances are not permitted to decrease the accessibility of a building.

B1 Follow the guidelines for entrances in new construction to the maximum extent possible when altering an existing building. **ADAAG: 1998 4.1 & ADA Standards: 2010 202**

B2 When planning alterations (where the accessibility of primary function areas may be affected), ensure that the entrances to the altered areas are accessible to the maximum extent possible. **ADAAG: 1998 4.1 & ADA Standards: 2010 202**

Exception: When altering an existing entrance to a building (where other entrances are accessible), the altered entrance is not required to be accessible unless modifying the entrance is necessary to make the primary function accessible. ADAAG: 1998 4.1 & ADA Standards: 2010 202, 206

Exception: If it is "technically infeasible" to alter an entrance to the standards for new construction, then ensure that the entrance is accessible to the maximum extent feasible. ADAAG: 1998 4.1 & ADA Standards: 2010 202

B3 If the only entrance to an existing building or to a tenant space within an existing building is a service entrance, ensure that it is accessible. **ADAAG: 1998 4.1 & ADA Standards: 2010 206**

B4 Identify and eliminate steps at, and in near proximity of, entrances and doorways. ca

Single step at entrance door – unsafe and not accessible

C Doors and Passageways

C1 Provide at least one accessible door with appropriate maneuvering space at each accessible entrance to the building. **ADAAG: 1998 4.1 & ADA Standards: 2010 206**

C2 Inside the building, provide at least one accessible door or passageway to each accessible room or space. **ADAAG: 1998 4.1 & ADA Standards: 2010 206**

See DR Doors for specific requirements.

Steps at entrance doors – unsafe and not accessible

Settlement adjacent to doorway landing resulting in tripping hazard

D Signs

Provide signs along routes to direct people to accessible entrances. The ADA Standards does not require that you install signs at entrances to buildings where all entrances are accessible.

Signs must comply with ADA Standards requirements for height, placement, and design. **See SN Signs for details.**

D1 In buildings where not all entrances are accessible, provide signs that
   a. identify accessible entrances, and
   b. direct people to accessible entrances.
   ADAAG: 1998 4.1 & ADA Standards: 2010 216

D2 Identify accessible entrances with signs that display the International Symbol of Accessibility. **ADAAG: 1998 4.1 & ADA Standards: 2010 216**
See Figure EN.1

EN.1 International symbol of accessibility

D3 Place signs in the appropriate locations so that people do not have to backtrack along a route after arriving at an inaccessible entrance. Place signs at the beginning of the route to direct people to the nearest accessible entrance. **ADAAG: 1998 4.1**

D4 Comply with all sign requirements for Braille, character proportion, character height, finish, contrast, and mounting location and height as described in **SN Signs**. **ADAAG: 1998 4.30 & ADA Standards: 2010 703**

E Vestibules

Small vestibules and inappropriate locations of automatic door activators make entering and exiting buildings much more difficult.

E1 Increase the space between doors in vestibules beyond ADA minimum dimensions to make the user experience easier.
See DR.F

Wide space between vestibule doors

E2 Locate automatic door activators where they are easy to get to and easy to use.

F Maintenance

F1 Inspect entrance areas and vestibules frequently for moisture and debris (water, slush, snow, dirt, sand, and salt) that is tracked in on shoes and boots.

F2 Ensure floor mats are high quality, heavy mats with flush edges that don't roll up.

F3 Eliminate loose and worn floor mats and/or replace them with integrated floor mats where practical.

F4 Clean floor mats frequently.

Design for All: The Best Path Forward — Dr. Arvid E. Osterberg

G Warnings

G1 Provide warnings when appropriate but also correct unsafe conditions as soon as possible. Ca

G2 Place folding *Wet Floor* signs or warning cones on wet floors and clean up spills as soon as possible. Ca

G3 Remove folding *Wet Floor* signs and warning cones soon after floors are dry. Ca

DR Doors

A	New Construction: Number and Location	77
B	Alterations to Existing Conditions:	78
C	Revolving Doors and Turnstiles	78
D	Gates	78
E	Double-Leaf Doors	78
F	Doors in a Series	78

Clear Opening Width at a Door — 79
G Measuring Clear Opening Width — 79

Maneuvering Space at a Door — 81
H Maneuvering Spaces at Hinged Doors: Front Approach — 81
I Maneuvering Spaces at Hinged Doors: Hinge Side Approach — 83
J Maneuvering Spaces at Hinged Doors: Handle Side Approach — 84
K Maneuvering Spaces at Folding and Sliding Doors and at Passageways — 86
L Headroom — 87
M Traveling Surfaces — 87
N Thresholds at Doorways — 87
O Opening and Locking Hardware — 88
P Door Opening Force — 88
Q Door Closers — 89
R Door Surfaces and Kickplates — 89
S Vision Lites and Side Lites — 90
T Automatic and Power-Assisted Doors and Gates — 91

Proper design and installation of doors is essential for independent access to buildings and within buildings. A *doorway* includes the door, doorframe, hardware, doorstop, and closer. A *door* is the movable leaf that closes an opening in a wall. In some cases, a doorway will not include a door. A doorway with no door is referred to here as a *passageway*. For simplicity, in this chapter, *door* may refer to either a door or a doorway.

The distinction between door and doorway is important because the clear opening width required in a doorway is not necessarily the same as the door size. This section includes information on accurately measuring the clear opening width.

For a door to be usable, people need to be able to position themselves to open the door and to pass through the doorway. Accessibility issues include clear width; threshold profile; maneuvering space in front of and to the sides of doors; type and placement of door hardware; force required to open doors; and door safety features such as the height and position of view panels.

This chapter uses the following terms (adapted from ADA Standards) to describe the orientation of a person to a door, including the direction from which a person approaches the door (*handle side or hinge side*), and a person's position relative to the direction of the door swing on approach to the door (*pull face or push face*).

The various combinations of the hinge or handle side approach, the direction of the door swing, and the presence of latches and closers influence the minimum required maneuvering space at a doorway.

Handle side. The handle side refers to the side of the door where the moving edge of the door leaf meets the doorway. This is the side where the handle (lever, loop, or knob) is located. Latches may also be installed on the handle side. However, not all doors have handles, knobs, or latches.

Handle side refers to the direction of travel of a person approaching the door where the person reaches the handle side of the door first, without passing by the door. (The ADA Standards refers to this side as the latch side.)

Hinge side. The hinge side refers to the side of the door where the door is attached to the doorway with hinges or pivots.

Hinge side refers to the direction of travel of a person approaching the door where the person has to pass by the hinge side of the door to get to the handle side of the door.

Pull face. The pull face refers to the approach to a door where people must pull the door toward themselves to open the door and maneuver through the doorway.

Push face. The push face refers to the approach to a door where people must push the door away from themselves to open and maneuver through the doorway.

Stop. The part of the door jamb that stops the door and helps to hold it in a closed position.

Latch. A mechanism that may be included on the handle side of a door to hold the door in the closed position. A latch may require people to operate the handle to release the latch. A lock or other door fastening hardware may also be included as part of the latch or latch set.

Closer. A mechanism that automatically returns the door to a closed position. Different types of closers include those at the top of the door (attached to the doorway and the door), those integrated in the hinge mechanism, and spring-loaded devices that are added to hinge pins.

A closer regulates the speed of the closing door. Some closers are adjustable and must be set to meet fire, life-safety, and accessibility requirements.

See Figure DR.1

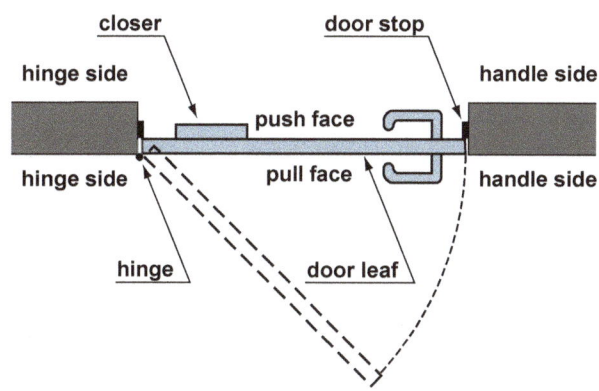

DR.1 Door and doorway components

A New Construction

A1 Ensure that every door that is part of an accessible route is accessible. **ADAAD: 1998 4.1 & ADA Standards: 2010 404**

A2 Ensure that doors and doorways that are part of an accessible route meet all accessibility requirements. **ADAAD: 1998 4.1 & ADA Standards: 2010 404**
Exception: Manual and automatic doors and gates that are operated only by security personnel do not have to meet accessibility requirements if security

personnel have sole control of the doors at all times. **ADA Standards: 2010 404 (Advisory)**

A3 Ensure that every door is accessible that
    a. serves as part of an accessible means of egress, and
    b. connects to an area of refuge. **ADAAG: 1998 4.3 See EG Egress and AR Areas of Refuge.**

A4 Ensure that at least one door or passageway at each accessible entrance to a building is accessible. **ADAAG: 1998 4.1 & ADA Standards: 2010 206**

A5 Ensure that at least one door or passageway to each accessible space within a building is accessible. **ADAAG: 1998 4.1 & ADA Standards: 2010 206**

A6 Install wider doors for easier access and increased safety. Ca

A7 Install high quality doors, door closers, and door hardware. Ca

B Alterations to Existing Conditions

It is best to install accessible egress doors wherever possible. Check state and local building and life-safety codes for egress requirements regarding doors.

B1 Follow the guidelines for doors in new construction to the maximum extent feasible in alterations. **ADAAG: 1998 4.1 & ADA Standards: 2010 202**

B2 Identify *steps* at, and in near proximity of, doorways, provide warning, and eliminate hazards as soon as possible. Ca

B3 Identify *high thresholds* at doorways, provide warning, and replace them with low profile thresholds as soon as possible. Ca

B4 Where possible, remove doors to increase access and safety. Ca

C Revolving Doors and Turnstiles

Many people who have limited mobility find revolving doors and turnstiles difficult to use.

C1 Manual revolving doors and turnstiles are not permitted as part of an accessible route. **ADAAG: 1998 4.13 & ADA Standards: 2010 404**

C2 Where a revolving door or turnstile is present, provide an alternative such as an accessible door or gate. Configure the entrance and route to ensure that the accessible door or gate is adjacent to the revolving door or turnstile. **ADAAG: 1998 4.13** Ca

C3 Ensure that the accessible alternative to the revolving door or turnstile accommodates the same pattern of traffic as the revolving door or turnstile. **ADAAG: 1998 4.13** Ca

D Gates

D1 Ensure that gates (including ticket gates) that are part of an accessible route meet all accessibility requirements that apply to accessible doors, including clear width, reach ranges, maneuvering space, threshold height, and opening and closing force. **ADAAG: 1998 4.13 & ADA Standards: 2010 404**

E Double-Leaf Doors

Double-leaf doors are where two door leaves open to form a common doorway.

E1 When a doorway has two or more independently operated door leaves, ensure that at least one active leaf meets guidelines for door width and maneuvering space. **ADAAG: 1998 4.13 & ADA Standards: 2010 404**

F Doors in a Series

Doors in a series should be designed to provide space between doors that allows for wheelchair maneuvering and for safe, comfortable passage by all people.

Doors in a series are easier to use if they both swing in the same direction. When doors in a series swing in opposite directions into a vestibule or hallway, they can create hazards by reducing the space necessary for maneuvering safely.

F1 Between two hinged or pivoted doors in a series, provide a minimum space of 48in. (1220mm), plus the width of any door swinging into the space. **ADAAG: 1998 4.13 & ADA Standards: 2010 404**
60in. (1525 mm) preferred ca
See Figure DR.2

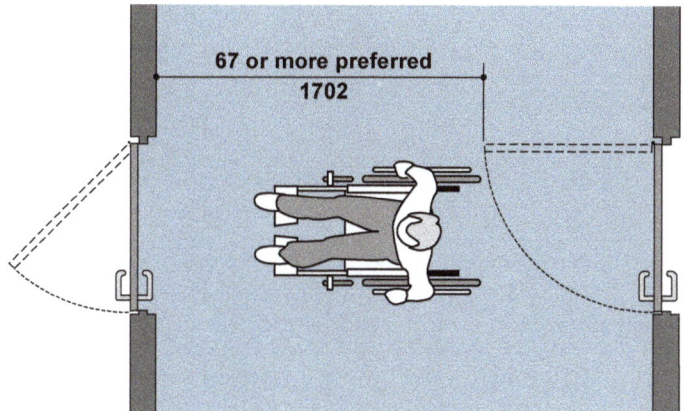

DR.2 Preferred space between two hinged doors in a series that swing in the same direction

F2 **Install doors in series so that they swing either in the same direction or away from the space between the doors. ADAAG: 1998 4.13** ca

F3 In cases where doors in a series both swing towards the space between the doors, ensure 48in. (1220mm) minimum clear space is maintained between door swings. **ADA Standards: 2010 404 (New)**
60in. (1525 mm) preferred ca
See Figure DR.3

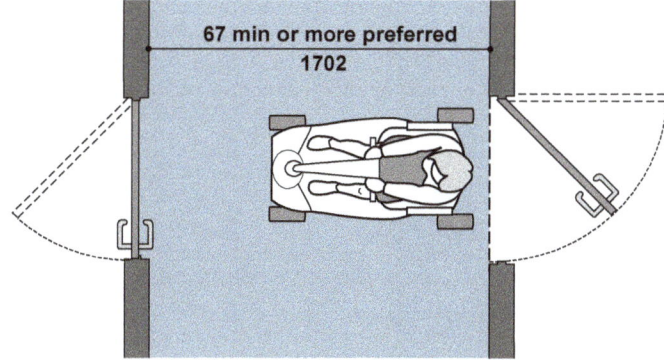

DR.3 Preferred space between two hinged doors in a series that swing in opposite directions

Clear Opening Width at a Door

Wider doorways are easier for most people to use. Doors that are 36in. (915mm) wide minimum are generally required by building and life-safety codes for egress and are preferred for accessibility because they provide a wider clear opening width. The additional width at doors is helpful in areas of heavy traffic, for people who use crutches or other walking aids, and when people using wheelchairs need to maneuver to turn into a doorway.

G Measuring Clear Opening Width

To measure the clear opening in a doorway of a hinged door, open the door to 90°. Measure the clear opening from the face or leading edge of the open door to the opposite door stop.
See Figures DR.4, DR.5, and DR.6

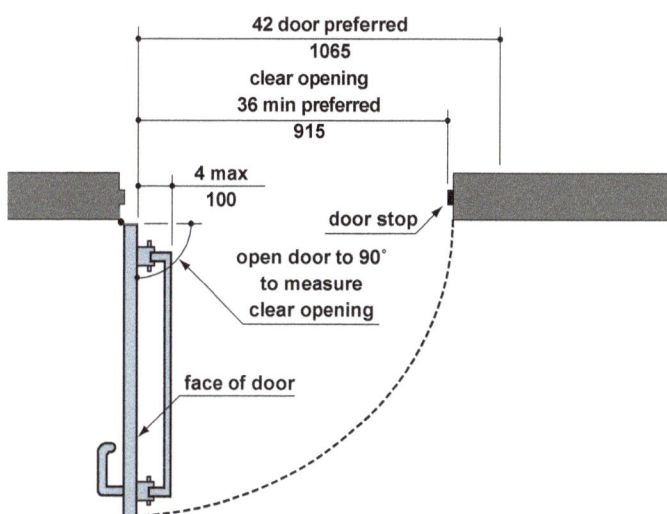

DR.4 How to measure the clear opening at a doorway with a hinged door

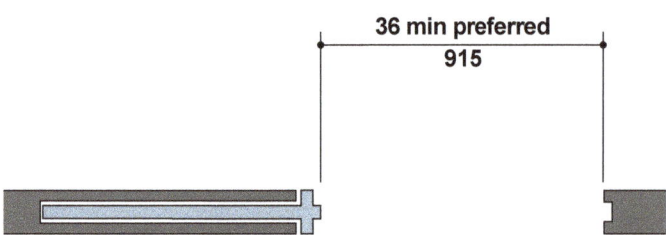

DR.5 How to measure the clear opening at a pocket door or sliding door

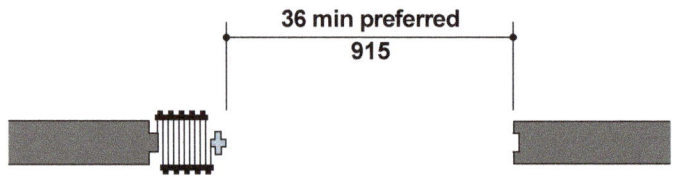

DR.6 How to measure the clear opening at a folding door

Door hardware and other projections (including door stops) up to 4in. (100mm) are permitted to protrude into the door clear opening space between 34in. (865mm) and 80in. (2030mm) above the floor. *No projections* are permitted below 34in. (865mm). **ADAAG: 1998 4.4 & ADA Standards: 2010 404**

G1 Provide a minimum clear opening of 32in. (815mm) at doorways that have no recess or that are recessed 24in. (610mm) or less. **ADAAG: 1998 4.13 & ADA Standards: 2010 404**
Doors that are 36in. (915mm) wide are preferred. ca

Exception: In existing buildings where it is technically infeasible to comply with clear opening requirements, a maximum projection of 5/8in. (16mm) is permitted for the doorstop. This reduces the minimum clear space to 31-3/8in. (797mm). ADAAG: 1998 4.1 & ADA Standards: 2010 404

G2 Increase clear opening width in existing doorways by installing offset hinges. Offset hinges are designed to allow the door leaf to open past the 90° position so that the door leaf is moved completely out of the doorway clear opening. ca
See Figure DR.7

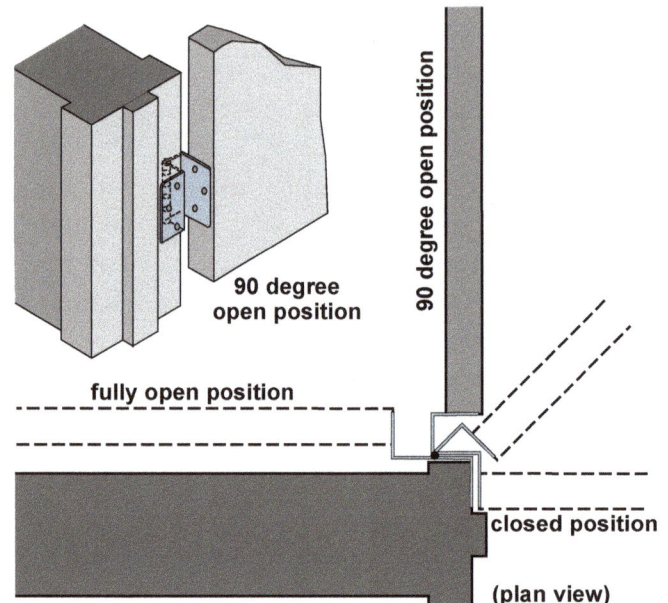

DR.7 A door with offset hinges

Side swinging hinges increase clear width ca

G3 Provide a minimum clear opening of 36in. (915mm) at doorways that are recessed more than 24in. (610mm). **ADAAG: 1998 4.13, 4.2, 4.3 & ADA Standards: 2010 404**

G4 Provide a minimum clear opening of 20in. (510mm) at doors where people do not need full passage, such as shallow closets less than 18in. (455mm) deep. Although such doors do not affect egress or accessibility of a route, people should be able to access shallow spaces, such as linen closets. ADAAG: 1998 4.13

See Figure DR.8

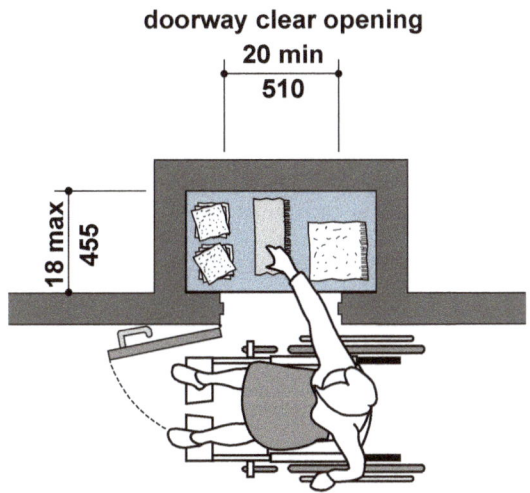

DR.8   Minimum clear opening at a door that does not require full passage

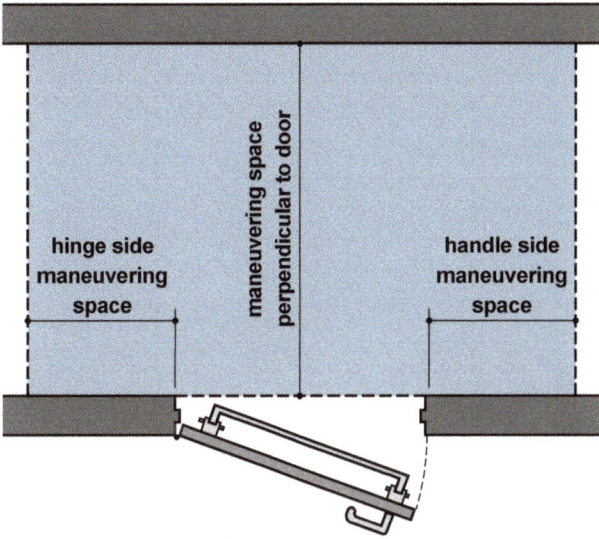

DR.9   How to measure maneuvering space at a doorway with a hinged door

Maneuvering Space at a Door

In addition to providing sufficient clear opening space for a person to pass through a door, sufficient maneuvering space in front of both faces and at the sides of doors must be provided. Door swings are permitted to overlap the clear maneuvering space of accessible routes and spaces.

When determining the maneuvering space at a door, consider both the perpendicular maneuvering space and the space beyond the handle or hinge side of the door. Dimensions for maneuvering space beyond a doorway are measured from the edge of the door frame, excluding the stop.
See Figure DR.9

DR-H through DR-K provide minimum maneuvering spaces at manual doors based on the door type (hinged, swinging, folding, double-leaf, etc.), approaches to doors (front, hinge or handle side), door swings (pull or push face), and whether or not the doors include latches and closers. For definitions and usage of these terms, see the beginning of this chapter.

People can approach a door from one of three directions: perpendicular to the door (where the door is directly in front of them); parallel to the door from the hinge side (where they pass the hinge side to get to the handle), or parallel to the door from the handle side (where they reach the handle side of the door first). It is important to consider approach, door swing, and hardware to determine clear floor space on both sides of all doors. Keep in mind that every door has a pull face and a push face depending on which side of the door a person is facing.

Because complying strictly with minimum required maneuvering spaces sometimes results in restrictive situations, **DR-H through DR-K** provide preferred dimensions that reflect universal design principles and result in situations where the door is more accessible.

H   Maneuvering Spaces at Hinged Doors: Front Approach

Doors are sometimes recessed due to wall thickness, placement of millwork, or other conditions. Maneuvering spaces for front approaches apply to both recessed and non-recessed doors.

H1   Provide maneuvering space for a front approach to the pull face of a door that is
  a.   60in. (1525mm) minimum perpendicular to the doorway, and

b. 18in. (455mm) minimum beyond the handle side of the doorway; 24in. (610mm) is preferred. ADAAG: 1998 4.13 & ADA Standards: 2010 404

See Figure DR.10

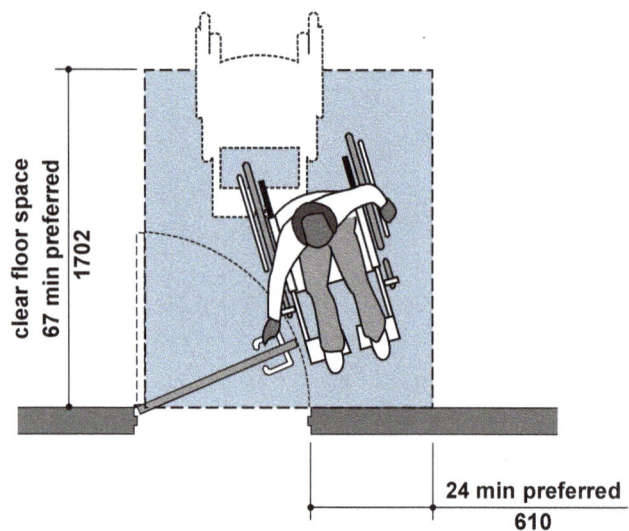

DR.10 **Preferred** minimum maneuvering space for a front approach to the pull face of a door

Adequate space on pull sides of restroom doors

H2 Provide maneuvering space and configure doors and door hardware for doors recessed more than 8in. (205mm) as a front approach only. **ADA Standards: 2010 404** (NEW)

A recessed door condition may result from placement of cabinetry or furniture adjacent to a door opening, as well as from a permanent wall configuration. **ADA Standards: 2010 404** (ADVISORY)

See Figure DR.11

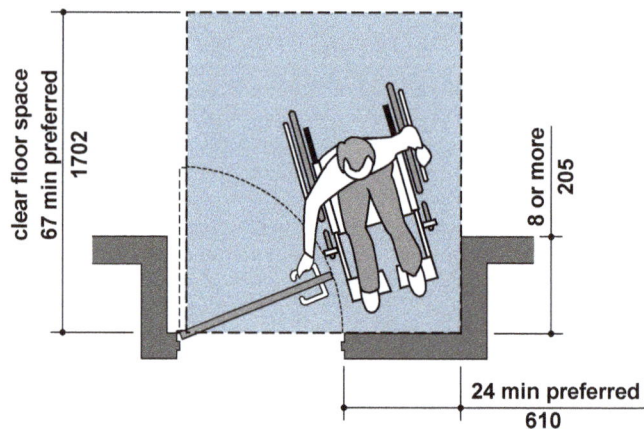

DR.11 **Preferred** minimum maneuvering space for a front approach to the pull face of a door recessed 8in. (205mm) or more

H3 Provide space for a front approach to the push face of a door with a closer and latch that is
a. 48in. (1220mm) minimum perpendicular to the doorway, and
b. 12in. (305mm) minimum beyond the handle side of the doorway. **ADAAG: 1998 4.13 & ADA Standards: 2010 404**

See Figure DR.12

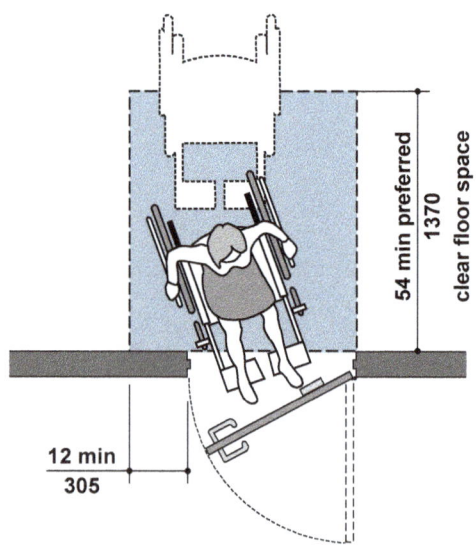

DR.12 **Preferred** minimum maneuvering space for a front approach to the push face of a door *with a closer and latch*

H4 Provide space for a front approach to the push face of a door without a closer and latch that is
a. 48in. (1220mm) minimum perpendicular to the doorway, and
b. at least the width of the doorway.

ADAAG: 1998 4.13 & ADA Standards: 2010 404

See Figure DR.13

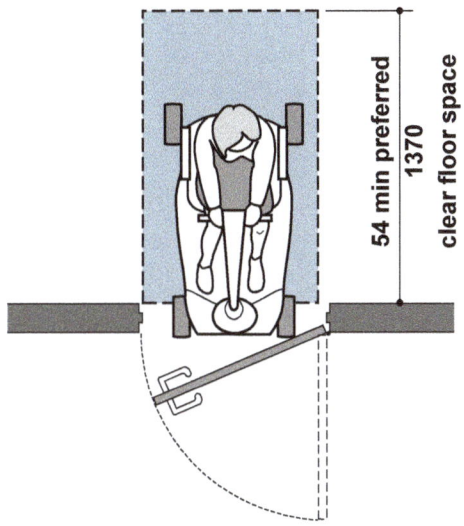

DR.13 Preferred minimum maneuvering space for a front approach to the push face of a door *without* a closer and latch

H5 Ensure that the clear floor space on the pull side of doors is kept clear and is not used for trash receptacles, recycling bins, or other items.

Clear floor space obstructed on pull side of door

I Maneuvering Spaces at Hinged Doors: Hinge Side Approach

When people approach a door from the hinge side, they must pass in front of the door to reach the door handle. In this case, people who use wheelchairs need additional space for maneuvering to reach the door handle and to pull the door open toward them.

The maneuvering space required for a hinge side approach to a door depends on the clear space available in front of the door and the maneuvering space available beyond the handle side of the door.

I 1 Provide maneuvering space for a hinge side approach to the pull face of a door that meets one of the following conditions.
  a. 60in. (1525mm) minimum perpendicular to the doorway, with a 36in. (915mm) minimum required maneuvering space beyond the handle;
     42in. (1065mm) preferred;
  or
  b. 54in. (1370mm) minimum perpendicular to the doorway, with a 42in. (1065mm) minimum required maneuvering space beyond the handle; **ADAAG: 1998 4.13 & ADA Standards: 2010 404**
     48in. (1220mm) preferred.

See Figures DR.14 and DR.15

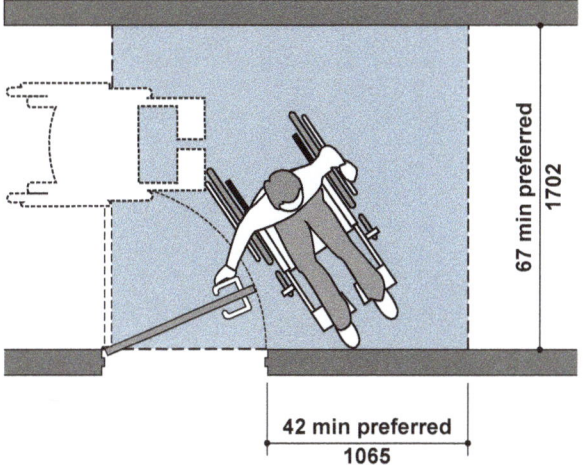

DR.14 Preferred minimum maneuvering space for a hinge side approach to the pull face of a door

Design for All: The Best Path Forward — Dr. Arvid E. Osterberg

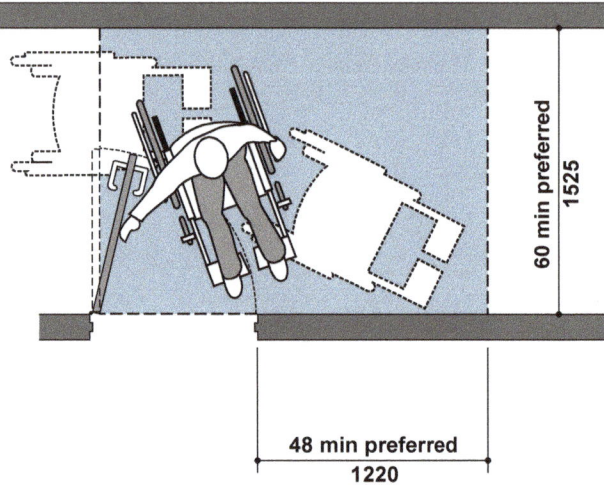

DR.15 Preferred minimum maneuvering space for a handle side approach to the pull face of a door

I 2 Provide space for a hinge side approach to the push face of a door with a closer and latch that is
  a. 48in. (1220mm) minimum perpendicular to the doorway;
    60in. (1525mm) preferred; and
  b. 22in. (560mm) minimum beyond the hinge side of the doorway; **ADAAG: 1998 4.13 & ADA Standards: 2010 404**
    36in. (915mm) preferred.

See Figure DR.16

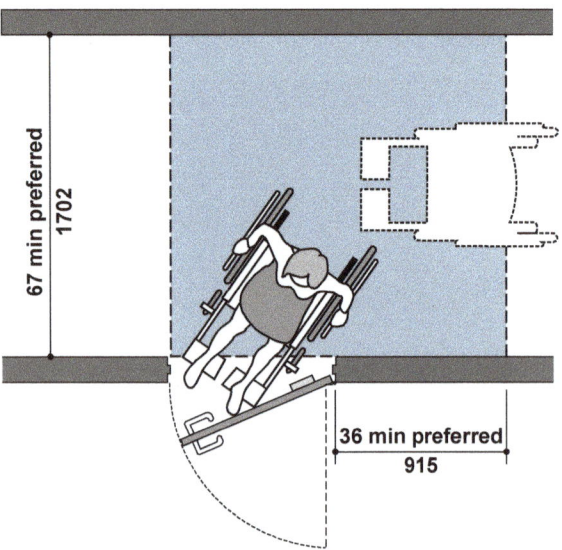

DR.16 Preferred minimum maneuvering space for a hinge side approach to the push face of a door *with* a closer and latch

I 3 Provide space for a hinge side approach to the push face of a door without a closer or latch that is
  a. 42in. (1065mm) minimum perpendicular to the doorway;
    54in. (1370mm) preferred;
    and
  b. 22in. (560mm) minimum beyond the hinge side of the doorway; **ADAAG: 1998 4.13 & ADA Standards: 2010 404**
    36in. (915mm) preferred.

See Figure DR.17

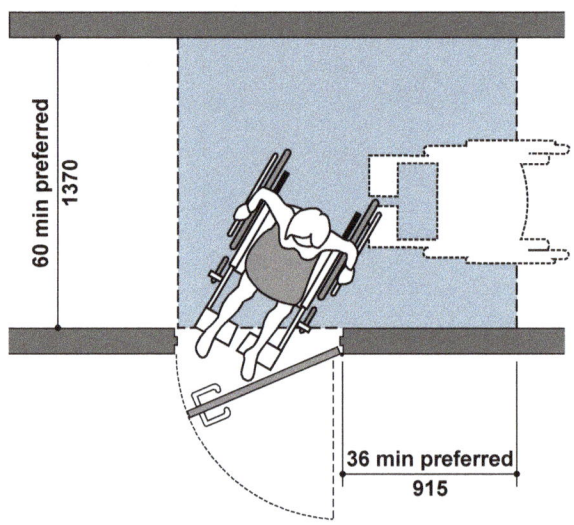

DR.17 Preferred minimum maneuvering space for a hinge side approach to the push face of a door *without* a closer and latch

J Maneuvering Spaces at Hinged Doors: Handle Side Approach

J1 Provide space for a handle side approach to the pull face of a door with a closer and latch that is
  a. 54in. (1370mm) minimum perpendicular to the doorway;
    60in. (1525mm) preferred;
    and
  b. 24in. (610mm) minimum beyond the handle side of the doorway; **ADAAG: 1998 4.13 & ADA Standards: 2010 404**
    36in. (915mm) preferred.

See Figure DR.18

J2 Provide space for a handle side approach to the pull face of a door without a closer and latch that is
  a. 48in. (1220mm) minimum perpendicular to the doorway;
    54in. (1370mm) preferred;

and
b. 24in. (610mm) minimum beyond the handle side of the doorway; **ADAAG: 1998 4.13 & ADA Standards: 2010 404**
36in. (915mm) preferred. ca

See Figure DR.19

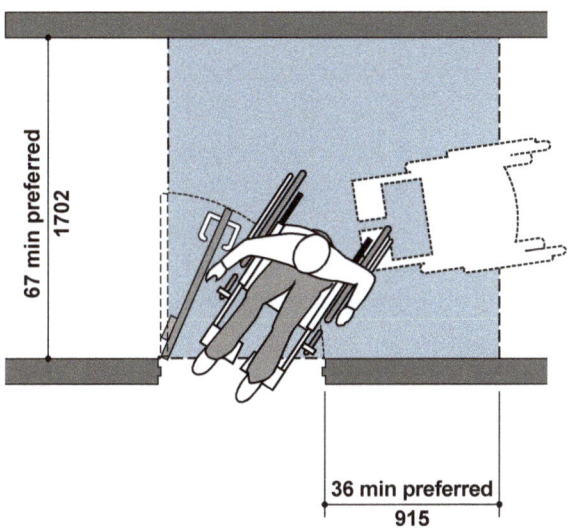

DR.18 Preferred minimum maneuvering space for a handle side approach to the pull face of a door *with* a closer and latch

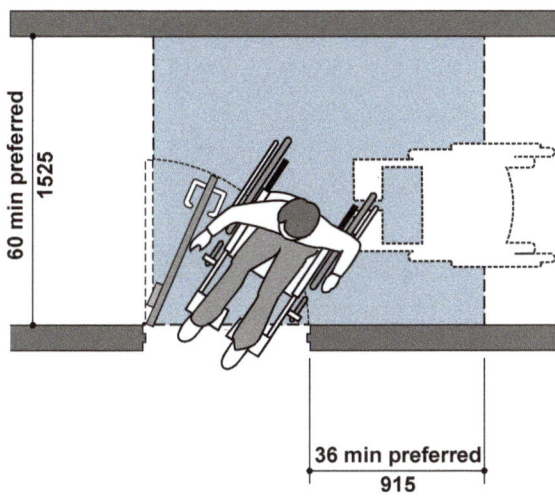

DR.19 Preferred minimum maneuvering space for a handle side approach to the pull face of a door *without* a closer and latch

J3 Provide space for a handle side approach to the push face of a door with a closer and latch that is
 a. 48in. (1220mm) minimum perpendicular to the doorway;
 54in. (1370mm) preferred; ca and

b. 24in. (610mm) minimum beyond the handle side of the doorway; **ADAAG: 1998 4.13 & ADA Standards: 2010 404**
36in. (915mm) preferred. ca

See Figure DR.20

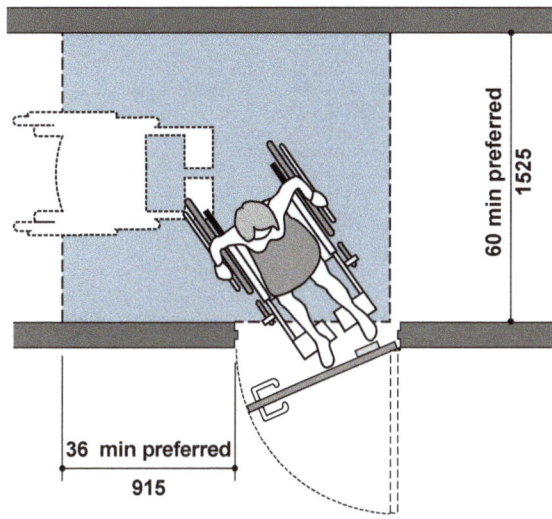

DR.20 Preferred minimum maneuvering space for a handle side approach to the push face of a door *with* a closer and latch

J4 Provide space for a handle side approach to the push face of a door without a closer and latch that is
 a. 42in. (1065mm) minimum perpendicular to the doorway; **ADAAG: 1998 4.13 & ADA Standards: 2010 404**
 54in. (1370mm) preferred; ca and
 b. 24in. (610mm) minimum beyond the handle side of the doorway; **ADAAG: 1998 4.13 & ADA Standards: 2010 404**
 36in. (915mm) preferred. ca

See Figure DR.21

Design for All: The Best Path Forward — Dr. Arvid E. Osterberg

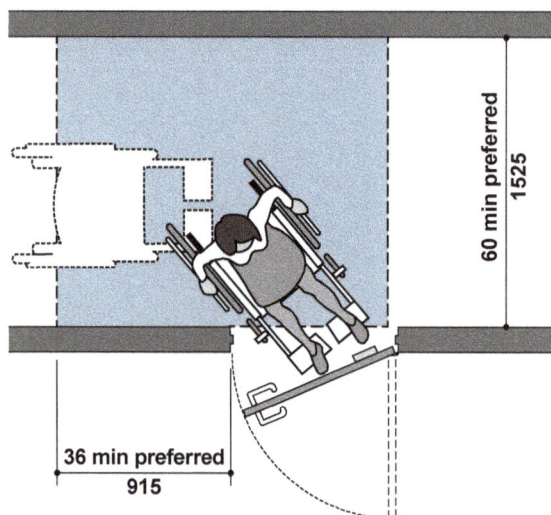

DR.21 Preferred minimum maneuvering space for a handle side approach to the push face of a door *without* a closer and latch

K Maneuvering Spaces at Folding and Sliding Doors and at Passageways

Approaches to folding doors and sliding doors can be from the front, from the handle side of the door, or from the side where one leaf of a sliding door recesses behind another leaf or into a pocket. The dimensions below apply to folding doors and sliding doors (including pocket doors) and at open passageways without doors.

K1 Provide space for a front approach that is
   a. 48in. (1220mm) minimum perpendicular to the doorway, and
   b. at least the width of the doorway. **ADAAG: 1998 4.13 & ADA Standards: 2010 404**

See Figure DR.22

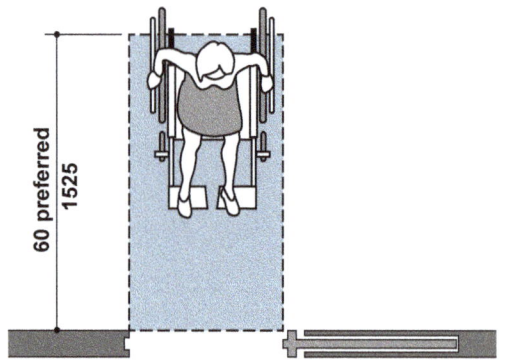

DR.22 Preferred minimum maneuvering space for 1) a front approach to a folding or sliding door, and 2) at a passageway *without* a door

K2 Provide space for a handle side approach to a folding or sliding door that is
   a. 42in. (1065mm) minimum perpendicular to the doorway;
      54in. (1370mm) preferred; Ca
      and
   b. 24in. (610mm) minimum beyond the handle side of the doorway; **ADAAG: 1998 4.13 & ADA Standards: 2010 404**
      36in. (915mm) preferred. Ca

K3 Provide space for a side approach at a passageway (a doorway where no door leaf is installed) that is
   a. 42in. (1065mm) minimum perpendicular to the doorway,
      54in. (1370mm) preferred; Ca
      and
   b. at least the width of the doorway. **ADA Standards: 2010 404** (NEW)

See Figure DR.23

K4 Provide space for a recess side or fold side approach that is
   a. 42in. (1065mm) minimum perpendicular to the doorway;
      54in. (1370mm) preferred; Ca and
   b. 22in. (560mm) minimum beyond the side of the door where the door recesses or folds; **ADAAG: 1998 4.13 & ADA Standards: 2010 404**
      36in. (915mm) preferred. Ca

See Figure DR.24

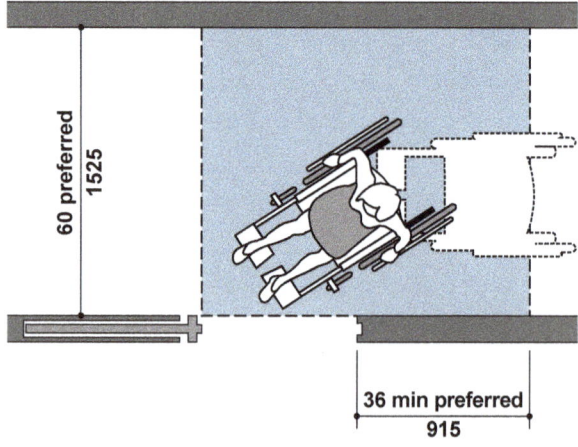

DR.23 Preferred minimum maneuvering space for 1) a handle side approach at a folding or sliding door, and 2) at a passageway *without* a door

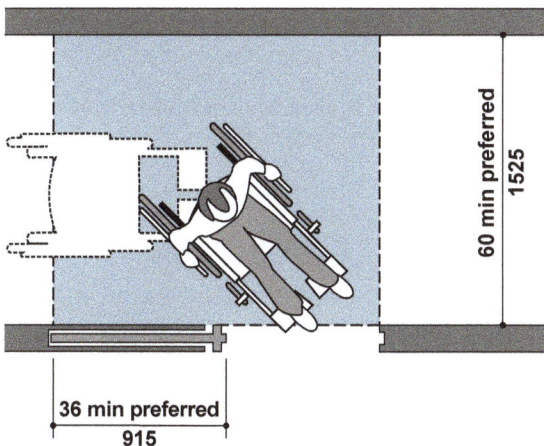

DR.24 **Preferred** minimum maneuvering space for 1) a recess side or fold side approach to a folding or sliding door, and 2) at a **passageway** *without* a door

K5 Provide space for a side approach at a passageway (a doorway where no door leaf is installed) that is
   a. 42in. (1065mm) minimum perpendicular to the doorway,
      54in. (1370mm) preferred; 🆑
      and
   b. at least the width of the doorway. **ADA Standards: 2010 404 (NEW)**

L Headroom

Adequate headroom in doorways allows safe, comfortable passage for people walking through doorways.

L1 Provide headroom a minimum of 80in. (2030mm) above the floor in doorways. **ADAAG: 1998 4.4 & ADA Standards: 2010 307**

Exception: Door closers and stops are permitted to be as low as 78in. (1980mm) above the floor in doorways. ADAAG: 2010 307, 404 (NEW)
See Figure DR.25

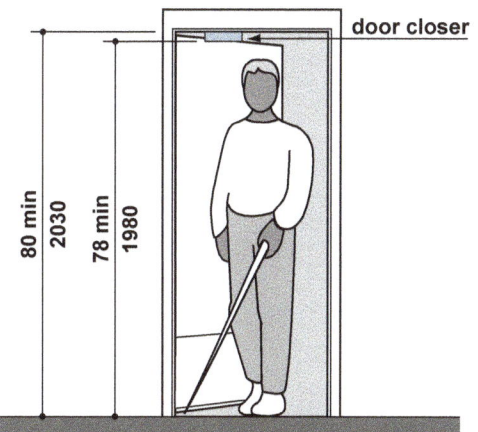

DR.25 Headroom and placement of a door closer or stop at a doorway or passageway

M Traveling Surfaces

M1 Ensure that traveling surfaces in doorways and maneuvering spaces of doors are level, with a maximum slope of 1:48 (approx. 2%), and clear of obstructions. **ADAAG: 1998 4.13 & ADA Standards: 2010 404, 302**

N Thresholds at Doorways

Level changes and thresholds in doorways can cause difficulty for people who use mobility devices (such as wheelchairs and walkers) and can be tripping hazards for all people. Wherever possible, use flush thresholds to provide safe, smooth transitions.

N1 Ensure that the maximum threshold height at doors does not exceed 0.5in. (12.7mm). **ADAAG: 1998 4.13 & ADA Standards: 2010 404**

N2 Bevel the edges of raised thresholds that are between 0.25in. (6.4mm) and 0.5in. (12.7mm) in height with a slope no greater than 1:2 (50%). Level changes less than 0.25in. (6.4mm) can be vertical. **ADAAG: 1998 4.13, 4.5 & ADA Standards: 2010 303**

Exception: Existing thresholds that are greater than 0.5in. (12.7mm) and less than 0.75in. (19mm) that have beveled edges 1:2 maximum slope (50%) on both sides, may remain. ADAAG: 1998 4.1, 4.5 & ADA Standards: 2010 404
See Figure DR.26

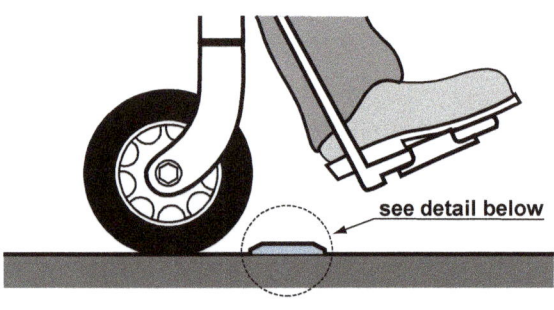

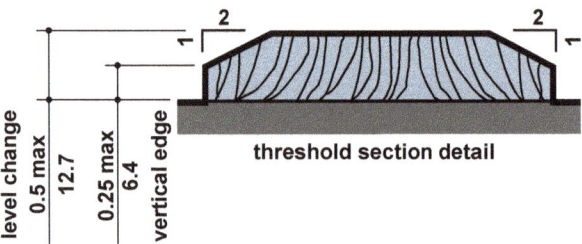

DR.26 Level changes at a threshold with beveled edges

N3 Replace thresholds and transition strips that are tripping hazards with safe, low profile thresholds and transition strips. ca

High threshold at doorway: unsafe and not accessible

O Opening and Locking Hardware

Lever-operated mechanisms, push-type mechanisms, and U-shaped handles are examples of accessible door hardware.

To make it easier for people who use wheelchairs or other assistive devices to close doors, add auxiliary pulls to doors that are not equipped with closers.

O1 Choose and install hardware that does not protrude more than 4in. (100mm) into the clear opening of the doorway. **ADAAG: 1998 4.13 & ADA Standards: 2010 404**
Refer to Figure DR.4

O2 Mount door hardware, including panic bars, at least 34in. (865mm) and no more than 48in. (1220mm) above the traveling surface. **ADAAG: 1998 4.13 & ADA Standards: 2010 404**

O3 Ensure that door hardware (including handles, pulls, locks, and other operating devices)
   a. has an easy to grasp shape;
   b. is operable with one hand; and
   c. does not require tight grasping, pinching, or twisting of the wrist. **ADAAG: 1998 4.13, 4.27 & ADA Standards: 2010 404, 309**

O4 Ensure that when sliding glass doors are fully open, operating hardware is exposed and usable from both sides. **ADAAG: 1998 4.13 & ADA Standards: 2010 404**

O5 On a door without a closer, install a 4in. (100mm) to 6in. (150mm) long auxiliary handle (door pull) between the hinge side and the center of a door where needed.

Install auxiliary door pulls 12in. (305mm) to 18in. (455mm) from the hinge side of the door. ca

See Figure DR.27

P Door Opening Force

Due to wind and pressure differences between the inside and outside of buildings, it is difficult to prescribe maximum opening force requirements for exterior doors.

Therefore, the ADA Standards does not specify a maximum door opening force for exterior hinged doors at exits. Whenever possible, it is best to equip exterior doors at accessible entrances with automatic or power-assisted door openers.

See Entrances: Automatic and Power Assist Doors.

Door opening forces must comply with state and local building and life-safety codes.
Exception: Door opening force requirements do not apply to latch bolts or other devices that may hold the door in a closed position. ADAAG: 1998 4.13 & ADA Standards: 2010 404

P1 Ensure that the force for pushing or pulling open doors complies with the following.
  a. Interior hinged, sliding, or folding doors: 5 lbs. (22.2N) maximum force.
  b. Fire doors: the minimum opening force allowable by the appropriate administrative authority is the maximum force allowed by ADA Standards. **ADAAG: 1998 4.13 & ADA Standards: 2010 404**

Exception: Door opening force requirements do not apply to the initial force needed to overcome latch-bolts or disengage other devices. ADAAG: 1998 4.13 & ADA Standards: 2010 404

P2 Provide magnetic hold open devices on fire doors in corridors and other areas wherever possible. ca

Fire doors with magnetic hold-open devices ca

Q Door Closers

Improperly adjusted door closers make passage through doorways difficult for many people. Door closers that close too quickly and those that take too much force to open can trap people and wheelchairs in doorways.

Q1 Adjust the sweep period of a door closer so that the door will take at least 5 seconds to move from an open position of 90° to a partially open position of 12°. **ADA Standards: 2010 404 (Modified-More Restrictive)**

Q2 Adjust spring hinges so that a door will take at least 1.5 seconds to move from a 70° open position to the closed position. **ADA Standards: 2010 404 (Modified-More Restrictive)**

Q3 Install delayed reaction features on door closers. **ADAAG: 1998 4.13** ca

Q4 Adjust the door closers on all interior doors so that the opening force does not exceed 5 lbs. (22.2N). **ADAAG: 1998 4.18 & ADA Standards: 2010 309**

Q5 Replace door closers that cannot be adjusted properly. ca

Q6 Ensure that the bottom edge of door closers are installed no lower than 78in. (1980mm) above the floor. **ADA Standards: 2010 307 (New)**
Refer to Figure DR.26

R Door Surfaces and Kickplates

People using assistive devices for mobility frequently push against the bottom of doors to open them. Kickplates help protect doors from damage.

R1 Ensure that at least the bottom 10in. (255mm) of swinging doors have a smooth surface or kickplate on the push face of the door. **ADA Standards: 2010 404 (New)**
  A smooth surface of 16in. (405mm) is preferred. ca

See Figure DR.28

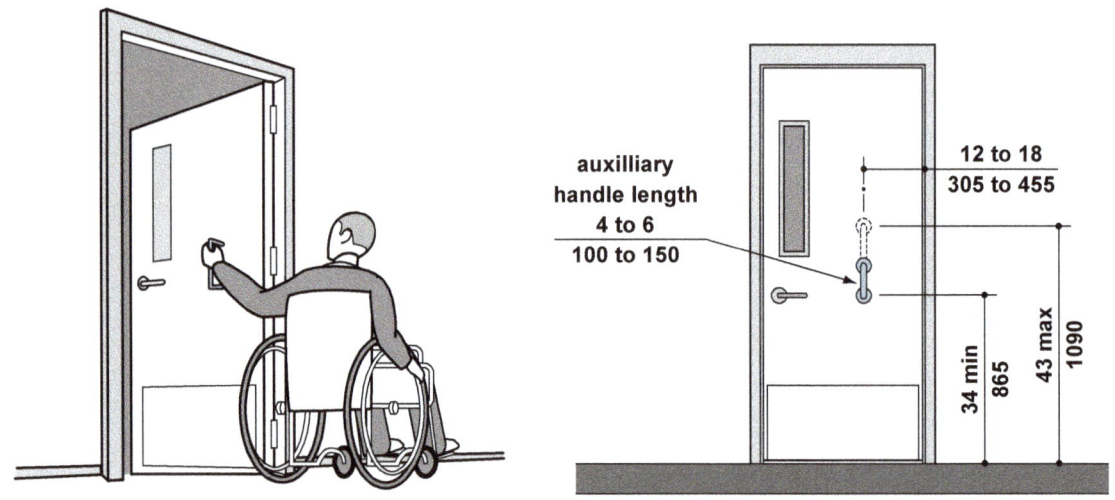

DR.27 Placement of an auxiliary door handle on a door *without* a closer

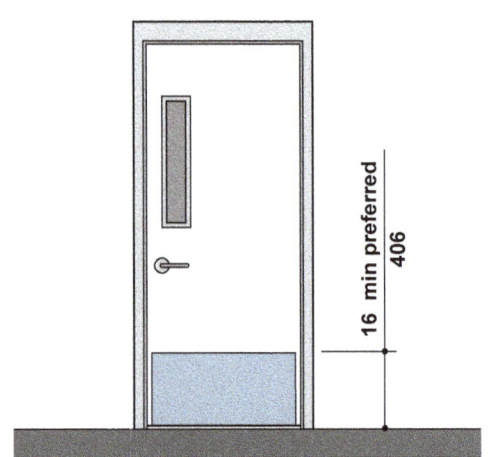

DR.28 Smooth surface or kickplate on a door

R2 Ensure that the exposed edges of kickplates are rounded to prevent scraping or catching of skin or clothing. ᶜᵃ

R3 Provide solid backing for kickplates, particularly on hollow-core doors. ᶜᵃ

R4 Ensure that all parts of a door that create horizontal or vertical joints in the door surface (such as kickplates or decorative panels) do not protrude more than 1/16in. (1.6mm). **ADA Standards: 2010 404 (NEW)**
Exception: The requirements for door surfaces do not apply to some types of tempered glass doors or sliding doors. **ADA Standards: 2010 404 (NEW)**
Exception: The requirements for door surfaces do not apply where the bottom of a door is 10in.

(255mm) or more above the floor (such as a toilet stall door). **ADA Standards: 2010 404 (NEW)**

S   Vision Lites and Side Lites

A vision lite is a glazed panel in a door that permits viewing and improves safety. A side lite is a glazed panel adjacent to a door and is an acceptable alternative to a vision lite. Building and life-safety codes may limit the amount of glass permitted in doors. Based on the amount of glass permitted in doors, provide windows that are proportioned to accommodate both people using wheelchairs and people who are ambulatory.

S1 Install a vision lite or side lite so that the bottom edge of the glazed panel is located no more than 43in. (1090mm) above the floor. **ADA Standards: 2010 404 (NEW)**

S2 Provide vision panels in doors and/or glass sidelights at doorways to public use spaces including classrooms, conference rooms, laboratories, lecture halls, assembly spaces, and break rooms. ᶜᵃ
See Figure DR.29

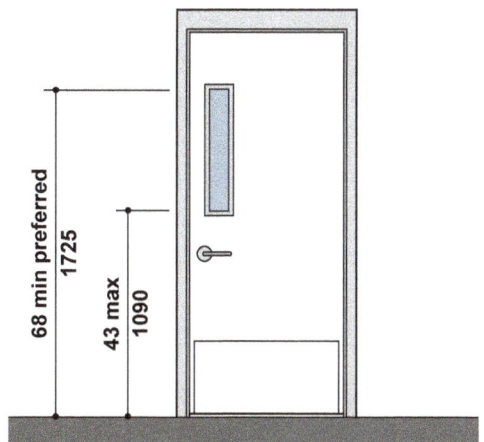

DR.29 Vision lite in a door

Vision panel in door and glass side light

S3 Install a vision lite or side lite so that the top edge of at least one glazed panel is located no less than 68in. (1725mm) above the floor.
Exception: The ADA Standards requirements do not apply to doors where the bottom edge of the vision lite is more than 66in. (1675mm) above the floor. ADA Standards: 2010 404 (NEW)

T Automatic and Power-Assisted Doors and Gates

Automatic and power-assisted doors and gates greatly improve accessibility at entrances. Without these, most entrance doors are difficult for many people to open. Due to problems with building pressurization and wind, door opening devices make entering buildings much easier.

Automatic door openers are generally preferred to power assist door openers, because they require no force to be applied directly to the door surface. However, power assist doors, which open automatically when moderated force is applied to the door surface, are helpful in many situations.

Automatic and power-assisted doors are recommended but not required by ADA Standards. Wherever an automatic or power-assisted door is installed, the door must comply with ADA Standards requirements for power-assisted doors, maneuvering space at doors, and thresholds at doors. **ADAAG: 1998 4.13 & ADA Standards: 2010 404 See DR-H through DR-K and DR-N**

Many people rely on automatic and power-assisted doors or openers for access to buildings. If you install automatic or power-assisted doors or openers, implement a program of monitoring and scheduled maintenance to ensure that doors always operate properly.

T1 Ensure that automatic doors comply with requirements in *ANSI/BHMA A156.10*. **ADAAG: 1998 4.13 & ADA Standards: 2010 404**

T2 To facilitate maneuver to and through doorways, place all auto door activators in appropriate locations that are unobstructed, easy to get to, and easy to use. Consult with wheelchair users to determine the best locations for exterior and interior auto door activators.

T3 Ensure that slow-opening, low-powered, power-assisted doors comply with requirements in *ANSI/BHMA A156.19*. **ADAAG: 1998 4.13 & ADA Standards: 2010 404**

T4 Provide a clear door opening width of 32in. (815mm) minimum in power-on and power-off mode. **ADA Standards: 2010 404 (NEW)**
A width of 36in. (915mm) is preferred.
The minimum clear width for automatic door systems is based on the clear opening provided by all door leafs in the open position.

T5 Ensure that *slow-opening, low-powered* automatic doors
   a. take more than 3 seconds to open to the back check (stopping position), **ADAAG: 1998 4.13**

    b.   require a force of less than 15 lbs. (67N) to stop door movement, **ADAAG: 1998 4.13** ca and,

    c.   have an automatic detection device that will stop or slow the door before contacting an obstruction. ca

T6 Ensure that the manual door opening force of power-assisted doors does not exceed the requirements for door opening force in DR-P. **ADAAG: 1998 4.13** ca

T7 Ensure that controls for automatic and power-assisted doors are located outside of door swings. **ADA Standards: 2010 404 (New)**

T8 Provide clear maneuvering space, configured for a forward or parallel approach, of 30in. (760mm) by 48in. (1220mm) minimum. **ADA Standards: 2010 404 (New)**

T9 Ensure that any automatic or power-assisted door controls are within the appropriate maneuvering space and reach range. **ADAAG: 1998 4.27 & ADA Standards: 2010 309**
See RR Reach Ranges.

T10 Provide controls and operating mechanisms for automatic and power-assisted doors that
    a.   are operable with one hand;
    b.   do not require tight grasping, pinching, or twisting of the wrist; and
    c.   are operable with a force no greater than 5 lbs. (22.2N). **ADAAG: 1998 4.27 & ADA Standards: 2010 309**

T11 Provide signs that
    a.   identify automatic doors and any related hazards, and
    b.   meet industry requirements. ca

T12 Inspect automatic doors and power assist doors for proper operation on a regularly scheduled basis (at least once a day for high usage doorways). ca

T13 To avoid confusion, do not install activators near card readers, switches, outlets, thermostats, or other controls. ca

T14 Specify auto door activators with 'Wave to Open' text and a hand icon that make sounds and light up when activated. ca

T15 Uniformly place standardized *Auto Door* decals on both sides of all activated doors. ca

EL Elevators

All Elevators 93
A   General Requirements 93

Standard Passenger Elevators 94
B   Safety Code Compliance 94
C   Signs 94
D   Automatic Leveling 94
E   Hall Call Buttons 96
F   Hall Signals 96
G   Labels on Elevator Entrances 96
H   Elevator Car Dimensions 97
I   Handrails in Elevators 99
J   Elevator Doors 99
K   Car Floor Surfaces 100
L   Illumination Levels 100
M   Elevator Car Controls and Indicators: Location 101
N   Car Control Buttons 101
O   Car Position Indicators 103
P   Emergency Communications 103

Destination-Oriented Elevators 104
Q   Destination Controls 104
R   Hall Signals 104
S   Elevator Car Controls and Indicators: Location 104

Limited Use/Limited Application (LULA) Elevators 105
T   LULA Elevator Doors 105
U   LULA Car Dimensions 105
V   LULA Controls 105

Elevators greatly improve accessibility by providing vertical access to multiple floors or levels in buildings. The ADA Standards contains requirements for elevators in new and existing construction.

The ADA Standards contains requirements for several types of elevators in new construction including standard passenger elevators, destination-oriented elevators, and limited use/limited application elevators. Standard passenger elevators (referred to in this chapter as elevators) provide service to all levels in a building. Destination-oriented elevators provide service to specific floors in a building. Limited-Use/Limited-Application (LULA) elevators can be used in a building that is not required to include a passenger elevator. LULA elevators are smaller and slower than other passenger elevators and are generally used for low-traffic, low-rise installations, including residential buildings. LULA elevators are allowed: 1) where standard elevators are not required, 2) as an alternative to platform lifts, and 3) in residential dwelling units, including private residence elevators.

The ADA Standards also contains requirements for existing elevators. Generally, existing elevators must comply with the requirements for new elevators. We have included differences allowed for existing elevators as exceptions under the items to which they apply. Where existing elevators are altered, or where the control panels or car indicators are changed, the new equipment must meet all the requirements for new elevators.

In multi-story buildings where elevators are not provided, guidelines for accessible routes and stairways apply to floors above the ground level that are used by the public.

Information in this chapter is grouped in four headings: All Elevators, Standard Passenger Elevators, Destination-oriented Elevators, and LULA Elevators.

All Elevators

A   General Requirements
All new and existing elevators, except service elevators, must meet accessibility requirements.

A1 In buildings where any accessible floor is four or more stories above or below a level with an exit to the outside of the building, ensure that at least one required accessible means of egress is an accessible elevator. **ADA Standards: 2010 207 See IBC: 2003 1007.**

A2 Locate elevators in easy to fine, predictable locations near stairways, and/or restrooms. ca

Elevator next to stairway ca

Elevator next to stairway serving short vertical distance ca

A3 Ensure that all accessible elevators that are part of an egress route
    a. meet the current requirements of Rule 211 of *ASME A17.1.*, **ADAAG: 1998 4.10 & ADA Standards: 2010 105 (Advisory)**
    b. are equipped with standby power, and **ADA Standards: 2010 105 (Advisory)**
    c. can be accessed from either an accessible area of refuge or a horizontal exit. **ADA Standards: 2010 105 (Advisory)** ca
    See AR Areas of Refuge.

Exception: Elevators in buildings protected throughout by a supervised automatic sprinkler system are not required to be adjacent to an area of refuge or horizontal exit. See IBC: 2003 1003. See EG Egress.

A4 Ensure that every passenger elevator provided meets all accessibility requirements and serves all levels, including accessible mezzanines. **ADAAG: 1998 4.1 & ADA Standards: 2010 206**

A5 Ensure that the horizontal clearance between the car platform (floor) door sill and the edge of any hoistway landing floor is no more than 1.25in. (32mm). **ADAAG: 1998 4.10 & ADA Standards: 2010 407** See EL-H.

A6 Consult experienced elevator system specialists who are familiar with accessibility requirements before specifying or installing any elevator or elevator controls. ca

Refer to Figures EL.2 through EL.5

Standard Passenger Elevators

Standard passenger elevators provide service to all public levels in a building, unlike destination oriented elevators, which only provide access to specific floors.

B   Safety Code Compliance

When choosing and installing standard passenger elevators in new construction, work with the elevator supplier, manufacturer, and installer to ensure that the elevator meets all federal, state, and local building and life-safety codes and ADA Standards requirements.

B1 Ensure that all passenger elevators meet or exceed the standards for passenger elevators in Safety Code for Elevators and Escalators. *ASME A17.1.* **ADAAG: 1998 4.10 & ADA Standards: 2010 105, 407**

C   Signs

When all elevators in a building are accessible, signs containing the International Symbol of Accessibility are not required at elevators.

C1 When only a portion of the elevators in a building are accessible, identify accessible elevators with signs containing the International Symbol of Accessibility. **ADA Standards: 2010 216 (New)** See SN Signs.

D   Automatic Leveling

Proper and consistent leveling is important because it reduces the risk of tripping and falling for all people. An elevator with an automatic leveling system automatically adjusts when it stops so that the floor of the elevator car is even with the floor of the adjacent hall.

D1 Install self-leveling elevator car features to automatically bring and maintain the elevator car floor level with floor landings within a vertical tolerance of 0.5in. (12.7mm), preferably less. Elevator cars should be level within this tolerance when the car is empty as well as when the car is full to its rated capacity. **ADAAG: 1998 4.10 & ADA Standards: 2010 407**

E Hall Call Buttons

Hall call buttons are the devices located on hallway or corridor walls adjacent to elevators that are used to call elevator cars. The location and characteristics of the hall call buttons must ensure equal access for all people, regardless of ability. Keypads may also be provided for hall controls.

When hall call buttons are equipped with small signal lights people often have difficulty recognizing whether or not the hall call buttons have been activated.
See Figure EL.1

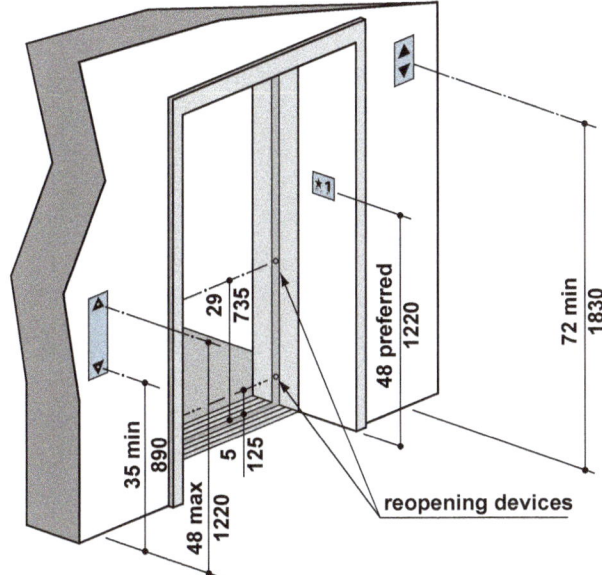

EL.1 Elevator controls and indicators on the hallway side at an elevator entrance

Note: The hall call buttons in the vertical panel are shown to the left of the elevator door. The Up button is shown at the maximum height for an elevator call button while the Down button is shown at the minimum height for a hall call button.

E1 Provide a clear floor space in front of hall call buttons, oriented for either a front or side approach, that is a minimum of 30in. (760mm) by 48in. (1220mm). **ADA Standards: 2010 407, 305 (New)**

E2 Locate hall call buttons between 35in. (890mm) minimum and 48in. (1220mm) maximum above the floor measured to the centerline of the highest operable part. **ADA Standards: 2010 407 (Modified–Less Restrictive)**

Exception: At existing elevators, hall call buttons may be 54in. (1370mm) maximum above the floor measured to the centerline of the highest operable part. ADA Standards: 2010 407 (New)

A maximum height of 48in. (1220mm) is preferred. ca

E3 Include visual signal lights on call buttons to indicate when each call is registered and answered. **ADAAG: 1998 4.10 & ADA Standards: 2010 407**

E4 *Provide hall call buttons that fully illuminate and are bright and easy to recognize when activated.* ca

E5 Use flush or raised buttons. **ADAAG: 1998 4.10 & ADA Standards: 2010 407**
Flat-surfaced, raised buttons are preferred because they can be operated by means other than fingertips and because they are easier to activate than convex buttons. ca
Exception: Recessed buttons are permitted at existing elevators. ADA Standards: 2010 407 (New)

E6 Ensure that the size of the button is at least 0.75in. (19mm) in the smallest dimension. **ADAAG: 1998 4.10 & ADA Standards: 2010 407**
Exception: Buttons at existing elevators are not required to comply with this size requirement. ADA Standards: 2010 407 (New)

E7 Install the **Up** button above the **Down** button on the wall. **ADAAG: 1998 4.10 & ADA Standards: 2010 407**

E8 Ensure that any object mounted under call buttons does not protrude from the wall more than 4in. (100mm) into the clear floor space provided in front of the button. **ADAAG: 1998 4.10 & ADA Standards: 2010 305, 307**

E9 Ensure that, where one elevator car is altered, all cars that respond to the same hall call are altered. **ADA Standards: 2010 206 (New)**

E10 Where keypads are provided for hall controls, ensure that all keypads meet the requirements listed in **EL-N**. **ADA Standards: 2010 407 (New)**

Confusing hall call buttons

Easy-to-see and understand hall call buttons

F   Hall Signals

Hall signals are the visual and audible indicators at elevators that alert people to the presence of an elevator car and indicate the direction in which the car will travel. The best location for hall signals is outside the elevator. The ADA Standards permits the use of in-car indicators if they are visible from the floor area adjacent to the call buttons. However, most people expect to find, and therefore benefit from, signals located outside the elevator car.

Refer to Figure EL.1

F1 Provide visible and audible signals outside each elevator entrance (at each hoistway) to indicate which car is answering the call and the direction of travel. **ADAAG: 1998 4.10 & ADA Standards: 2010 407**

Exception: Audible signals indicating the direction of travel are not required at existing elevators. ADA Standards: 2010 206 (New)

F2 Provide one of the following:
  a. audible signals that sound once for cars going **Up** and twice for cars going **Down**, or
  b. verbal annunciators that announce **Up** and **Down** in words. **ADAAG: 1998 4.10 & ADA Standards: 2010 407**

F3 Ensure that the sound (measured at the hall call button) of the audible signals or verbal annunciators meets the following requirements:
  a. audible signal frequency of 1500Hz maximum **ADAAG: 1998 4.10 & ADA Standards: 2010 407**
  b. verbal annunciator frequency of 300Hz minimum and 3000Hz maximum **ADA Standards: 2010 407 (New)**
  c. sound of signals and verbal annunciators between 10dB minimum above ambient and 80dB maximum measured at the hall call button. **ADA Standards: 2010 407 (Modified-More Restrictive)**

F4 Mount visual signals centered at 72in. (1830mm) minimum above the floor. **ADAAG: 1998 4.10 & ADA Standards: 2010 407**

F5 Use visual signals that are a minimum of 2.5in. (64mm) in height. **ADAAG: 1998 4.10 & ADA Standards: 2010 407**

F6 Ensure that signals are visible from the floor area adjacent to the hall call button. **ADAAG: 1998 4.10 & ADA Standards: 2010 407**

G   Labels on Elevator Entrances

Labels on the outside of elevator entrances need to accommodate people of differing sensory abilities. All people should be able to easily locate and interpret the information contained in labels (such as the floor or level of the elevator landing).

G1 Provide tactile and Braille floor designations on both jambs of each elevator entrance. **ADAAG: 1998 4.10 & ADA Standards: 2010 407**

G2 Ensure that the tactile and Braille floor designations are
   a. 48in. (1220) minimum above the floor, measured to the baseline of the characters; and
   b. 60in. (1525mm) maximum above the floor, measured to the top of characters. **ADA Standards: 2010 407, 703 (Modified-Less Restrictive)**

Refer to Figure EL.1

G3 Provide a tactile star on both jambs at the main entry level. **ADAAG: 1998 4.10 & ADA Standards: 2010 407**

Refer to Figure EL.1

G4 Provide a tactile elevator car identification label immediately below the hoistway entrance floor designation. **ADA Standards: 2010 407 (New)**

G5 Use 2in. (51mm) high raised characters for designations that meet all other requirements for Braille and tactile signs. **ADAAG: 1998 4.10 & ADA Standards: 2010 407 See SN Signs.**

H Elevator Car Dimensions

Elevator cars and doors must provide enough space for people who use wheelchairs to enter the car, maneuver within the car to reach controls, and exit the car in a forward-facing position.

Elevator car floor plans, door types, and dimensions vary and a range of solutions is permissible. The ADA Standards specifies the minimum requirements for elevator car dimensions and configurations but permits alternative car designs that provide wheelchair turning space when the elevator doors are closed.

See RT Routes and Spaces for information about wheelchair turning spaces.

H1 Install elevators that meet or exceed ADA Standards minimum requirements for interior car dimensions, door location, and door clear width. **ADAAG: 1998 4.10 & ADA Standards: 2010 407**

H2 Ensure that elevators with a centered door meet the following minimum dimension requirements:
   a. clear door width 42in. (1065mm) **ADA Standards: 2010 407 (Modified-More Restrictive)**
   b. side-to-side 80in. (2030mm) **ADAAG: 1998 4.10 & ADA Standards: 2010 407**
   c. back wall to front wall 51in. (1295mm)
      57in (1448mm) min preferred Ca
      ADAAG: 1998 4.10 & ADA Standards: 2010 407
   d. back wall to door face 54in. (1370mm)
      60in (1525mm) min preferred Ca
      ADAAG: 1998 4.10 & ADA Standards: 2010 407

See Figure EL.2

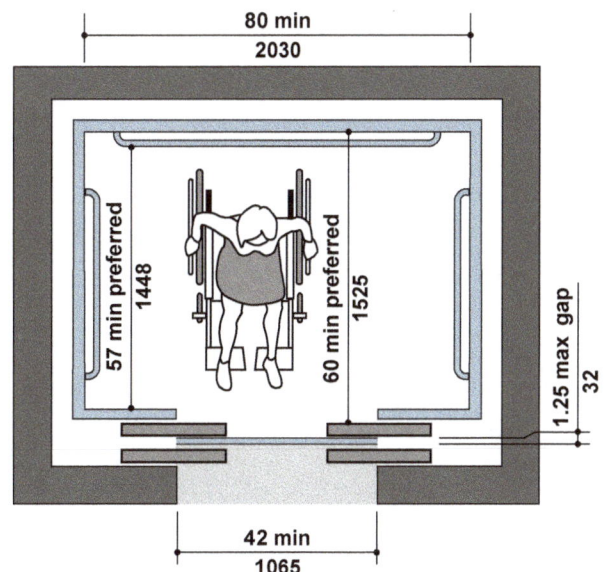

EL.2 Elevator with a *centered* door

H3 Ensure that elevators with off-centered doors meet the following minimum dimension requirements:
   a. clear door width 36in. (915mm)
      42in (1065mm) preferred Ca
      tolerance permitted 5/8in. (16mm)
   b. side-to-side 68in. (1725mm)
   c. back wall to front wall 51in. (1295mm)
      57in (1448mm) min preferred Ca
   d. back wall to door face 54in. (1370mm)
      60in (1525mm) preferred Ca
      ADAAG: 1998 4.10 & ADA Standards: 2010 407

See Figure EL.3

Design for All: The Best Path Forward — Dr. Arvid E. Osterberg

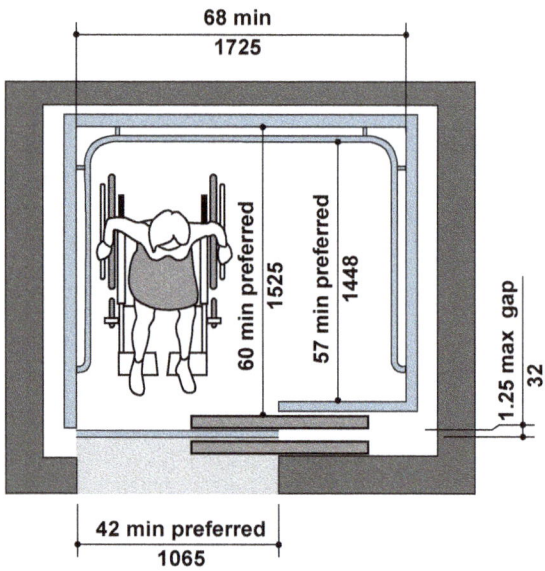

EL.3 Elevator with a side an *off-centered* door

H4 Ensure that elongated, or hospital type, elevators with centered or side (off-centered) doors meet the following minimum dimension requirements:
  a. clear door width 36in. (915mm)
     42in (1065mm) preferred ca
     tolerance permitted 5/8in. (16mm)
  b. side-to-side 54in. (1370mm)
     60in (1525mm) min preferred ca
  c. back wall to front wall 80in. (2030mm)
  d. back wall to door face 80in. (2030mm)
     ADA Standards: 2010 407 (New)

See Figure EL.4

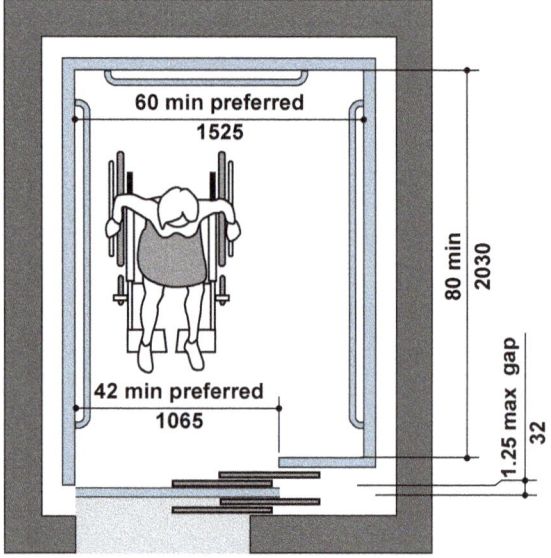

EL.4 *Elongated* elevator with a centered or off-centered door

H5 Ensure that square elevators with centered or side (off-centered) doors meet the following dimension requirements:
  a. clear door width 36in. (915mm)
     42in (1065mm) preferred ca
     tolerance permitted 5/8in. (16mm)
  b. side-to-side 60in. (1525mm)
  c. back wall to front wall 60in. (1525mm)
     67in (1702mm) min preferred ca
  d. back wall to door face 60in. (1525mm)

The minimum car size provides just enough room for a person in a standard size wheelchair to turn around. **ADA Standards: 2010 407 (New)**

See Figure EL.5

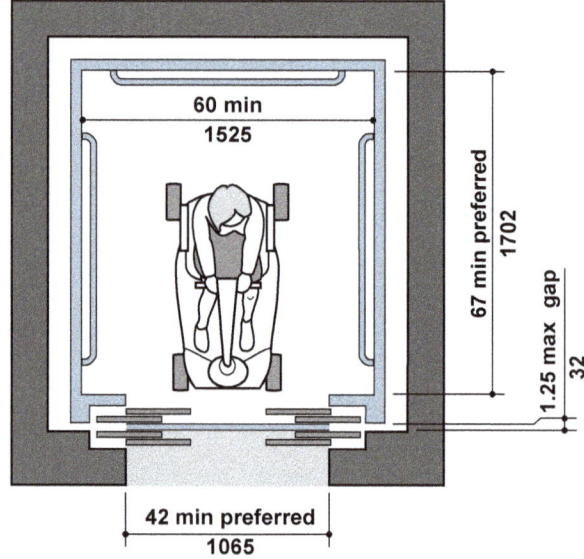

EL.5 *Square* elevator with a centered or off-centered door

EL-A provides an overview of the minimum dimensions, door location, and clear door width for elevator cars described in **EL-H2 through EL-H5**. Other car configurations that provide a wheelchair turning space consistent with ADAAG requirements are also permitted. For general specifications for turning spaces. **See RT Routes and Spaces.**

Door dimensions		Minimum inside car dimensions		
door location	door clear width	side to side	back to front wall	back to door face
EL.2 centered	42in 1065mm	80in 2030mm	51in 1295mm	54in 1370mm
EL.3 off-centered	36in 915mm	68in 1725mm	51in 1295mm	54in 1370mm
EL.4 centered or off-centered	36in 915mm	54in 1370mm	80in 2030mm	80in 2030mm
EL.5 centered or off-centered	36in 915mm	60in 1525mm	60in 1525mm	60in 1525mm

EL-A Minimum elevator car dimensions, door placement, and clear door width

H6 Ensure that existing elevator cars comply with the dimensions in **EL-H2 through EL-H5** (or in **Table EL-A**) unless they meet these conditions. The existing elevator car provides
  a. a minimum clear floor area of 16ft² (1.5m²),
  b. a minimum of 54in. (1370mm) inside clear depth, and
  c. a minimum of 36in. (915mm) inside clear width. **ADA Standards: 2010 407 (New)**

I Handrails in Elevators

Handrails (or bumpers) are often provided in elevators. Because people use the handrails or bumpers to steady themselves, ensure that they are accessible and easy to use.

I 1 Specify easy to grip handrails, rather than flat bars, in elevators. Ca

I 2 Follow the guidelines for handrails in **RP Ramps** regarding handrail profiles and space between handrails and walls. Ca

High and low handrails double as bumpers Ca

Aesthetically pleasing handrails Ca

J Elevator Doors

When an elevator responds to a call, the doors should remain open long enough for people to safely and comfortably move to and enter the elevator car.

Door protection and reopening devices work with automatic elevator doors to allow people to safely enter or exit an elevator car as the elevator car door(s) begin to close. These devices ensure that door(s) reopen and will not push, squeeze, or injure passengers.

Gates are not permitted in new or existing passenger elevators.

J1 Install elevator doors that are the horizontalsliding type. **ADA Standards: 2010 407 (New)**

J2 Ensure that elevator doors meet the requirements for clear width. **ADAAG: 1998 4.10 & ADA Standards: 2010 407**
Refer to Table EL-A
Exception: In existing elevators with power-operated doors, ensure that doors open to a minimum width of 32in. (815mm) and maintain that clear width as long as they are open. ADA Standards: 2010 404, 407 (New)
Exception: In existing elevators with manually-operated swing doors, ensure that the doors meet all the requirements for clear width and door opening force. ADA Standards: 2010 407 (New) See DR Doors.

J3 Install elevator hoistway and car doors that open and close automatically. **ADAAG: 1998 4.10 & ADA Standards: 2010 407**

J4 Provide adequate time between the signal when an elevator car has arrived and the point when the doors begin to close.
The time between the signal and when the doors begin to close depends on the distance between the elevator doors and a point 60in. (1525mm) in front of the farthest call button. The minimum amount of time allowed between the signal and the start of door closing is 5 seconds. **ADAAG: 1998 4.10 & ADA Standards: 2010 407**
Use this formula to compute the time elevators doors must remain open:

T = D/(1.5 ft/s) or T = D/(455 mm/s)

T is the time in seconds that the door should remain open. The time begins when the call signal is visible from a point 60in. (1525mm) directly in front of the farthest hall call button and when the audible signal sounds.
D is the distance someone has to go from a point 60in. (1525mm) directly in front of the farthest call button to the centerline of the open hoistway door.
Example: If a person must travel 9ft. (2.75m) from the call button to the elevator, then the car door should remain open for 6 seconds:

9/(1.5 ft/s) = 6 seconds

J5 Set the elevator door delay to keep the elevator door completely open for at least 3 seconds in response to a call. **ADAAG: 1998 4.10 & ADA Standards: 2010 407**

J6 Install reopening devices ("electric eyes") to stop and reopen elevator car and hoistway doors when they are obstructed by objects or persons. **ADAAG:1998 4.10 & ADA Standards: 2010 407**

J7 Ensure that reopening devices
  a. detect and are activated by an obstruction passing through the opening, without contacting the obstruction, at heights of exactly 5in. (125mm) and 29in. (735mm) above the floor; and
Refer to Figure EL.1
  b. stop and reopen the doors for at least 20 seconds before closing. **ADAAG: 1998 4.10 & ADA Standards: 2010 407**

K Car Floor Surfaces
Floor surfaces on routes to and from elevators and inside elevators must meet accessibility guidelines.

K1 Provide floor surfaces that are firm, stable, and slip-resistant. **ADAAG: 1998 4.5 & ADA Standards: 2010 302**

K2 Carpet installed in elevators must be
  a. attached securely;
  b. backed with firm padding or not backed;
  c. level or textured loop, level cut pile, or cut/uncut pile texture;
  d. no more than 0.5in. (12.7mm) pile thickness; and
  e. fastened to floor surfaces with carpet edge trim if there are any exposed edges. **ADAAG: 1998 4.5 & ADA Standards: 2010 407, 302, 303**

L Illumination Levels
All people benefit when light levels are sufficient for people to move about comfortably and safely.

L1 Provide illumination levels of at least 5 footcandles (54 lux) at elevator controls, platforms, car thresholds, and landings. **ADAAG: 1998 4.10 & ADA Standards: 2010 407**

M Elevator Car Controls and Indicators: Location

Elevator car controls are the devices (usually buttons) and information sources inside the elevator car. Elevator car controls initiate car movement, convey car emergency status, and allow passengers to manually control elevator functions. Controls need to be located and configured so that they are accessible to all people.

M1 Install car controls in one of the following locations.
  a. For a car with a side opening door, locate controls on the side or front wall next to the door.
  b. For a car with a center opening door, locate the controls on the front wall of the car. **ADAAG: 1998 4.10** ca

M2 Locate car controls within the appropriate reach range. **ADAAG: 1998 4.27 & ADA Standards: 2010 407, 308** See RR Reach Ranges.

Exception: In existing elevators or in elevators that serve more than 16 floors, where a parallel approach is provided, control panels are permitted to be 54in. (1370mm) above the floor. ADA Standards: 2010 407 (New)
See Figure EL.6

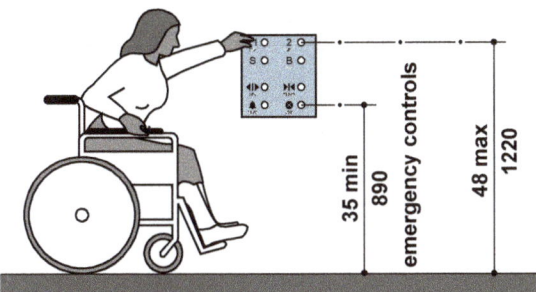

EL.6 Elevator controls inside an elevator car

M3 Group emergency controls, including *Alarm* and *Stop*, at the bottom of the panel with center lines 35in. (890mm) minimum above the car floor. **ADA Standards: 2010 407 (New)**
Refer to Figure EL.6

N Car Control Buttons

The ADA Standards contains very specific requirements pertaining to the dimensions of and spacing between call buttons, tactile characters, pictograms and Braille messages for elevator controls and control panels.

The information below covers general requirements for accessible button types, sizes, and mounting heights, and provides illustrations of required symbols.

When car control buttons are equipped with small signal lights people often have difficulty recognizing whether or not the car control buttons have been activated.

N1 Work with qualified elevator contractors to ensure all ADAAG requirements and elevator industry standards are met. ca

N2 Ensure that the minimum size of buttons is 0.75in. (19mm) in the smallest dimension. **ADAAG: 1998 4.10 & ADA Standards: 2010 407**

N3 Use buttons that are flush with or raised from the faceplate. **ADAAG: 1998 4.10 & ADA Standards: 2010 407**
  Flat-surfaced, raised buttons are preferred because they can be operated by means other than fingertips and because they are easier to activate than convex buttons. ca

Exception: In existing elevators, buttons may be recessed. ADA Standards: 2010 407 (New)

N4 Identify control buttons with both Braille and tactile designations. **ADAAG: 1998 4.10 & ADA Standards: 2010 407, 703**

N5 Provide car control buttons that fully illuminate and are bright and easy to recognize when activated. ca
See Figure EL.7

N6 Use floor buttons with visual signals that illuminate when each call is registered and turn off when each call is answered. **ADAAG: 1998 4.10 & ADA Standards: 2010 407**

	Control Button	Tactile Symbol	Braille Message
DOOR OPEN			OP"EN" (3 cells)
REAR/SIDE OPEN			OP"EN" (3 cells)
DOOR CLOSE			CLOSE (5 cells)
REAR/SIDE CLOSE			CLOSE (5 cells)
MAIN FLOOR			MA"IN" (3 cells)
ALARM			AL"AR"M (4 cells)
PHONE			PH"ONE" (4 cells)
EMERGENCY STOP			"ST"OP (3 cells)

EL.7 Standard symbols used on elevator car control buttons

N7 Identify the call button for the main entry floor with a raised star to the left of the floor designation. **ADAAG: 1998 4.10 & ADA Standards: 2010 407**

N8 Place raised character and Braille designations immediately to the left of the button or control to which they refer. **ADAAG: 1998 4.10 & ADA Standards: 2010 407**
For specific requirements for Braille and other character styles, contrasts, proportions, and sizes.
See SN Signs.
Exception: Where the space on an existing control panel does not allow for tactile designations to the left of the controls, place the tactile designations as close to the corresponding control as possible. **ADA Standards: 2010 407 (New)**

N9 Arrange car control buttons with numbers in ascending order. **ADA Standards: 2010 407 (New)**

N10 Arrange two or more columns of buttons to read from left to right. **ADA Standards: 2010 407 (New)**

N11 Designate all control buttons using standard symbols. **ADA Standards: 2010 407 (New)**
See Figure EL.8

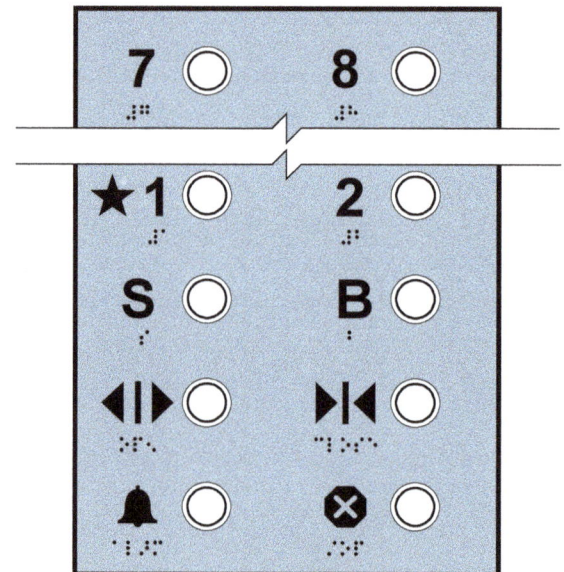

EL.8 Placement of designations on an elevator car control panel

N12 Where keypad controls are provided,
  a. arrange buttons on keypads in a standard telephone keypad arrangement,
  b. identify keypad buttons with tactile characters centered on the corresponding keypad button (Braille is not required), and
  c. identify the number 5 with a single raised dot that is 0.118in. (3mm) to 0.120in. (3.05mm) wide and meets other requirements for tactile character in **SN Signs**. **ADA Standards: 2010 407 (New)**

N13 Specify control panel layouts and car control buttons that are easy to see and understand.

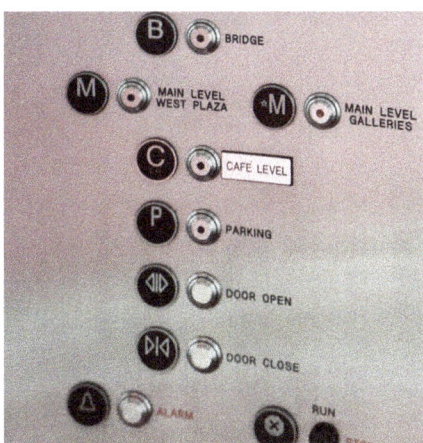
Confusing car control button arrangement

Legible and easy-to-understand control panel ca

Well-organized buttons arrangement ca

O Car Position Indicators

The position of elevator cars must be indicated both visually, with an indicator that lights as the elevator car reaches a level served by the elevator, and audibly, with a tone that meets audibility standards that announces when the elevator car reaches a level.

A special button may be provided to activate the audible signal when needed instead of maintaining constant operation of an audible signal.
See SN Signs and AL Alarms for more specific information.

O1 Provide a visual car position indicator above the car control panel or above the elevator door that includes the following features:
   a. car position indicators illuminate the corresponding floor number and sound an audible signal as the elevator car passes or stops at each floor it serves, **ADAAG: 1998 4.10 & ADA Standards: 2010 407**
   b. numerals on indicators that are 0.5in. (12.7mm) minimum high, **ADAAG: 1998 4.10 & ADA Standards: 2010 407** and
   c. audible signals must be automatic verbal announcements of the location of stop that are between 10dB above ambient and 80dB maximum, **ADA Standards: 2010 407 (Modified-More Restrictive)** with a frequency between 300Hz and 3000Hz, measured at the annunciator. **ADA Standards: 2010 407 (Modified-Less Restrictive)**

Exception: For elevators that have a rated speed of 200 feet per minute (1 meter/second) or less, an audible signal with a maximum frequency of 1500Hz that sounds as the car passes or stops at a floor served by the elevator is permitted. ADA Standards: 2010 407 (New)

P Emergency Communications

Emergency communication systems must be provided so that elevator passengers can quickly and safely report problems they encounter.

Systems that operate without handsets are *preferred* because they are easier to use for people who have difficulty reaching. Similarly, systems without doors are preferred because some people have difficulty grasping.

Emergency communication systems must be appropriately located and labeled. For additional requirements for Braille and other character styles, contrasts, proportions, and sizes. **See SN Signs.** For more information on anticipating and providing for emergency situations. **See AR Areas of Refuge.**

P1 When provided, two-way communication systems between elevators and a point outside elevators must comply with *ASME A17.1*. **ADAAG: 1998 4.10 & ADA Standards: 2010 407**

P2 Install two-way communication systems so that the highest operable part is no more than 48in. (1220mm) above the car floor. **ADAAG: 1998 4.10 & ADA Standards: 2010 407, 308**

P3 Identify two-way communication systems by a raised symbol and lettering located adjacent to the device. Use raised and Braille characters and pictograms that are
  a. 0.625in. (16mm) minimum to 2in. (51mm) maximum high,
  b. raised 0.0313in. (0.8mm),
  c. upper case,
  d. sans serif or simple serif type, and
  e. Grade 2 Braille. **ADAAG: 1998 4.30 & ADA Standards: 2010 407, 703**

P4 If the two-way communication system is located in a closed compartment, ensure that the door to the compartment
  a. is operable with one hand;
  b. does not require tight grasping, pinching, or twisting of the wrist; and
  c. is operable with a force no greater than 5 lbs. (22.2N). **ADAAG: 1998 4.10, 4.27 & ADA Standards: 2010 309**

Destination-Oriented Elevators

Destination-oriented elevators provide access to specific floors in a building. New destination-oriented elevators must be passenger elevators as classified by *ASME A17.1* and must meet all of the accessibility requirements for other passenger elevators except as follows.

Q Destination Controls

Q1 Provide a keypad or other means for entering destination information. **ADA Standards: 2010 407** (New)
  a. Where keypads are provided, ensure that the buttons are arranged in the standard telephone keypad arrangement and follow the requirements in **EL-M, and EL-N**. **ADA Standards: 2010 407** (New)

Q2 Provide both audible and visible signals that indicate which elevator car to enter. **ADA Standards: 2010 407** (New)

R Hall Signals

Destination-oriented elevators must include the same type of audible and visible signals as regular passenger elevators to indicate elevator car destination. **See EL-F**

In addition, destination-oriented elevators should meet the following guidelines.

R1 Provide the same audible tone and verbal announcement as those provided at the call button or call button keypad. **ADA Standards: 2010 407** (New)

R2 Provide both audible and visible means for differentiating each elevator in a bank of elevators. **ADA Standards: 2010 407** (New)

S Elevator Car Controls and Indicators: Location

Follow the guidelines for standard passenger elevators. **See EL-M**

In addition, destination-oriented elevators should meet the following guidelines.

S1 Install emergency controls, including the emergency alarm, so that their centerlines are 35in. (890mm) minimum and 48in. (1220mm) maximum above the elevator car floor. **ADA Standards: 2010 407** (New)

S2 Install visual car indicators above the car control panel or above the door.
   a. Provide a display of visible indicators inside the car that shows car destinations.
   b. Ensure that the numerals included in the visual indicator are at least 0.5in. (12.7mm) high.
   c. Ensure that the visible indicators switch off when the call has been answered. **ADA Standards: 2010 407 (New)**

S3 Provide an automatic verbal announcement that announces the floor where the car has stopped. Ensure that the sound of the verbal annunciator is 10dB minimum above ambient and 80dB maximum, measured at the hall call button. **ADA Standards: 2010 407 (New)**

Limited Use/Limited Application (LULA) Elevators

Limited-Use/Limited-Application (LULA) elevators can be used in a building that is not required to include a passenger elevator. LULA elevators are smaller and slower than other passenger elevators and are generally used for low-traffic, low-rise installations, including residential buildings.

LULA elevators must meet all of the accessibility requirements for other passenger elevators except as follows.

T LULA Elevator Doors
T1 Provide either swinging or sliding type doors. **ADA Standards: 2010 408 (New)**

T2 Ensure that swinging doors
   a. are low-energy power-operated,
   b. comply with *ANSI/BHMA A156.19*,
   c. close automatically, and
   d. remain open for a minimum of 20 seconds when activated. **ADA Standards: 2010 408 (New)**

U LULA Car Dimensions
U1 For new construction, provide cars that have the following minimum inside dimensions:
   a. a clear width of 42in. (1065mm), and
   b. a clear depth of 54in. (1370mm). **ADA Standards: 2010 408 (New)**

U2 In existing LULA elevators, ensure that cars have the following minimum inside dimensions:
   a. a clear width of 36in. (915mm),
   b. a clear depth of 54in. (1370mm), and
   c. a net clear platform area of 15ft^2 (4.57m^2). **ADA Standards: 2010 408 (New)**

Exception: For elevator cars that have a clear width of 51in. (1295mm) minimum, a clear depth of 51in. (1295mm) minimum is allowed where the car doors provide a clear opening of 36in. (915mm) wide minimum. ADA Standards: 2010 408 (New)

U3 Position elevator doors at the narrow end of cars and provide a minimum clear width of 32in. (815mm). **ADA Standards: 2010 407 (New)**

V LULA Controls
V1 Install elevator controls that are centered on a side wall of the elevator car. **ADA Standards: 2010 408 (New)**

PL   Platform Lifts

A	All Platform Lifts	106
B	New Construction	106
C	Alterations to Existing Conditions	107
D	Safety Code Compliance	107
E	Operation	107
F	Headroom	107
G	Doors and Gates	107
H	Clear Floor Space at Platform Lift Entrances	107
I	Level Change	108
J	Clear Floor Space Inside a Platform Lift	108
K	Floor Surfaces in Platform Lifts	109
L	Operable Parts	109
M	Handrails in Platform Lifts	109

Platform lifts (also referred to as mechanical lifts or wheelchairs lifts) are not recommended in new construction and many states severely limit or prohibit their use in both new and existing construction. Platform lifts typically result in a separate, stigmatizing experience for people who use them, a situation that violates the spirit of the ADA as well as the principles of *design for all*.

In most circumstances, platform lifts do not provide adequate solutions to accessibility problems in public buildings. For example, exterior platform lifts are subject to problems due to exposure to weather. Platform lifts may be appropriate for adapting existing single-family housing. However, elevators and ramps are preferred.

Platform lifts are allowed by ADA Standards in some situations where existing conditions make it infeasible to install a ramp or elevator. Such conditions generally occur where it is essential to provide access to small raised or lowered areas where space is not available for a ramp or to meet line-of-sight requirements in assembly areas.

The ADA Standards requirements for platform lifts also cover vertical and inclined wheelchair lifts. Always consult state and local building codes to determine whether the proposed lift is permitted for the purpose it will serve and to ensure that it meets ADA Standards as well as all applicable state and local codes and ordinances.

Consult experienced platform lift specialists familiar with accessibility requirements before specifying or installing a platform lift.

A   All Platform Lifts

A1   Do not install platform lifts in new construction, additions, and existing conditions where other solutions are possible. ca

A2   Although the use of platform lifts is permitted by ADA Standards under certain circumstances, check state and local codes and ordinances that may further restrict their use. ca

A3   Wherever a platform lift is installed, specify a high-quality lift that is mechanically reliable that meets or exceeds ADA Standards standards for ease of operation. ca

A4   Ensure that all platform lifts have an alternative operation system in the event of a power outage. ca

B   New Construction

Avoid platform lifts in new construction and additions wherever possible. Although the use of platform lifts is permitted by ADA Standards under certain circumstances, check state and local codes and ordinances that may further restrict their use.

B1   In new construction, ADA Standards permits the use of platform lifts only in the following situations:
- **a.** to provide an accessible route to a performing area or speaker's platform in an assembly area;
- **b.** to comply with wheelchair viewing position, line-of-sight, and dispersion requirements;
- **c.** to provide access to incidental, occupiable spaces with a maximum occupancy of five persons that are not open to the public (such as control rooms or projection booths); and
- **d.** to provide access to raised courtroom stations including: judges' benches, clerks' stations, bailiff's stations and court reporter's stations, or other areas of court rooms that require a level change.

ADAAG: 1998 4.1 & ADA Standards: 2010 206

C Alterations to Existing Conditions

Where existing exterior site constraints make the use of a ramp or an elevator infeasible, the use of platform lifts may be permitted. Check state and local codes and requirements.

C1 Wherever a platform lift is used as part of an accessible route in an existing building or facility, ensure that it complies with all ADA Standards requirements and applicable state and local codes. **ADAAG: 1998 4.1 & ADA Standards: 2010 206**

D Safety Code Compliance

If a platform lift must be used, it must comply with all applicable safety codes.

D1 Ensure that all platform lifts comply with *ASME A17.1*. **ADAAG: 1998 4.11 & ADA Standards: 2010 410**

D2 Provide standby power in accordance with *IBC section 1007.5* for platform lifts used as part of an accessible means of egress. **ADA Standards: 2010 207** (New)

E Operation

E1 Wherever a platform lift is installed, ensure that it facilitates unassisted entry, operation, and exit. **ADAAG: 1998 4.11 & ADA Standards: 2010 410**

F Headroom

To be part of an accessible route, headroom (vertical clearance) must meet accessibility guidelines. In particular, inclined stairway chair lifts and inclined and vertical platform lifts may not provide sufficient headroom.

F1 Select a lift that can accommodate people standing in the lift as well as people using wheelchairs. **ADA Standards: 2010 410** (Advisory)

F2 Ensure that headroom above the floor of the lift at any point in the lift's path of travel is at least 80in. (2030mm). **ADAAG: 1998 4.4 & ADA Standards: 2010 307**

G Doors and Gates

A lift door or gate can be at the end of a lift for a forward approach or at the side of a lift for a parallel approach. Door or gate controls that can be operated with a closed fist are preferred.

G1 Provide end doors or gates with a 32in. (815mm) minimum clear width. **ADA Standards: 2010 410** (New)

A clear width of 36in. (915mm) is preferred.

G2 Provide side doors or gates with a minimum clear width of 42in. (1065mm). **ADA Standards: 2010 410** (New)

A clear width of 54in. (1370mm) is preferred.

G3 Provide low-energy, power-operated doors or gates complying with the requirements for power-assisted doors and gates in **DR Doors**. **ADA Standards: 2010 410** (New)

   a. Ensure that doors and gates remain open for a minimum of 20 seconds. **ADA Standards: 2010 410** (New)

Exception: Pass-through type lifts that serve only two landings, and have doors or gates on opposite sides are permitted to have self-closing manual doors or gates. ADA Standards: 2010 410 (New)

G4 Install entrance controls for manual doors or gates that
   a. are operable with one hand;
   b. do not require tight grasping, pinching, or twisting of the wrist; and
   c. are activated with a force less than or equal to 5 lbs. (22.2N). **ADAAG: 1998 4.27 & ADA Standards: 2010 309, 410**

G5 Provide lift entrance controls at appropriate heights. **ADAAG: 1998 4.27 & ADA Standards: 2010 309** See RR Reach Ranges.

H Clear Floor Space at Platform Lift Entrances

The doors to platform lifts may be on one end, on both ends, on one side, or on one side and one end. However, keep in mind that it is easier for a person using a wheelchair to maneuver in and out of a platform lift that has doors on both ends.

People need adequate clearance and maneuvering space adjacent to a platform lift to approach, enter, operate, and exit the lift at every level served by the lift. The clear floor space can overlap an adjacent accessible route or another adjacent clear floor space.

H1 Provide clear floor space to facilitate approaches and maneuvering as follows:
    a. if the door or gate is on the end of the platform lift, provide a minimum clear maneuvering space of 30in. (760mm) by 48in. (1220mm) for a forward approach; 60in (1525mm) preferred or
    b. if the door or gate is on the side of the platform lift, provide a minimum clear maneuvering space of 30in. (760mm) by 60in. (1525mm) for a parallel approach. **ADAAG: 1998 4.11, 4.2 & ADA Standards: 2010 410, 305**

H2 Provide clear floor space to allow proper forward or parallel approaches to all lift controls. **ADAAG: 1998 4.11, 4.2 & ADA Standards: 2010 410, 305** See RR Reach Ranges.

H3 Ensure that the clear floor spaces adjacent to the lift are level, or have a slope of 1:48 (approx. 2%) or less. **ADA Standards: 2010 403 (Modified-Less Restrictive)**

I Level Change

On lifts that include an entrance ramp or threshold, any level change at the entrance of the lift should be minimal.

I 1 Where level changes are from 0.25in. (6.4mm) to 0.5in. (12.7mm), bevel edges with a maximum slope of 1:2 (50%). **ADAAG: 1998 4.5 & ADA Standards: 2010 303**
Refer to Figure DR.27

I 2 Ensure that the clearance between the outer edge of the platform and adjacent landing is 1in. (25mm) maximum. **ADA Standards: 2010 410 (New)**
A clearance of 0.5in. (16mm) is preferred.

J Clear Floor Space Inside a Platform Lift

Dimensions for platform lifts are not specified by ADA Standards (except for door clear opening width). However, clear floor space inside lifts must meet ADA Standards minimum requirements for clear floor space in general.

Platform lifts are manufactured in various sizes and configurations. Platform lifts that do not meet ADA Standards requirements for clear floor space may be sufficient for residential remodeling but are not appropriate for public buildings.

The configuration of space in an existing building often dictates the size of the lift and the location of doors. To select a platform lift that meets ADA Standards requirements and users' needs, consider whether the available space for the lift allows a forward or parallel approach. Provide the clear floor space necessary for maneuvering in and out of the lift.
See PL-G.

J1 Inside a platform lift with an end door, ensure that the clear floor space is 36in. (915mm) wide minimum on the door side **ADAAG: 1998 4.3 & ADA Standards: 2010 410,**
An inside clear floor space of 42in. (1065mm) wide by 67in. (1702mm) long is preferred.
See Figure PL.1

J2 Inside a platform lift with a side door, ensure that the clear floor space is 36in. (915mm) wide minimum by 60in. (1525mm) long minimum on the door side.
An inside clear floor space of 42in. (1065mm) wide by 67in. (1702mm) long is preferred.
See Figure PL.2

J3 If the configuration of the lift, lift doors, and/or controls is such that knee and toe space is required, follow the guidelines for knee and toe clearance in **RT Routes and Spaces, RT-Q.**

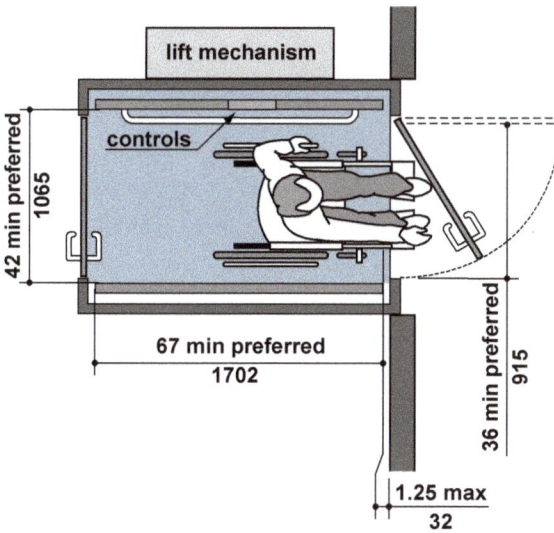

PL.1 Platform lift with end doors

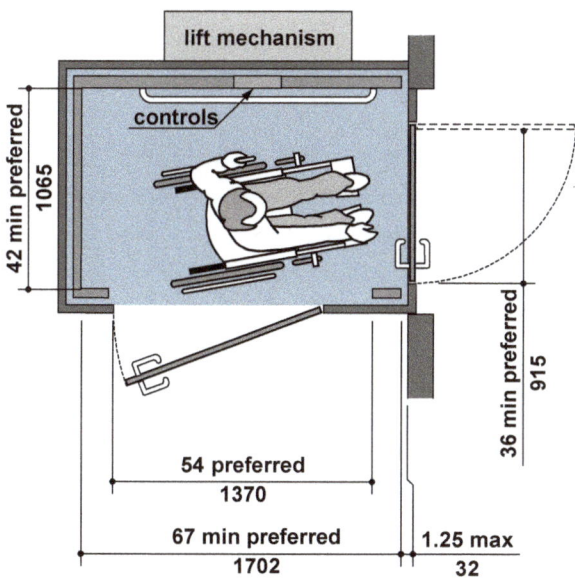

PL.2 Platform lift with a side door and an end door

K Floor Surfaces in Platform Lifts

K1 Provide floor surfaces on platform lifts that are firm, stable, and slip-resistant. **ADAAG: 1998 4.11, 4.5 & ADA Standards: 2010 410, 302, 303**

K2 Ensure that carpet installed in platform lifts is
   a. attached securely;
   b. backed with firm padding, or not backed;
   c. a level or textured loop, level cut pile, or level cut/uncut pile texture;
   d. no more than 0.5in (12.7mm) pile thickness; and

   e. fastened to floor surfaces with carpet edge trim if there are any exposed edges. **ADAAG: 1998 4.11, 4.5 & ADA Standards: 2010 410, 302**

L Operable Parts

L1 Mount controls and operating mechanisms within the lift at appropriate heights. **ADAAG: 1998 4.27 & ADA Standards: 2010 309** See **RR Reach Ranges.**

L2 Provide controls and mechanisms that
   a. are operable with one hand;
   b. do not require tight grasping, pinching, or twisting of the wrist; and
   c. are activated with a force less than or equal to 5 lbs. (22.2N). **ADAAG: 1998 4.11, 4.27 & ADA Standards: 2010 410, 309**

M Handrails in Platform Lifts

Handrails (or bumpers) are often provided in platform lifts. Because people use the handrails or bumpers to steady themselves, ensure that they are accessible and easy to use.

M1 Follow the guidelines for handrails in **RP Ramps** regarding handrail profiles and space between handrails and walls. 🅒🅐

ST Stairs

A	All Stairs	110
B	New Construction	111
C	Alterations to Existing Conditions	111
D	Clear Width	112
E	Treads and Risers	112
F	Nosings	113
G	Tread Surfaces	113
H	Handrails: Location and Placement	113
I	Handrails: Mounting and Profiles	115
J	Stairways in Hazardous or Unexpected Locations	117

It is essential that stairs be designed for safety because falls on stairs result in more than one million hospital treated injuries each year in the United States. Single stairs in unexpected locations are hazardous. Inadequate lighting, insufficient visual or tactile contrast between stairs and surrounding floor surfaces, confusing patterns on stair treads, missing handrails, and handrails without extensions are all factors that increase the number of falls on stairs.

Stairs should be accessible even when elevators or other forms of vertical access are available because many people with disabilities can and do use stairs. All people benefit from the increased safety and ease of use of stairs that meet accessibility guidelines. Stairs cannot be part of a *wheelchair*-accessible route.

It is imperative to maintain quality control during the construction of stairs and handrails. Handrails on both sides of stairs, dimensional uniformity of treads and risers, proper handrail extensions, and consistent handrail height are essential features of safe stairways. Adequate lighting is also important for safe travel on stairs. Stairways that are part of an egress route must meet additional requirements as described in **EG Egress, EG-D.**

Technically, a stair is a single riser. Stairs refers to a series of treads and risers connected by landings. A stairway is the structure containing a single flight or multiple flights of stairs that includes supports, frameworks, and handrails. For simplicity, in this chapter stairs may refer to a series of stairs, flights of stairs, or a stairway.

A All Stairs

A1 Ensure that all stairways, and all treads in stairways, are visually prominent and easy to recognize. ca

A2 Increase the visibility of stairways by contrasting tread and riser color with adjacent wall color. ca

A3 Increase visibility for people *ascending* stairs by specifying all risers in the stairway to be the same, solid color. ca

A4 Ensure that landings at the top and bottom of interior stairways have distinct and contrasting color to stair treads. ca

A5 Ensure that the lighting level on all stairs is at least equal to (or greater than) the lighting level of adjacent areas. ca

A6 Identify and eliminate distractions (such as mirrors, artwork, and posters) near stairways. ca

A7 Increase visibility for people *descending* stairs by including 2in (51mm) contrasting edge strips on the leading edges of all treads in all stairways. ca

A8 Increase visibility for people *descending existing stairways* by installing 2in (51mm) contrasting edge strips on the leading edges of the top stair tread, on the bottom stair tread, on the leading edge of stairway landings, and on the stair tread immediately above stairway landings. (Installing contrasting edge strips on all existing stair treads in a stairway is preferred). ca

A9 Increase visibility by having floor material at the top of stairways extend to the nosing above the top riser in the stairway, and by having floor color contrast stair tread color. ca

A10 Ensure that there is only one strip or marking per tread (two strips per tread can increase visual confusion). ca

Contrasting edge strips added to existing stair treads

Exterior stairway with setbacks at top and bottom, intermediate landing, edge protection, contrasting edge strips on all stair treads, and handrails with extentions

B New Construction

B1 To increase safety and accessibility ensure that all new interior and exterior stairs comply with accessibility requirements.

B2 Ensure that all interior and exterior stairs that are part of an egress route comply with accessibility requirements. **ADA Standards: 2010 207, 210 (New) See EG Egress and AR Areas of Refuge.**

B3 Follow all applicable building and life-safety code requirements for new stairs.

B4 Do not design or construct small level changes that result in unsafe single risers in any exterior or interior routes or at doorways.

B5 Ensure that all interior and exterior stairs connecting levels that are not served by an alternate, accessible means of vertical access (such as an elevator, ramp, or platform lift) comply with accessibility requirements. **ADAAG: 1998 4.1 & ADA Standards: 2010 210**

C Alterations to Existing Conditions

The ADA Standards does not require that stairs in alterations to an existing buildings meet all accessibility requirements for new construction as long as vertical access is provided by an alternative means, such as an elevator.

C1 To increase safety and accessibility ensure that all *existing* interior and exterior stairs comply with accessibility requirements to the maximum extent possible.

C2 Replace or reconstruct unsafe stairways (e.g. stairways that are too steep) that cannot be adequately improved due to restrictive *existing* conditions.

C3 When modifying an *existing* stairway to meet building and life-safety codes, ensure that all modifications also meet all requirements for accessible stairs in new construction.

C4 In *existing conditions* where a level change in a route or space is caused by a single step or stair, modify the level change and eliminate the single step by grading or by installing a low-slope (1:20 preferred) ramp.

C5 In alterations to existing conditions where levels are connected by both a stairway and an

Design for All: The Best Path Forward — Dr. Arvid E. Osterberg

accessible route (such as a ramp or elevator), install accessible handrails on stairways. **ADA Standards: 2010 210 (NEW)**

C6 In alterations to *existing* conditions improve stairways by
   a. installing proper accessible handrails on both sides of stairways,
   b. providing contrasting color from stairs to landings,
   c. increasing lighting on stairs.
   d. ensuring that the leading edge of all treads contrasts in color with the rest of the treads to increase visibility and safety (where conditions merit). **ADA Standards: 2010 405 (ADVISORY)** Ca

C7 In alterations and additions where an escalator or stairway is added through major structural modifications, provide an accessible route (such as an elevator or ramp) between the levels served by the added escalator or stairway. **ADAAG: 1998 4.1 & ADA Standards: 2010 206 See RT Routes and Spaces, RT-D2 for exceptions.**

D Clear Width

The ADA Standards does not specify a minimum clear width for stairways except where stairways are part of egress routes or areas of rescue. For additional information, **see EG Egress and AR Areas of Refuge.**

D1 Ensure that exit stairways that are part of egress routes and stairways that are adjacent to areas of rescue have a minimum clear width of 48in. (1220mm) measured between the handrails. **ADAAG: 1998: 4.3 & ADA Standards: 2010 207 See IBC: 2003 1003**

Exception: The minimum clear width requirement for exit stairways that are part of an egress route (or are adjacent to an area of rescue) does not apply to; 1) exit stairways in buildings protected throughout by a supervised automatic sprinkler system, 2) exit stairways accessed from a horizontal exit, and 3) or exit stairways serving open parking structures. See IBC: 2003 1003.

E Treads and Risers

Treads are the walking surfaces of stairs. Risers are the vertical surfaces between treads.
See Figures ST.1 and ST.2

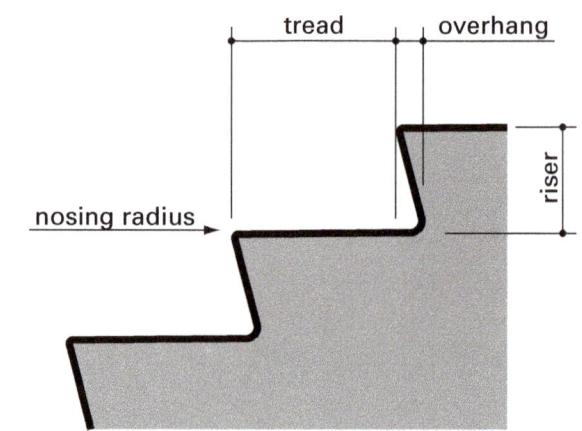

ST.1 Stair components

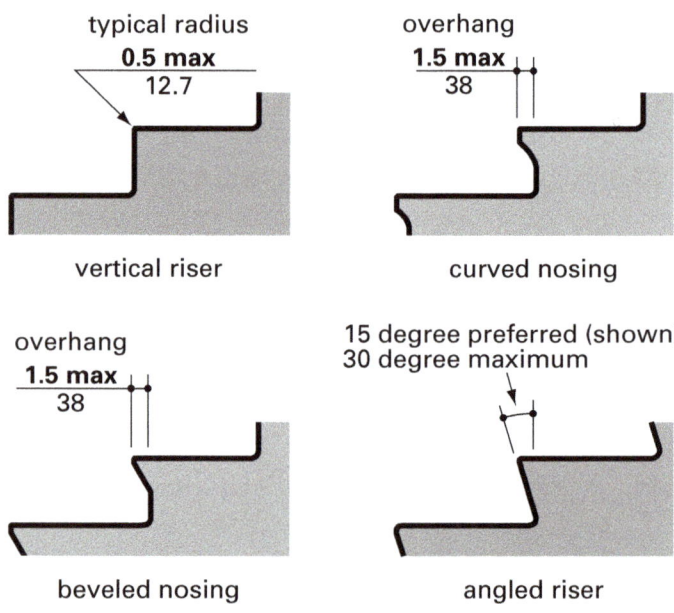

ST.2 Accessible stair profiles

E1 Provide uniform riser heights and tread depths on all stairs in a flight. **ADAAG: 1998 4.9 & ADA Standards: 2010 504** Ca

E2 Provide vertical or slightly angled risers to eliminate tripping hazards. **ADAAG: 1998 4.9**

E3 Ensure that angled risers slope under the tread at a maximum angle of 30° from vertical. **ADAAG: 1998 4.9 & ADA Standards: 2010 504**
   An angle of 15° or less is preferred. Ca

E4 Ensure that the minimum depth of treads is 11in. (280mm) measured from riser to riser. **ADAAG: 1998 4.9 & ADA Standards: 2010 504**

E5 Ensure that the height of risers is between a minimum of 4in. (100mm) and a maximum of 7in. (180mm). **ADA Standards: 2010 504 (New)**

E6 To reduce tripping and falling hazards, do not design or construct stairs with open risers (where the supports for the treads are only on the sides and there is no vertical surface between treads). **ADAAG: 1998 4.9 & ADA Standards: 2010 504**

E7 Inspect the top and bottom risers in *existing stairways* for dimensional uniformity and reconstruct if excessive variations exist. Ca

F Nosings

A nosing is the leading edge of a tread and is the horizontal projection from the vertical surface of the stair. Nosings that overhang the front edges of stair treads are often tripping hazards for people ascending stairs. **Refer to Figure ST.2.**

F1 Do not design or construct stairs with overhanging nosings. Ca

F2 Eliminate overhanging nosings in *existing stairways* where possible. Ca

F3 Ensure that the radius of the curvature at the nosing of a tread does not exceed 0.5in. (12.7mm). **ADAAG: 1998 4.9 & ADA Standards: 2010 504**

F4 Where nosings project beyond the riser, ensure that the underside of the nosings are either curved or beveled. **ADA Standards: 2010 504 (New)**

F5 Ensure that nosings do not overhang more than 1.5in. (38mm) beyond the rear of the tread below. **ADAAG: 1998 4.9 & ADA Standards: 2010 504**

G Tread Surfaces

Poor visibility of stair treads can increase the likelihood of falls. Many factors, including tread color and lighting, contribute to the visibility of stair treads. The slope of stair treads should be only enough to allow for drainage where necessary. For specifics on traveling surfaces, including carpeting, **see RT Routes and Spaces, RT-L.**

G1 Ensure that the slope of stair treads and landing surfaces does not exceed 1:48 (approx. 2%) in any direction. **ADAAG: 1998 4.3 & ADA Standards: 2010 504**
A slope of 1:100 (1%) is preferred. Ca

G2 Design stairs, approaches, and landings that are subject to wet conditions to prevent the accumulation of water. **ADAAG: 1998 4.9 & ADA Standards: 2010 504**

G3 Ensure that surfaces of stairs, approaches, and landings are firm, stable, and slip-resistant. **ADAAG: 1998 4.5 & ADA Standards: 2010 504, 302**

G4 Ensure that the leading edge of treads contrasts in color with the rest of the treads to increase visibility and safety where appropriate. **ADA Standards: 2010 504 (ADVISORY)** Ca

G5 When the leading edges of stair treads have either: 1) slip resistant strips, or 2) marked or painted edges for visual prominence, ensure that all treads in the flight of stairs have strips or marked edges that
  a. are securely and permanently attached
  b. are between 1.0in. (25mm) and 2.0in. (51mm) wide
  c. extend the full width of each tread, and
  d. extend to the leading edge of each tread Ca

H Handrails: Location and Placement

Properly designed and installed handrails provide support that is essential for reducing injuries resulting from tripping and falling.

Handrail extensions at the top and bottom of stairs reduce the likelihood of falls by providing 1) additional support for people entering or leaving stairs, and 2) visual cues to alert people to the top and bottom of stairways.

The open ends of handrails are hazardous when they catch shirt and coat sleeves. All handrail extensions must be returned in order to eliminate this hazard.

H1   Install or replace missing or inadequate handrails on *existing stairways* with handrails that meet ADA Standards. ca

H2   Provide handrails on both sides of all stairways. **ADAAG: 1998 4.9 & ADA Standards: 2010 505**
Exception: Only one handrail is required on aisle stairs in assembly areas. The handrail can be at either side or within the aisle width but cannot reduce the required route width. ADA Standards: 2010 505 (New)

H3   Provide handrails on both sides of all stairways, including those with only one or two risers. ca

H4   Install continuous handrails along the full length of each stair flight, including around columns or other structural elements. **ADAAG: 1998 4.9 & ADA Standards: 2010 505**
Exception: Handrails are not required to be continuous in aisles serving seating in assembly areas. ADAAG: 1998 4.8 & ADA Standards: 2010 505
   Provide continuous handrails along walls serving seating areas where possible. ca

H5   Provide continuous handrails around the perimeter of landings (with no doors) where possible. ca

H6   Install continuous inside handrails on switch-back stairs. **ADAAG: 1998 4.9 & ADA Standards: 2010 505**
See Figure ST.3

H7   Install center and intermediate handrails on wide stairways. Check state and local building and life-safety codes to determine whether intermediate handrails are required and to determine the maximum spacing permitted between handrails. ca

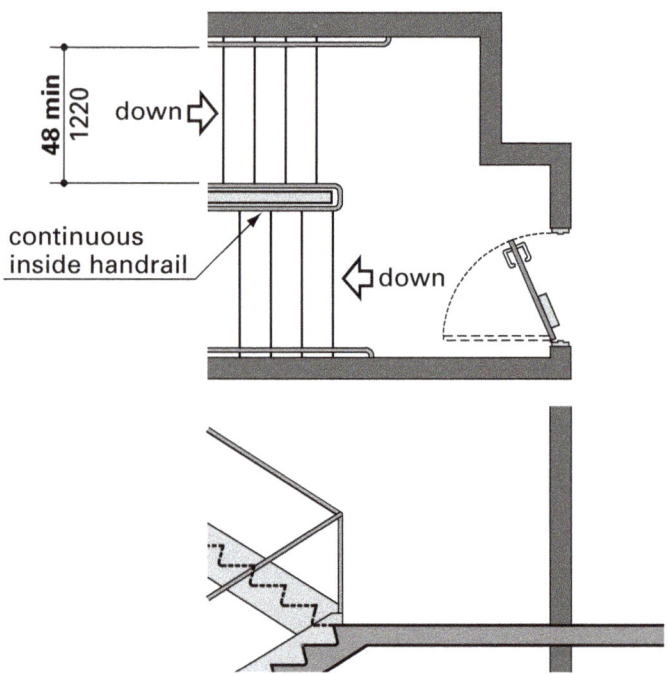

ST.3   A continuous stair handrail at a switch-back

H8   Extend handrails beyond the top and bottom of stair flights and ensure that they are parallel to the landing surface. **ADAAG: 1998 4.9 & ADA Standards: 2010 505**
   a.   Extend handrails at the bottom of stair flights by continuing the handrails to follow the slope of the stair flight for a distance of at least one tread depth beyond the last riser nosing. **ADAAG: 1998 4.9 & ADA Standards: 2010 505**
   b.   Extend handrails horizontally above the landing at the top of flights 12in. (305mm) minimum measured from directly above the top riser nosing. **ADAAG: 1998 4.9 & ADA Standards: 2010 505**
See Figures ST.4 and ST.5
Exception: Full handrail extensions are not required in alterations where site limitations would make it impossible to add extensions or where extensions would create a hazard. ADA Standards: 2010 505 (New)

Exception: Handrail extensions are not required at the inside turns of switch-back stairs. ADAAG: 1998 4.9 & ADA Standards: 2010 505
   c.   In existing conditions ensure that all handrails extend at least to top and bottom of stairways. **ADAAG: 1998 4.9 & ADA Standards: 2010 505**

d. Locate stairs to avoid handrail extension(s) protruding into adjoining routes. ca

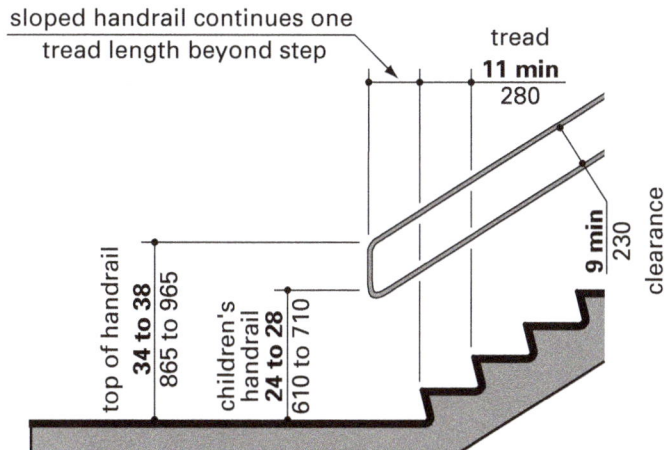

ST.4 Handrail with the *required* extension at the bottom of a stair flight

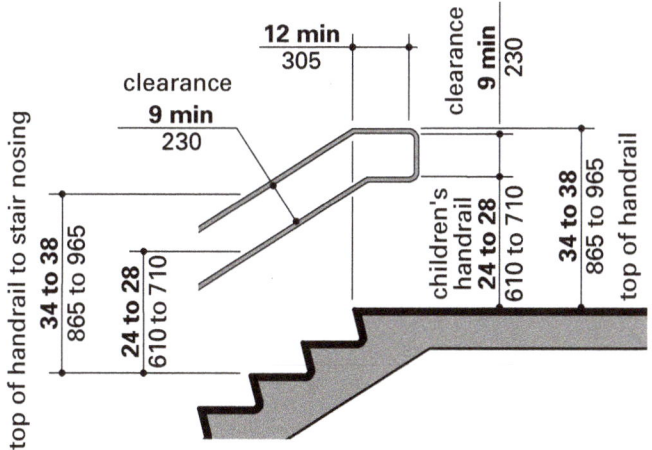

ST.5 Handrail with the *required* horizontal extension at the top of a stair flight

H9 Ensure that handrails are continuous with the handrails of adjacent stairways or that handrail extensions return to a wall, post, guard, or walking surface so they are not sleeve catchers.. **ADAAG: 1998 4.9 & ADA Standards: 2010 505**

H10 Install handrails so the top of the gripping surface is at a consistent height of 34in. (865mm) minimum to 38in. (965mm) maximum, measured from the top of the stair nosings. **ADAAG: 1998 4.9 & ADA Standards: 2010 505**

A top surface height of 36in. (915mm) is preferred. ca

H11 Provide a second, lower set of handrails if children are primary or frequent users of the stairway.
   a. Install children's handrails so the top of the gripping surface is at a consistent height of 24in. (610mm) minimum to 28in. (710mm) maximum measured from the top of the stair nosings. **ADA Standards: 2010 505 (Advisory)**
   A top surface height of 26in. (655mm) is preferred. ca
   b. Ensure that there is a 9in. (230mm) minimum clear space between the children's handrail and any handrail or obstruction above it to prevent children from becoming trapped between rails.
   ADA Standards: 2010 505 (Advisory)

Note: Most building codes require 4in. (100mm) maximum between handrails to prevent entrapment. The 9in. (230mm) minimum allows the correct height for both children's and adults' handrails. Check with your state and local code authorities to determine if the 9in. (230mm) minimum also complies with entrapment requirements.
Refer to Figures ST.4 and ST.5

H12 Ensure that there is adequate color contrast between handrails and walls. ca

I Handrails: Mounting and Profiles

Properly designed and mounted handrails reduce falls and mishaps on stairs.

I 1 Provide gripping surfaces on handrails that meet one of the following profiles:
   a. circular with a diameter or width of 1.25in. (32mm) to 2in. (51mm). **ADA Standards: 2010 505 (Modified-Less Restrictive)**
   b. non-circular with a perimeter dimension of 4in. (100mm) minimum to 6.25in. (160mm) maximum, and a cross-section dimension of 2.25in. (57mm) maximum. **ADA Standards & 2010 505 (New)**
   Circular profiles are preferred. ca

See Figure ST.6

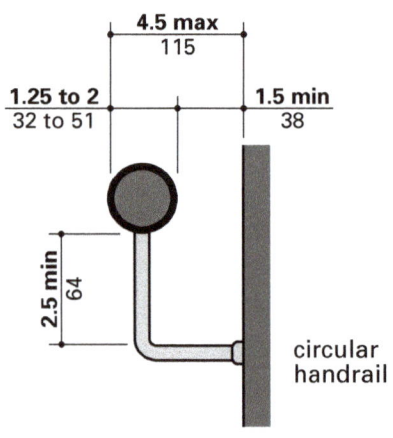
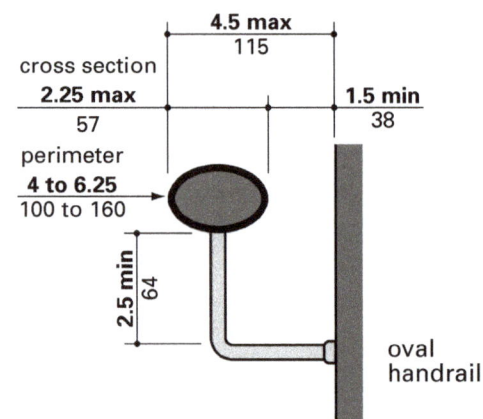
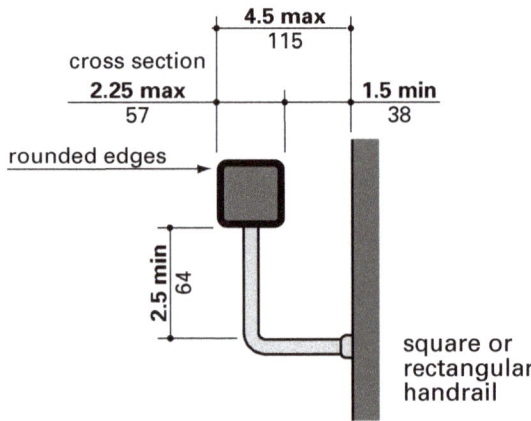

ST.6 Accessible handrail dimensions and profiles

I 2 Secure handrails so they do not rotate in their fittings. **ADAAG: 1998 4.9 & ADA Standards: 2010 505**

I 3 Ensure that handrails and adjacent surfaces are free of abrasive or sharp elements and have rounded edges. **ADAAG: 1998 4.26 & ADA Standards: 2010 505**

I 4 Provide 1.5in. (38mm) minimum clear space between handrails and walls or adjacent objects and surfaces. **ADAAG: 1998 4.9 & ADA Standards: 2010 505**

I 5 Ensure that handrails protrude from a wall no more than 4.5in. (115mm) and do not extend into any minimum required clear width of the stairway (such as the minimum required width for an egress stairway). **ADA Standards: 2010 307, 405 (MODIFIED-MORE RESTRITIVE)**

I 6 Provide a continuous gripping surface on handrails that is not obstructed by posts or other elements. **ADAAG: 1998 4.9 & ADA Standards: 2010 505**

I 7 If handrails are attached from underneath by balusters (posts) or brackets, ensure that
   a. not more than 20% of the handrail is obstructed by the bracket or baluster;
   b. any horizontal projections beyond the sides of the handrail are 1.5in. (38mm) minimum below the bottom of the handrail;
   2.5in. (64mm) preferred Ca
   and
   c. all edges must be rounded. **ADA Standards: 2010 505 (New)**

Exception: Handrail brackets or balusters that are attached to the bottom of railings are not considered obstructions (1) if they do not obstruct more than 20% of the handrail, and (2) if any horizontal projections beyond the sides of the handrail are 1.5in. (38mm) minimum below the bottom of the handrail. ADA Standards: 2010 505 (New)

I 8 Locate handrails in recesses only if the recesses are a maximum of 3in. (75mm) deep and extend a minimum of 18in. (455mm) above the top of the handrail. **ADAAG: 1998 4.26** Ca

See Figure ST.7

I 9 Ensure there is adequate color contrast between handrails and adjacent walls and panels. Ca

I 10 Where appropriate, increase the visibility of stairs by specifying continuous LED lighting on the bottom of handrails and/or guardrails. Ca

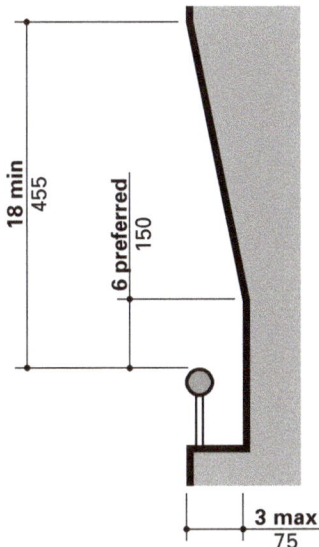

ST.7 Accessible recessed handrail profile

Additional lighting on stairway and handrail

Light strips under guardrail provide additional lighting on handrail and stairway

J Stairways in Hazardous or Unexpected Locations

Open stairways that are in unexpected locations within or adjacent to routes can be particularly hazardous for people with limited vision.

J1 In new construction, avoid locating open stairways in primary routes wherever possible.

J2 In an existing conditions where a stairway is in an unexpected location within or adjacent to a route, increase lighting and visual contrast at the top and bottom of the stairway.

Design for All: The Best Path Forward — Dr. Arvid E. Osterberg

Chapters in Alarms, Safety Areas, and Signs

AL Alarms   120
EG Egress   122
AR Areas of Refuge   125
SN Signs   129

Section 2. Alarms, Safety Areas, and Signs

The chapters in this section provide information on several aspects of buildings and sites that directly affect peoples' safety, including alarms, egress, areas of refuge, and signs. The ADA Standards provides a number of very specific requirements for meeting the needs of people with mobility, hearing, and vision disabilities. As you review safety issues, consider the different needs that people have for navigating the environment.

In all buildings, including new buildings and modifications to existing buildings, ensure that alarms, egress, areas of refuge, and signs fully comply with ADA Standards requirements.

Alarms
Alarms include both visual and audible signals to alert people of emergencies.

Safety Areas
Proper egress includes a fire-safe path of travel to a fire-safe area or to the outside of a building. Areas of refuge are fire-safe spaces where people can wait for assistance to exit a building. Means of egress and areas of refuge need to be accessible. So that all people can locate and reach these areas, they must be well-lit and free of obstructions.

Signs
Signs serve several important functions, including
1) directing people through buildings and sites and to specific spaces
2) allowing people to move through spaces independently, and
3) providing information and instructions
In addition, signs are an important consideration in creating a safe environment. During emergencies, signs are crucial in assisting people to find and use exits and safe places to wait for assistance. Signs should also provide important information about hazards and emergency procedures.

Technical Assistance
The ADA Standards and other codes contain very specific technical criteria for alarms, areas of refuge, egress, and signs. To meet the needs of all people and to comply with specific requirements, consult applicable codes, state and local officials, and expert consultants who are knowledgeable about code requirements and accessibility issues.

AL Alarms

A	Alarm Systems	120
B	Visual Alarms	120
C	Audible Alarms	121
D	Auxiliary Alarms	121

Alarm systems are not specifically required by ADA Standards. However, state and local building and life-safety codes require them in most public buildings. Where alarms are planned or included as part of public areas in a building, or when systems are replaced or upgraded in alterations, they must be accessible.

Prior to 2010, the ADAAG contained specific technical guidelines for accessible visual and audible alarms. Beginning with the 2010 ADA Standards, the guidelines include primarily scoping requirements for visual and audible alarms and the ADA Standards technical guidelines have been largely replaced by the general requirement to meet the standards in *National Fire Protection Association Life Safety Code (NFPA) 72, Chapter 4* unless otherwise noted.

This chapter provides ADA Standards scoping information on alarms. Public areas refers to all areas in buildings that are accessible by the public (such as routes, lobbies, restrooms, corridors, and assembly areas). Common areas (such as restrooms, break rooms, and corridors) refers to spaces that are shared by employees, residents, visitors, and/or other people. For alarm requirements in guest rooms, residential facilities, employee work areas, and medical facilities that differ from the requirements covered in this section, **see TL Transient Lodging, DU Dwelling Units, and WA Work Areas.**

This chapter includes information on issues related to alarms and accessibility and references to additional information on accessible alarms.

A Alarm Systems
Most public buildings are required to have fire alarms. Buildings in different areas of the country may also include alarm systems for hurricane, tornado, and/or earthquake warnings. The best solution is to always follow current industry practices for all alarm systems.

A1 Where fire alarm systems are required in public use and common areas, ensure that the systems include permanently installed audible and visual signals that meet the requirements of *NFPA 72.* **ADA Standards: 2010 215, 702 (NEW)**

A2 Where an emergency warning system (for emergencies other than fire) is provided in public use or common use areas, ensure that the system meets the following requirements:
  a. It provides both audible and visual signals,
  b. It provides a signal that is different than the fire alarm system signal. ca

A3 Ensure that alarms comply with all applicable state and local building and life-safety codes. ca

A4 Consult experienced electrical engineers or alarm system specialists with expertise on accessibility issues before specifying or installing any alarm or alarm system. ca

B Visual Alarms
Features of visual alarms include the type and color of the lights, pulse rate and duration, and flash rate. The flash rate is the interval between repetitive bursts of high-intensity light. Flash rates must be checked carefully because those that exceed five flashes per second may be disturbing to people who are photosensitive, particularly to people with certain forms of epilepsy.

The pulse duration is the interval between the signal build-up and decay, or the time interval between initial and final points of 10% of the maximum signal. The pulse durations should be such that the intensity of alarm flashes will not have the effect of temporarily blinding people.

Signals provided by alarms must be visible either by direct view or by reflection from all parts of the area they cover. To be effective, visual alarms need to raise the overall level of the light in a space significantly.

The number and intensity of signals is dependent on the size of the area covered by each signal.

Generally only one visual alarm is permitted in a single area. Multiple alarms are permitted to cover single areas only where the size, shape, building construction, or furniture obstruct total coverage by a single alarm. When multiple visual signals in a single space are not synchronized, the combined effect may produce a composite flash rate that could trigger an adverse response in some people.

Many factors are involved in proper placement and intensity of alarm signals, including ambient lighting, surface reflection, and space configuration. Ensuring that visual alarm signals function effectively (especially in very large or irregularly shaped areas or where building-wide systems are installed) requires careful planning and installation based on exacting calculations.

B1 Ensure that visual alarms meet the standards of *NFPA 72*. **ADA Standards: 2010 702 (New)**
Exception: Visible alarms are not required in existing buildings unless a fire alarm system is upgraded, or replaced, or a new fire alarm system is installed. ADA Standards: 2010 215 (New)

B2 Avoid problems caused by multiple visual signals by
   a. decreasing the number of fixtures and raising the intensity of lamps,
   b. decreasing the flash rate of multiple lamps, or
   c. synchronizing the flash rates of fixtures.

B3 Exercise caution when installing visual alarms near windows, mirrors, or other areas with very reflective surfaces where reflections will increase the intensity of the flash rate.

B4 Consult professionals familiar with accessibility requirements when specifying or installing alarms.

C Audible Alarms

Audible emergency signals need to be of an intensity and frequency that can attract the attention of individuals who have partial hearing loss and/or difficulty perceiving frequencies higher than 10,000 Hz. Alarm signals with a periodic element (such as single stroke bells, hi-low, or a fast on-off-on-off *whoop*) are best. Avoid continuous or reverberating tones.

Factors involved in proper placement and intensity of audible alarm systems include space configuration and the potential for reverberations or sound intensification due to echoes. These factors, singly or combined, may raise the audible alarm signal to uncomfortable or harmful levels.

C1 Ensure that audible alarms meet the standards of *NFPA 72*. **ADA Standards: 2010 702 (New)**

C2 Ensure that sound levels for audible alarm signals do not exceed 110dB at the minimum hearing distance from the audible appliance. **ADA Standards: 2010 702 (Modified-More Restrictive)**

C3 Ensure that alarms in guest rooms that are required to provide communication features comply with *NFPA 72*. **ADA Standards: 2010 702 (New)**

D Auxiliary Alarms

Auxiliary alarms ensure that people who have hearing disabilities are warned in an emergency. Auxiliary alarms must be located and oriented to spread signals and reflections throughout a space or to raise the overall light level significantly and instantly. However, light-based auxiliary signals are not always effective when people are asleep. An alternative for sleeping areas is to also install signal-activated vibrating devices under mattresses or pillows.

D1 Install auxiliary alarms so that they will be activated in the event of an emergency by one of the following methods:
   a. connect visual alarms in dwelling and sleeping accommodations to the building emergency alarm system,
   b. provide standard 110-volt electrical receptacles for connecting an alarm, or
   c. provide a means for a signal from the building emergency alarm to trigger the auxiliary alarm. **ADAAG: 1998 4.28**

D2 Install visual signals so that they are visible from all areas of the room or dwelling unit. **ADAAG: 1998 4.28** Ca

D3 Provide instructions for the use of auxiliary alarms and/or receptacles. **ADAAG: 1998 4.28** Ca

EG Egress

A	New Construction: Location and Number	123
B	Alterations & Existing Conditions: Location and Number	123
C	Egress Routes	123
D	Egress Stairways	123
E	Egress Elevators	124
F	Egress Signs	124
G	Egress Areas of Refuge	125

Accessible egress is a major safety concern because all people need safe, clear exit routes, particularly in an emergency. To coordinate more effectively with existing fire and life-safety codes, in the 2010 ADA Standards the Access Board replaced most of the technical requirements for egress (previously included in the 1998 ADAAG, section 4.1 and 4.3) with the requirement that egress meet the standards included in the (IBC) 1003.2.13. The information in this chapter is based on ADA Standards scoping requirements and remaining technical requirements as well as IBC requirements. Also consult the National Fire Protection Association Life Safety Code for information concerning egress elevators.

Accessible egress is a continuous, unobstructed path of travel along an accessible route from any accessible area in a building to an area of refuge, a public way, or a horizontal exit.

A horizontal exit is a fire-safety concept included in building codes that in effect creates a fire safe means of egress, such as a fire-resistive corridor leading to the outside.
Example: A floor level in a building is divided into areas separated by fire-resistive construction. In the event of a fire, occupants can move away from the area of the fire into an area that is protected by fire-resistive walls and doors.

Multi-level new construction must also include fire-rated areas of refuge on levels where direct accessible routes to the outside of the building is not available. **See AR Areas of Refuge**.

A NEW Construction: Number and Location

A1 Ensure that accessible means of egress comply with the requirements of **IBC: 2003 1007**. **ADA Standards: 2010 207** (NEW)

A2 Provide at least one accessible means of egress from each accessible space in a building to the outside of the building. **ADA Standards: 2010 105 (ADVISORY)** Ca

A3 Where more than one means of egress is required from an accessible space, ensure that each accessible portion of the space is served by at least two accessible means of egress. **ADA Standards: 2010 105 (ADVISORY)** Ca

A4 Ensure that each required accessible means of egress provides a continuous and uninterrupted path of travel to a public way. **ADA Standards: 2010 106** (NEW)

A5 Comply with all state and local building and life-safety codes for egress. Ca

B Alterations and Existing Conditions: Number and Location

While the standards do not require accessible means of egress in existing buildings, providing accessible egress will increase safety for all people using the building. **ADAAG: 1998 4.1, 4.3**

B1 In an alteration, provide accessible egress that meets the guidelines for new construction whenever possible. Ca

B2 Comply with all state and local building and life-safety codes for egress. Ca

C Egress Routes

Safe egress involves accessibility of both interior and exterior routes. People need direct, unobstructed interior egress routes to reach exit points and to exit buildings safely. When people are outside of buildings, they also need accessible exterior routes to safely and quickly move away from buildings to an area of safety.

To ensure that egress routes are accessible, follow all accessibility requirements for interior and exterior routes, entrances, and doors. **See RT Routes and Spaces, EN Entrances, and DR Doors.**

C1 Connect accessible means of egress to the level of exit discharge by an accessible route unless the level of discharge is 30in. (760mm) or more above or below the level of discharge. **ADA Standards: 2010 702** (NEW)

Exception: Where means of egress are permitted by local building or life-safety codes to share a common path of egress travel, the accessible means of egress may share a common path of egress travel. ADA Standards: 2010 207 (NEW)

C2 Ensure that all the components of each accessible means of egress meet accessibility requirements including:
   a. Route(s); See RT Routes and Spaces.
   b. Exit stairway(s); See EG-D and ST Stairs.
   c. Elevator(s); See EG-E and EL Elevators.
   d. Platform lifts(s); See PL Platform Lifts.
   e. Horizontal exit(s) or smoke barrier(s). **ADAAG: 1998 4.3** Ca

C3 Ensure that exit doors on egress routes meet the following requirements:
   a. 36in. (915mm) wide minimum,
   b. meet all state and local building and life-safety code requirements, and
   c. swing in the direction of travel, **IBC: 2003 1008**

C4 Where automatic doors and gates that are not equipped with standby power are part of an accessible means of egress, ensure that the clear breakout opening at swinging or sliding doors and gates is 32in. (815mm) minimum when operated in emergency mode. **ADA Standards: 2010 404** (NEW)

D Egress Stairways

Exit stairways are often used as part of a means of egress. To be considered a means of egress, a stairway must be enclosed. **IBC: 2003 1003**

D1 Ensure that interior and exterior stairs that are part of a means of egress meet all ADA Standards requirements for stairs. **ADA Standards: 2010 504 (New) See ST Stairs**.

D2 Provide a minimum clear width between handrails of 48in. (1220mm) on stair flights that are part of an egress route. **IBC: 2003 1007**

D3 Stairways used as a means of egress must meet one of the following conditions:
  a. incorporate areas of refuge that meet accessibility guidelines, or
  b. be reachable directly from either an area of refuge or a horizontal exit. **IBC: 2003 1007**

Exception: These requirements do not apply to exit stairways serving a single guest room. IBC: 2003 1007

Exception: These requirements do not apply to exit stairways in buildings that are fully sprinklered by a supervised automatic sprinkler system. IBC: 2003 1007

Exception: These requirements do not apply to exit stairways serving open parking structures. IBC: 2003 1007

E Egress Elevators

Safe egress out of multi-story buildings is a serious concern for people with disabilities. In some multi-story buildings, accessible means of egress may include egress elevators that are specially designed and constructed for evacuation. These specially designed and equipped egress elevators include standby power and other safety features. **IBC: 2003 1007 See EL Elevators.**

E1 Wherever an accessible floor is four or more stories above or below a level of exit discharge, provide an egress elevator as part of at least one of the required accessible means of egress. **IBC: 2003 1007**

E2 Locate egress elevators so they can be reached from either a horizontal exit or an accessible area of refuge. **IBC: 2003 1007**

E3 Work with the elevator manufacturer to choose and install elevators that meet or exceed the standards in *ASME A17.1, Rule 211*, including requirements for emergency operation and signaling devices. **IBC: 2003 1007**

E4 Provide standby power to egress elevators so that emergency or other authorized personnel can use the elevator for evacuation after the loss of primary electrical power. **IBC: 2003 1007**

Exception: In buildings and facilities protected throughout by a supervised automatic sprinkler system, egress elevators are not required to be adjacent to an area of refuge or a horizontal exit. IBC: 2003 1007

F Egress Signs

Accessible signs that identify egress routes and exit doors are critical for safety. The purpose and location of signs determine whether signs must include tactile characters in addition to visual characters. **See SN Signs.**

F1 Install directional signs containing visual characters to indicate the location and direction of accessible means of egress. **ADA Standards: 2010 216 (New)**

F2 Install signs containing both visual and tactile characters at egress doors to identify them. **ADAAG: 1998 4.1 & ADA Standards: 2010 216**

F3 Install directional signs containing accessible visual characters at exit stairways and elevators that are not accessible to direct people to the nearest accessible exit. **ADAAG 1998 4.1 & ADA Standards: 2010 216**

F4 Where possible, install tactile signs at stairways and elevators that are not accessible to direct people to the nearest accessible exits. Ca

F5 Ensure that each accessible sign meets the requirements for size, characters, finish and contrast, and mounting height. **ADAAG: 1998 4.1 & ADA Standards: 2010 216**

See SN Signs for additional information on signs.

G Egress Areas of Refuge

Areas of refuge are fire-resistive spaces where people can wait for rescue assistance. The specific requirements for accessible areas of refuge are covered in **AR Areas of Refuge.**

G1 Wherever areas of refuge are provided, ensure that the maximum travel distance to an area of refuge does not exceed the travel distance permitted for the occupancy by state and local building and life-safety codes and by **IBC: 2003 1007.**

AR Areas of Refuge

A	Location	126
B	Dimensions	126
C	Construction	127
D	Elevator Lobby	127
E	Communication and Instructions	127
F	Signs	128
G	Emergency Plans	128

Areas of refuge are fire-rated spaces where people can wait in safety for evacuation assistance by emergency personnel. Areas of refuge are critical for people who use wheelchairs and other people who have mobility problems that make using stairs difficult.

The 2010 ADA Standards does not include information on areas of refuge, but does require that egress, including areas of refuge, meet the requirements of the International Building Code (IBC).

In this chapter, we have included information and recommendations pertaining to areas of refuge that are included in the 1998 ADAAG and the 2010 ADA Standards, and that are consistent with IBC (with references to the ADA Standards and to IBC where applicable). In addition, we provide applicable requirements covered under other sections of the ADA Standards. Also consult the National Fire Protection Association (NFPA) Life Safety Code. Areas of refuge are generally not required in buildings with an approved, supervised, building-wide automatic sprinkler system.

NEW multi-level construction that is not equipped with an approved, supervised, building-wide automatic sprinkler system may be required to include areas of refuge on levels where direct, level, accessible egress to the outside of the building is not available.

Horizontal exits that meet the requirements of state and local building and life-safety codes may satisfy requirements for areas of refuge. A horizontal exit is a fire-safety concept included in building codes that, in effect, creates a fire safe means of egress (such as a fire-rated construction corridor leading to the outside of the building).

A designated area of refuge is an area that is fire-rated construction where people are instructed to gather in an emergency.

Example: A designated area of refuge is enclosed by fire-rated doors. The area between the doors has fire-rated construction including walls, ceiling panels, and smoke-actuated, fire-rated dampers.

In the event of a fire, the fire-rated doors close automatically so that occupants can move away from the area of the fire and/or smoke into the designated area of refuge that is protected by the fire-rated construction.

A   Location

Areas of refuge are required in multi-level new construction where accessible egress routes are on floors above or below the level where people can exit the building. Where areas of refuge are required, people must be able to reach them from accessible routes that are used for egress. **IBC: 2003 1007**
Exception: Areas of refuge are not required in alterations to existing buildings but are recommended to ensure the safety of people using the area. **IBC: 2003 1007**
Exception: Areas of refuge are not required in spaces that are not occupied. **IBC: 2003 1007**
See Figure AR.1

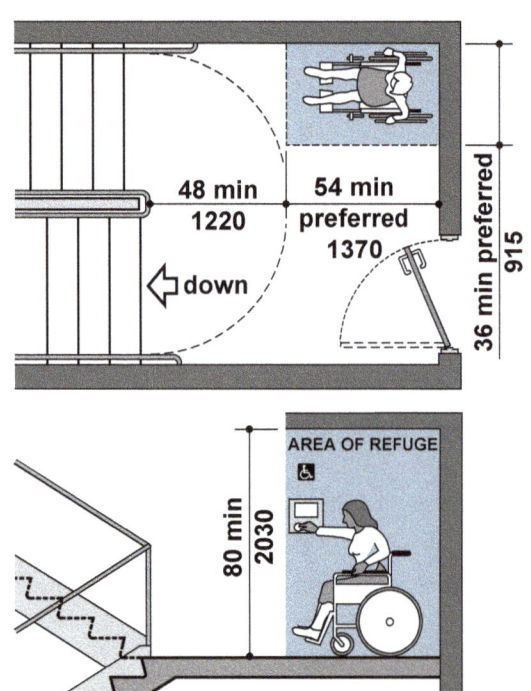

AR.1   Area of refuge located in a stairway

A1   Equip buildings with building-wide supervised automatic sprinkler systems.
Where such a system is installed, areas of refuge may not be required. Consult with building code officials and/or refer to IBC: 2003 for specific requirements.

A2   Where accessible areas of refuge are required, locate them on every occupiable level above and below the level where accessible exits are provided. Consult with building code officials and/or refer to IBC: 2003 for specific requirements.

A3   Review all applicable state and local fire and life-safety codes to ensure that all code requirements are met.

A4   Ensure that each area of refuge can be reached by an accessible means of egress from the space it serves. ADAAG: 1998 4.3 See EG Egress.

A5   Ensure that the maximum travel distance to an area of refuge does not exceed the travel distance permitted for the occupancy according to state and local building and life-safety codes. **IBC: 2003 1007**

A6   Provide direct access from every area of refuge to an accessible exit stairway or an egress elevator. **IBC: 2003 1007 See EG Egress, EG-D and EG-E**

B   Dimensions

All areas of refuge must include space for at least one wheelchair for every 200 people (or fraction of 200) based on occupant load. Clear floor space for wheelchairs must meet the following minimum size requirements. **ADAAG: 1998 4.3 IBC: 2003 1003**

B1   Provide a minimum clear floor space of 30in. (760mm) by 48in. (1220mm) for each required wheelchair space. **ADAAG: 1998 4.3 & ADA Standards: 2010 305**

B2   Ensure that all required wheelchair spaces can be reached without having to go through more than one adjoining wheelchair space. **IBC: 2003 1007**

B3 Ensure that the clear floor space provided for wheelchairs does not overlap any clear floor space for the exit route required by ADA Standards or by state and local building and life-safety codes. **ADAAG: 1998 4.3 See EG Egress and ST Stairs.** ca

B4 Provide a minimum of 80in. (2030mm) clear headroom. **ADAAG: 1998 4.4 & ADA Standards: 2010 307**
Refer to Figure AR.1

C Construction

Ensure that the floor plan and features of all areas of refuge in a building are designed and constructed to be predictable and easily understood.

C1 Separate areas of refuge from the rest of the floor level using a smoke barrier (such as fire-rated wall construction and fire-rated doors) with a fire-resistance rating of one-hour or greater. **IBC: 2003 1007**

C2 Design every area of refuge to prevent the intrusion of smoke and promote the safety of people. **IBC: 2003 1007**
Exception: This requirement does not apply to areas of refuge located within an exit stair enclosure. IBC: 2003 1007

C3 Comply with all state and local building and life-safety codes for areas of refuge and fire-rated construction. ca

D Elevator Lobby

Wherever an elevator lobby is used as an area of refuge, pressurize the elevator hoistway and lobby to comply with the requirements for smoke-proof enclosures. **IBC: 2003 1007**
Exception: This requirement does not apply where elevators are in an area of refuge formed by a horizontal exit or smoke barrier. IBC: 2003 1007

D1 Follow state and local life-safety codes and consult **IBC: 2003 709.** ca

E Communication and Instructions

Two-way communication systems that use both audible and visual signals must be provided in areas of refuge. Visible means of communication can include LEDs, screen displays, or lighted buttons that indicate help is on the way when the message is answered at the point of entry.

Signs and signals that provide information about emergency procedures, egress, and areas of refuge must be designed to accommodate people with limited vision, hearing impairment, and other disabilities.

E1 Provide a system of two-way communication between each area of refuge and the primary building entry (or other location approved by local fire department or other authority). **ADAAG: 1998 4.3** ca

E2 Provide both audible and visual communication or signals. **ADAAG: 1998 4.3** ca

E3 Provide audible signals using voice output or recorded messages. ca

E4 Include tactile and Braille labeling on signs at two-way communication systems. **See SN Signs.** ca

E5 Install communication controls
   a. within reach from spaces provided for wheelchairs, and
   b. 48in. (1220mm) maximum above the floor. **ADAAG: 1998 4.2 & ADA Standards: 2010 308**

E6 Install controls and mechanisms that
   a. are operable with one hand;
   b. do not require grasping, pinching, or twisting of the wrist; and
   c. are operable with a force no greater than 5 lbs. (22.2N). **ADAAG: 1998 4.27 & ADA Standards: 2010 309**

E7 Connect the communication system to the building's emergency power supply. ca

E8 Post instructions adjacent to the communications system that
    a. explain how to use the area and the communication devices in an emergency,
    b. meet the requirements of **IBC: 2003 1003**, and
    c. meet requirements for accessible visual signs. **See SN Signs. ADAAG: 1998 4.3 & ADA Standards: 2010 216**

E9 Ensure that the posted instructions
    a. include directions to follow routes to other means of egress, **ADAAG: 1998 4.3**
    b. advise people able to use the exit stairs to do so as soon as possible unless they are assisting others, **IBC: 2003 1007**
    c. provide information on the availability of assistance in the use of stairs or supervised operation of elevators, **IBC: 2003 1007**
    d. explain how to summon assistance, **IBC: 2003 1007** and
    e. provide directions for using the emergency communications system. **IBC: 2003 1007**

F Signs

F1 At exits, stairways, and elevators serving accessible routes (but not used for egress), install accessible visual signs to direct people to areas of refuge. **ADAAG: 1998 4.1 & ADA Standards: 2010 216**

F2 Ensure that all signs meet the requirements for characters, finish and contrast, and mounting heights in **SN Signs. ADAAG: 1998 4.1 & ADA Standards: 2010 216, 702**

F3 Install signs at doors serving areas of refuge that include
    a. tactile and visual characters,
    b. the words *Area of Refuge*, and
    c. the International Symbol for Accessibility. **ADAAG: 1998 4.3**

F4 Wherever illuminated exit signs are required at exit doors leading to areas of refuge, provide area of refuge signs that are all illuminated in the same manner. **ADAAG: 1998 4.3**

G Emergency Plans

Building occupants need to know what to do in an emergency. Check the Access Board website at www.access-board.gov for additional information about accessibility and emergency planning.

G1 Develop an effective emergency plan that includes procedures for helping people with disabilities and ensures that occupants of the building are familiar with emergency procedures before an emergency occurs.

G2 Provide instructions at the communication system that include information about assistance for people using areas of refuge. **IBC: 2003 1007**

G3 Check state and local fire and life-safety codes for additional requirements.

SN Signs

A	All Signs	130

Tactile Signs — 131
- B Mounting Location — 131
- C Mounting Height — 132
- D Tactile Characters — 132
- E Tactile Character Spacing — 132
- F Line Spacing for Tactile Characters — 133
- G Braille — 133
- H Pictograms — 133

Visual Signs — 134
- I Mounting Height — 134
- J Visual Characters — 134
- L Visual Character Spacing — 135
- L Line Spacing for Visual Characters — 135

Symbols of Accessibility — 135
- M Types of Symbols — 135
- N Finish and Contrast — 136
- O Illumination Levels — 136
- P Additional Signs and Messaging — 137

Unfortunately, signs often have inappropriate words, symbols, and messages. Many signs are also confusing and difficult to understand.

Well-designed signs facilitate wayfinding through sites and in buildings. However, even the best signage does not compensate for confusing arrangements and layouts and designers should not rely on signs to make the environment understandable.

Directional signs help people to get to their destinations, especially when site or building layouts and routes are complex or confusing. They can be a great benefit for everyone, and especially for first time users, people with memory problems, and people with cognitive limitations. Directional signs also help minimize unnecessary backtracking.

As a society, we continue to evolve and improve our attitudes and language about accessibility. Over the past several decades many outdated accessibility

Poorly designed and confusing accessibility signs

Design for All: The Best Path Forward — Dr. Arvid E. Osterberg

signs have been replaced with more appropriate signs. But unfortunately signs with the words 'disabled' or 'handicapped' are still commonplace. Additionally, accessibility signs for ramps, restrooms and other building and site features are often complex and confusing, and in some cases they are totally unnecessary, as seen in the photos shown.

Although an international symbol for accessibility is necessary, it would be better to emphasize 'access' rather that disabilities and wheelchairs. Since the majority of people who have state tags for accessible parking are not wheelchair users, it is time to replace the traditional symbol with a simple straightforward symbol that communicates 'access.'

The author proposes that new standardized access symbols be developed and endorsed by the Access Board for accessible parking, van accessible parking, ramps, elevators, restrooms and other building and site features. Accessibility signage should be as simple and straightforward as possible, with standardized color and layout, and without wheelchair depictions, unnecessary words and phrases, and/or confusing messages.

This chapter covers specific ADA requirements for signs. Other chapters that discuss specific areas of buildings provide information about where you need to locate signs. Additionally, signs that provide directions to rooms or spaces and to accessible means of egress also need to be accessible **ADA Standards: 2010 216, 703 (New)**

Signs that are not required to be accessible include building directories, menues, seat and row designations in assembly areas, occupant names, building addresses, and company names and logos. Even though these signs are not required to meet accessibility requirements, we recommend making the information readily available to all people wherever possible.

Signs provide important information about accessible locations and services. All people should have access to all types of information provided by signs. To assist the greatest number of people, signs should be placed at appropriate locations and heights, contain characters and backgrounds that meet specific requirements for readability, and use symbols that have been adopted internationally to indicate accessible locations and features.

The design and placement of signs should be uniform in and around buildings and sites. People will be able to find and use signs more easily and quickly if the placement and height of signs is consistent.

Accessible signs may include tactile characters (such as raised characters, Braille, and/or pictograms), visual characters, or both visual and tactile features. Where signs are required to be both tactile and visual, you may install one sign that includes both types of information or you may install two signs, one visual and the other tactile.

Symbols of accessibility may also be required in various locations to indicate the availability of accessible spaces and features.
See Figure SN.1

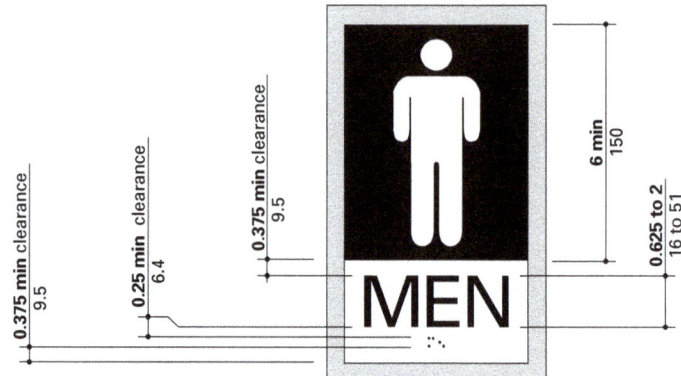

SN.1 A sign with visual and tactile characters, a pictogram, and Braille

All Signs

A1 **Do not display signs that convey messages such as, "for disabled only" or "for wheelchair users only" near automatic doors, elevators, or other accessible building and site features. Access should be for everyone.** ca

A2 **Use simple, straightforward and easy to understand symbols, words, and fonts on all signs.** ca

Do not display sign stating "For Disabled Use Only"

Do not display sign stating "For Wheelchair Only"

A3 Provide well organized and easy to read and understand directory information outside and inside major building entrances, where appropriate. ca

A4 Provide adequate lighting and eliminate glare on all signs. ca

Tactile Signs

The following guidelines apply to signs that include tactile characters. Mounting locations and heights apply to signs that require both tactile and accessible visual characters.

B Mounting Location

Signs that designate permanent rooms and spaces, or that provide information about spaces, are commonly mounted next to doors. To prevent injury to people reading tactile signs, ensure that the clear floor space in front of signs is out of the way of any door swing. Measure for the placement of signs in relation to clear floor space and door swings.

B1 Where a sign with tactile characters is provided at a door, locate the sign next to the door at the latch side. **ADAAG: 1998 4.30 & ADA Standards: 2010 703**
Exception: Tactile signs may be installed at the push side of doors that have closers but do not have hold-open devices. ADA Standards: 2010 703 (New)
See Figure SN.2

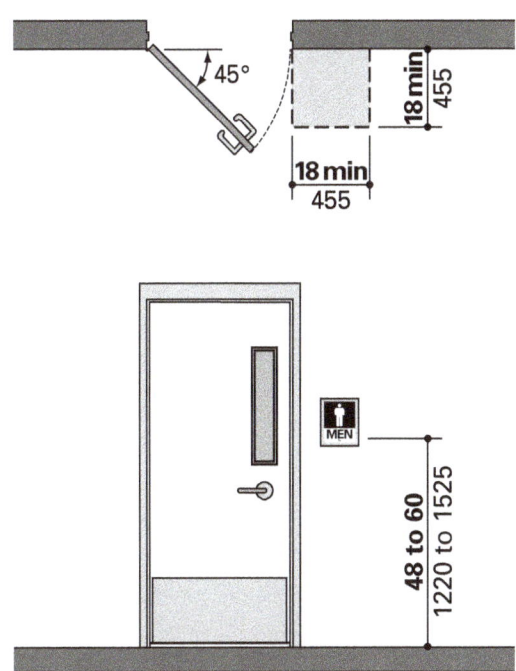

SN.2 Placement of a sign at a door

B2 Where a sign with tactile characters is provided at double doors,
  a. locate the sign to the right of the right-hand door if the double door has two active leaves, or
  b. locate the sign on the inactive leaf if the double door has only one active leaf. **ADA Standards: 2010 703 (New)**

B3 Where there is no wall space at the latch side of a single door or to the right side of double doors, locate signs on the nearest adjacent wall outside the door swing. **ADAAG: 1998 4.30 & ADA Standards: 2010 703**

B4 Wherever signs with tactile characters are installed near doors in any of the above configurations, provide clear floor space in front of the sign that meets the following requirements:
    a. 18in. (455mm) by 18in. (455mm) minimum,
    b. centered on the sign, and
    c. beyond the arc of any door swing between the closed position and the 45° open position. **ADA Standards: 2010 703 (New)**

Refer to Figure SN.2

C Mounting Height

The mounting height of a sign with tactile characters and/or Braille is based on the placement of the characters in the sign rather than on the outside edges of signs. Check state and local fire and life-safety codes for any additional requirements.

C1 Mount signs with tactile characters
    a. 48in. (1220mm) minimum above the floor, measured to the baseline of the lowest tactile character; and
    b. 60in. (1525mm) maximum above the floor measured to the baseline of the highest tactile character. **ADA Standards: 2010 703 (Modified-Less Restrictive)**

D Tactile Characters

Characters that are elaborate or unusual (such as italic, oblique, script, or highly decorative forms) are more difficult to read than plain styles and should not be used. The size of all characters is determined by the size of guide letters, such as **I** and **O**.

D1 Use sans serif fonts. **ADAAG: 1998 4.30 & ADA Standards: 2010 703**

D2 Use uppercase characters. **ADAAG: 1998 4.30 & ADA Standards: 2010 703**

D3 Ensure that tactile characters are raised a minimum 1/32in. (0.8mm) above their background. **ADAAG: 1998 4.30 & ADA Standards: 2010 703**

D4 Separate raised tactile characters from borders and decorative elements by 3/8in. (9.5mm) minimum. **ADA Standards: 2010 703 (New)**

D5 Ensure that the width of characters is 55% minimum and 110% maximum of the height of the character, with the width based on the uppercase letter O and the height based on the uppercase letter I. **ADA Standards: 2010 703 (Modified-More Restrictive)**

D6 Ensure that the height of characters is a minimum of 5/8in. (16mm) and a maximum of 2in. (51mm) based on the uppercase letter I and measured vertically from the baseline of the character. **ADA Standards: 2010 703 (New)**

Exception: Where both raised tactile and visual characters are provided on the same sign, the height of tactile characters may be 0.5in. (12.7mm) minimum. ADA Standards: 2010 703 (New)

D7 Ensure that stroke thickness of the uppercase letter I is 10% minimum and 15% maximum of the height of the character. **ADA Standards: 2010 703 (Modified-More Restrictive)**

E Tactile Character Spacing

Measure character spacing between the two closest points of adjacent characters within a message, excluding word spaces.

E1 Where characters have rectangular cross sections, ensure that the spacing between individual raised characters is 1/8in. (3.2mm) minimum and 4 times the raised character stroke width maximum. **ADA Standards: 2010 703 (New)**

E2 Where characters have cross sections other than rectangular, ensure that the spacing between individual raised characters is 1/16in. (1.6mm) minimum and 4 times the raised character stroke width maximum at the base of the cross sections, and 1/8in. (3.2mm) minimum and 4 times the raised character stroke width maximum at the top of the cross sections. **ADA Standards: 2010 703** (New)

F Line Spacing for Tactile Characters

F1 Ensure that the spacing between the baselines of separate lines of tactile characters in a sentence or paragraph is 135% minimum and 170% maximum of the character height. **ADA Standards: 2010 703** (New)

G Braille

Where Braille is required on a sign, the ADAAG requires the use of Grade 2 Braille. The requirements for Grade 2 Braille provided here are absolute. Because Braille is read with a light sweep of the finger pads, the dots must have a domed or rounded shape.

G1 Ensure that Grade 2 Braille is used where Braille is required on a sign. **ADAAG:1998 4.30 & ADA Standards: 2010 703**

G2 Ensure that the Grade 2 Braille dots have a domed or rounded shape. **ADA Standards: 2010 703** (New)

G3 Ensure that uppercase symbols are used before letters that need to be capitalized (before the first word of a sentence, before proper nouns and names, before individual letters of the alphabet, before initials, and before acronyms). **ADA Standards: 2010 703** (New)

G4 Locate Braille below corresponding text. **ADA Standards: 2010 703** (New)
   a. If text is multi-lined, place Braille below the entire block of text. **ADA Standards: 2010 703** (New)

G5 Separate Braille from any other tactile characters by 0.375in. (9.6mm) minimum. **ADA Standards: 2010 703** (New)

G6 Separate Braille from raised borders and decorative elements by 3/8in. (9.5mm) minimum. **ADA Standards: 2010 703** (New)

G7 Provide Braille in the exact dimensions for Grade 2 Braille characters. **ADAAG: 1998 4.30 & ADA Standards: 2010 703**

See SN-A

		Minimum	Maximum
a	Dot base diameter	0.059 in. (1.5mm)	0.063 in. (1.6mm)
b	Distance between two dots in the same cell *	0.090 in. (2.3mm)	0.100 in. (2.5mm)
c	Distance between corresponding dots in adjacent cells	0.241 in. (6.1mm)	0.300 in. (7.6mm)
d	Dot height	0.025 in. (0.6mm)	0.037 in. (0.9mm)
e	Distance between corresponding dots in cell directly below *	0.395 in. (10.0mm)	0.400 in. (10.2mm)
* measured center to center			

SN-A Required dimensions for Grade 2 Braille

H Pictograms

A pictogram is a symbol that represents an activity, place, or concept. Pictograms are not required on signs unless specified in the requirements for a particular type of sign in a specific area.

Pictograms do not have to be raised, but tactile text descriptions are required for pictograms that identify permanent rooms or spaces. Pictograms that provide information about a room or space (such as no smoking or occupant load) are not required to have text descriptions.

The pictograms shown in this chapter have a light (white) figure on a dark (black) background. Many times, though, pictograms are depicted using a dark figure (blue or black) on a light (white) background. Either option is acceptable as long as there is sufficient figure/ground distinction.

H1 Use a field height of 6in. (150mm) minimum in pictograms. **ADAAG: 1998 4.30 & ADA Standards: 2010 703**

H2 Locate characters and/or Braille outside the pictogram field. **ADA Standards: 2010 703 (New)**

H3 Where text descriptors for pictograms are provided, locate text directly below the pictogram field. **ADA Standards: 2010 703 (New)**

H4 Ensure that text used to describe pictograms complies with the guidelines for accessible tactile and visual signs. **ADA Standards: 2010 703 (New)**

Visual Signs

Factors affecting the readability of signs with visual characters include the distance from which the sign will be viewed; character height; the ratio of the stroke width to the height of characters; the contrast between characters and the background; and the font style. The character size should be based on the intended viewing distance.

To increase recognition and legibility, higher mounting heights and larger characters are required for signs that are viewed from greater distances.

I   Mounting Height

The mounting height of a sign is based on the placement of the characters in the sign rather than on the placement of the outside edges of the sign. Minimum viewing distance is measured horizontally from the point where any obstruction prevents further approach toward the sign. That point is called the viewing position.

In some instances, the floor level of the viewing position may be higher or lower than the floor level where the sign is installed. The height of a sign is always based on the floor level at the viewing position.

Where visual and tactile characters are included on the same sign, the visual characters must be above the tactile characters and the height and position of the sign is determined by the requirements for tactile characters.

I 1 Locate an overhead sign so that the bottom edge of the sign is 80in. (2030mm) minimum above the floor or ground (suspended or projected). **ADAAG: 1998 4.4 & ADA Standards: 2010 307**
See Figure SN.3

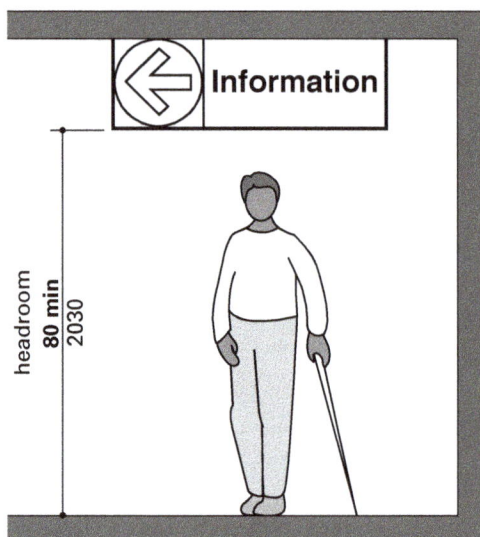

SN.3   Minimum required headroom for an overhead sign

I 2 Locate visual characters 40in. (1015mm) minimum above the floor or ground level of the viewing position. **ADA Standards: 2010 703 (New)**
See SN-B
Example: When the viewing distance to a sign is 25ft. (7.62m), the mounting height must be greater than 10ft. (3.01m) and the character height is required to be 3-1/8in. (78mm).

J   Visual Characters

Characters that are elaborate or unusual (such as italic, oblique, script, or highly decorative fonts) are often more difficult to read than plain styles and should not be used. Characters may be uppercase or lowercase or a combination of both. **ADA Standards: 2010 703 (New)**

J1 Use sans serif fonts where possible.

J2 Use upper and lower case rather than all upper case, where appropriate.

	Mounting height from floor to character baseline	Viewing distance	Minimum character height
a	less than **40 in.** (1015 mm)	only allowed in elevators	only allowed in elevators
b	**40 in.** (1015 mm) to less than or equal to **70 in.** (1780 mm)	less than **72 in.** (1830 mm)	**0.625 in.** (16 mm)
c	**40 in.** (1015 mm) to less than or equal to **70 in.** (1780 mm)	**72 in.** (1830 mm) and greater	**0.625 in.** (16mm), + **0.125 in.** (3.2 mm) per **12 in.** (305 mm) of viewing distance above **72 in.** (1830 mm)
d	**70 in.** (1780 mm) to less than or equal to **10 ft.** (3.01 m)	less than **15 ft.** (4.57 m)	**2 in.** (51 mm)
e	**70 in** (1780 mm) to less than or equal to **10 ft.** (3.01 m)	**15 ft.** (4.57 m) and greater	**2 in.** (51 mm), + **0.125 in.** (3.2 mm) per **12 in.** (305 mm) of viewing distance above **15 ft.** (4.57 m)
f	greater than **10 ft.** (3.01 m)	less than **21 ft.** (6.40 m)	**3 in.** (75 mm)
g	greater than **10 ft.** (3.01 m)	**21 ft.** (6.40 m) and greater	**3 in.** (75 mm), + **0.125 in.** (3.2 mm) per **12 in.** (305 mm) of viewing distance above **21 ft.** (6.40 m)

SN-B Information used to determine the size of visual characteristics based on mounting height and viewing distance

J3 Ensure that character width is 55% minimum and 110% maximum the height of the character with the width based on the uppercase letter O and the height based on the uppercase letter I. **ADA Standards: 2010 703** (NEW)

J4 Follow the guidelines in Table SN-B to determine the height of characters based on the viewing location and the minimum viewing distance.
   a. Base character height on the uppercase letter **I**.
   b. Measure minimum character height from the baseline of the character.
   c. Ensure that stroke thickness of the uppercase letter **I** is 10% minimum and 30% maximum of the height of the character. **ADA Standards: 2010 703** (NEW)

K Visual Character Spacing

K1 Measure character spacing between the two closest points of adjacent characters, excluding word spaces. **ADA Standards: 2010 703** (NEW)

K2 Ensure that the spacing between individual characters is 10% minimum and 35% maximum of character height. **ADA Standards: 2010 703** (NEW)

L Line Spacing for Visual Characters

L1 Ensure that the spacing between the baselines of separate lines of characters is 135% minimum and 170% maximum of the character height. **ADA Standards: 2010 703** (NEW)

Symbols of Accessibility

Several symbols that are used to indicate accessibility have been adopted internationally. The ADAAG requires these to be displayed in various areas. These symbols should be consistent in appearance and location throughout the building and site.

M Types of Symbols

M1 Wherever signs incorporate text with the International Symbol for Accessibility, use the word *Accessible* rather than *Handicapped* or *Disabled* (or avoid using words altogether).

M2 Display the International Symbol of Accessibility where required to indicate the locations of accessible spaces and features. **ADAAG: 1998 4.30 & ADA Standards: 2010 703**

See Figure SN.4

SN.4 International Symbol of Accessibility

M3 Where text-based telephones are provided, identify them by displaying the International Symbol of TTY. **ADAAG: 1998 4.30 & ADA Standards: 2010 703**
See Figure SN.5

SN.5 International Symbol of TTY

M4 Identify volume controlled telephones by displaying a pictogram of a telephone handset with radiating sound waves on a square field. **ADAAG: 1998 4.30 & ADA Standards: 2010 703**
See Figure SN.6

SN.6 International Symbol of Volume Controlled Telephones

M5 Where assistive listening systems are provided, indicate their availability by displaying the International Symbol of Access for Assistive Listening Systems. **ADAAG: 1998 4.30 & ADA Standards: 2010 703**
See Figure SN.7

SN.7 International Symbol of Assistive Listening Systems

N Finish and Contrast

Signs are more legible for persons with low vision when characters contrast with their background by approximately 70%.

N1 Use a non-glare finish for characters, pictograms, and backgrounds. **ADAAG: 1998 4.30 & ADA Standards: 2010 703**

N2 Contrast characters, pictograms, and symbols with backgrounds by using either light characters and symbols on a dark background, or dark characters and symbols on a light background. **ADAAG: 1998 4.30 & ADA Standards: 2010 703**

O Illumination Levels

Due to difficulty in controlling variable conditions in buildings and sites, requirements for illumination levels are currently not included in ADAAG. The following guidelines are recommendations based on previous ADA Standards recommendations.

O1 Provide illumination levels on sign surfaces between 10 to 30 footcandles (100 to 300 lux) wherever possible. **Ca**

O2 Ensure that the illumination level is uniform over the surface of the sign. **Ca**

O3 Locate signs and lighting so that the illumination level on the surface of signs is brighter than the ambient light in the space and brighter than the visible bright lighting source behind or in front of the sign. **Ca**

P Additional Signs and Messaging

The following signs and messaging systems assist people with disabilities in accessing information that is generally not included in tactile and non-tactile signs.

P1 Provide interpretive guides, audio tape devices, or other methods to convey descriptive information about public buildings, monuments, and objects of cultural interest. ca

P2 Provide tactile maps or pre-recorded instructions in large complexes (such as office parks, academic or corporate campuses) where people may routinely need to find locations independently. ca

Chapters in Restrooms and Bathrooms

TB	Toilet/Bath Rooms	140
TS	Toilet Stalls	150
UR	Urinals	159
FX	Fixtures	160
SS	Shower Stalls	167
SE	Tub/Shower Seats	173
BT	Bathtubs	175
GB	Grab Bars	179

Section 3. Restrooms and Bathrooms

The chapters in this section address accessibility issues related to restrooms, bathrooms, and bathing and changing areas that are designed to accommodate all people. Providing accessible public restrooms is particularly important to ensure that all people can work, use services, and participate in activities away from home.

Access

People need to easily locate, enter, and use restrooms and bathrooms. The best solution is to ensure that all restrooms and bathrooms are accessible. Where this is not possible:

1) locate restrooms and bathrooms close to main routes and entrances
2) provide signs that indicate routes to accessible restrooms and bathrooms, and
3) design doors and/or entry areas that allow easy access and ensure privacy

Space

All people need restrooms and bathing rooms that provide adequate maneuvering room. Space is particularly important for people who need extra room for wheelchairs, electric carts, walkers, or crutches or who may need the assistance of another person.

Consider the overall floor plan of restrooms and bathrooms to ensure that the space in stalls and aisles and around sinks and other fixtures allows people to comfortably move around.

Support

Many people need seating and grab bars for additional support while using restrooms and bathrooms. Support is essential for people who need to transfer from wheelchairs to toilets or bathing areas. Support is also helpful for people with limited mobility or vision. To ensure that grab bars and seating provide adequate and safe support, follow the guidelines in this section.

Controls

People should be able to use restrooms and bathrooms independently. In addition to providing access, space, and support, ensure that fixtures and controls are accessible by

1) Installing automatic controls or lever handles at sinks, showers, tubs, and toilets that can be easily manipulated by users with limited dexterity, and
2) ensuring that fixtures (such as toilet paper and paper towel holders, shelves, and hand dryers) are easy to use and are mounted at appropriate heights in correct locations.

TB Toilet/Bath Rooms

A	New Construction: Number and Location	140
B	Alterations to Existing Conditions: Number and Location	141
C	Toilet Rooms and/or Bathrooms: Private Use	141
D	Single-User Toilet Rooms and/or Bathrooms: Number and Location	142
E	Portable Toilets: Number and Location	143
F	Multiple-User Toilet Room and/or Bathroom Toilet Stalls: Type and Number	143
G	Multiple-User Toilet Room and/or Bathroom Fixtures: Type and Number	144
H	Signs	145
I	Doors	145
J	Clear Floor Space	145
K	Floor Surfaces	146
L	Legroom	146
M	Dispensers and Controls	148
N	Coat Hooks and Shelves	148
O	Baby-Changing Tables	149
P	Lactation Rooms	149
Q	Waste Receptacles	149

All public toilet rooms and/or bathrooms should be accessible to allow for safe and convenient use by all people. Public toilet rooms and/or bathrooms are those that are provided for the public or that are located in common areas of buildings used by visitors and/or employees. Accessible toilet rooms and/or bathrooms must be located on accessible routes and should be centrally located for convenient access.

Both individual fixtures and combinations of fixtures must be carefully analyzed to ensure that toilet rooms and/or bathrooms meet all accessibility requirements. Plan the areas to allow maneuvering room for wheelchairs and adequate clear floor space in front of fixtures and outside toilet stalls. Fixtures and accessories need to be installed within appropriate reach ranges to make toilet rooms and/or bathrooms convenient and easy to use.

This chapter provides information on the location, number, and general requirements for accessible public toilet rooms and/or bathrooms. It also provides specific information regarding the type and number of accessible fixtures and accessories that must be included in accessible toilet rooms and/or bathrooms.

Other chapters in the **Restrooms and Bathrooms** section address requirements for specific features of toilet rooms and/or bathrooms. General accessibility requirements that apply to toilet rooms and/or bathrooms (such as routes and spaces, doors, signs, and alarms) are provided in chapters **RT Routes and Spaces, DR Doors, SN Signs, and AL Alarms.**

The requirements in this chapter do not apply to toilet rooms and/or bathrooms that are part of resident or patient rooms in medical care facilities, guest rooms in transient lodging, or dwelling units that are not required to be accessible. For information pertaining to those areas, see the chapters in **Specific Use Areas.**

A   New Construction: Number and Location

A1 Where toilet rooms and/or bathrooms are provided in public areas or on accessible levels, ensure that they are accessible. **ADAAG: 1998 4.1 & ADA Standards: 2010 213**

A2 Locate all accessible toilet rooms and/or bathrooms on accessible routes. **ADAAG: 1998 4.1, 4.22 & ADA Standards: 2010 206**

A3 If toilet rooms and/or bathrooms are included on an inaccessible level in a multi-story building, provide accessible toilet rooms and/or bathrooms on an accessible level (connected by an accessible route to an accessible entrance). **ADA Standards: 2010 213 (New)**

A4 To make maneuverability and access easier for everyone, design and construct public restrooms without entrance doors wherever possible. ca

A5 Increase visibility in public restrooms by using non-glare materials and appropriate lighting. ca

A6 Do not use busy designs and confusing patterns on floors and walls. ca

See Figure TB.1

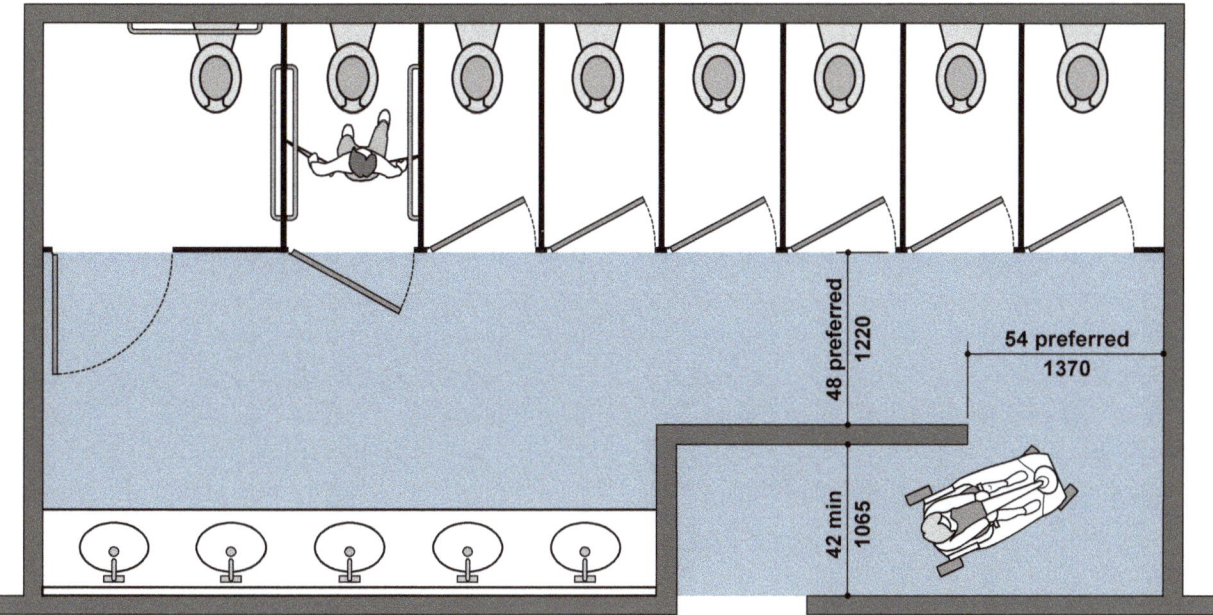

TB.1 Minimum and preferred clearances for an accessible public restroom entrance *without a door*

Public restrooms without doors ca

B   Alterations to Existing Conditions: Number and Location

Existing toilet rooms and/or bathrooms that are provided in public areas must be evaluated to ensure that they meet accessibility guidelines.

B1 Whenever possible, remove existing entrance doors to public restrooms to make access easier for everyone. ca

B2 When altering existing conditions, follow the requirements for toilet rooms and/or bathrooms in new construction to the maximum extent feasible. ca

Exception: Where it is technically infeasible to meet the requirements for new construction, install at least one accessible single-user toilet room and/or bathroom per floor in the same area as existing inaccessible toilet rooms and/or bathrooms. **ADAAG: 1998 4.1 & ADA Standards: 2010 213**

B3 When alterations to a primary function area require you to provide an accessible route, ensure that toilet rooms and/or bathrooms on that route are accessible. **ADAAG: 1998 4.1, 4.19 & ADA Standards: 2010 202**

B4 Ensure that toilets are positioned properly and not too close, or too far away, from adjacent walls or partitions. ca

B5 Install securely attached high quality toilet partitions that do not shake when doors are opened. ca

B6 Specify self-closing toilet partition doors that hang slightly open so that people can see if stalls are occupied. ca

C   Toilet Rooms and/or Bathrooms: Private Use

All new construction should be fully accessible. However, toilet rooms and/or bathrooms that are provided for private use (such as a private toilet room for a private office) are not required to meet all accessibility requirements. If, however, you provide toilet rooms and/or bathrooms for private use by occupants, it is best to construct the rooms so that they can be adapted for future accessibility.

C1 Provide sufficient access to (and space within) the toilet and/or bathroom to accommodate a wheelchair.

C2 Construct the space so that it can be adapted for accessibility by reinforcing the walls in toilet, shower, and tub areas so that grab bars can be added. **ADAAG: 1998 4.1**

D Single-User Toilet Rooms and/or Bathrooms: Number and Location

Single-user toilet rooms and/or bathrooms are permitted in specific situations where it is technically infeasible to alter existing single-user toilet rooms and/or bathrooms to meet accessibility requirements.

Providing accessible single-user toilet rooms in addition to accessible women's and men's toilet rooms offers several benefits. Single-user toilet rooms accommodate people who need personal care attendants. Single-user toilet rooms make more toilet rooms available for all people during times of increased demand for toilets (such as during breaks or intermissions).

D1 Reuse existing spaces in public buildings to install single-user and family restrooms where the need exists.

D2 Ensure that toilets are positioned properly and not too close, or too far away, from adjacent walls or partitions.

D3 Where multiple single-user toilet rooms are clustered at a single location, ensure that at least 50%, but not less than one, toilet room in each cluster is accessible. **ADA Standards: 2010 213 (New)**
Toilet rooms in a "cluster" are those that are within sight of, or adjacent to, one another (e.g. in medical care facilities). **ADA Standards: 2010 213 (Advisory)**

D4 Ensure that each accessible single-user toilet room contains
   a. no more than one accessible toilet and one accessible urinal or two accessible toilets, **ADA Standards: 2010 213 (New)** and
   b. one accessible lavatory. **ADAAG: 1998 4.1 & ADA Standards: 2010 213** See FX Fixtures.

D5 Ensure that each accessible single-user bathroom contains
   a. one accessible shower or one accessible bathtub and one accessible shower, **ADA Standards: 2010 213 (New)**
   b. one accessible toilet, **ADAAG: 1998 4.1 & ADA Standards: 2010 213** and
   c. one accessible lavatory. **ADAAG: 1998 4.1 & ADA Standards: 2010 213** See SS Shower Stalls, BT Bathtubs, FX Fixtures, and TS Toilet Stalls.

D6 Install accessible privacy latches on doors to single-user toilet rooms and/or bathrooms. **ADAAG: 1998 4.1 & ADA Standards: 2010 213**

D7 Ensure that all fixtures and accessories included in single-user toilet rooms and/or bathrooms are accessible. **ADAAG: 1998 4.1 & ADA Standards: 2010 213** See FX Fixtures.

D8 Include easy-to-read hardware indicating 'vacant' (green) or 'in use' (red) on single-user and family restroom doors.

Single-user restroom door hardware indicating 'Vacant' and 'In Use'

Single-user/family restroom with accessible features and floor-to-wall contrast ^{Ca}

E Portable Toilets: Number and Location

Where portable toilet rooms and/or bathrooms are provided, a portion of portable toilets must meet accessibility guidelines unless they are located on a construction site and are provided for exclusive use of construction personnel.

E1 Ensure that at least 5%, but not less than one, of single-user portable toilets is accessible. ^{Ca}

E2 Where portable toilets are clustered in different locations, ensure that at least 5%, but not less than one, of portable toilets in each cluster is accessible. ^{Ca}

E3 Identify accessible portable toilets with the International Symbol of Accessibility. **ADA Standards: 2010 213 (New) See SN Signs.**

F Multiple-User Toilet Room and/or Bathroom Toilet Stalls: Type and Number

There are two types of accessible toilet stalls: wheelchair accessible stalls and ambulatory accessible stalls. Wheelchair accessible stalls are large enough to accommodate wheelchairs and allow people to comfortably transfer to toilets, and they include accessible features, such as grab bars. Ambulatory accessible stalls are not wide enough for wheelchairs but provide accessible features (such as grab bars) for people who need additional support.

Locating a wheelchair accessible stall at the end of a row is preferred because the stall is larger and the door that swings in. **Refer to Figure TB.1**

This chapter includes information on the number of each type of compartment that must be provided. **See TS Toilet Stalls** for specific information on size, configuration, and features of accessible stalls.

Wherever urinals are provided, at least one urinal must be accessible. Where urinals are provided, include the number of urinals in the total count of toilet stalls when determining the number of accessible toilet compartments.

Example: Where there are four toilet stalls and six urinals in a men's restroom (to be counted as ten toilet compartments), one toilet stall must be wheelchair accessible, another toilet stall should be ambulatory accessible (preferred), and one urinal must also be accessible. See UR Urinals for specific information on urinals.

F1 In rooms that include from one to five toilet stalls, provide at least one wheelchair accessible stall. **ADAAG: 1998 4.22 & ADA Standards: 2010 213**

F2 In rooms that include six or more toilet stalls, provide at least one wheelchair accessible stall and at least one ambulatory accessible stall. **ADAAG: 1998 4.22 & ADA Standards: 2010 213**

F3 In rooms that include two or more toilets, provide at least one ambulatory accessible stall and one wheelchair accessible stall. ^{Ca}
See Figure TB.2

F4 Provide ambulatory accessible stalls in at least one men's public restroom and one women's public restroom in all buildings. ^{Ca}

F5 In large public restrooms, provide multiple accessible stalls of both types (wheelchair accessible and ambulatory accessible). ^{Ca}

F6 Where multiple toilet stalls are provided, and where room configuration allows, locate wheelchair accessible stalls at the end of rows of stalls to provide additional space within the wheelchair accessible stalls. Ca

Refer to Figure TB.2

F7 **In rooms that include urinals, provide at least one accessible urinal.** ADAAG: 1998 4.22 Ca

F8 **Provide vertical grab bars in wheelchair accessible toilet stalls to comply with ANSI A117.1 Standards and the Uniform Building Code (UBC).** Ca

G Multiple-User Toilet Room and/or Bathroom Fixtures: Type and Number

All people benefit from access to comfortable, safe, and easy-to-use fixtures. Accessible toilet rooms and/or bathrooms must include an adequate number of each type of accessible fixture and accessory. **ADAAG: 1998 4.1 & ADA Standards: 2010 213**

When planning toilet rooms and/or bathrooms in new construction, it is usually more efficient, cost effective, and aesthetically pleasing to equip toilet rooms and/or bathrooms with uniform accessible fixtures and accessories.

In new construction, public restrooms should be planned following universal design principles. Is best to follow the same standard for alterations to existing conditions. However at a minimum, you must provide at least the minimum number of accessible fixtures required by ADA Standards.

G1 **Equip all public restrooms with uniform accessible counters, lavatories, faucets, mirrors, and other features** *instead of* **installing 'special' accessible features (such as sloped mirrors).** Ca

G2 Ensure that at least one lavatory is accessible. **ADAAG: 1998 4.22 & ADA Standards: 2010 213**

G3 Where only one accessible lavatory is provided in a multi-user toilet room, ensure that it is not located within a toilet stall. **ADAAG: 1998 4.22 & ADA Standards: 2010 213 See FX Fixtures.**

G4 Ensure that at least one mirror is accessible and is installed at the appropriate height. **ADAAG: 1998 4.22 & ADA Standards: 2010 213 See FX Fixtures, FX-J**

G5 Ensure that at least one of each type of control, dispenser, receptacle, coat hook, shelf, and other fixture is accessible. **ADAAG: 1998 4.22 & ADA Standards: 2010 213 See FX Fixtures and RR Reach Ranges.**

G6 Where bathtubs and/or showers are provided, ensure that at least one bathtub or shower is accessible. **ADAAG: 1998 4.23 & ADA Standards: 2010 213**

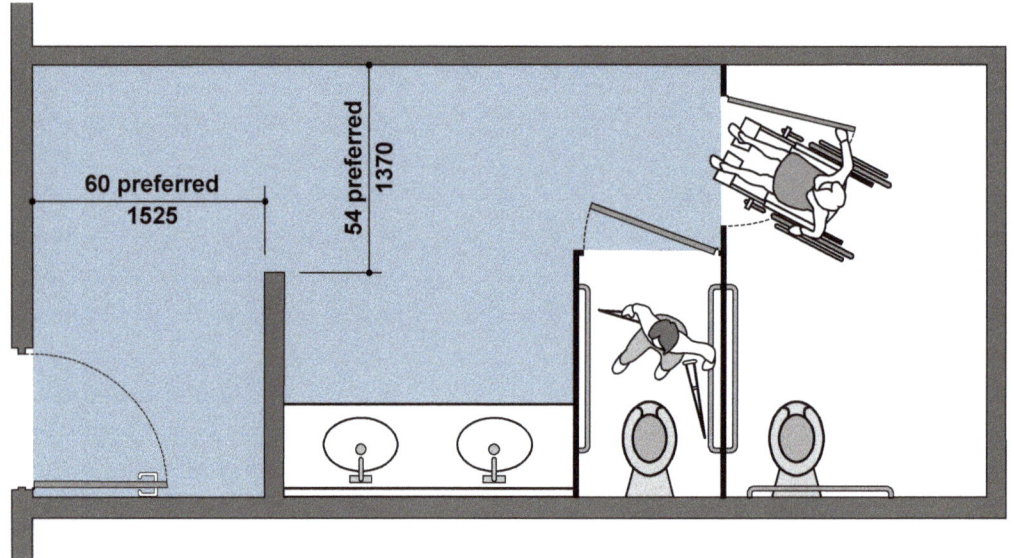

TB.2 Ambulatory accessible and wheelchair-accessible stalls in a public bathroom

G7 Locate liquid-soap dispensers over sinks to prevent liquid-soap from spilling on counters and floors. ⓒa

H Signs

Provide accurate, accessible signs in all appropriate locations in new or existing buildings to identify accessible restrooms. For specific sign requirements, including features of characters, mounting locations, and heights, **see SN Signs**.

H1 Where not all toilet rooms and/or bathrooms are accessible, install accessible visual signs that include the International Symbol of Accessibility to
   a. identify permanent accessible toilet rooms, bathrooms, or clusters of single user toilet rooms; and
   b. direct people to the nearest accessible toilet room or bathroom. **ADAAG: 1998 4.1 & ADA Standards: 2010 216 See SN Signs.**

I Doors

Convenient entry to toilet rooms and/or bathrooms is essential for accessibility. Doors along accessible routes to toilet rooms and bathrooms must be accessible. In toilet rooms and/or bathrooms that have vestibules or double door entries, both doors should open in the same direction. If the doors both swing into a small entryway, navigating with a wheelchair or crutches is difficult.

The ADA Standards does permit doors to swing into the wheelchair turning space in vestibules, however, it is best to provide sufficient space so that doors do not swing into wheelchair turning space. **ADAAG: 1998 4.22, 4.23 & ADA Standards: 2010 603 See DR Doors.**

Entryways that have privacy walls or panels rather than doors may be easier to use. The space between privacy walls or panels and interior walls must be sufficiently wide to allow for maneuvering. **See RT Routes and Spaces.**

I 1 Ensure that doors to accessible toilet rooms and bathrooms are accessible. **See DR Doors. ADAAG: 1998 4.22, 4.23 & ADA Standards: 2010 603**

I 2 Install doors so that they do not swing into required clear floor space or other required space for any fixture. **ADAAG: 1998 4.22, 4.23 & ADA Standards: 2010 603**
Exception: This requirement does not apply where (1) the toilet room and/or bathroom is for private use (such as in a private office) and where the door is hung so it can be reversed to meet the standard, or (2) the clearfloor space beyond the arc of the door swing is a minimum of 30in. (760mm) by 48in. (1220mm). ADA Standards: 2010 603 (New)

I 3 Design and construct public restrooms with continuous, level floor surfaces through entrance doorways. ⓒa

J Clear Floor Space

Wheelchair turning spaces should be located to provide the greatest access possible to accessible fixtures and toilet stalls. Toilet rooms and/or bathrooms should be designed to minimize the amount of backing up required to use accessible fixtures and accessories. It is especially important to provide adequate approach and maneuvering space outside toilet stalls. Check the required clearances at all fixtures and provide appropriate total clear floor space. **See TS Toilet Stalls, BT Bathtubs, SS Shower Stalls, and FX Fixtures.**

J1 Locate all accessible fixtures and toilet stalls along accessible routes. The clear floor space in front of fixtures and controls may overlap accessible routes and/or turning space. **ADAAG: 1998 4.22, 4.23 & ADA Standards: 2010 603**

J2 Ensure adequate unobstructed wheelchair turning space in toilet rooms and/or bathrooms by providing one of the following:
   a. a circular area 60in. (1525mm) in diameter; or
   b. a **T**-intersection 60in. (1525mm) deep with legs at least 36in. (915mm) wide. For additional provisions for **T**-intersections **ADAAG: 1998 4.22, 4.23 & ADA Standards: 2010 603 See RT Routes and Spaces, RT-G.**

J3 Where turns around a privacy wall are necessary to enter a restroom, ensure that a minimum of 48in. (1220mm) is provided between the end of the privacy wall and any wall or obstruction. **ADAAG: 1998 4.3 & ADA Standards: 2010 403 See RT Routes and Spaces.**
Refer to Figures TB.2 and TB.3

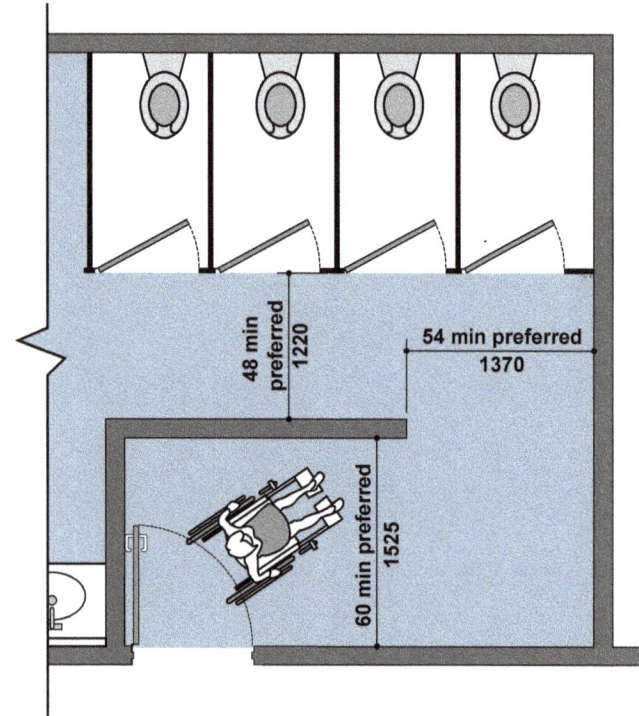

TB.3 Preferred minimum clearances for a restroom entrance with a door and closer

J4 Provide clearance of 42in. (1065mm) minimum from the door side of toilet compartments to any walls or other obstructions. **ADAAG: 1998 4.17 & ADA Standards: 2010 604**

J5 Eliminate unnecessary and obstructive wing walls where possible. When wing walls are necessary, ensure that adequate clearances are maintained. Larger clearances are needed in high use public restroom. Ca

J6 Outside of toilet stalls, ensure that toilet stall doors do not swing into the clear floor space required for any fixture. Door swings may overlap wheelchair turning spaces. **ADA Standards: 2010 603 (New)**

K Floor Surfaces

Because of the presence of water, liquid soap, and shampoo, and because people transferring to and from fixtures are sometimes off balance, floor materials in toilet rooms and/or bathrooms must be carefully selected to minimize the risks of slipping and falling.

K1 Install floor surfaces that are firm, stable, and slip-resistant. **ADAAG: 1998 4.5 & ADA Standards: 2010 302**

K2 Ensure that floor surfaces are level. Where floor drains are present, ensure that slopes to floor drains are gradual and minimal. Ca

K3 Ensure that floor drain openings are smaller than 0.5in. (12.7mm) and that elongated openings are placed so that the long dimension is perpendicular to the dominant direction of travel. **ADAAG: 1998 4.5 & ADA Standards: 2010 302**

K4 Ensure that drain covers are level and are not slipping or tripping hazards. Ca

L Legroom

People need adequate legroom under toilet room and/or bathroom fixtures, counters, sinks, and other objects or surfaces to approach, sit at, and use them comfortably. Legroom is particularly important for people who use wheelchairs and need additional clearance under surfaces. Legroom is also a key safety factor for people who use wheelchairs and cannot detect potentially dangerous conditions (such as exposed drain pipes) where they might be bruised, burned, cut, or scraped by an obstruction.

When determining the appropriate space for legroom, consider the space three dimensionally. Legroom has requirements for the width, height, and depth of the space. Legroom coincides with required clear floor space. To ensure that adequate space under surfaces and fixtures is provided (to accommodate the height and angle of wheelchair foot and leg rests and people's toes), ADA Standards divides the legroom under surfaces vertically into toe clearance and knee clearance.

Many surfaces and fixtures include obstructions

underneath them (such as pipes or base cabinets under sinks and lavatories and walls or other support structures), which can limit the amount of legroom available. The ADA Standards includes a provision for tapering the knee clearance under fixtures and other objects in toilet rooms and bathrooms.

L1 Legroom may extend any distance under a fixture beyond the 17in. [430mm] minimum depth. Additional space for legroom is preferred. **Ca**

L2 Ensure that the space provided for legroom is unobstructed. Legroom under any toilet room and/or bathroom fixture, counter, or object must be at a height between 27in. (685mm) and 30in (760mm). **ADAAG: 1998 4.19 & ADA Standards: 2010 306**

A height of 30in. (760mm) is preferred. **Ca**

See Figure TB.4

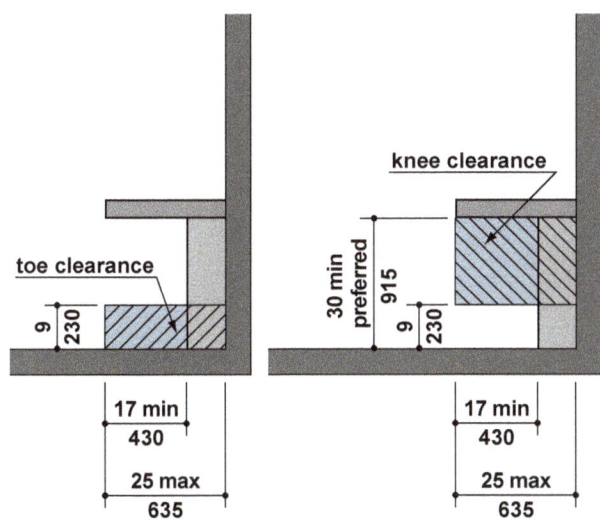

TB.4 Required legroom dimensions at accessible fixtures or counters

L3 Ensure that legroom measures at least 30in. (760mm) from side to side. **ADAAG: 1998 4.2 & ADA Standards: 2010 306**

L4 Where the fixture, surface, or object is in an alcove that is 24in. (610mm) deep or deeper, or is bounded on both sides by walls or other objects, ensure that the width of the legroom measures 36in. (915mm) wide so that people using wheelchairs can maneuver more easily **ADAAG: 1998 4.2 & ADA Standards: 2010 305**

L5 Ensure that legroom provides adequate toe clearance that
  a. includes vertical space from the floor to 9in. (230mm) above the floor, and
  b. extends horizontally under the counter or fixture at least 17in. (430mm) measured from the front edge of the counter or fixture. **ADAAG: 1998 4.19 & ADA Standards: 2010 306**

L6 Ensure that legroom provides adequate knee clearance. Knee clearance extends horizontally, measured from the front of the fixture, surface, or object
  a. at least 8in. (205mm) deep at a height of 27in. (685mm) above the floor, and
  b. at least 11in. (280mm) deep at a height of 9in. (230mm) above the floor. **ADAAG: 1998 4.19 & ADA Standards: 2010 306**

L7 Where the knee clearance must be reduced at an angle because of plumbing, angled vertical supports, or other obstructions, taper the depth of the vertical knee clearance at a rate of 1in. (25mm) horizontally for each 6in. (150mm) of vertical rise. **ADA Standards: 2010 306 (New)**

See Figure TB.5

L8 Where people need to reach over a surface or object to access controls or other objects, ensure that the horizontal depth of the legroom is at least equal to the reach length above the fixture, surface, or object to 25in. (635mm) maximum. **ADA Standards: 2010 308 (New) See RR Reach Ranges.**

Refer to Figure TB.5

Design for All: The Best Path Forward — Dr. Arvid E. Osterberg

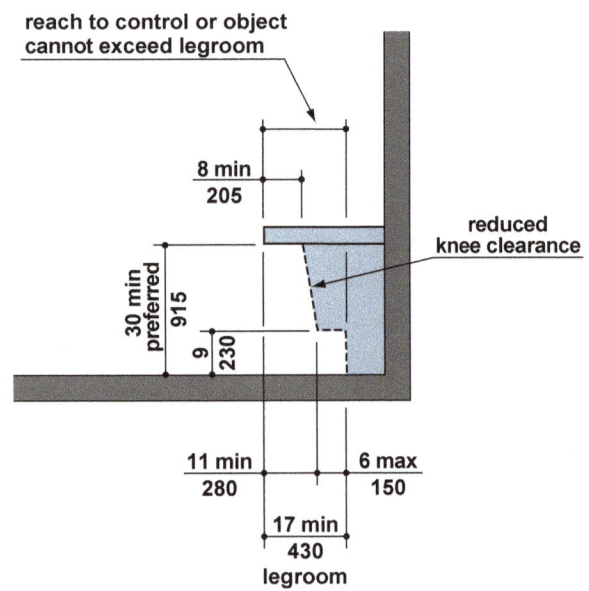

TB.5 Permitted reduced knee clearance

M Dispensers and Controls

People should be able to safely and comfortably use fixtures, dispensers, and controls in toilet rooms and/or bathrooms.

Soap dispensers in public rest rooms are often mounted on mirrors above lavatories. However, if they are not placed in appropriate locations they can be difficult or impossible for some people to reach. Additionally, soap dispensers on mirrors that are centered above lavatories block the view of people of short stature and people in wheelchairs.

M1 Where controls, dispensers, receptacles, and other equipment are provided, ensure that at least one of each type is installed on an accessible route and complies with clear floor space and reach range requirements. **ADAAG: 1998 4.23 & ADA Standards: 2010 213 See RT Routes and Spaces and RR Reach Ranges.**

M2 Ensure that soap dispensers are mounted in locations that
   a. are within allowable reach ranges, and
   b. do not block the view of mirrors for people of short stature and people using wheelchairs.

M3 Ensure that dispensers have color contrast with wall color.

M4 Ensure that *dispenser controls* have color contrast with dispenser color.

M5 Ensure that any controls and mechanisms
   a. are operable with one hand;
   b. do not require grasping, pinching, or twisting of the wrist; and
   c. are operable with a force no greater than 5 lbs. (22.2N). **ADAAG: 1998 4.27 & ADA Standards: 2010 309**

N Coat Hooks and Shelves

When coat hooks and/or shelves are provided, both high and low mounting heights are necessary to meet the needs of all people.

N1 Where coat hooks are provided in toilet rooms and/or bathrooms, install at least one of each type of coat hook within the specified reach range. **ADA Standards: 2010 213 (New) See RR Reach Ranges.**
   A height of 43in. (1090mm) is preferred.

N2 Where shelves are provided in toilet rooms and/or bathrooms, install at least one permanent or fold-down shelf between 40in. (1015mm) and 48in. (1220mm) above the floor. **ADA Standards: 2010 213 (New)**
   A height of 40in. (1015mm) is preferred.
See Figure TB.6

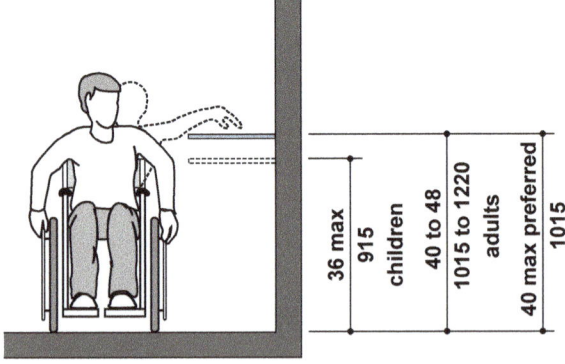

TB.6 Reach ranges for accessible storage shelves

N3 If shelves are provided in toilet rooms and/or bathrooms primarily for use by children, install shelves 36in. (915mm) maximum above the floor. **ADA Standards: 2010 308 (New)**

N4 Ensure that accessible shelves and coat hooks are located out of circulation paths so that people cannot walk into them. ca

N5 Locate coat hooks and shelves in appropriate locations where they do not become hazardous obstructions. ca

O Baby-Changing Tables

The ADA Standards do not require accessible seating and fixtures for infants and nursing mothers in accessible toilet rooms. However providing them will meet the needs of parents and children.

O1 Provide accessible baby-changing tables in accessible men's, women's, and single-user toilet rooms and/or bathrooms. **See FX Fixtures.** ca

O2 Design restrooms with adequate space for baby changing stations in appropriate locations. It is recommended not to locate them in traffic areas or in accessible toilet stalls. ca

O3 Provide appropriate space and seating for nursing mothers in *existing* women's and single-user toilet rooms and/or bathrooms. ca

P Lactation Rooms

P1 Provide lactation rooms in appropriate locations in all public buildings. ca

P2 Ensure that lactation rooms have enough space and amenities for comfort and relaxation including appropriate lighting, floor and wall coverings, and furnishings. ca

Q Waste Receptacles

Poorly located trash cans and waste receptacles become obstacles for people using wheelchairs, canes, walkers, or even pushing strollers. This problem occurs when the type and location of waste cans is not properly specified, when trash cans are too large for the space, and when custodial staff are not properly educated about the issue. Additionally, some people use paper towels to cover door lever handles (for sanitary reasons) when leaving rest rooms and if trash cans are not located close to exit doors paper towels often get thrown on the floor.

Q1 Where restroom doors have handles for exiting, ensure that trash dispensers are located within reach, but not in the required clear floor space. ca

Q2 Specify accessible trash can locations that
  a. do not intrude on required clear floor space and maneuvering space, and
  b. are within the reach of lavatories, and
  c. are within the reach of restroom doors. ca

Trash dispenser within reach of restroom door ca

TS Toilet Stalls

All Accessible Toilet Compartments &
Single-User Toilet Rooms — 150
- A Clear Floor Space — 150
- B Toilet Stall Doors — 150
- C Toilet Stall Door Hardware — 152
- D Toilets — 152
- E Toilet Flush Controls — 153
- F Grab Bars — 153
- G Toilet Paper Dispensers — 154
- H Coat Hooks and Shelves — 155

Wheelchair Accessible Stalls — 155
- I Wheelchair Accessible Stalls: Number — 155
- J Toilet Stall Access — 156
- K Toilet Stall Dimensions — 156
- L Toe Clearance — 157

Ambulatory Accessible Stalls — 158
- M Ambulatory Accessible Stalls: Number — 158
- N Ambulatory Toilet Stall Dimensions — 158

This chapter provides specific requirements for ensuring that toilets in toilet rooms, compartments, and stalls are accessible. The requirements in this chapter are grouped under three headings: All Accessible Toilet Compartments & Single-User Toilet Rooms, Wheelchair Accessible Stalls, and Ambulatory Accessible Stalls. The items listed under the first heading discuss requirements that pertain to features of all types of toilet rooms, compartments, and stalls. The items under the second and third headings specifically address the dimensions and configuration for two different types of accessible toilet stalls. When planning new construction or renovating existing buildings that include multi-user toilet rooms, providing both wheelchair accessible stalls and ambulatory accessible stalls will meet the needs of most people. To determine the number and type of accessible toilets stalls that you need to provide in accessible toilet rooms and bathrooms, **see TB Toilet/Bath Rooms.**

All Accessible Toilet Compartments & Single-User Toilet Rooms

The following requirements apply to all accessible toilet compartments and single-user toilet rooms. For each item under this heading, we indicate variations in requirements for wheelchair accessible stalls, ambulatory accessible stalls, and toilet rooms primarily used by children.

A Clear Floor Space

The dimensions of accessible toilet rooms and compartments include required clear floor space. Fixtures, grab bars, and the wheelchair turning space can overlap the required clear floor space.

A1 Provide clearance around the toilet fixture that
- **a.** is 60in. (1525mm) minimum measured perpendicular from the side wall, and
- **b.** is 56in. (1420mm) minimum measured perpendicular from the rear wall, **or**
- **c.** that meets the requirements for either a wheelchair accessible or ambulatory accessible toilet stall. **ADAAG: 1998 4.17 & ADA Standards: 2010 604**

A2 Ensure that no other fixtures or obstructions (such as a trash can or cleaning supplies) are located within the required toilet fixture clearance. **ADA Standards: 2010 604 (NEW)**

A3 Ensure that doors do not swing into the minimum required compartment area. **ADAAG: 1998 4.17 & ADA Standards: 2010 604, 603**

A4 Increase visibility in public toilet stalls by using non-glare materials and appropriate lighting. Ca

A5 Do not use busy designs and confusing patterns on toilet stall floors and walls. Ca

B Toilet Stall Doors

Toilet stall doors must meet the same requirements for width and maneuvering clearances as other accessible doors. The clear floor space required at a wheelchair accessible toilet stall door depends on the approach to the stall and the placement of door hardware. Where latches on toilet stall doors do not require people to unlatch a door to enter a stall, use the maneuvering clearance requirements for doors without latches and closers. Requirements below pertain only to stall doors.

B1 Outside wheelchair accessible toilet stalls, provide adequate maneuvering space. **ADAAG: 1998 4.13 & ADA Standards: 2010 404 See DR Doors.**

Exception: If the approach is to the latch side of a compartment door, the minimum clearance may be reduced to 42in. (1065mm) between the door side of the stall and any wall or obstruction. **ADAAG: 1998 4.17 & ADA Standards: 2010 604**
See Figure TS.1

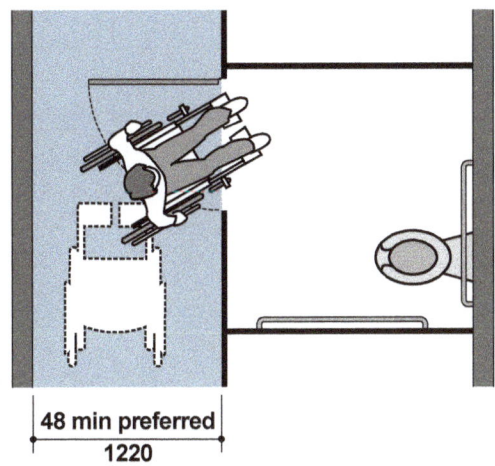

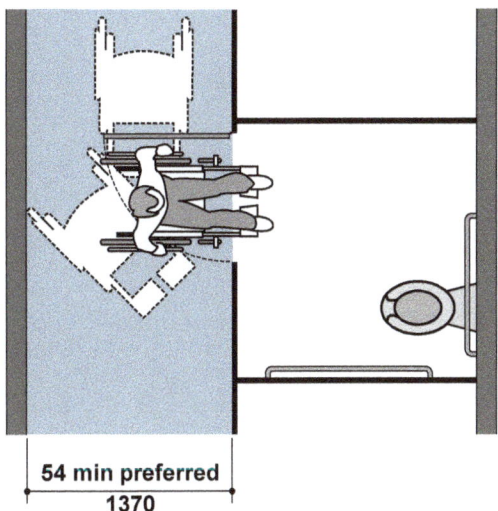

TS.2 **Preferred** maneuvering clearance for both hinge side and latch side approaches to a wheelchair accessible toilet stall

TS.1 **Preferred** minimum maneuvering clearance for a latch side approach to a wheelchair accessible stall

B2 To allow for both hinge side and latch side approaches to a wheelchair accessible stall, provide 48in. (1220mm) minimum clearance between the door side of the stall and any wall or obstruction. **ADAAG: 1998 4.17 & ADA Standards: 2010 404**

A 54in. (1370mm) clearance is preferred. Ca

See Figure TS.2

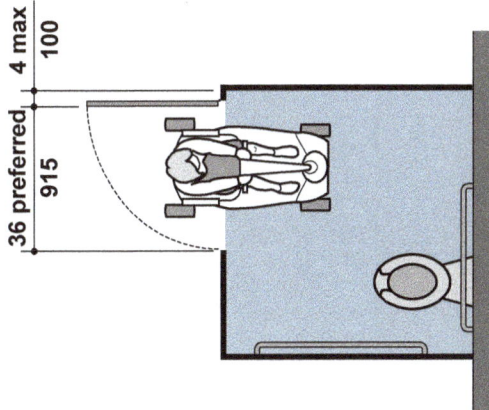

B3 Provide a minimum clear width of 32in. (815mm) at all accessible toilet stall doors. **ADAAG: 1998 4.13 & ADA Standards: 2010 404**

A 36in. (915mm) width is preferred. Ca

See Figure TS.3

TS.3 **Preferred** minimum clear door width for both a wheelchair accessible and a ambulatory accessible toilet stall

B5 Install self-closing doors. **ADA Standards: 2010 604** (NEW)

B4 In wheelchair accessible stalls, mount doors so that they are hinged a maximum of 4in. (100mm) from the side wall or partition opposite the toilet fixture. **ADAAG: 1998 4.17 & ADA Standards: 2010 604**

B6 Ensure that doors to wheelchair accessible toilet stalls swing out from the stalls unless there is a 30in. (760mm) by 48in. (1220mm) minimum clear floor space within the stall (on fixture side) that is not in the path of the swinging door. **ADA Standards: 2010 603** (NEW)

Toilet partition doors that hang shut make it difficult to see if occupied

Toilet partition doors that hang slightly open make it easy to see if occupied Ca

B7 Install securely attached high-quality toilet partitions that do not shake when doors are opened. Ca

B8 Specify self-closing toilet partition doors that hang slightly open so that people can see if stalls are occupied. Ca

C Toilet Stall Door Hardware

High quality, durable toilet stall door hardware is important for ensuring accessibility.

C1 Install handles, pulls, latches, locks, and other operable parts on accessible doors between 34in. (865mm) minimum and 48in. (1220mm) maximum above the floor. **ADA Standards: 2010 404 (Modified-Less Restrictive)**
A height of 43in. (1090mm) is preferred. Ca

C2 Install door pulls on both sides of the door near the latch. **ADAAG: 1998 4.13 & ADA Standards: 2010 604**

C3 Provide door handles, pulls, latches, locks, and other operable parts that
   a. are operable with one hand;
   b. do not require tight grasping, pinching, or twisting of the wrist; and
   c. are activated with a force less than or equal to 5 lbs. (22.2N). **ADAAG: 1998 4.27 & ADA Standards: 2010 309**

D Toilets

Configure toilet rooms or compartments for either a left side or right side approach to the toilet.

D1 Locate the toilet with the wall or partition to the rear and to one side of the toilet. **ADAAG: 1998 4.17 & ADA Standards: 2010 604**

D2 Install the toilet so that the centerline is between 16in. (405mm) minimum and 18in. (455mm) maximum measured from the near side wall or partition. **ADA Standards: 2010 604 (Modified-Less Restrictive)**
See Figure TS.4

D3 Ensure that toilets are positioned properly and not too close or too far away from adjacent walls or partitions. Ca

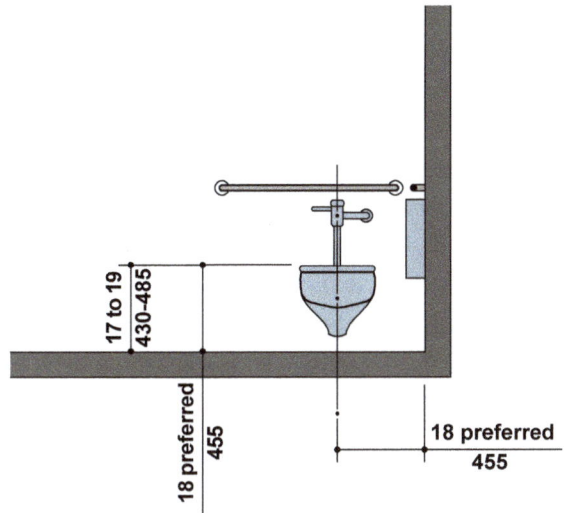

TS.4 **Preferred** placement of the toilet

D4 Where children are the primary users of the toilet room, install the toilet so that the centerline is
- a. between 12in. (305mm) minimum and 18in. (455mm) maximum measured from the near side wall or partition, **ADAAG: 1998 4.17 & ADA Standards: 2010 604** or
- b. centered between partitions in a ambulatory stall. **ADA Standards: 2010 604 (New)**

D5 Ensure that the height of a toilet is 17in. (430mm) minimum to 19in. (485mm) maximum measured from the floor to the top of the toilet seat. **ADAAG: 1998 4.17 & ADA Standards: 2010 604**

A height of 18in. (455mm) is preferred.
Refer to Figure TS.4

D6 Where children are the primary users of the toilet room, ensure that the height of a toilet is 11in. (280mm) minimum to 17in. (430mm) maximum measured from the floor to the top of the toilet seat. **ADAAG: 1998 4.17 & ADA Standards: 2010 604**

D7 Install toilet seats that do not return automatically to a lifted position. **ADA Standards: 2010 604 (New)**

E   Toilet Flush Controls

E1 Install automatic flush controls where possible.

E2 Locate flush controls on the rear wall.

E3 Locate flush controls to the open side of the toilet in all single-user toilet rooms or compartments, and in all wheelchair accessible stalls. **ADA Standards: 2010 604 (New)**

E4 Install hand-operated flush controls within appropriate reach ranges. **ADAAG: 1998 4.16 & 2010 605, 309** See RR Reach Ranges.

E5 Where children are the primary users of the toilet room, install flush controls 36in. (915mm) maximum above the floor.

E6 Ensure that flush controls
- a. are operable with one hand;
- b. do not require tight grasping, pinching, or twisting of the wrist; and
- c. are activated with a force less than or equal to 5 lbs. (22.2N). **ADAAG: 1998 4.18 & ADA Standards: 2010 309**

F   Grab Bars

Grab bars are not required in wheelchair accessible toilet rooms that are used by a single occupant and that are unavailable for public use as long as reinforcement has been installed in walls to permit the future installation of grab bars. However, another recommends that grab bars be installed in all accessible toilet rooms and stalls.

If toilet flush controls are required to be located in a position that conflicts with the location of the rear grab bar, rear grab bars may be divided into two shorter segments or shifted to the open side of the toilet area.

For grab bars in single-user toilet rooms and wheelchair accessible toilet stalls, follow all requirements in this section. For ambulatory accessible toilet stalls, follow the requirements for side grab bars that are necessary for the safety of people who need additional support.

Design for All: The Best Path Forward — Dr. Arvid E. Osterberg

F1 To ensure safety, always install all grab bars in a horizontal position. **ADAAG: 1998 4.20, 4.26 & ADA Standards: 2010 609**

F2 In single-user toilet rooms and in wheelchair accessible stalls, install
   a. a grab bar on the side wall or partition closest to the toilet, and
   b. a grab bar on the rear wall behind the toilet. **ADAAG: 1998 4.17 & ADA Standards: 2010 604**

F3 In ambulatory accessible stalls, install grab bars on both side walls or partitions. **ADAAG: 1998 4.17 & ADA Standards: 2010 604**

F4 Ensure that side wall or partition grab bars meet the following requirements:
   a. are 42in. (1065mm) long minimum, **ADAAG: 2010 604 (MODIFIED- MORE RESTRICTIVE)**
   b. are located 12in. (305mm) maximum from the rear wall, **ADAAG: 1998 4.17 & ADA Standards: 2010 604** and
   c. extend 54in. (1370mm) minimum from the rear wall. **ADA Standards: 2010 604 (MODIFIED-MORE RESTRICTIVE)**

See Figure TS.5

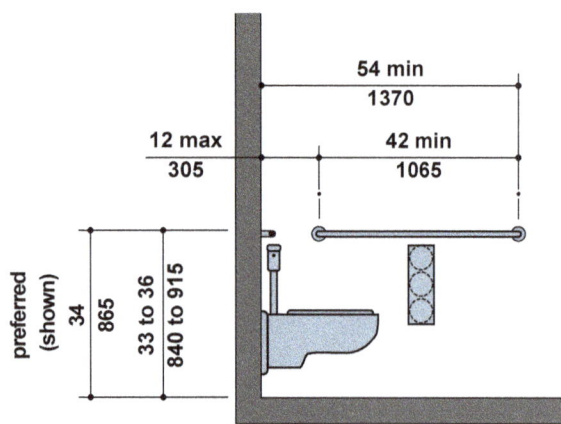

TS.5 Grab bar on a side wall or partition in an accessible toilet stall

F5 Ensure that rear wall grab bars meet the following requirements:
   a. are 36in. (915mm) long minimum; and
   b. extend 12in. (305mm) toward the side partition from the centerline of the toilet.

The remaining length extends to the transfer side of the toilet. **ADAAG: 1998 4.17 & ADA Standards: 2010 604**

Exception: In single-user toilet rooms or compartments, where the rear wall includes a recessed area for a fixture (such as a lavatory) that limits the amount of wall space available, a grab bar 24in. (610mm) long minimum (centered on the toilet) is permitted. ADA Standards: 2010 604 (NEW)
See Figure TS.6

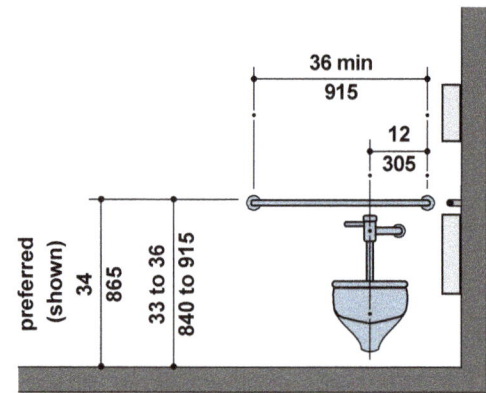

TS.6 Grab bar on the rear wall in a wheelchair accessible toilet stall

F6 Mount all toilet room or toilet stall grab bars 33in. (840mm) minimum to 36in. (915mm) maximum above the floor. **ADAAG: 1998 4.17 & ADA Standards: 2010 609**
   A height of 34in. (865mm) is preferred.
Refer to Figures TS.5 and TS.6

F7 Ensure that grab bars meet the requirements for size, surface shape, and strength. **See GB Grab Bars.**

F8 Provide vertical grab bars in wheelchair-accessible toilet stalls to comply with ANSI A117.1 Standards and the Uniform Building Code (UBC)

G **Toilet Paper Dispensers**
G1 Install a toilet paper dispenser between 7in. (180mm) and 9in. (230mm) in front of the toilet measured from the front of the toilet to the centerline of the outlet of the dispenser.

ADA Standards: 2010 604 (Modified-More Restrictive)
See Figure TS.7

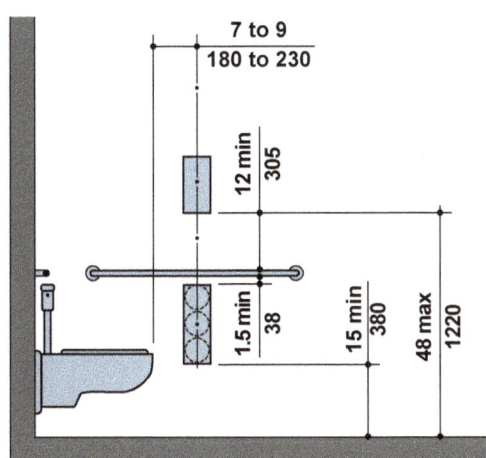

TS.7 Toilet paper dispensers in an accessible toilet stall

G2 Locate the dispenser so that the outlet is between 15in. (380mm) minimum and 48in. (1220mm) maximum above the floor. **ADA Standards: 2010 604 (Modified-Less Restrictive)**
Dispensers mounted below grab bars are preferred. Ca
Refer to Figure TS.7

G3 Where children are the primary users of the toilet room, locate the dispenser so that the outlet is between 14in. (355mm) minimum and 19in. (485mm) maximum above the floor. **ADAAG: 1998 4.16 & ADA Standards: 2010 604**

G4 Ensure that there is minimum clearance of 1.5in. (305mm) between the bottom of a grab bar and any dispenser below it. **ADA Standards: 2010 604 (New)**
Refer to Figure TS.7

G5 Ensure that there is minimum clearance of 12in. (380mm) between the top of a grab bar and any dispenser above it. **ADA Standards: 2010 604 (New)**
Refer to Figure TS.7

G6 Install dispensers that provide continuous paper flow and that do not control delivery. **ADA Standards: 2010 604 (New)**

G7 Ensure that toilet paper dispensers meet the guidelines in **FX Fixtures**. **ADA Standards: 2010 604 (New)**

G8 When installing a waste receptacle for feminine hygiene products in a toilet stall, follow the dimensional requirements for a toilet paper dispenser. Ca

H Coat Hooks and Shelves

Coat hooks and shelves are not required in toilet stalls by ADA Standards, but if provided, they must be accessible.

H1 If coat hooks are provided in toilet stalls, install them within the appropriate reach range. **ADA Standards: 2010 604 (New)** See RR Reach Ranges.
A height of 43in. (1090mm) is preferred. Ca

H2 If shelves are provided in toilet stalls, install fold-down shelves mounted between 40in. (1015mm) minimum and 48in. (1220mm) maximum above the floor. **ADA Standards: 2010 604 (New)**
A height of 43in. (1090mm) is preferred. Ca

Wheelchair Accessible Stalls

Wheelchair accessible toilet stalls must be large enough to accommodate devices that assist mobility, such as wheelchairs, walkers, and strollers. The space must be sufficient for a person to maneuver in the stall and transfer from a wheelchair to the toilet fixture. Adequate space also allows an attendant to assist without excessive crowding or awkward bending.

I Wheelchair Accessible Stalls: Number

I 1 Ensure that all public restrooms have at least one wheelchair accessible toilet stall. **ADAAG: 1998 4.22 & ADA Standards: 2010 213**

I 2 In larger public restrooms, provide one wheelchair accessible toilet stall for every ten toilet stalls. Ca

J Toilet Stall Access

In planning and configuring multiple-user toilet rooms, it is important to provide adequate clear aisle width and room for maneuvering wheelchairs both inside and outside toilet stalls. When turning is required to enter stalls, wider aisles are necessary. Locating a larger wheelchair accessible stall at the end of a row of stalls allows for a forward approach, which permits a narrow clear floor space in front of the door, and provides additional space within the stall.

J1 Provide a larger end-of-row accessible toilet stall where space permits. Ca

See Figure TS.8

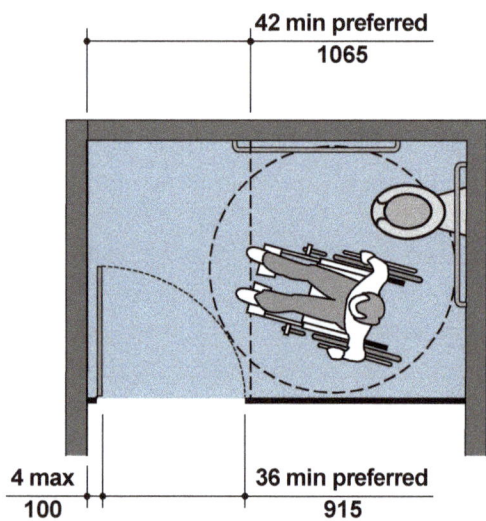

TS.8 End-of-row wheelchair accessible toilet stall

K Toilet Stall Dimensions

The dimensional requirements of wheelchair accessible toilet stalls are different for stalls with wall-mounted toilets and stalls with floor-mounted toilets. Toilet stalls that meet only minimum dimensions require toe clearance. Toe clearance in toilet stalls refers to the space between the bottom of toilet stall partitions and the floor.

See TS-L for specific toe clearance requirements.

K1 Stall width: wall-hung or floor-mounted toilet. Ensure that the width of the stall (side to side) meets one of the following minimum requirements:
  a. 66in. (1675mm) minimum clear floor space between partitions (toe clearance is not required);

   67 in (1702mm) preferred Ca
   ADA Standards: 2010 604 (Modified-More Restrictive)
   or
  b. 60in. (1525mm) minimum clear floor space between partitions (toe clearance must be provided under at least one side partition).

   67 in (1702mm) preferred Ca
   ADAAG: 1998 4.17 & ADA Standards: 2010 604

See Figure TS.9

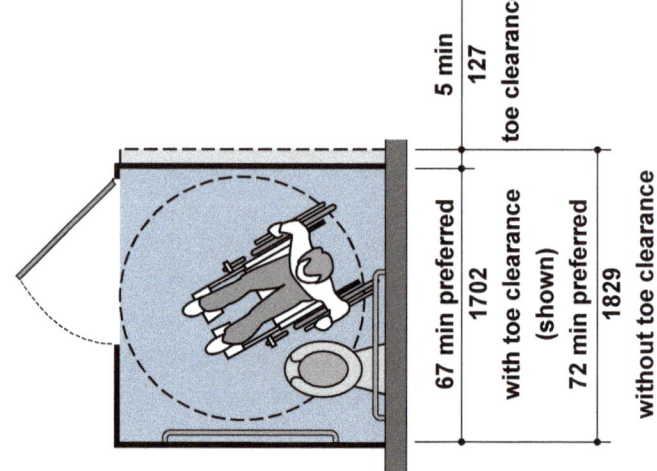

TS.9 Wheelchair accessible toilet stall width

K2 Stall depth: wall-hung toilet. Ensure that the depth of the stall (back wall to front wall or partition) meets one of the following minimum requirements:
  a. 62in. (1575mm) minimum clear floor space between partitions (toe clearance is not required);

   67 in (1702mm) preferred Ca
   ADA Standards: 2010 604 (Modified-More Restrictive) or
  b. 56in. (1420mm) minimum clear floor space between partitions (toe clearance must be provided under the front partition).

   62in (1575mm) preferred Ca
   ADAAG: 1998 4.17 & ADA Standards: 2010 604

See Figure TS.10

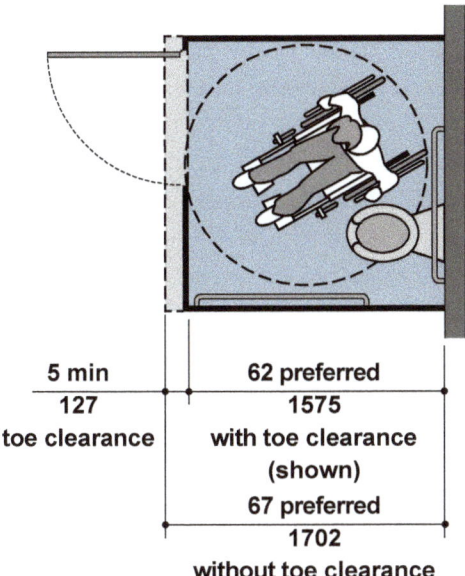

5 min	62 preferred
127	1575
toe clearance	with toe clearance (shown)
	67 preferred
	1702
	without toe clearance

TS.10 Wheelchair accessible toilet stall depth for a *wall-hung toilet*

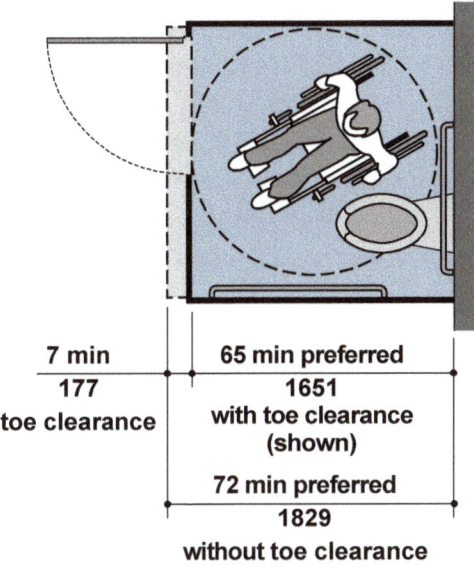

7 min	65 min preferred
177	1651
toe clearance	with toe clearance (shown)
	72 min preferred
	1829
	without toe clearance

TS.11 Wheelchair accessible toilet stall depth for a *floor-mounted toilet*

K3   Stall depth: floor-mounted toilet. Ensure that the depth of the stall (back wall to front wall or partition) meets one of the following minimum requirements:

- **a.** 65in. (1650mm) minimum clear floor space between partitions (toe clearance is not required);
  72in (1829mm) preferred Ca
  ADA Standards: 2010 604 (MODIFIED-MORE RESTRICTIVE) or
- **b.** 59in. (1500mm) minimum clear floor space (toe clearance must be provided under the front partition). **ADAAG: 1998 4.17 & ADA Standards: 2010 604**
  65in (1651mm) preferred Ca

See Figure TS.11

L   Toe Clearance

Toe clearance in toilet stalls refers to the space between the bottom of a toilet stall partition and the floor. The requirements for providing toe clearance depend on the dimensions of the stall and the type of toilet in the stall.

L1   In *any* toilet stall that is less than 66in. (1675mm) wide, provide toe clearance under at least one side partition. **ADA Standards: 2010 604 (MODIFIED-MORE RESTRICTIVE)**

L2   In toilet stalls less than 62in. (1575mm) deep with *wall-hung* toilets, provide toe clearance under the front partition. **ADA Standards: 2010 604 (MODIFIED-MORE RESTRICTIVE)**
Refer to Figure TS.10

L3   In toilet stalls less than 65in. (1650mm) deep with *floor-mounted* toilets, provide toe clearance under the front partition. **ADA Standards: 2010 604 (MODIFIED-MORE RESTRICTIVE) Refer to Figure TS.11**

L4   Where toilet stalls meet only the minimum dimensions for both width and depth, provide toe clearance under the front partition and at least one side partition. **ADAAG: 1998 4.17 & ADA Standards: 2010 604**

Design for All: The Best Path Forward — Dr. Arvid E. Osterberg

L5 Where toe clearance is required, provide toe clearance under a partition that extends
  a. vertically 9in. (230mm) minimum above the floor; **ADAAG: 1998 4.17 & ADA Standards: 2010 604** and
  b. horizontally 6in. (150mm) minimum beyond the compartment-side face of the partition. **ADAAG: 2010 604, 304 (New)**

See Figure TS.12

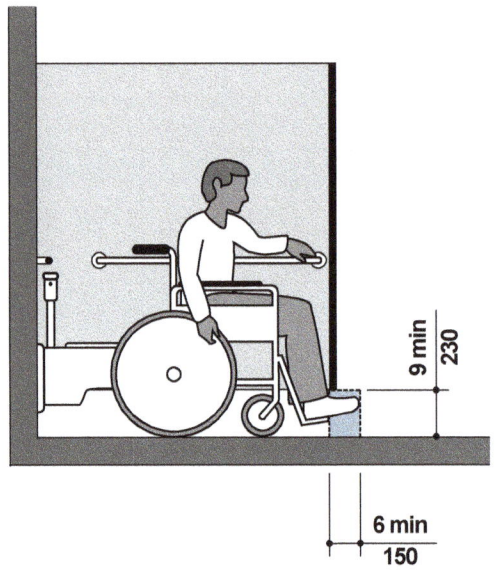

TS.12 Dimensions for toe clearance under a toilet stall partition

Ambulatory Accessible Stalls

Ambulatory accessible stalls meet the needs of people with mobility limitations and other people who need additional support. The ADA Standards refers to ambulatory accessible stalls as "ambulatory accessible stalls."

M Ambulatory Accessible Stalls: Number

M1 In rooms that include two or more toilets, provide at least one ambulatory stall and one wheelchair-accessible stall. ca

M2 Provide 36in. (915mm) wide ambulatory accessible toilet stalls (with higher toilet seats, grab bars on both sides, and out-swinging doors) in all restrooms that have two or more toilet stalls. ca

M3 To comply with the ADA minimum requirements, where there are six or more toilets in a women's restroom, provide at least one wheelchair accessible toilet stall and one ambulatory accessible toilet stall. **ADAAG: 1998 4.22 & ADA Standards: 2010 213**

M4 Where there are six or more toilets and urinals in a men's restroom (including both toilets and urinals), provide at least one wheelchair accessible toilet stall and one ambulatory accessible toilet stall. **ADA Standards: 2010 213 (New)**

N Ambulatory Stall Dimensions

N1 Ensure that the dimensions of the toilet stall are
  a. 60in. (1525mm) minimum front to back, and
  b. 35in. (889mm) minimum to 37in. (940mm) maximum side to side. **ADA Standards: 2010 604 (Modified-Less Restrictive)**

N2 Locate the toilet so that the centerline of the toilet is 17in. (432mm) minimum to 19in. (483mm) maximum from the side wall of the compartment. **ADA Standards: 2010 604 (Modified-Less Restrictive)**

N3 Center the toilet between the side walls (or partitions) of the compartment. ca

See Figure TS.13

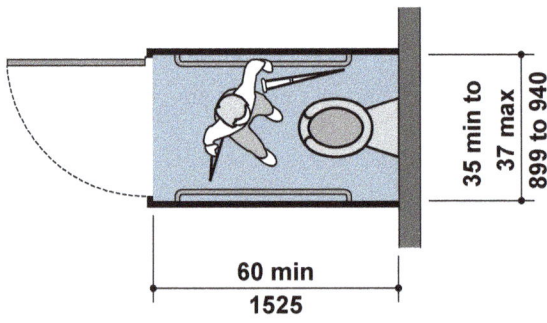

TS.13 Ambulatory accessible toilet stall

UR Urinals

A	Urinals: Number	159
B	Urinal Mounting Height	159
C	Urinal Depth at the Rim	159
D	Clear Floor Space	159
E	Urinal Flush Controls	160

Where urinals are provided, at least one urinal must be accessible. Both stall-type urinals and unenclosed wall-hung urinals are acceptable if they are configured and installed according to the requirements.

A Urinals: Number

A1 Provide at least one accessible urinal in all restrooms where urinals are provided. **ADAAG: 1998 4.22**

A2 Provide at least one accessible urinal, one ambulatory accessible toilet stall, and one wheelchair accessible toilet stall in all men's restrooms with three or more fixtures.

B Urinal Mounting Height

B1 Mount wall-hung urinals with the rim a maximum of 17in. (430mm) above the floor. **ADAAG: 1998 4.18 & ADA Standards: 2010 605**

See Figure UR.1

C Urinal Depth at the Rim

C1 Ensure that the urinal depth measures a minimum of 13.5in. (345mm) from the outer face of the urinal rim to the back of the fixture. **ADA Standards: 2010 605** (New)

Refer to Figure UR.1

D Clear Floor Space

D1 Provide a minimum clear floor space of 30in. (760mm) by 48in. (1220mm) in front of the urinal to allow for a forward approach. 36in (1062mm) by 54in (1370mm) preferred **ADAAG: 1998 4.18 4.2 & ADA Standards: 2010 605, 305**

Refer to Figure UR.1

D2 Ensure that the clear floor space overlaps or adjoins an accessible route. **ADAAG: 1998 4.18, 4.2 & ADA Standards: 2010 605, 305** See RT Routes and Spaces.

D3 Ensure that privacy panels do not obstruct the required clear floor space. **ADAAG: 1998 4.2 & ADA Standards: 2010 305** Privacy panels or partitions 24in. (610mm) deep or less are recommended.

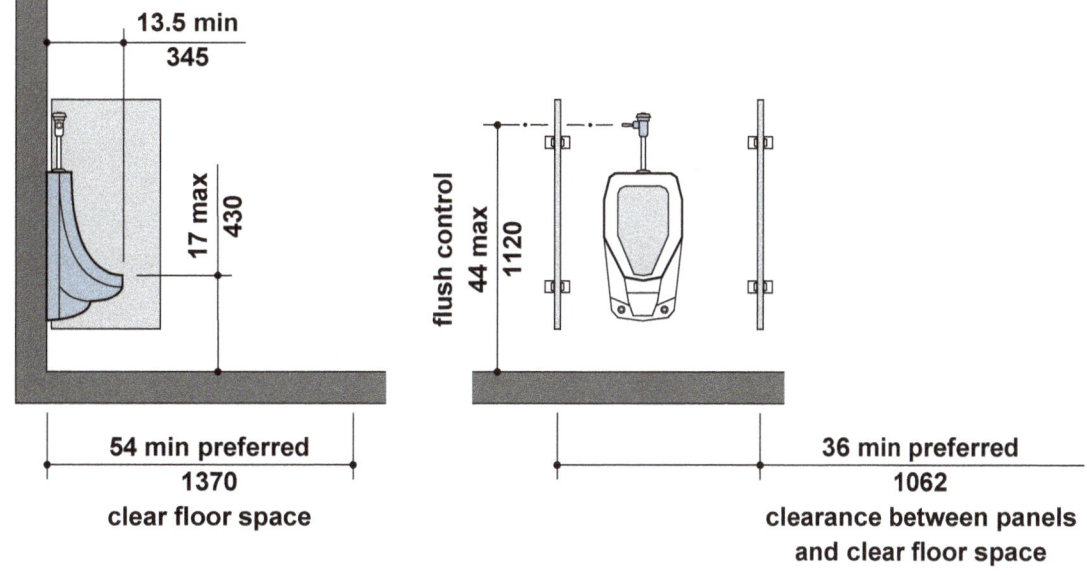

UR.1 Mounting dimensions for a wall-hung urinal

Design for All: The Best Path Forward — Dr. Arvid E. Osterberg

D4 When privacy panels or partitions are more than 24in. (610mm) deep, ensure that the clear floor space is 36in. (915mm) by 48in. (1220mm) in front of the urinal.
36in (1062mm) by 54in (1370mm) preferred ca
ADAAG: 1998 4.2 & ADA Standards: 2010 305

E   Urinal Flush Controls

E1 Install automatic flush controls where possible. ca

E2 Install hand-operated flush controls 44in. (1120mm) maximum above the floor. **ADAAG: 1998 4.18, 4.27 & ADA Standards: 2010 605, 309**
Refer to Figure UR.1

E3 Ensure that flush controls
  a. are operable with one hand;
  b. do not require tight grasping, pinching, or twisting of the wrist; and
  c. are activated with a force less than or equal to 5 lbs. (22.2N). **ADAAG: 1998 4.18, 4.27 & ADA Standards: 2010 605, 309**

FX   Fixtures

A	All Fixtures	161
B	New Construction: Number and Location	161
C	Alterations to Existing Conditions: Number and Location	161
D	Clear Floor Space	161
E	Height	162
F	Legroom	162
G	Exposed Pipes and Surfaces	164
H	Sinks and Lavatories	164
I	Faucets and Operable Parts on Fixtures	164
J	Mirrors	165
K	Medicine Cabinets	165
L	Coat Hooks and Shelves	165
M	Children's Accommodations	166
N	Baby-Changing Tables	166
O	Windows	167

Sinks, lavatories, wet bars, kitchenettes, baby changing tables, and other fixtures need to be accessible where they are provided in public use or common areas.

In this chapter, lavatory refers to the sinks and surrounding counters and cabinetry that are installed in restrooms and bathrooms. A sink is a plumbing fixture consisting of a water supply, a basin, and a drain connection.

Special sinks, lavatories, mirrors, and fixtures (often identified as handicapped or hospital) are not required and are inappropriate in most situations. Specialty fixtures are often more expensive than universally designed fixtures that work equally well for most people.

In addition to selecting the most appropriate fixture, it is important to consider the heights, depths, and clear spaces around lavatories, mirrors, and fixtures; the location of exposed pipes; the types of faucets and other operable mechanisms used; and the size and position of mirrors.

When designing or remodeling restrooms or bathrooms for multiple users it is best to plan and install uniform counters, lavatories, mirrors, and fixtures. This approach is cost effective, inclusive, and will provide a uniform look in restrooms and bathrooms.

It is important to select and install fixtures (such as towel dispensers, soap dispensers, hand dryers, coat racks, shelves, and medicine cabinets) that can be used by persons with disabilities.

A   All Fixtures

A1   Ensure that all accessible fixtures are located on an accessible route. **ADAAG: 1998 4.3 & ADA Standards: 2010 213 See RT Routes and Spaces.**

A2   Install fixtures that are designed for universal use and do not install special fixtures that only accommodate some people. ca

A3   Ensure that all mirrors, lavatories, and fixtures are accessible in all public use toilet rooms and/or bathrooms. ca

A4   Choose appropriate sinks and faucets to prevent water from splashing onto counters and floors. ca

A5   Ensure that all restroom accessories, including mirrors, soap dispensers, paper towel dispensers, and blow dryers are within reach range. ca

B   New Construction: Number and Location

B1   In each toilet room and/or bathroom, provide at least the following:
  a. One accessible toilet
  b. One accessible lavatory
  c. One accessible mirror
  d. One accessible unit of each type of fixture and accessory provided in the restroom area (such as dispensers, hand-dryers, and receptacles) **ADAAG: 1998 4.19, 4.22, 4.23 & ADA Standards: 2010 213**

B2   In each room or space where sinks or lavatories are provided, ensure that 5%, but not less than one, of each type is accessible. **ADA Standards: 2010 212 (New)**

C   Alterations to Existing Conditions: Number and Location

C1   In altered toilet rooms and/or bathrooms, provide at least the following (by either modifying existing fixtures and clearances or by installing new fixtures):
  a. One accessible toilet
  b. One accessible lavatory
  c. One accessible mirror
  d. One accessible unit of each type of fixture and accessory provided in the restroom area (such as dispensers, hand-dryers, and receptacles) **ADAAG: 1998 4.1, 4.19, 4.22, 4.23 & ADA Standards 2010 213, 202**

D   Clear Floor Space

Clear floor space refers to the space in front of lavatories and other fixtures. Space beneath fixtures for knees and toes must also be provided, but that space is not considered part of the clear floor space. **See FX-F.**

Lavatories that include base cabinets restrict the legroom for a forward approach. If you install base cabinets under sinks and lavatories that are not required to be accessible, use removable units for adaptability whenever possible. Other fixtures (such as hand dryers and towel dispensers) should be installed at appropriate heights and must not protrude into clear floor spaces.

D1   Ensure that the clear floor space in front of lavatories and other fixtures adjoins or overlaps an accessible route. **ADAAG: 1998 4.19, 4.24 & ADA Standards: 2010 305**

D2   Provide a minimum clear floor space of 30in. (760mm) by 48in. (1220mm) in front of lavatories and other accessible fixtures to allow for a forward approach.
  36in (1062mm) by 54in (1370mm) preferred ca
  ADAAG: 1998 4.19, 4.24 & ADA Standards: 2010 305 See RT Routes and Spaces, RT-P for additional information on clear floor space.

D3   Where the bottom edge of a wall-mounted fixture on a circulation path is between 27in. (685mm)

and 80in. (2030mm) above the floor, ensure that it does not protrude into the accessible route more than 4in. (100mm). **ADAAG: 1998 4.4 & ADA Standards: 2010 307**

D4 Where clear floor space is confined on both sides by more than 24in. (610 mm), provide clear floor space measuring 36in. (915mm) wide by 48in. (1220mm) deep to allow for a forward approach in an alcove. **ADAAG: 1998 4.19, 4.24 & ADA Standards: 2010 305** See **RT Routes and Spaces, RT-P** for additional information on clear floor space.

E Height

People must be able to reach counters, lavatories, vanities, and sinks. Also, fixtures (such as hand dryers, paper towel holders, and soap dispensers) must be within easy reach. For fixtures to be accessible, proper mounting height, reach range, and the space under the fixture are all important.

E1 Install sinks, lavatories, countertops, and vanities so that highest point in front (either the rim of the sink or the top of a counter) is no higher than 34in. (865mm) above the floor. **ADAAG: 1998 4.24 & ADA Standards: 2010 606**

E2 Mount fixtures (including hand dryers, paper towel holders, and soap dispensers) within appropriate reach ranges. **ADA Standards: 2010 309 (NEW)**
A height of 43in. (1090mm) to the operable control is preferred for all fixtures and dispensers. See **RR Reach Ranges.**
See Figure FX.1

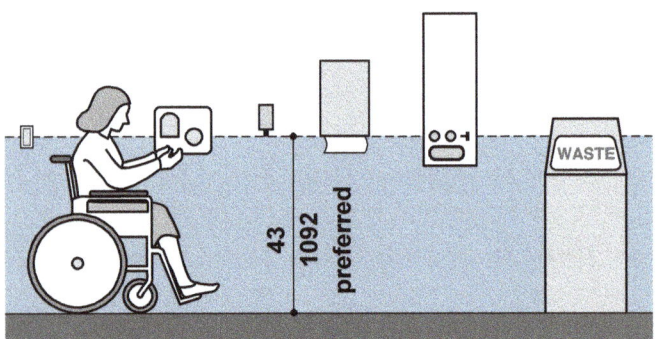

FX.1 Maximum and preferred height for operable parts of fixtures and dispensers

F Legroom

People need adequate legroom under counters, lavatories, sinks, and other fixtures and dispensers to approach and use them comfortably. For additional information pertaining to legroom in restrooms and bathrooms, **see TB Toilet/Bath Rooms, TB-L.**

F1 Ensure that the space provided for legroom is unobstructed and that the legroom under any toilet room and/or bathroom fixture, counter, or object is a height of 27in. (685mm) minimum. **ADAAG: 1998 4.19 & ADA Standards: 2010 306**
A height of 30in. (760mm) is preferred.
See Figure FX.2

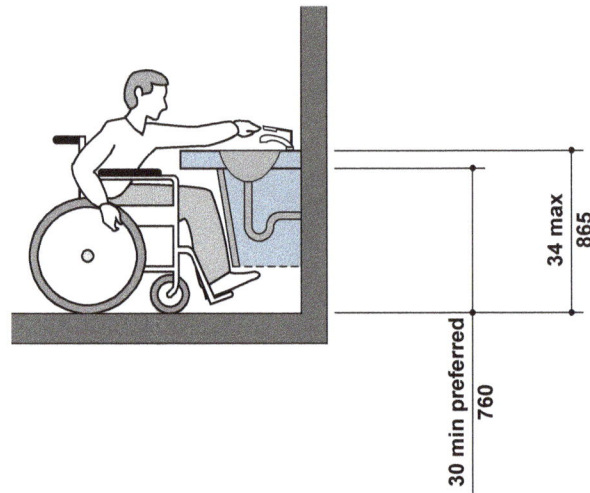

FX.2 Legroom height under a lavatory

F2 Ensure that the legroom provided under a sink has adequate knee and toe clearance, see **TB Toilet/Bath Rooms, TB-L. ADAAG: 1998 4.24 & ADA Standards: 2010 306**

F3 Ensure that the legroom measures at least 30in. (760mm) from side to side. **ADAAG: 1998 4.24 & ADA Standards: 2010 306**

F4 Where a fixture, surface, or object is in an alcove that is 24in. (610mm) deep or deeper, or is bounded on both sides by walls or other objects, ensure that the width of the legroom measures 36in. (915mm) wide so that people using wheelchairs can maneuver more easily. **ADAAG: 1998 4.3 & ADA Standards: 2010 305**

F5 Ensure that the legroom provides adequate toe clearance that
   a. includes the vertical space from the floor to 9in. (230mm) above the floor, and
   b. extends horizontally under the counter or fixture at least 17in. (430mm) measured from the front edge of the counter or fixture. **ADAAG: 1998 4.19 & ADA Standards: 2010 306**

See Figure FX.3

a. Ensure that a fixture overlaps required clear floor space no more than 25in. (635mm). **ADAAG: 1998 4.3 & ADA Standards: 2010 306**

See Figure FX.4

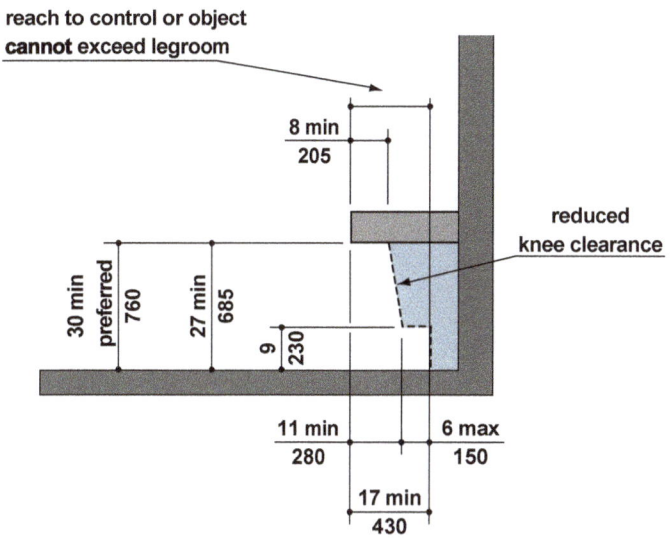

FX.4 Permitted reduced knee clearance

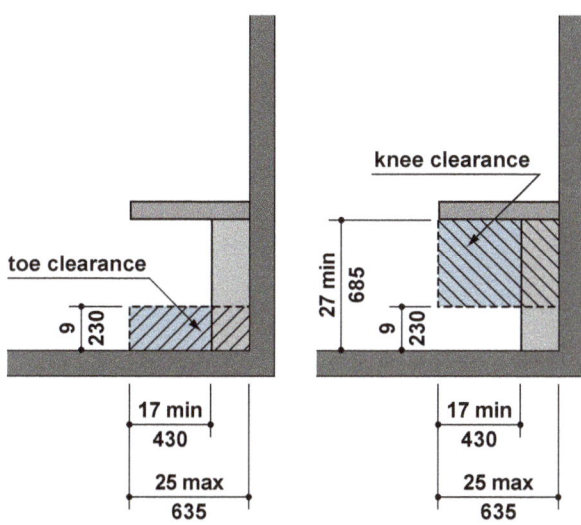

FX.3 Minimum required legroom dimensions under a counter

F6 Ensure that the legroom provides adequate knee clearance. Knee clearance extends horizontally, measured from the front of the fixture, surface, or object,
   a. at least 8in. (205mm) deep at a height of 27in. (685mm) above the floor, and
   b. at least 11in. (280mm) deep at a height of 9in. (230mm) above the floor. **ADAAG: 1998 4.19 & ADA Standards: 2010 306**

Refer to Figure FX.3

F7 Legroom may extend any distance under a fixture (beyond the 17in. [430mm] minimum depth). **Additional space for legroom is preferred.**

F8 Only a maximum of 25in. (635mm) under a fixture measured from the front edge of the fixture can also be part of any required clear floor space. **ADAAG: 1998 4.3 & ADA Standards: 2010 306**

F9 Where the knee clearance must be reduced at an angle because of plumbing, angled supports, or other obstructions, taper the depth of the vertical knee clearance at a rate of 1in. (25mm) horizontally for each 6in. (150mm) of vertical rise. **ADA Standards: 2010 306 (NEW)**

F10 Ensure that the reach to a control or object above counter does not exceed the legroom under the counter. **ADAAG: 1998 4.3 & ADA Standards: 2010 308**

Refer to Figure FX.4

F11 Where people need to reach over a counter or fixture to access controls or objects, ensure that the horizontal depth of the legroom is at least equal to the reach length above the surface or counter to a maximum of 25in. (635mm). **ADAAG: 1998 4.3 & ADA Standards: 2010 308 See RR Reach Ranges** for additional information.

G Exposed Pipes and Surfaces
Sharp or abrasive edges and exposed pipes, which often go unnoticed when they are under fixtures and counters, can be hazardous for all people.

G1 Insulate or install hot water and drain pipes in such a manner that people are protected against direct contact with pipes. **ADAAG: 1998 4.19, 4.24 & ADA Standards: 2010 606**

G2 Check for and remove or cover any sharp or abrasive surfaces or edges under sinks, lavatories and other fixtures. **ADAAG: 1998 4.19, 4.24 & ADA Standards: 2010 606**

G3 Provide coverings and/or insulation on all hot and cold water pipes and drainpipes under all sinks, including those that are not intended to be accessible. ca

H Sinks and Lavatories
The sinks and surrounding counters and cabinetry that are installed in restrooms and bathrooms are generally referred to as lavatories. Sinks include free-standing and wall-hung units that are located in restrooms, bathrooms, and other areas for hand-washing and other purposes.

All types of sinks, lavatories, and vanities that are provided for public use or for use in common areas (such as sinks in laboratories, classrooms, dormitories, break rooms, and other areas) must be accessible. Where sinks, lavatories, and other fixtures are provided in work areas for the use of employees only, they are not required to be accessible. However, providing accessible fixtures may prevent expensive modifications in the future. See WA Work Areas. Sinks used for custodial purposes (such as mop basins) are not required to be accessible.

Lavatories are not permitted to be installed in toilet compartments or stalls.

H1 Ensure that there is at least one accessible sink provided in all public spaces (including break rooms, conference rooms, classrooms and laboratories) where sinks are provided. **ADAAG: 1998 4.24 & ADA Standards: 2010 606, 305**

H2 Ensure that the approach to a sink is a forward approach. **ADAAG: 1998 4.24 & ADA Standards: 2010 606, 305**

H3 Mount accessible sinks, lavatories, and other fixtures so that the highest part in front (either the rim of the sink or the top of a counter) is no higher than 34in. (865mm) above the floor. **ADAAG: 1998 4.24 & ADA Standards: 2010 606**

Note: The depth of a sink basin is not specifically addressed by ADA Standards, but can be determined by the maximum height of the sink or counter and the minimum amount of knee space required below the sink basin.

H4 Contrast the color of sink bowls with the color of surrounding counters. ca

I Faucets and Operable Parts on Fixtures
Lever-operated, push-type, and electronically controlled mechanisms are examples of accessible faucet designs.

I 1 Install automatic faucets and controls where possible. ca

I 2 Choose appropriate faucets to prevent water from splashing onto counters and floors. ca

I 3 Provide catch areas (or locate liquid-soap dispensers over sinks) to prevent liquid-soap from spilling on counters and floors. ca

I 4 Install faucets and other fixtures with controls that
- **a.** are operable with one hand; **ADAAG: 1998 4.27 & ADA Standards: 2010 309**
- **b.** do not require tight grasping, pinching, or twisting of the wrist; **ADAAG: 1998 4.27 & ADA Standards: 2010 309**
- **c.** are activated with a force less than or equal to 5 lbs. (22.2N); **ADAAG: 1998 4.27 & ADA Standards: 2010 309** and
- **d.** include temperature and pressure regulating valves. **ADA Standards: 2010 309** (New)

I5 If you install a faucet with a self-closing (self-metering) valve, ensure that the faucet valve is set to remain open for at least 10 seconds. **ADAAG: 1998 4.19, 4.27 & ADA Standards: 2010 606**
See Figure FX.5

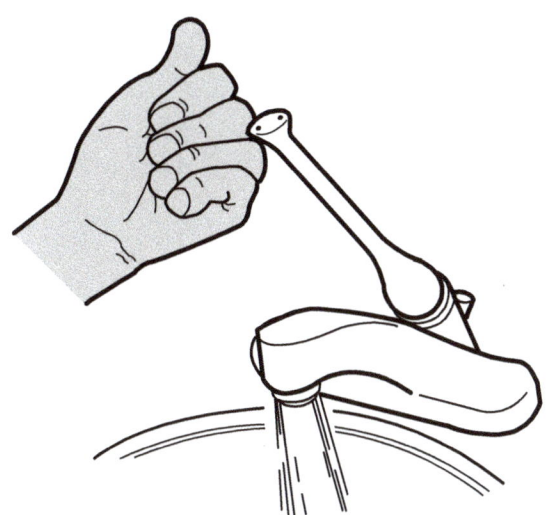

FX.5   Accessible faucet control

J   Mirrors

The bottom edge of mirrors mounted above sinks, lavatories, vanities, or counter tops should extend down as close as possible to the edge of the counter top or splash-guard.

To meet the needs of people of different heights, it is best to also install a full-length mirror on a wall where adequate clear floor space can be provided in front of it.

J1 Mount mirrors so that
  a. the bottom edge of the mirror is a maximum of 40in. (1015mm) above the floor, where the mirror is located above a lavatory or countertop, **ADAAG: 1998 4.19 & ADA Standards: 2010 603**
   A 36in. (915mm) height is preferred, 🌀
   or
  b. the bottom edge of the mirror is a maximum of 35in. (890mm) above the floor where the mirror is not located above a lavatory or a countertop, **ADA Standards: 2010 603 (Modified-More Restrictive)**

J2 Mount mirrors so that the top edge of the mirror is a minimum of 74in. (1880mm) above the floor. **ADA Standards: 2010 603 (New)**
See Figure FX.6

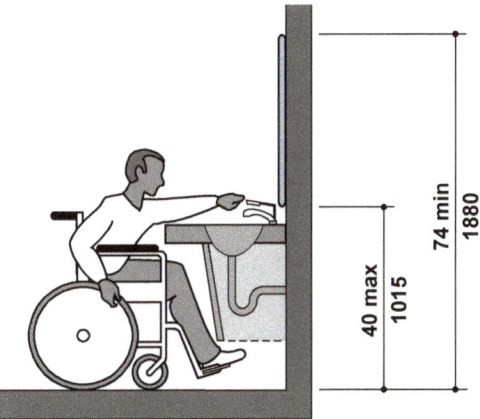

FX.6   Mouting heights for a mirror above a lavatory

K   Medicine Cabinets

Mounting height and reach range requirements should be considered when choosing and installing medicine cabinets. To be accessible, medicine cabinets should include shelves that can be easily reached and hardware that is easy to use. Medicine cabinets should be mounted so that people can reach them, open them, and store items in them.
See RR Reach Ranges.

K1 Where medicine cabinets are provided, mount at least one cabinet so that at least one usable shelf is no higher than 44in. (1120mm) above the floor. **ADAAG: 1998 4.23** 🌀

L   Coat Hooks and Shelves

Accessible coat hooks and shelves should be available to all people.

L1 Wherever shelves are provided, install a fold-down shelf between 40in. (1015mm) and 48in. (1220mm) above the floor. **ADA Standards: 2010 603 (New)**
   A 40in. (1015mm) height is preferred. 🌀

L2 Mount a portion of available coat hooks and shelves within the appropriate reach range. **ADA**

Design for All: The Best Path Forward — Dr. Arvid E. Osterberg

Standards: 2010 308 (NEW) See RR Reach Ranges.

A 43in. (1090mm) height is preferred. Ca

M Children's Accommodations

Where children are the primary users of the space, adjust reach ranges and clearances to meet their needs.

M1 Provide wall or partition mounted infant seats in accessible toilet stalls where appropriate. Ca

M2 Mount fixtures and accessories within the appropriate reach range for children. **ADA Standards: 2010 308, 309** (NEW) See RR Reach Ranges.

Infant seat in accessible toilet stall Ca

M3 For children ages 6 through 12, install sinks, lavatories, lavatory fixtures, and vanities so that highest point in front (either the rim of the sink or the top of a counter) is no higher than 31in. (785mm) above the floor. **ADA Standards: 2010 606** (NEW)

M4 For children ages 6 through 12, provide knee space under sinks, lavatories, vanities, countertops and other protruding fixtures that is 24in. (610mm) minimum above the floor. **ADA Standards: 2010 606** (NEW)

M5 For children ages 5 and younger, configure fixtures and clear floor space for either a parallel or forward approach to lavatories and sinks. **ADA Standards: 2010 606** (NEW)

N Baby-Changing Tables

Wherever baby-changing tables are installed, they should be accessible.

N1 Design restrooms with adequate space for baby-changing stations in appropriate locations. It is recommended *not to* locate them in accessible toilet stalls, Ca

N2 Provide baby changing stations in appropriate locations for ease-of-use and privacy in all public restrooms. Ca

N3 Locate baby-changing tables adjacent to an accessible route but out of the way of the circulation path. Ca

N4 Ensure that stored baby-changing tables do not protrude more than 4in. (100mm) into an accessible route. **ADAAG: 1998 4.4 & ADA Standards: 2010 307**

N5 Provide a clear floor space in front of the baby changing table at least 30in. (760mm) by 48in. (1220mm) to accommodate a single, stationary wheelchair. **ADAAG: 1998 4.2 & ADA Standards: 2010 305**

N6 Where possible, configure the clear floor space for a forward approach to the baby-changing table. Ca

N7 Install baby-changing tables so that the front edge of the usable surface is between 34in. (865mm) minimum and 48in. (1220mm) maximum above the floor.
A 34in. (865mm) height is preferred. Ca

N8 Provide adequate knee and toe clearance under baby changing tables. **ADAAG: 1998 4.24 & ADA Standards: 2010 306** See FX-F.

N9 If the baby-changing table is a fold-down type, install pull-down handles and other hardware that
 a. are operable with one hand;
 b. do not require tight grasping, pinching, or twisting of the wrist; and
 c. are activated with a force less than or equal to 5 lbs. (22.2N). **ADAAG: 1998 4.19,**

4.27 & ADA Standards: 2010 309
See Figure FX.7

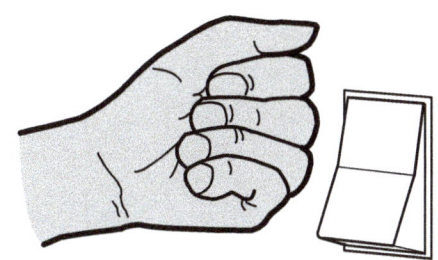

FX.7   Accessible light switch

O   Windows

All accessible rooms and spaces that have windows that are operable by occupants are required to have at least one accessible window.

O1   Ensure that at least one window that is operable by occupants has controls and mechanisms that
- a. are operable with one hand;
- b. do not require grasping, pinching, or twisting of the wrist;
- c. are operable with a force no greater than 5 lbs. (22.2N); and
- d. are within the appropriate reach range; **ADAAG: 1998 4.2, 4.27 & ADA Standards: 2010 229 See RR Reach Ranges.**

O2   **Ensure that the bottom edges of all viewing windows from corridor to interior rooms are no more than 43in (1090mm) above the floor.** ca
Refer to Figure RT.32

SS   Shower Stalls

All Shower Stalls	168
A All Shower Stalls: Controls and Spray Units	168
B All Shower Stalls: Curbs	168
C All Shower Stalls: Enclosures	168
D Location and Number	169
Transfer Shower Stalls	169
E Transfer Shower Stalls: Dimensions and Clear Floor Space	169
F Transfer Shower Stalls: Grab Bars	169
G Transfer Shower Stalls: Controls	170
Roll-in Shower Stalls	170
H Standard Roll-in Shower Stalls: Dimensions and Clear Floor Space	170
I Alternative Roll-in Shower Stalls: Dimensions and Clear Floor Space	171
J Standard Roll-in Shower Stalls: Controls	171
K Alternative Roll-in Shower Stalls: Controls	172
L All Roll-in Shower Stalls: Grab Bars	172
M Standard Roll-in Shower Stalls: Grab Bars	172

Transfer shower stalls and roll-in shower stalls are the two types of accessible shower stalls. Transfer shower stalls are designed for easy transfer from wheelchairs onto seats in shower stalls.

Roll-in shower stalls allow people who use wheelchairs to enter and use showers while in their wheelchairs. Roll-in shower stalls include two variations, a standard roll-in stall and an alternative roll-in stall, which incorporates features of both roll-in and transfer shower stalls.

This chapter discusses requirements specific to each type of accessible shower stall and common requirements for all types of shower stalls.
See SE Seats for information about the placement, dimensions, and structural strength of seats required in accessible shower stalls.

All Shower Stalls

The following requirements apply to transfer, standard roll-in and alternative roll-in shower stalls.

A All Shower Stalls: Controls and Spray Units

A hand-held shower spray unit that can also be mounted to serve as a fixed shower head accommodates the needs of most people.

A1 Install a shower spray unit that
 a. includes a hose at least 59in. (1500mm) long; **ADA Standards: 2010 607 (MODIFIED-LESS RESTRICTIVE)**
 b. can be used as both a fixed position shower head and a hand-held shower; **ADAAG: 1998 4.20 & ADA Standards: 2010 607** and
 c. includes water-on/water-off controls with a non-positive shut-off. **ADA Standards: 2010 607 (NEW)**

A2 Ensure that shower spray units deliver water that is limited to a maximum temperature of 120°F (49°C). **ADA Standards: 2010 607 (NEW)**

A3 Install valves that are both pressure and temperature regulated. Ca

A4 If you install hand-operated, metered faucets with self-closing valves, ensure that the faucet valves are set to remain open for at least 10 seconds. **ADAAG: 1998 4.19 & ADA Standards: 2010 606**

A5 If you install an adjustable-height shower head on a vertical bar,
 a. install the bar so that it does not obstruct the grab bars. **ADA Standards: 2010 608 (NEW)**
 b. mount the vertical bar so that the shower head can be lowered to 43in. (1090mm) above the floor. Ca

Refer to Figure SS.3.

A6 If the shower stall is located anywhere other than in medical care, transient lodging, long-term care units, or residential dwelling units, or if vandalism is a consideration, you may install a fixed shower head instead of a hand-held type.
 a. Mount the fixed shower head 48in. (1220mm) above the shower stall floor. **ADAAG: 1998 4.21 & ADA Standards: 2010 608**

A7 Use controls that
 a. are operable with one hand;
 b. do not require grasping, pinching, or twisting of the wrist; and
 c. require a force no greater than 5 lbs. (22.2N). **ADAAG: 1998 4.20, 4.27 & ADA Standards: 2010 309, 608**

A8 Provide high quality fixtures that stay in place, operate effectively, and hold up well to heavy use. Ca

B All Shower Stalls: Curbs

While thresholds at the entrances to shower stalls help contain the runoff from showers, they can present a barrier for some users. Shower stalls with no thresholds increase the accessibility of bathrooms because the shower area provides additional maneuvering space.

B1 If you install thresholds at shower stalls, ensure that they are less than 0.5in. (12.7mm) high. **ADA Standards: 2010 303, 608 (MODIFIED-LESS RESTRICTIVE)**

B2 Where thresholds between 0.25in. (6.4mm) and 0.5in. (12.7mm) are installed, bevel the edges of the thresholds so that wheelchairs can be maneuvered over the thresholds easily. **ADAAG: 1998 4.5 & ADA Standards: 2010 303, 608**

Exception: In existing conditions, thresholds are permitted to be up to 2in. (51mm) high where altering thresholds would disturb the structural reinforcement of shower floor slabs. ADA Standards: 2010 608 (NEW)

C All Shower Stalls: Enclosures

C1 Ensure that shower stall enclosures do not obstruct access to shower controls or inhibit transfer from a wheelchair to the shower seat.

ADAAG: 1998 4.21 & ADA Standards: 2010 608

D Location and Number

D1 Where bathtubs or shower stalls are provided, ensure that at least one shower stall or bathtub is accessible. **ADAAG: 1998 4.23 & ADA Standards: 2010 213, 608** See BT Bathtubs.

Transfer Shower Stalls

Transfer showers are designed to allow people to easily transfer from a wheelchair to the shower stall seat. Transfer showers do not accommodate wheelchairs.

E Transfer Shower Stalls: Dimensions and Clear Floor Space

Transfer shower stalls that are too small do not provide adequate room for comfortable transfer and use. Transfer shower stalls that are too large pose hazards. People may have difficulty transferring if grab bars are not within easy reach, and people can slip and fall when reaching from the seat to shower controls that are too far away.

E1 Ensure that the inside finished dimensions of transfer shower stalls are exactly 36in. (915mm) by 36in. (915mm). **ADAAG: 1998 4.21 & ADA Standards: 2010 608**

E2 Provide an entry on the front side of the transfer shower stall that is 36in. (915mm) wide. **ADAAG: 1998 4.21 & ADA Standards: 2010 608**

E3 Provide clear floor space outside the front of the transfer shower stall that is a minimum of 36in. (915mm) wide by a minimum of 48in. (1220mm) long. **ADAAG: 1998 4.21 & ADA Standards: 2010 608**

The 48in. (1220mm) minimum length dimension includes the 36in. (915mm) width of the shower stall plus 12in. (305mm) minimum beyond the seat wall to facilitate transfer. **ADAAG: 1998 4.21 & ADA Standards: 2010 608**

E4 Ensure that fixtures (such as lavatories, toilets, or trash receptacles) do not protrude into the minimum clear floor space outside of a transfer shower stall. Ca
See Figure SS.1

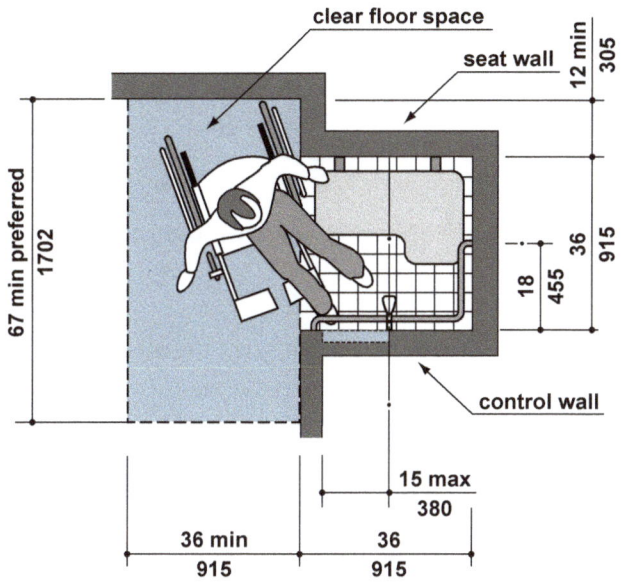

SS.1 Transfer shower stall dimensions

F Transfer Shower Stalls: Grab Bars

Grab bars are an essential safety feature of transfer shower stalls and must meet these requirements.

F1 Install a continuous grab bar extending across the full length of the control wall and half-way across the back wall to a point 18in. (455mm) from the control wall. **ADA Standards: 2010 608** (MODIFIED-MORE RESTRICTIVE)
Refer to Figure SS.1

F2 Install grab bars between 33in. (840mm) minimum and 36in. (915mm) maximum above the shower stall floor. **ADAAG: 1998 4.21 & ADA Standards: 2010 608, 609**
A height of 34in. (865mm) is preferred. Ca
See Figure SS.2

F3 Install all horizontal grab bars at a consistent height. Ca

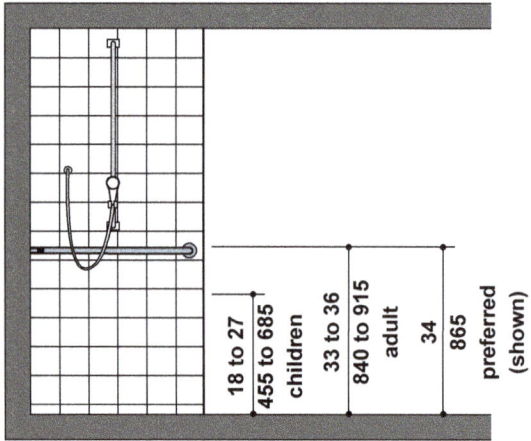

SS.2 Grab bar heights in transfer and roll-in shower stalls

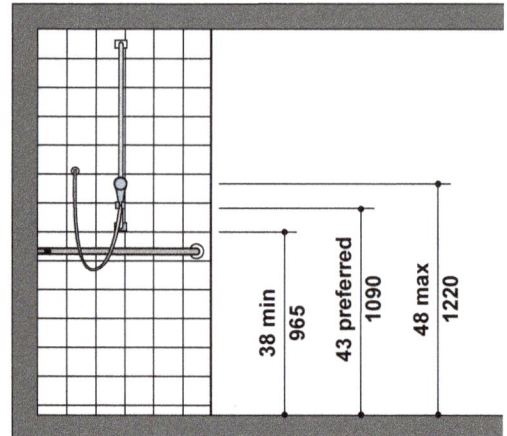

SS.3 Control heights in transfer and roll-in shower stalls

F4 If children will be the primary users of the shower stall, install grab bars between 18in. (455mm) minimum and 27in. (685mm) maximum above the shower stall floor. **ADA Standards: 2010 609** (NEW)

See GB Grab Bars for additional information about the requirements for and structural strength of grab bars. **ADAAG: 1998 4.21, 4.26 & ADA Standards: 2010 608, 609**

G Transfer Shower Stalls: Controls

Lever-operated, push-type, and electronically controlled mechanisms are all accessible faucet designs.

G1 Install controls, including faucets and spray units, on the wall opposite the seat wall. **ADAAG: 1998 4.21 & ADA Standards: 2010 608**
Refer to Figure SS.1.

G2 Mount controls no more than 15in. (380mm) from the centerline of the seat toward the shower entry. **ADA Standards: 2010 608** (NEW)
Refer to Figure SS.1.

G3 Mount controls above the grab bar 38in. (965mm) minimum to 48in. (1220mm) maximum above the shower stall floor. **ADAAG: 1998 4.21 & ADA Standards: 2010 608**
A height of 43in. (1090mm) is preferred. Ⓒa
See Figure SS.3

Roll-in Shower Stalls

Roll-in shower stalls accommodate wheelchairs or bathing chairs. Two roll-in shower stall variations are acceptable. Standard roll-in shower stalls use the same amount of space as accessible bathtubs. Alternative roll-in shower stalls are wider, but have a narrower entrance. Both types of roll-in shower stalls may incorporate a folding seat (but not a fixed seat) which provides more flexibility for people using them.

H Standard Roll-in Shower Stalls: Dimensions and Clear Floor Space

The clear floor space outside the roll-in shower stall must meet or exceed the minimum dimensions to comfortably and safely accommodate all users.

H1 Ensure that the inside clear finished dimensions of a standard roll-in shower stall is a minimum of 30in. (760mm) by 60in. (1525mm). **ADAAG: 1998 4.21 & ADA Standards: 2010 608**
A space of 42in. (1065mm) by 60in. (1525mm) or larger is preferred. Ⓒa

H2 Provide an entry on the front side of the standard roll-in shower stall that is 60in. (1525mm) wide minimum. **ADAAG: 1998 4.21 & ADA Standards: 2010 608**

H3 Provide a clear floor space that is
  a. 30in. (760mm) wide minimum; **ADAAG: 2010 608** (MODIFIED-LESS RESTRICTIVE)
  A width of 36in. (915mm) preferred. Ⓒa
  and

b. by 60in. (1525mm) long minimum adjacent to the entrance. **ADAAG: 1998 4.21 & ADA Standards: 2010 608**

H4 **Locate lavatories outside the clear floor space where possible.**

Lavatories may be located at the end of the clear floor space opposite the side of the shower stall where the seat and controls are located or on either side where no seat is installed. The lavatory may overlap the clear floor space. **ADA Standards: 2010 608 (New)**

See Figure SS.4

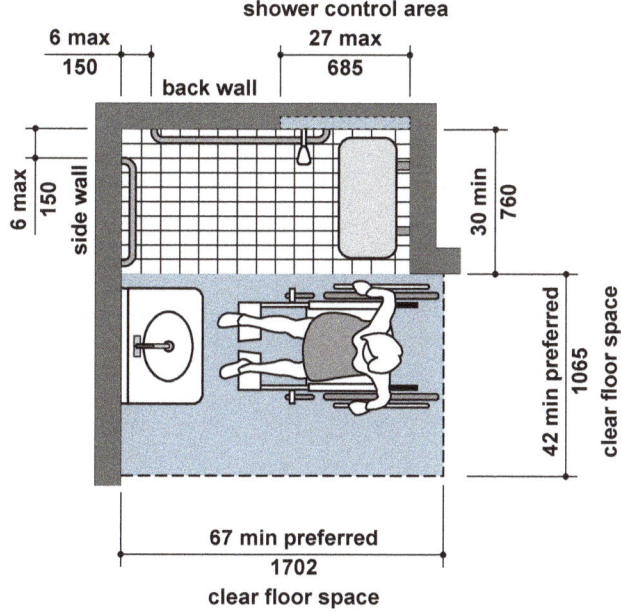

SS.4 **Standard roll-in shower stall with a folding seat**

I **Alternative Roll-in Shower Stalls: Dimensions and Clear Floor Space**

In an alternative roll-in shower stall, the inside clear dimensions are larger than in a standard roll-in shower stall. However, the dimensions at the entry are smaller. Alternative roll-in shower stalls can be provided in any type of building and are required in hotel rooms and other types of transient lodging. **See TL Transient Lodging.**

I 1 Ensure that the minimum inside clear finished dimensions of an alternative roll-in shower stall are 36in. (915mm) by 60in. (1525mm). **ADA Standards: 2010 608 (New)**

I 2 Provide an entry on one end of the long side of the alternate roll-in stall that is 36in. (915mm) wide minimum. **ADA Standards: 2010 608 (New)**

See Figure SS.5

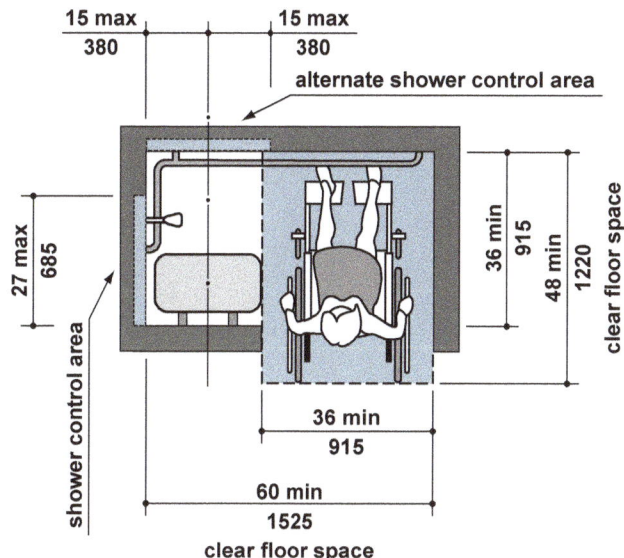

SS.5 **Alternative roll-in shower stall with a folding seat**

J **Standard Roll-in Shower Stalls: Controls**

The placement of shower controls and spray units is important for accessibility.

J1 In a standard roll-in shower stall without a seat, install the controls and shower unit on any of the three walls of the shower stall. **ADAAG: 1998 4.21 & ADA Standards: 2010 608**

J2 In a standard roll-in shower stall with a folding seat, install the controls and shower unit on the wall adjacent to the seat. **ADAAG: 1998 4.21 & ADA Standards: 2010 608**

J3 Mount controls above the grab bar 38in. (965mm) minimum to 48in. (1220mm) maximum above the shower stall floor. **ADAAG: 1998 4.21 & ADA Standards: 2010 608**

A height of 43in. (1090mm) is preferred.

Refer to Figure SS.3

J4 In a standard roll-in shower stall with a folding seat, install the controls a maximum of 27in.

(685mm) from the seat wall. **ADAAG: 1998 4.21 & ADA Standards: 2010 608**
Refer to Figures SS.4

K Alternative Roll-in Shower Stalls: Controls

The placement of shower controls and spray units is important for accessibility.

K1 In an alternative roll-in shower stall without a seat, install the controls and shower unit on the side wall farthest from the compartment entry. **ADA Standards: 2010 608 (NEW)**

K2 In an alternative roll-in shower stall with a folding seat, install the controls and shower unit
   a. on the wall adjacent to the seat; or
   b. on the back wall opposite the seat 15in. (380mm) maximum, left or right, of the centerline of the seat. **ADA Standards: 2010 608 (NEW)**
Refer to Figure SS.5

K3 Mount controls above the grab bar 38in. (965mm) minimum to 48in. (1220mm) maximum above the shower stall floor. **ADAAG: 1998 4.21 & ADA Standards: 2010 608**
A height of 43in. (1090mm) is preferred. Ca
Refer to Figure SS.3

K4 In an alternative roll-in shower stall with a folding seat, install the controls a maximum of 27in. (685mm) from the seat wall. **ADAAG: 1998 4.21 & ADA Standards: 2010 608**
Refer to Figures SS.5

L All Roll-in Shower Stalls: Grab Bars

L1 To ensure safety, always install all grab bars in a horizontal position. **ADAAG: 1998 4.20, 4.26 & ADA Standards: 2010 609**

L2 If a shower seat is not included, install grab bars on all three walls of the shower stall. **ADAAG: 1998 4.21 & ADA Standards: 2010 608, 610**

L3 If a seat is provided, install grab bars on walls adjacent to the seat wall so that grab bars do not extend over the seat. Grab bars are not required on the wall opposite the control wall. **ADAAG: 1998 4.21 & ADA Standards: 2010 608**

L4 Install grab bars at a height between 33in. (840mm) minimum to 36in. (915mm) maximum. **ADAAG: 1998 4.21 & ADA Standards: 2010 608, 609**
A 34in. (865mm) height is preferred. Ca

L5 If children will be the primary users of the shower stall, install grab bars between 18in. (455mm) minimum and 27in. (685mm) maximum above the shower stall floor. **ADA Standards: 2010 609 (NEW)**

See GB Grab Bars for additional information about requirements for and structural strength of grab bars.

M Standard Roll-in Shower Stalls: Grab Bars

M1 Locate grab bars no more than 6in. (150mm) from the adjacent wall to the wall the grab bar is mounted on. **ADAAG: 1998 4.21 & ADA Standards: 2010 608**
Refer to Figure SS.4

SE Tub/Shower Seats

A   Bathtub Seats   173
B   Transfer Shower Stall Seats   173
C   Standard Roll-in and Alternative Roll-in
        Shower Stall Seats   174
D   Rectangular Shower Stall Seats   174
E   L-shaped Shower Stall Seats   174
F   Structural Strength   175

Seats are required in all accessible bathtubs and transfer shower stalls. Folding seats also may be included (but are not required) in roll-in shower stalls. However, transient lodging *does require* folding seats in roll-in shower stalls. To ensure safe conditions for users of seats in bathtubs and shower stalls, follow the requirements in this section for placement, size, shape, and strength of seats.

The measurement for the depth of a seat refers to the dimension from the front of the seat to the back of the seat. The measurement for the width of a seat refers to the dimension from side to side. In a bathtub, the width is measured from the back wall of the tub to the outside edge of the tub.

The foot end of the tub is the end where the controls are located. The head end is opposite the foot end. The back wall connects the two ends of the tub.

A Bathtub Seats
A seat in a bathtub may be an in-tub portable seat or a permanent, built-in seat.

A1 In bathtubs, install a permanent rectangular seat or a removable rectangular seat that can be placed securely and that will remain stable. **ADAAG: 1998 4.20 & ADA Standards: 2010 607, 610**

A2 Provide a removable in-tub seat or a permanent seat at the head end of the tub. **ADAAG: 1998 4.20 & ADA Standards: 2010 607**

A3 Ensure that the seat is as wide as the bathtub, including the width of the tub sides. **ADA Standards: 2010 610 (New)**

A4 Ensure that the top of a bathtub seat is 17in. (430mm) minimum to 19in. (485mm) maximum above the bathroom floor. **ADA Standards: 2010 607, 610 (New)**

A5 If a portable in-tub seat is used, ensure that it is mounted securely to prevent the seat from slipping during use. **ADAAG: 1998 4.20 & ADA Standards: 2010 607, 610**

A6 If a permanent seat is installed at the head of the tub, ensure that the seat is 15in. (380mm) minimum deep. **ADAAG: 1998 4.20 & ADA Standards: 2010 607, 610**
Refer to Figure SE.1

A7 If a portable in-tub seat is used, ensure that the seat is 15in. (380mm) minimum to 16in. (405mm) maximum deep. **ADA Standards: 2010 607, 610 (Modified-Less Restrictive)**
See Figure SE.1

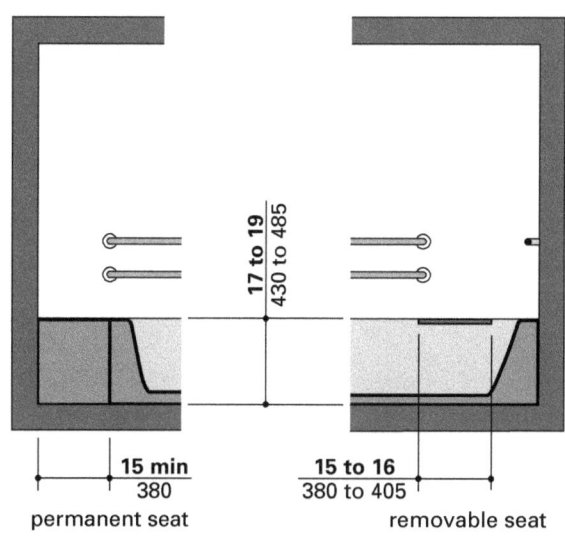

SE.1   Dimensions for bathtub seats

B Transfer Shower Stall Seats
Both **L**-shaped and rectangular seats are permitted in transfer shower stalls. **See SE-D and SE-E** for specific dimensional requirements for seat type.

B1 In a transfer shower stall, install an L-shaped or rectangular permanent seat or provide an attachable seat. **ADAAG: 1998 4.21 & ADA Standards: 2010 608, 610**

B2 Install the seat on the wall opposite the control wall. **ADAAG: 1998 4.21 & ADA Standards: 2010 608, 610**

B3 Locate the seat to extend from the back wall to a point within 3in. (75mm) of the compartment entry. **ADA Standards: 2010 608, 610 (MODIFIED-LESS RESTRICTIVE)**

B4 Mount the seat so that the top is 17in. (430mm) minimum to 19in. (485mm) maximum above the floor. **ADAAG: 1998 4.21 & ADA Standards: 2010 610**
   A height of 18in. (455mm) is preferred. ca

C Standard Roll-in and Alternative Roll-in Shower Stall Seats

Both **L**-shaped and rectangular seats are permitted in roll-in stalls. **See SE-D and SE-E** for specific dimensional requirements for seat type.

C1 In transient lodging, folding seats are required in both standard and alternative roll-in shower stalls. **ADA Standards: 2010 608 (NEW) See TL Transient Lodging.**

C2 Install an L-shaped or rectangular folding seat on the wall adjacent to the controls. **ADAAG: 1998 4.21 & ADA Standards: 2010 608, 610**

C3 Locate the seat adjacent to the stall entry, extending from the control wall to a point within 3in. (75mm) of the stall entry. **ADA Standards: 2010 608, 610 (MODIFIED-LESS RESTRICTIVE)**

C4 Mount the seat so that the top is 17in. (430mm) minimum to 19in. (485mm) maximum above the floor. **ADAAG: 1998 4.21 & ADA Standards: 2010 608, 610**
   A height of 18in. (455mm) is preferred. ca

D Rectangular Shower Stall Seats

D1 In shower stalls, install rectangular seats so that
   a. the rear edge of the seat is 2.5in. (64mm) maximum from the seat wall; **ADA Standards: 2010 610 (MODIFIED-LESS RESTRICTIVE)**
   b. the front edge of the seat is 15in. (380mm) minimum to 16in. (405mm) maximum from the seat wall; **ADAAG: 1998 4.21 & ADA Standards: 2010 610**
   c. the side edge of the seat next to the wall is 1.5in. (38mm) maximum from the wall. **ADAAG: 1998 4.21 & ADA Standards: 2010 610**

See Figure SE.2

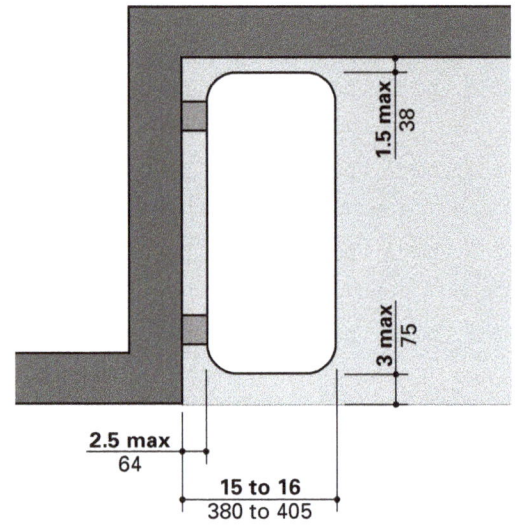

SE.2 A rectangular shower stall seat

E L-shaped Shower Stall Seats

E1 In shower stalls, install L-shaped seats so that
   a. the rear edge of the main seat is 2.5in. (64mm) maximum from the seat wall; **ADA Standards: 2010 610 (MODIFIED-LESS RESTRICTIVE)**
   b. the front edge of the main seat is 15in. (380mm) minimum to 16in. (405mm) maximum from the seat wall; **ADAAG: 1998 4.21 & ADA Standards: 2010 610**
   c. the rear edge of the **L**-portion of the seat is 1.5in. (38mm) maximum from the wall and the front edge of the **L**-portion of the seat is 14in. (355mm) minimum to 15in. (380mm) maximum from the wall; **ADA Standards: 2010 610 (MODIFIED-LESS RESTRICTIVE)** and
   d. the long side of the short leg of the **L** is 22in. (560mm) minimum to 23in. (585mm) maximum from the main seat wall. **ADAAG: 1998 4.21 & ADA Standards: 2010 610**

See Figure SE.3

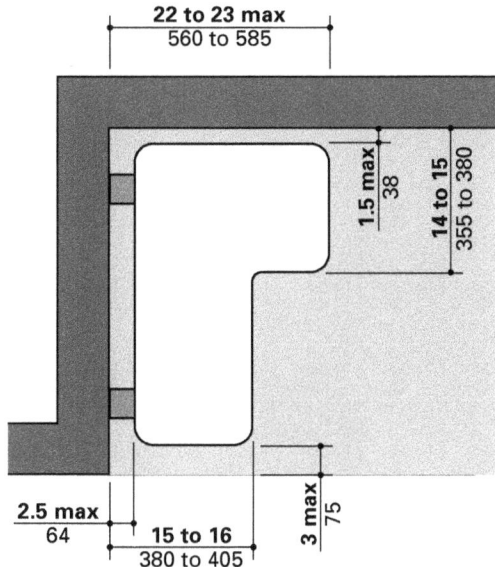

SE.3   An *L*-shaped shower stall seat

F   Structural Strength
Install seats and mounting devices that meet the following requirements for strength.

F1 Ensure that the seat and all materials used for mounting the seat support a vertical or horizontal force of 250 lbs. (1112N) applied at any point on the seat, fastener, mounting device, or supporting structure. **ADAAG: 1998 4.26 & ADA Standards: 2010 610**

BT   Bathtubs

A	Number	175
B	Clear Floor Space	175
C	Bathtub Grab Bars	177
D	Bathtub Controls	177
E	Bathtub Spray Units	179
F	Bathtub Enclosures	179

Accessible bathtubs or accessible showers are required by ADA Standards where bathing facilities are provided for public use. The ADA Standards does not specify requirements for tub depth, but the height of tub sides is limited by the maximum height allowed for tub seats as listed below.

You may choose to provide an accessible shower instead of, or in addition to, an accessible bathtub because transfers into and out of bathtubs can be difficult for many people. Showers are generally safer than tubs, particularly for older people. We recommend installing accessible shower stalls where possible.

See SE Seats for information about the placement, dimensions, and structural strength of seats required in accessible bathtubs. Portable tub chairs also may be needed to assist people in transferring in and out of tubs.

The control-end of the tub is the end where the controls are located. The 1998 ADAAG refers to the control-end as the foot end of the tub. The head end is opposite the foot end. The back wall connects the two ends of the tub.

A   Number
A1 Wherever bathtubs and showers are provided for public use, ensure that at least one bathtub or shower is accessible. **ADAAG: 1998 4.23, 4.20 & ADA Standards: 2010 213 See SS Shower Stalls.**

B   Clear Floor Space
Approaches to bathtubs are generally from the head end or from the side. Provide sufficient clear floor space to allow for a convenient approach and transfer into the tub and onto the tub seat. Where tubs

include permanent seats, provide additional clear floor space past the seat-end of the tub to permit easier transferring to the seat.

B1 Clear floor space at bathtubs can overlap turning space required in the room.

   a. A lavatory or sink may overlap the clear floor space at the control-end (foot end) of the tub, but ensure that the lavatory or sink extends only as far as necessary into the bathtub's clear floor space.

   b. Ensure that the placement of lavatories, sinks, and toilets does not interfere with access to bathtub controls. **ADAAG: 1998 4.20 & ADA Standards: 2010 607**

See FX Fixtures for specific information on lavatories and sinks and the requirements for legroom.

B2 Ensure that at least the minimum required clear floor space at bathtubs is provided based on the type of tub seat installed and the approach to the tub.

   a. **In-tub or portable seat, parallel approach:** Where an in-tub seat or portable seat is installed and the approach to the tub is parallel, provide a 30in. (760mm) wide minimum clear floor space that extends the length of the tub. **ADAAG: 1998 4.20 & ADA Standards: 2010 305**

   A 42in. (1065mm) wide clear floor space is preferred. ca

See Figure BT.1

   b. **In-tub or portable seat, forward approach:** Where an in-tub seat or portable seat is installed and the approach to the tub is a forward approach, provide a 48in. (1220mm) wide minimum clear floor space that extends the length of the tub. **ADAAG: 1998 4.20 & ADA Standards: 2010 607**

   A 67in (1702mm) wide clear floor space is preferred. ca

See Figure BT.2

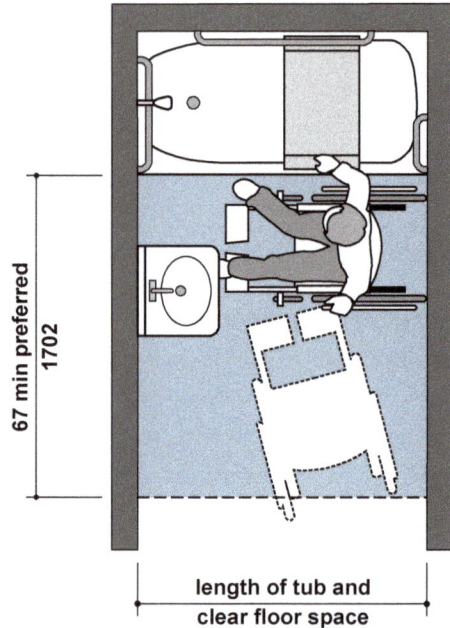

BT.2 Preferred clear floor space for a *forward* approach to a bathtub with an in-tub or portable seat

   c. **Permanent seat, parallel approach:** Where a permanent seat is installed at the head of the tub and the approach to the tub is parallel, provide a 30in. (760mm) wide minimum clear floor space that extends the length of the tub plus 12in. (305mm) beyond the seat. **ADA Standards: 2010 607 (New)**

   A 42in. (1065mm) wide clear floor space is preferred. ca

See Figure BT.3

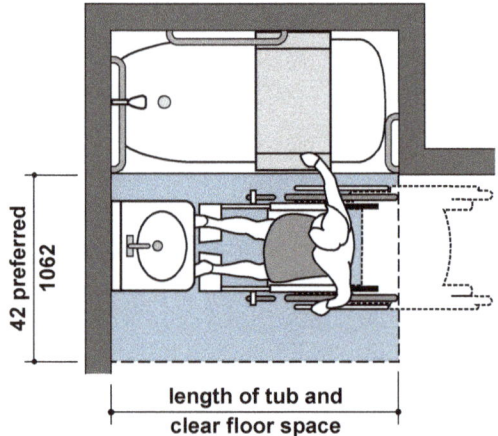

BT.1 Preferred clear floor space for a *parallel* approach to a bathtub with an in-tub or portable seat

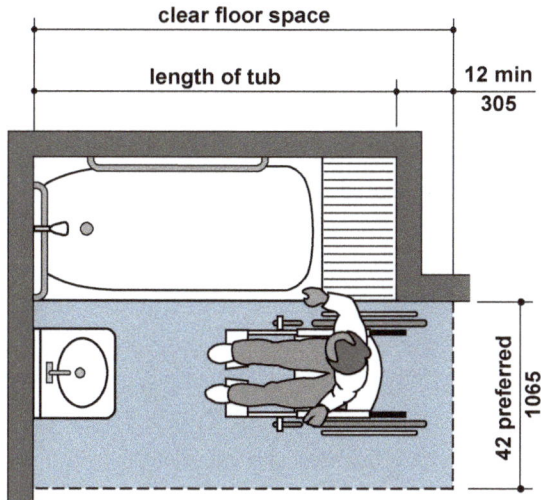

BT.3 Preferred clear floor space for a *parallel* approach to a bathtub with a permanent seat

C Bathtub Grab Bars

Grab bars are required in all bathrooms used by the public. Proper placement and stability of grab bars is essential for safe use.

Grab bars are not required in single-user bathing rooms that are accessed from private offices and that are not for public use. However, structural reinforcement to accommodate future installation of grab bars is required.

C1 To ensure safety, always install all grab bars in a horizontal position. **ADAAG: 1998 4.20, 4.26 & ADA Standards: 2010 609**

C2 In a bathtub with a permanent seat, install grab bars as follows:
  a. Install two grab bars on the back wall. **ADAAG: 1998 4.20 & ADA Standards: 2010 609**
      A grab bar length of 48in. (1220mm) minimum is preferred. 🌀a
  b. Mount one grab bar between 33in. (840mm) minimum and 36in. (915mm) maximum above the floor. **ADAAG: 1998 4.20 & ADA Standards: 2010 609**
  c. Mount a second grab bar between 8in. (203mm) minimum and 10in. (254mm) maximum above the rim of the tub. **ADA Standards: 2010 607 (Modified-Less Restrictive)**
  d. Install each grab bar 15in. (380mm) maximum from the head end wall and 12in. (305mm) maximum from the control-end wall (foot end wall). **ADAAG: 1998 4.20 & ADA Standards: 2010 607**
  e. Mount one grab bar on the control-end (foot end) wall that extends 24in. (610mm) minimum from the front edge of the tub. **ADAAG: 1998 4.20 & ADA Standards: 2010 607, 609**

See Figure BT.4

C3 In a bathtub without a permanent seat (where an in-tub or portable seat will be used), install grab bars as follows:
  a. Install two grab bars that are 24in. (610mm) long minimum on the back wall. Mount one grab bar between 33in. (840mm) minimum and 36in. (915mm) maximum above the floor. Mount the second grab bar between 8in. (203mm) minimum and 10in. (254mm) maximum above the rim of the tub. Install each grab bar a maximum of 24in. (610mm) from the head end wall and a maximum of 12in. (305mm) from the control-end (foot end) wall.
  b. Mount one grab bar on the control-end (foot end) wall that extends 24in. (610mm) minimum from the front edge of the tub.
  c. Mount one grab bar that extends 12in. (305mm) minimum along the head end wall from the front edge of the tub. **ADA Standards: 2010 607, 609 (New)**

See Figure BT.5

C4 Install optional, auxiliary grab bars in a vertical position. 🌀a

D Bathtub Controls

Specify and install high quality, durable controls that are usable by everyone.

D1 Install controls and operable parts (except drain stoppers) as follows:
  a. on the control-end (foot end) wall above the tub rim;
  b. between the front edge of the tub and the

mid-point of the width of the tub;

c. below the grab bar with at least 1.5in. (38mm) clearance between controls and grab bar; and

d. within the appropriate reach range; **see RR Reach Ranges. ADAAG: 1998 4.20, 4.27 & ADA Standards: 2010 607, 309**

Refer to Figures BT.4 and BT.5.

D2 Install faucets and other fixtures with controls that
    a. are operable with one hand; **ADAAG: 1998 4.27 & ADA Standards: 2010 309**

b. do not require tight grasping, pinching, or twisting of the wrist; **ADAAG: 1998 4.27 & ADA Standards: 2010 309**

c. are activated with a force less than or equal to 5 lbs. (22.2N); **ADAAG: 1998 4.27 & ADA Standards: 2010 309** and

d. include temperature and pressure regulating valves. Ca

D3 If you install hand-operated metered faucets, ensure that the faucet valve is set to remain open for at least 10 seconds. **ADAAG: 1998 4.19, 4.27 & ADA Standards: 2010 606**

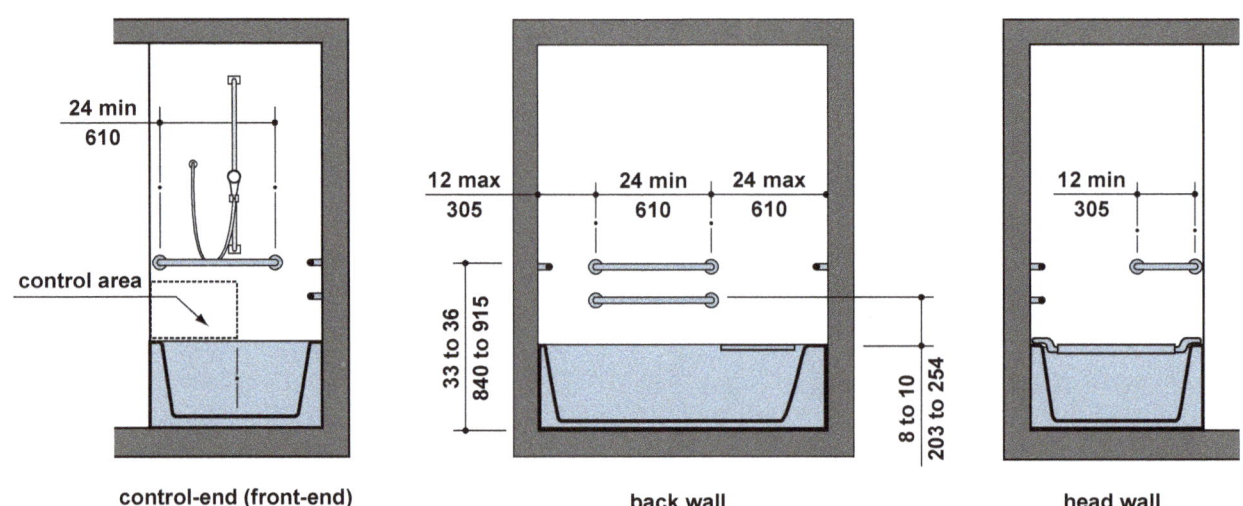

BT.4 Grab bars and controls in a bathtub with a *permanent* seat

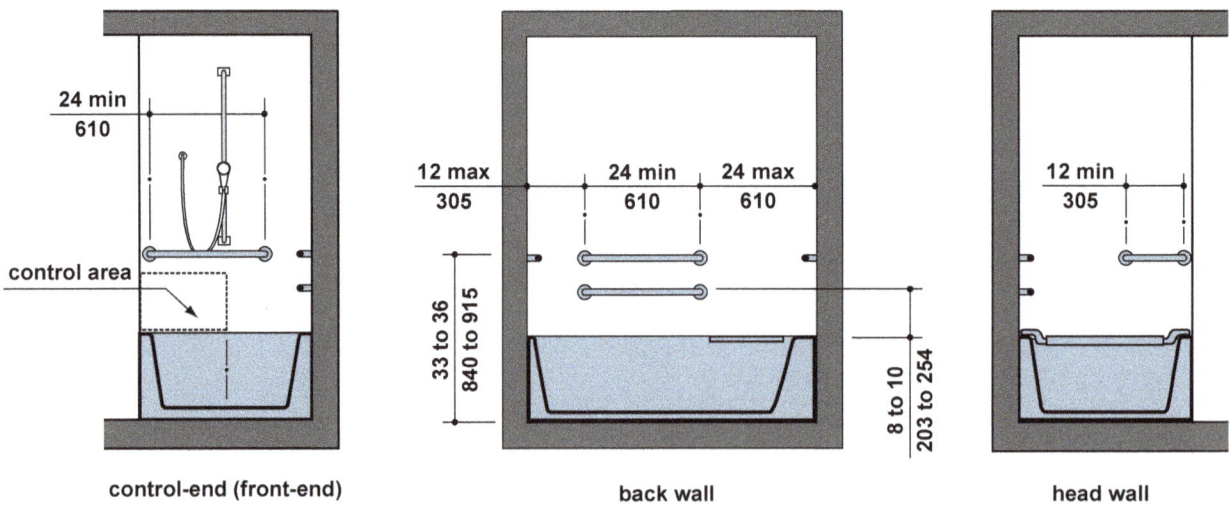

BT.5 Grab bars and controls in a bathtub with an *in-tub or portable* seat

E Bathtub Spray Units

Shower spray units make bathing without assistance easier for some people.

E1 Install a shower spray unit that
  a. includes a hose at least 59in. (1500mm) long,
  b. can be used as both a fixed position shower head and a hand-held shower, and
  c. includes water-on/water-off controls with a non-positive shut-off. **ADAAG: 1998 4.20 & ADA Standards: 2010 607**

E2 Mount the spray unit so that it
  a. does not obstruct the use of grab bars; and
  b. is within the appropriate reach range **See RR Reach Ranges**. **ADAAG: 1998 4.20 & ADA Standards: 2010 607**

E3 Ensure that any bathtub or shower spray unit delivers water that is limited to a maximum temperature of 120°F (49°C). **ADA Standards: 2010 607 (New)**
  A pressure and temperature regulator valve is preferred. Ca

F Bathtub Enclosures

A tub enclosure may be an obstacle for people getting into and out of the bathtub.

F1 Ensure that any tub enclosure does not obstruct access to controls or interfere with the transfer of a person from a wheelchair into the tub or onto a tub seat. **ADAAG: 1998 4.20 & ADA Standards: 2010 607**

F2 Do not use a bathtub enclosure that requires tracks to be mounted on the rim of the tub. **ADAAG: 1998 4.20 & ADA Standards: 2010 607**

GB Grab Bars

A Grab Bar Location and Installation	180
B Grab Bar Shape and Dimensions	180
C Grab Bar Structural Strength	180
D Grab Bar Positioning and Spacing	181

Grab bars help people to maintain their balance and avoid falling. For safety, it is important to install grab bars of the proper size and dimension, to provide adequate clearances between grab bars and walls or partitions, and to ensure that both the grab bars and the materials and methods used to mount grab bars to walls are of adequate strength.

Where grab bars are installed, or where grab bars may be installed in the future, walls should be reinforced with heavy plywood over studs or appropriate wood blocking. Walls reinforced with plywood are preferred because they allow for various mounting heights and locations.

Although some fiberglass and acrylic tubs, showers, tub enclosures, and wall panels are now reinforced for grab bar installation, many are not sturdy enough or adequately attached to walls for the attachment of grab bars without additional reinforcement. Unless these units are specifically labeled for grab bar installation, walls behind them need additional reinforcement where grab bars are attached.

A Grab Bar Location and Installation

Grab bars are required in accessible toilet stalls, bathtubs, and shower stalls. Consider installing additional grab bars in other locations where people would benefit from additional support.
See BT Bathtubs, SS Shower Stalls, and TS Toilet Stalls for specific requirements for grab bar installation.

A1 Install grab bars in a secure manner at specified locations. **ADAAG: 1998 4.26 & ADA Standards: 2010 609**

A2 Ensure that grab bars and adjacent wall surfaces are free from sharp edges or abrasive surfaces. **ADAAG: 1998 4.26 & ADA Standards: 2010 609**

A3 Install grab bars so that they do not rotate in their fittings. **ADAAG: 1998 4.26 & ADA Standards: 2010 609**

B Grab Bar Shape and Dimensions

The size and shape of grab bars determine how easy it is for people to grip them. Round grab bars are preferred. Grab bars with other shapes that provide equivalent graspability may also be used.
See Figure GB.1

B1 For round grab bars, ensure that the outside diameter is between 1.25in. (32mm) minimum and 2in. (51mm) maximum. **ADA Standards: 2010 609 (Modified-Less Restrictive)**

B2 For grab bars of other shapes, ensure that
  a. the maximum cross-section dimension does not exceed 2in. (51mm); **ADA Standards: 2010 609 (New)**
  b. the perimeter dimension is 4in. (100mm) minimum and 4.8in. (120mm) maximum; **ADA Standards: 2010 609 (New)** and
  c. the edges are rounded. **ADAAG: 1998 4.26 & ADA Standards: 2010 609**

C Grab Bar Structural Strength

Grab bars must be sufficiently strong to allow individuals to safely transfer between wheelchairs and toilets, bathtubs, and shower stall seats. People must be able to rely on them to support their entire weight. Both grab bars and grab bar mounting devices must meet minimum strength requirements.
Work with a knowledgeable supplier to choose grab bars that meet ADA Standards requirements.

C1 Carefully read product information and follow proper installation procedures to ensure that grab bars and mounting devices selected have sufficient structural strength. Ca

C2 Ensure that the materials used in grab bars and mounting devices can support a vertical or horizontal force of 250 lbs. (1112N) applied at any point on grab bars, fasteners, mounting devices, or supporting structures. **ADAAG: 1998 4.26 & ADA Standards: 2010 609**

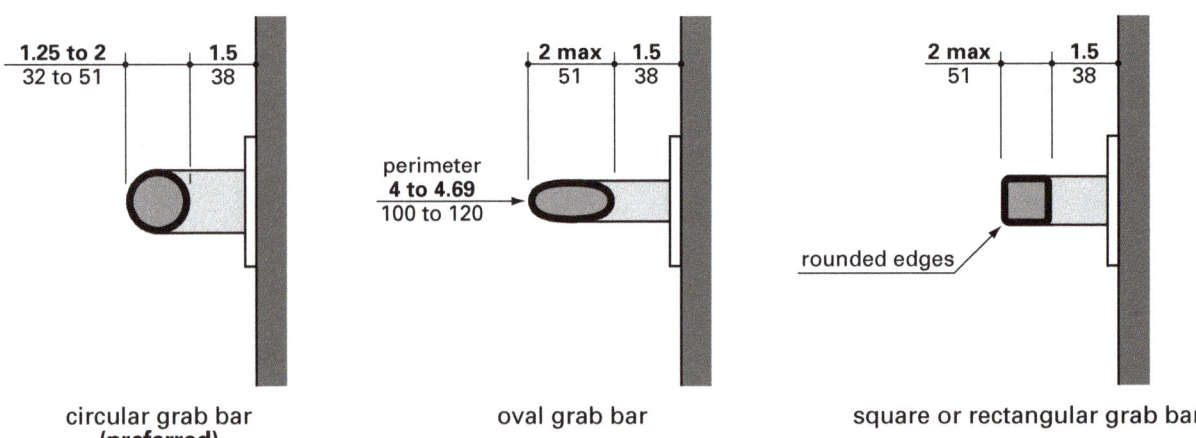

GB.1 Grab bar profiles and dimensions

D Grab Bar Positioning and Spacing

Grab bars must be placed for convenient, comfortable, and safe use. The following general guidelines apply to grab bars installed in any location.

D1 To ensure safety, always install all grab bars in a horizontal or vertical position where appropriate. Diagonally positioned grab bars do not comply with the ADA Standards and are not recommended. **ADAAG: 1998 4.20, 4.26 & ADA Standards: 2010 609**

D2 Install grab bars so that clear floor space is not obstructed. **ADAAG: 1998 4.3 & ADA Standards: 2010 609**

D3 Install grab bars in a horizontal position between 33in. (840mm) minimum and 36in. (915mm) maximum above the floor, measured to the top of the grab bar. **ADAAG: 4.17, 4.20, 4.21 & ADA Standards: 2010 609**
A mounting height of 34in. (865mm) is preferred. Ca

D4 In restrooms that are primarily used by children, install grab bars in a horizontal position 18in. (455mm) minimum to 27in. (685mm) maximum above the floor. **ADA Standards: 2010 609 (New)**

D5 Ensure that the space between grab bars, walls, and other objects meets accessibility requirements.
   a. Provide **exactly** 1.5in. (38mm) between grab bars and walls. **ADAAG: 1998 4.26 & ADA Standards: 2010 609**
   b. Provide at least 1.5in. (38mm) between grab bars and shower controls, shower fittings, and other grab bars. **ADA Standards: 2010 609 (New)**
   c. Position protruding objects (such as toilet paper dispensers) at least 1.5in. (38mm) below the bottom of grab bars. **ADA Standards: 2010 609 (New)** Protruding objects may be positioned beyond the ends of grab bars as long as the positioning meets reach range requirements. **See RR Reach Ranges.**
   d. Provide a minimum of 12in. (305mm) between grab bars and any protruding objects above them. **ADA Standards: 2010 609 (New)**

Refer to Figure TS.7

Chapters in Equipment, Tables, and Seating

DF	Drinking Fountains	184
PT	Public Telephones	187
TA	Tables & Seating	191
VS	Vending/Self-serve	196

Section 4. Equipment, Tables, and Seating

The chapters in this section cover additional features and furnishings of buildings and sites including drinking fountains, public telephones, tables and seating, and self-service machines (such as ATMs) and depositories. Use this section to identify and review features included in your building or site to ensure that they are safe, easy to use, and convenient for all people.

Convenience

Ensure that people can find and use accessible furnishings, fixtures, and machines by

1) locating accessible furnishings and features on or near main routes and entrances wherever possible
2) identifying areas that include accessible furnishings and features (in situations where not all spaces are accessible)
3) providing sufficient space around accessible furnishings and features for people to approach and use them, and
4) distributing accessible furnishings (such as tables and seating) throughout spaces to provide choices for all people

Control

People should be able to use furnishings and equipment independently. Install self-service machines, telephones, drinking fountains, and other equipment that allow independent use by people with a variety of different needs.

Ensure that handles, operating controls, and mechanisms of furnishings and features are easy to use and within reach for most people. **See RR Reach Ranges.**

Important Note

A number of elements covered in this chapter (e.g. telephones, drinking fountains, and self service machines) are factory built units. Many of the specific details of accessible features outlined here will be preconfigured by the manufacturer. We provide details to familiarize you with accessibility requirements so that you can ensure that the products you purchase and install meet ADA Standards standards.

DF Drinking Fountains

A	Location and Number	184
B	Wheelchair Accessible Drinking Fountains: Clear Floor Space	184
C	Wheelchair Accessible Drinking Fountains: Legroom	185
D	Wheelchair Drinking Fountains: Spout	185
E	Wheelchair Accessible Drinking Fountains: Water Flow	186
F	Standing Accessible Drinking Fountains: Spout	186
G	All Drinking Fountains: Operable Parts	186

All people should be able to use drinking fountains wherever they are available. Children, people of short or tall stature, people who use wheelchairs, and people who have difficulty manipulating controls all need drinking fountains that have spouts at convenient heights, adequate legroom, and appropriate controls.

The ADA Standards requirements for drinking fountains pertain to both standing and sitting persons. Since the needs of all groups must be met, at least two heights of drinking fountains (or a drinking fountain with two spouts mounted at different heights) are needed. This chapter contains requirements for both standing accessible and wheelchair accessible drinking fountain units.

A   Location and Number

The ADA Standards does not require that drinking fountains be provided. However, where they are provided, drinking fountains that accommodate different users are required.

A1 Where drinking fountains are available on a floor of a building, in an exterior area, or in a secured area inside or outside a building, ensure that at least two drinking fountains are provided. **ADAAG: 1998 4.1 & ADA Standards: 2010 211**

A2 Where only two drinking fountains are provided, ensure that
   a. One of the drinking fountains is wheelchair accessible, and
   b. One of the drinking fountains is accessible to standing persons. **ADAAG: 1998 4.1 & ADA Standards: 2010 211**

A3 Where more than two drinking fountains are provided, ensure that 50% are wheelchair accessible, and 50% are accessible to standing persons. **ADAAG: 1998 4.1 & ADA Standards: 2010 211**

Note: Where there is an odd number of drinking fountains, the 50% figure can be rounded up or down for either type of drinking fountain as long as all drinking fountains are accessible (either wheelchair accessible or standing accessible). ADAAG: 1998 4.1 & ADA Standards: 2010 211

Exception: Where only one drinking fountain is provided on a floor, in an exterior area, or in a secured area, the drinking fountain must meet requirements for both wheelchair accessible and standing accessible drinking fountains. A single, dual purpose drinking fountain (such as a "hi-low" unit) is an example of a type of drinking fountain that could meet all accessibility guidelines. ADAAG: 1998 4.1 & ADA Standards: 2010 211

A4 Where multiple drinking fountains are provided, disperse the drinking fountains to convenient locations to provide access to all people. ca

A5 Locate all wheelchair accessible drinking fountains along accessible routes. **ADAAG: 1998 4.1 & ADA Standards: 2010 206**
   Locating all drinking fountains on accessible routes is preferred. ca

B   Wheelchair Accessible Drinking Fountains: Clear Floor Space

Clear floor space must be provided for unobstructed access to drinking fountains.

B1 Provide a minimum clear floor space in front of drinking fountains that is
   a. 30in. (760mm) by 48in. (1220mm), 36in (915mm) by 54in (1370mm) preferred ca and
   b. configured for a forward approach. **ADAAG: 1998 4.2, 4.15 & ADA Standards: 2010 305, 602**

Exception: Where the primary users of the area are children, a parallel approach is permitted where the drinking fountain spout is 30in. (760mm) maximum above the floor ADAAG: 1998 4.15 & ADA Standards: 2010 602

and

the spout is 3.5in. (90mm) maximum from the edge of the unit including bumpers. ADA Standards: 2010 602 (NEW)

See Figure DF.1

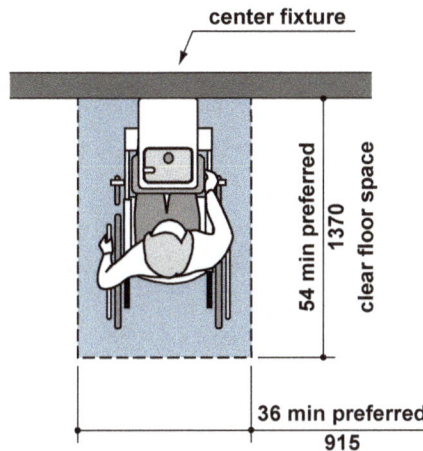

DF.1 **Preferred** minimum clear floor space at a wheelchair accessible drinking fountain

B2 Position the clear floor space so that it is centered on the drinking fountain. **ADA Standards: 2010 602 (NEW)**

B3 Ensure that one fully unobstructed side of the clear floor space overlaps or adjoins an accessible route. **ADAAG: 1998 4.2 & ADA Standards: 2010 305**

B4 Where a drinking fountain is in an alcove that is 24in. (610mm) deep or more, or is bounded on both sides by walls or other objects, provide clear floor space that is 36in. (915mm) wide. **42in (1065mm) min preferred** Ⓒa **ADAAG: 1998 4.2 & ADA Standards: 2010 305**

See Figure DF.2

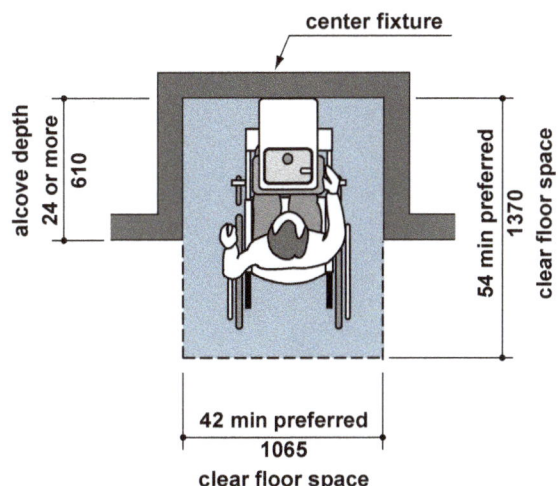

DF.2 **Preferred** minimum clear floor space for a forward approach to a drinking fountain in a deep alcove

C Wheelchair Accessible Drinking Fountains: Legroom

Adequate legroom must be provided for people to pull up to and use wheelchair accessible drinking fountains.

C1 Provide adequate legroom, including knee and toe clearance, under drinking fountains. **ADAAG: 1998 4.15 & ADA Standards: 2010 602, 306** See RT Routes and Spaces, RT-Q.

D Wheelchair Accessible Drinking Fountains: Spout

D1 Ensure that spout outlets are no higher than 36in. (915mm) above the floor. **ADAAG: 1998 4.15 & ADA Standards: 2010 602**

D2 Locate the spout at the front of the drinking fountains. **ADAAG: 1998 4.15 & ADA Standards: 2010 602**

D3 Ensure that spouts are located
  a. 15in. (380mm) minimum from the vertical support; **ADA Standards: 2010 602 (MODIFIED-MORE RESTRICTIVE)** and
  b. 5in. (125mm) maximum from the front edge of the unit, including bumpers. **ADA Standards: 2010 602 (NEW)**

Exception: Ensure that spouts on units configured for a parallel approach by children are located 3.5in.

(90mm) maximum from the front edge of the unit, including bumpers. **ADA Standards: 2010 602 (NEW)** See Figure DF.3

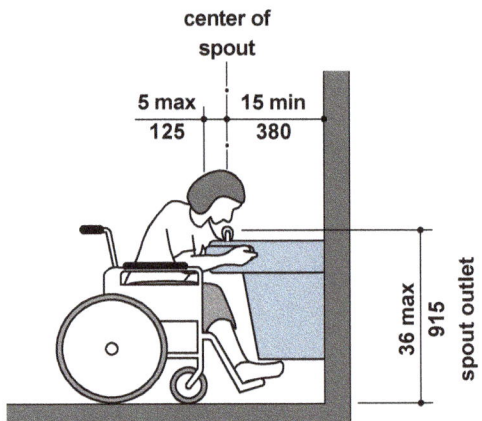

DF.3 Spout height and location for a wheelchair accessible drinking fountain

D4 Ensure that the legroom provided under drinking fountains has adequate knee and toe clearance. **Refer to TB-L** for specific requirements. **ADAAG: 1998 4.15 & ADA Standards: 2010 306**

E Wheelchair Accessible Drinking Fountains: Water Flow

The height of the water flow should be enough to allow people to put a glass or cup under the water stream.

E1 Provide water bottle fillers on all accessible height drinking fountains. ca

E2 Ensure that the spout provides a flow of water at least 4in. (100mm) high. **ADAAG: 1998 4.15 & ADA Standards: 2010 602**

E3 Ensure that the angle of the water stream is
  a. 30° maximum from the spout located within 3in. (75mm) of the front of the unit, and
  b. 15° maximum from the spout located between 3in. (75mm) and 5in. (125mm) from the front of the unit. **ADA Standards: 2010 602 (MODIFIED-MORE RESTRICTIVE)**

Accessible high-low drinking fountains with bottle filler ca

F Standing Accessible Drinking Fountains: Spout

F1 Ensure that spout outlets are 38in. (965mm) minimum and 43in. (1090mm) maximum above the floor. **ADA Standards: 2010 602 (NEW)**

G All Drinking Fountains: Operable Parts

G1 Mount the controls on the front of the unit or on the side near the front edge. ca

G2 Provide controls and mechanisms that
  a. are operable with one hand;
  b. do not require tight grasping, pinching, or twisting of the wrist; and
  c. do not require a force exceeding 5 lbs. (22.2N) to operate. **ADAAG: 1998 4.15, 4.27 & ADA Standards: 2010 602, 309**

PT Public Telephones

A   Volume Control   187

Wheelchair Accessible Telephones   188
B   Number and Location   188
C   Floor Space and Clearances   188
D   Cord Length   189
E   Operable Parts   189
F   Signs   189

TTY Telephones   189
G   TTYs on a Site: Number and Location   189
H   TTYs in Public Buildings:
     Number and Location   189
I   TTYs in Private Buildings:
     Number and Location   190
J   TTY: Heights and Clearances   190
K   TTY: Cord Length   190
L   Portable TTY Shelves   190
M   TTY Signs   191

Accessibility requirements for public telephones pertain to volume control, wheelchair access, and TTYs.

The ADA Standards requirements for volume control and wheelchair access cover coin-operated public pay telephones, coinless public pay telephones, public closed-circuit telephones, courtesy telephones, and any other types of public telephones that are provided on a site or in a building.

TTY access is required for all public pay telephones (where provided), but not all wheelchair accessible public pay telephones are required to have TTY access.

TTYs employ interactive text-based communications through the transmission of coded signals across the standard telephone network. TTYs typically include a simplified keyboard and provide an electronic readout.

The ADA Standards uses the designation TTY rather than text telephone or TDD. TTY is synonymous with text telephones and encompasses devices known as TDDs, a term which stands for telecommunication display devices (or telecommunication devices for deaf persons).

In this chapter, two or more adjacent telephones are referred to as a bank of telephones.

A   Volume Control

In accordance with the Telecommunications Act of 1996, Section 255, all public telephones are required to have volume control.

Amplifiers on pay telephones are built into the telephones and are located in either the base or the handset. Most are located in the base and are operated by pressing a button or key.

A mute button temporarily turns the amplifier off when it is not in use and also reduces the amount of background noise that the person hears in the earpiece. Work with knowledgeable suppliers to ensure that telephones are properly equipped.

A1   Ensure that all telephones on a site or in a building meet all specifications of the Telecommunications Act Accessibility Guidelines, Section 255. ᶜᵃ

A2   Provide volume controls for all public telephones. **ADAAG: 1998 4.1 & ADA Standards: 2010 217**

A3   Ensure that volume controls provide
   a.   a gain adjustable up to a minimum of 20dB, **ADA Standards: 2010 704 (MODIFIED-MORE RESTRICTIVE)** and
   b.   at least one intermediate step of 12dB of gain for incremental volume control. **ADAAG: 1998 4.31 & ADA Standards: 2010 704**

A4   Provide an automatic reset for the volume control. **ADA Standards: 2010 704 (Modified-More Restrictive)**

A5   In existing conditions where not all public phones have volume controls, identify volume controlled telephones with the International Symbol of Volume Controlled Telephones. ᶜᵃ

See Figure PT.1

PT.1 International Symbol of Volume Controlled Telephones

Wheelchair Accessible Telephones

Wheelchair accessible public telephones must be available for each type of public telephone provided.

B Number and Location

B1 Wherever public telephones are available (inside or outside a building or facility) provide at least the required minimum number of wheelchair accessible public telephones. **ADAAG: 1998 4.1 & ADA Standards: 2010 217**

Exception: This requirement does not apply where there are drive-up only public telephones. ADA Standards: 2010 217 (New)
See PT-A

Total number of public phones available	Minimum number of wheelchair accessible phones required
1 or more phones	1
1 bank of phones	1
2 or more banks	1 phone per bank

PT-A Minimum required number of wheelchair accessible public telephones (two or more adjacent phones are a bank of phones)

B2 Locate all wheelchair accessible public telephones along accessible routes. **ADAAG: 1998 4.1 & ADA Standards: 2010 206**

B3 Locating all public telephones on accessible routes is preferred. Ca

C Floor Space and Clearances

Clear floor space must be provided for unobstructed access to telephones.

C1 Provide a minimum clear floor space that is
  a. 30in. (760mm) by 48in. (1220mm), and
  b. configured for a forward or parallel approach. **ADAAG: 1998 4.2, 4.31 & ADA Standards: 2010 305, 704**

C2 For a parallel approach to a wheelchair accessible telephone with an enclosure or privacy panel, ensure that the distance from the edge of the telephone enclosure to the face of the telephone is 10in. (255mm) maximum. **ADAAG: 1998 4.31 & ADA Standards: 2010 704**
See Figure PT.2

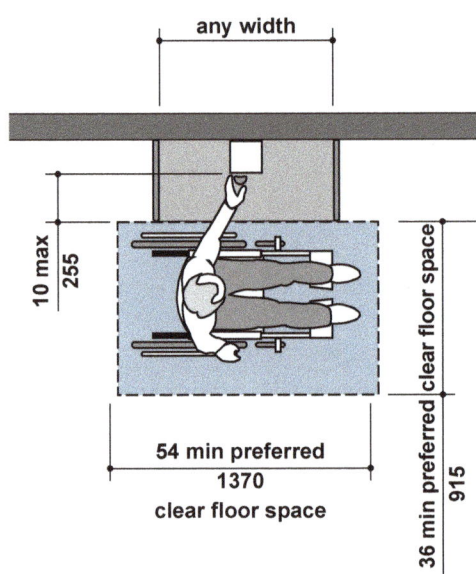

PT.2 Parallel approach to a wheelchair accessible telephone with an enclosure or privacy panel

C3 For a forward approach to a wheelchair accessible telephone with a counter, ensure that the distance from the front edge of the counter to the face of the telephone is a maximum of 20in. (510mm). **ADAAG: 1998 4.31 & ADA Standards: 2010 704**
See Figure PT.3

C4 Ensure that one side of the clear floor space overlaps or adjoins an accessible route. **ADAAG: 1998 4.2 & ADA Standards: 2010 305, 704**

C5 Ensure that the clear floor space is not restricted by bases, enclosures, or seats. **ADAAG: 1998 4.31 & ADA Standards: 2010 704, 305**

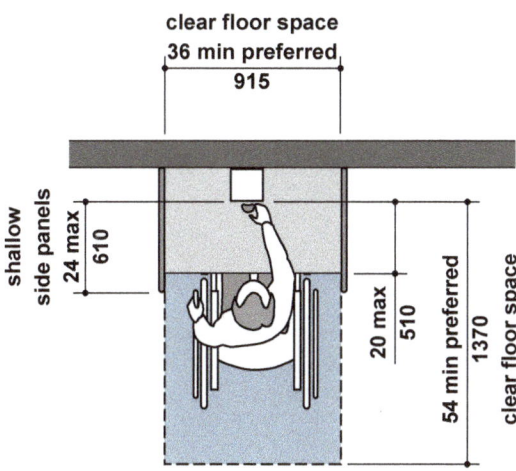

PT.3 Forward approach to a wheelchair accessible telephone with a counter

C6 Ensure that all telephones, enclosures, phone books, and related equipment on accessible routes meet all requirements for protruding objects. **ADAAG: 1998 4.31, 4.4 & ADA Standards: 2010 704, 305 See RT Routes and Spaces, RT-O.**

D Cord Length

D1 Provide a cord from the telephone to the handset that is a minimum of 29in. (735mm) long. **ADAAG: 1998 4.31 & ADA Standards: 2010 704**

E Operable Parts

E1 Install telephones that have push-button controls where push-button service is available. **ADAAG: 1998 4.31 & ADA Standards: 2010 704**

E2 Ensure that all other controls and mechanisms, including phone books,
   a. are operable with one hand;
   b. do not require tight grasping, pinching, or twisting of the wrist; and
   c. do not require force exceeding 5 lbs. (22.2N) to operate. **ADAAG: 1998 4.31, 4.27 & ADA Standards: 2010 704, 309**

E3 Ensure that the heights of operable parts of accessible telephones comply with reach range requirements. **ADAAG: 1998 4.31, 4.27 & ADA Standards: 2010 704, 308, 309 See RR Reach Ranges.**

F Signs

F1 Where wheelchair accessible public telephones are not provided at all banks of telephones, identify wheelchair accessible phones (wherever they are located) with accessible signs that include the International Symbol of Accessibility. **See SN Signs.**

TTY Telephones

When planning for the technical requirements of telephone systems that will support TTYs, consider installing systems that will accommodate both digital and analog TTYs. TTYs must be permanently installed within or adjacent to telephone enclosures.

TTYs may be permanently installed in a bank of public telephones. In some locations, shelves and outlets need to be provided for the use of personal portable TTYs.

The requirements for TTYs are based on the number of public pay telephones provided on a site, within a building, within a floor of a building, and at banks of telephones.

G TTYs on a Site: Number and Location

G1 Wherever four or more public pay telephones are provided on an exterior site, ensure that at least one public TTY is provided. **ADAAG: 1998 4.1 & ADA Standards: 2010 217**

G2 Where a public pay telephone is provided at a public rest stop, emergency roadside stop, or service plaza, ensure that at least one public TTY is provided. **ADA Standards: 2010 217 (New)**

H TTYs in Public Buildings: Number and Location

H1 Where four or more public pay telephones are provided at a bank of telephones (and where no TTY is available within 200ft. (61m) of the bank of telephones), ensure that at least one public TTY is provided. **ADA Standards: 2010 217 (New)**

H2 Where one or more public pay telephone is provided on a floor of a building, ensure that at least one public TTY is provided on that floor. **ADAAG: 1998 4.1 & ADA Standards: 2010 217**

H3 Where one or more public pay telephone is provided in a building, ensure that at least one public TTY is provided in the building. **ADAAG: 1998 4.1 & ADA Standards: 2010 217**

H4 Where one or more pay telephones are provided in a public use area, ensure that at least one TTY is provided. **ADA Standards: 2010 217 (NEW)**

I   TTYs in Private Buildings: Number and Location

I 1 Where four or more public pay telephones are provided at a bank of telephones in a private building (and where no TTY is available within 200ft. (61m) of the bank of telephones), ensure that at least one public TTY is provided. **ADA Standards: 2010 602 (Modified-More Restrictive)**

I 2 Where four or more public pay telephones are provided on a floor of a private building, ensure that at least one public TTY is provided on that floor. **ADAAG: 1998 4.1 & ADA Standards: 2010 217**

I 3 Where four or more public pay telephones are provided in a private building, ensure that at least one public TTY is provided in the building. **ADAAG: 1998 4.1 & ADA Standards: 2010 217**

J   TTY Heights and Clearances

Though ADAAG does not require that TTYs also be wheelchair accessible, we recommend that you follow the guidelines for wheelchair accessible telephones with regard to clear floor space and operable controls at one or more TTYs.

J1 Ensure that the touch surface of a TTY keypad is 34in. (865mm) maximum above the floor. **ADA Standards: 2010 704 (NEW)**
Exception: Where seats are provided at TTYs, the height requirement does not apply. ADA Standards: 2010 704 (NEW)
See Figure PT.4

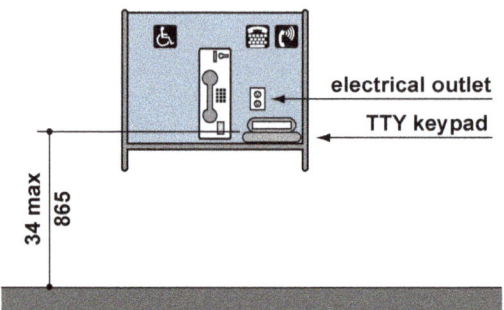

PT.4   TTY keypad height

K   TTY Cord Length

K1 Where an acoustic coupler is used, ensure that the telephone cord is long enough to permit the connection of the TTY and the telephone receiver. **ADAAG: 1998 4.31 & ADA Standards: 2010 704**

L   Portable TTY Shelves

In addition to public TTYs, shelves, electrical outlets, and TTY outlets are required at some banks of public telephones.

L1 Where a bank of telephones in the interior of a building includes three or more public pay phones, provide a shelf and an electrical outlet for at least one public pay telephone at the bank of phones to accommodate portable TTYs. **ADAAG: 1998 4.1 & ADA Standards: 2010 217**
Exception: Shelves and outlets are not required at a bank of telephones where a permanent TTY has been installed. ADA Standards: 2010 217 (NEW)

L2 Provide a shelf that is large enough to accommodate a portable TTY. **ADAAG: 1998 4.31 & ADA Standards: 2010 704**

L3 Install shelves with a 6in. (150mm) minimum vertical clearance in the area where the TTY is to be placed. **ADA Standards: 2010 704 (NEW)**

L4 Install shelves and outlets for TTYs within or adjacent to telephone enclosures where the TTYs are located. **ADAAG: 1998 4.31 & ADA Standards: 2010 704**

L5 Ensure that the telephone handset can be placed

flush on the shelf. **ADA Standards: 2010 704** (NEW)

M TTY Signs

In buildings and on floors where TTYs are required, signs must be installed to indicate the locations of TTYs.

M1 Identify public TTYs by the International Symbol of TTY. **ADAAG: 1998 4.30 & ADA Standards: 2010 216**
See Figure PT.5

PT.5   The International Symbol of TTY

M2 At all banks of public pay telephones that do not contain a public TTY, install directional signs indicating the location of the nearest public TTY. **ADAAG: 1998 4.30 & ADA Standards: 2010 216**

M3 Where signs provide directions leading to public pay telephones, include directions leading to public TTYs. **ADA Standards: 2010 216** (NEW)

M4 Include the International Symbol of TTY on signs providing directions to TTYs. **ADAAG: 1998 4.30 & ADA Standards: 2010 216, 703**

TA Tables & Seating

A	Number and Location	191
B	Dining and Work Surfaces	192
C	Clear Floor Space	193
D	Legroom	193
E	Benches	194

This chapter covers the requirements for providing accessible built-in furnishings and equipment (such as tables with fixed seating and benches) where these furnishings and equipment are provided for the public. The ADA Standards requirements for built-in furnishings apply to all types of public buildings including restaurants, banks, libraries, motels, stores, and service areas in other businesses.

Additional information about making the features of specific types of facilities accessible is provided in the chapters in **Special Purpose Areas.** For example, requirements for sales and service counters and checkout aisles, which must meet different requirements, are covered in **BU Businesses.**

All people should have access to built-in work and dining surfaces and seating that is provided for customers, employees, and visitors. These include conference rooms and work surfaces for people other than employees (such as check writing counters and dining surfaces including booths, tables, bars, counters and other surfaces provided for eating and drinking). In the past, built-in work and dining surfaces and seating generally have not had sufficient maneuvering space for people who use wheelchairs or for people with other mobility limitations. Built-in benches have also lacked adequate clear floor space and adequate support for assisting people in transferring from wheelchairs.

A Number and Location

People who use wheelchairs and people who have mobility disabilities should have access to all types of work and dining surfaces, tables, and other built-in furnishings that are provided. In addition, people should have options and choices for using built-in tables, seating and other types of furnishings.

Design for All: The Best Path Forward — Dr. Arvid E. Osterberg

A1 **Provide a variety of seating types, widths and heights, including some with armrests and back support, in all public seating and waiting areas.** ca

Seating accommodating various needs ca

A2 **Ensure that at least one seat in each seating cluster is fully accessible, including clear floor space for transferring on and off seating.** ca

A3 In each room or area where seating or standing space is provided at dining or work surfaces, ensure that at least 5%, but not less than one, of each type of sitting and standing space is accessible. **ADAAG: 1998 4.1 & ADA Standards: 2010 226**
Increasing the number of accessible sitting and standing spaces provided to 10-20% of the total is preferred. ca

A4 Distribute accessible dining and work surfaces throughout the area where they are included so that all people have options. **ADA Standards: 2010 226 (New)**

A5 Ensure that accessible furnishings are adjacent to accessible routes. **ADAAG: 1998 4.1 & ADA Standards: 2010 226**

Wheelchair-accessible seating with open end, back support, and clear floor space for transfer ca

B   Dining and Work Surfaces

People should be able to comfortably use accessible dining and work surfaces.

B1 Ensure that the tops of dining surfaces and work surfaces are between 28in. (710mm) minimum and 34in. (865mm) maximum above the floor. **ADAAG: 1998 4.32 & ADA Standards: 2010 902   See TA-D**

B2 Ensure that the height of the legroom under a dining surface or a work surface is a minimum of 27in (685mm). **ADAAG: 1998 4.32 & ADA Standards: 2010 306**
A legroom height of 30in. (760mm) is preferred. ca

B3 Where children are the primary users of the furniture, ensure that the tops of dining and work surfaces are 26in. (660mm) minimum and 30in. (760mm) maximum above the floor. **ADAAG: 1998 4.32 & ADA Standards: 2010 902**
Exception: Where the furnishings are used by children 5 and younger, the height and forward approach requirements do not apply. ADA Standards: 2010 902 (New)
See Figure TA.1

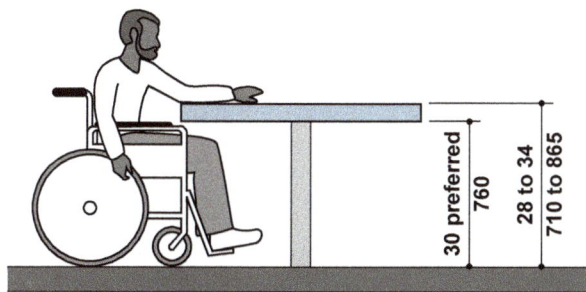

TA.1   Height of a wheelchair accessible dining or work surface

C   Clear Floor Space

Where accessible built-in furnishings are available, the clear floor space adjacent to the furniture should be adequate for approaching and maneuvering.

C1   Provide a minimum clear floor space of 30in. (760mm) by 48in. (1220mm) for each accessible space to accommodate a single, stationary wheelchair. **ADAAG: 1998 4.2, 4.32 & ADA Standards: 2010 305, 902**

C2   Configure clear floor space for a forward approach to dining and work surfaces. **ADA Standards: 2010 902 (New)**

C3   Ensure that one fully unobstructed side of the clear floor space overlaps or adjoins an accessible route. **ADAAG: 1998 4.2 & ADA Standards: 2010 305**

C4   If a clear floor space is confined on all or part of three sides or is in an alcove, provide additional maneuvering spaces as follows:
   a. If a forward approach clear floor space extends more than 24in. (610mm) into an alcove, provide a 36in. (915mm) wide minimum clear floor space in the alcove.
   b. If a parallel approach clear floor space extends more than 15in. (380mm) into an alcove, provide clear floor space in the alcove with a minimum length of 60in. (1525mm). **ADAAG: 1998 4.2 & ADA Standards: 2010 305**

Refer to Figures RT.26 and RT.27

C5   Ensure that the slope of the clear floor space does not exceed 1:48 (approx. 2%) in any direction.

ADA Standards: 2010 305 (Modified-Less-Restrictive)

C6   Ensure that there are no level changes in the clear floor space. **ADAAG: 1998 4.3 & ADA Standards: 2010 305**

C7   Ensure that accessible routes are maintained all the way around all table and seating areas and clusters.

D   Legroom

People need to have adequate legroom under tables, counters, desks, and other surfaces to approach them and to sit at and use them comfortably. Adequate leg room is a safety factor for wheelchair users who may not detect potentially dangerous conditions where they might be bruised, cut, or scraped by an obstruction.

To ensure that adequate space is provided under surfaces, fixtures, and other obstructions (for accommodating the height and angle of wheelchair foot and leg rests), ADA Standards divides the legroom under surfaces into toe clearance and knee clearance.

When you are determining the appropriate space for legroom, consider the space three dimensionally. The ADA Standards includes requirements for the width, height, and depth of toe clearance and knee clearance. Legroom coincides with required clear floor space where ADA Standards allows knee and toe clearance to be included as part of that space.

D1   Ensure that the space provided for legroom is unobstructed. Legroom under a table must be 27in. (685mm) high minimum. **ADAAG: 1998 4.32 & ADA Standards: 2010 306**
   A height of 30in. (760mm) is preferred.
See Figure TA.2

D2   Ensure that legroom under a table measures 30in. (760mm) wide minimum. **ADAAG: 1998 4.32 & ADA Standards: 2010 306**
   A width of 36in. (915mm) is preferred.

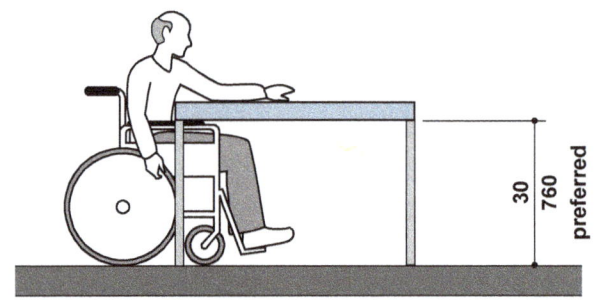

TA.2 Unobstructed legroom under a table

See Figure TA.3

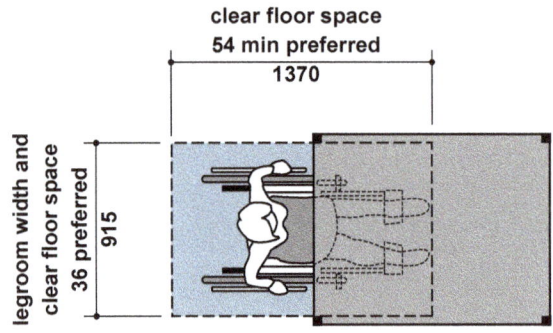

TA.3 *Preferred* minimum legroom width under a table

D3 Where a table is in an alcove that is 24in. (610mm) deep or deeper, or is bounded on both sides by walls or other objects, ensure that the width of the legroom measures 36in. (915mm) wide from side to side. **ADAAG: 1998 4.2 & ADA Standards: 2010 305**

D4 Ensure that legroom provides adequate toe clearance. Toe clearance
   a. includes the vertical space from the floor to 9in. (230mm) above the floor, and
   b. extends horizontally under the table at least 17in. (430mm) measured from the front edge of the table. **ADA Standards: 2010 306 (NEW)**

Refer to Figures RT.30 and RT.31

D5 Ensure that legroom provides adequate knee clearance. Knee clearance extends horizontally, measured from the front of the table
   a. at least 8in. (205mm) deep at a height of 27in. (685mm) above the floor, and
   b. at least 11in. (280mm) deep at a height of 9in. (230mm) above the floor. **ADA Standards: 2010 306 (NEW)**

Refer to Figure RT.31

D6 *Legroom may extend any distance under a table and additional space for legroom is preferred.* **Ca**

D7 Only a maximum of 25in. (635mm) under a table measured from the front edge of the table can also be part of any required clear floor space. **ADA Standards: 2010 306 (NEW)** Ensure that the table overlaps required clear floor space no more than 25in. (635mm). **ADA Standards: 2010 306 (NEW)**

D8 Where the knee clearance under a table must be reduced at an angle because of angled vertical supports or other obstructions, taper the depth of the vertical knee clearance at a rate of 1in. (25mm) horizontally for each 6in. (150mm) vertical rise. **ADA Standards: 2010 306 (NEW)**

D9 Where people need to reach over a table to access controls or objects, ensure that the horizontal depth of the legroom is at least equal to the reach length above the table to a maximum of 25in. (635mm). **ADA Standards: 2010 306 (NEW)** See RR Reach Ranges

E Benches

Accessible benches must be large enough and sturdy enough to ensure that people can transfer safely to them from a wheelchair. Accessible benches should also provide back support.

Where benches that are attached to walls are provided in dressing, fitting, shower and other rooms, consider providing grab bars on walls adjacent to the benches to assist people transferring.

E1 In rooms and areas where benches are provided, ensure that at least 5%, but not less than one, is accessible. **ADAAG: 1998 4.1 & ADA Standards: 2010 226**

Increasing the number of accessible benches to 10-20% of the total is preferred. **Ca**

The requirements for numbers of benches in specific locations (such as dressing, fitting, and locker rooms) may vary. **See DS Dressing Rooms** or other applicable chapters in *Design for All*.

E2 **Distribute accessible benches throughout areas where benches are included so that people have a range of seating options.**

E3 Configure clear floor space at benches for a parallel approach to the end of bench seats. **ADAAG: 1998 4.37 & ADA Standards: 2010 305, 903**

E4 **Where space permits, position the bench within the clear floor space so that the clear floor space extends 12in. (305mm) minimum behind the back of the bench to make maneuvering and transferring easier.**

See Figure TA.4

E5 Ensure that the top of an accessible bench seat is between 17in. (430mm) and 19in. (485mm) above the floor. **ADAAG: 1998 4.37 & ADA Standards: 2010 903**

E6 Ensure that accessible bench seats are
  a. 20in. (510mm) minimum to 24in. (610mm) maximum deep (from front to back), and
  b. 42in. (1065mm) minimum long. **ADAAG: 1998 4.37 & ADA Standards: 2010 903**

E7 Provide
  a. permanently installed back support that is a minimum of 42in. (1065mm) long, or
  b. attach the bench to a wall that provides back support. **ADA Standards: 2010 903 (NEW)**

E8 Ensure that the back support
  a. begins no more than 2in. (51mm) vertically, **ADAAG: 1998 4.37 & ADA Standards: 2010 903**
  b. 2.5in (64mm) maximum horizontally from the seat, **ADA Standards: 2010 903 (NEW)** and
  c. continues to at least 18in. (455mm) above the seat. **ADAAG: 1998 4.37 & ADA Standards: 2010 903**

E9 Do not install grab bars on the walls behind benches where people lean for back support. **ADA Standards: 2010 903 (NEW)**

E10 Ensure that the materials used for benches can support a vertical or horizontal force of 250 lbs. (1112N) applied at any point on the seat, fastener, mounting device, or supporting structure. **ADAAG: 1998 4.37 & ADA Standards: 2010 903**

E11 Wherever benches are installed in wet locations (such as locker or shower rooms) ensure that the surface of the bench seat is slip resistant and does not accumulate water. **ADAAG: 1998 4.37 & ADA Standards: 2010 903**

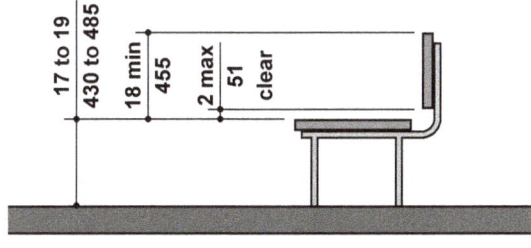

elevation view

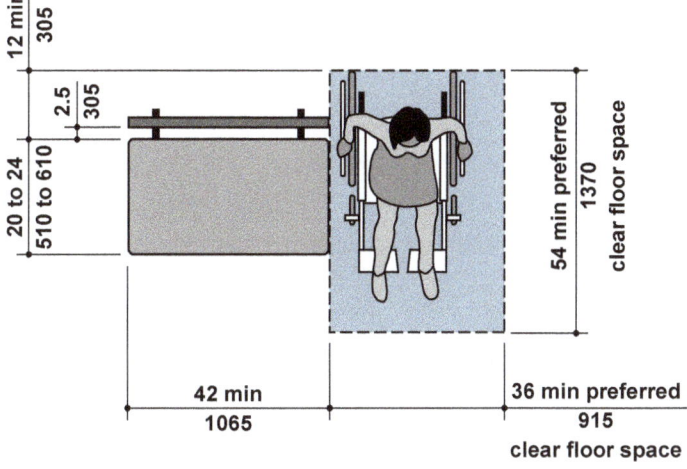

plan view

TA.4 An accessible bench

E12 Provide rounded corners on the ends of benches to reduce the hazard of sharp projecting surfaces. ca

Wheelchair-accessible picnic table next to accessible route ca

VS Vending/Self-serve

A	Number and Location	196
B	Clear Floor Space	197
C	Reach Ranges	198
D	Approach and Clearances	199
E	Controls and Operating Mechanisms	199
F	Automatic Teller Machines and Fare Vending Machines: Input Controls	199
G	Automatic Teller Machines and Fare Vending Machines: Output	200
H	Automatic Teller Machines and Fare Vending Machines: Display Screen	200
I	Automatic Teller Machines and Fare Vending Machines: Receipts and Verifications	200
J	Fare Cards and Tokens	201
K	Other Interactive Transaction Machines	201
L	Washers and Dryers: Number and Location	201
M	Washers and Dryers: Clear floor space	201
N	Washers and Dryers:Doors and Controls	201

Self-service machines and depositories share common features including buttons (for initiating and processing transactions), dispensers (for receipts, currency, fare cards, tokens, and products), and slots (for inserting items such as deposit envelopes, bill payments, library books, and mail).

To be accessible, self-service equipment must be located on accessible routes and must be configured so that controls and openings are easy to reach and have sufficient legroom where necessary. In addition, audible, visual, and tactile controls must be provided where appropriate.

This chapter covers specific types of self-service machines (such as Automatic Teller Machines [ATMs], fare machines, change machines, and vending machines) and depositories (such as bank deposit boxes and mailboxes). The chapter also includes requirements for washers and dryers.

A Number and Location

A1 Where self-service machines or depositories are provided, ensure that at least one of each type (including vending machines, change machines, automatic teller machines, and fare vending, collection, or adjustment machines) is accessible.
ADAAG: 1998 4.1 & ADA Standards: 2010 220, 228

A2 Where mailboxes are provided in an interior location, ensure that at least 5%, but not less than one, of each type is accessible. **ADA Standards: 2010 228 (NEW)**

A3 Where waste receptacles are provided, ensure that at least one of each type is accessible. **ADAAG: 1998 4.34 & ADA Standards: 2010 220**

A4 Locate accessible self-service machines and depositories on an accessible route. **ADAAG: 1998 4.1 4.34 & ADA Standards: 2010 220, 228, 707**

A5 Plan the location and arrangement of ATMs (and other machines that include personal information during a transaction) to provide the same degree of visual privacy to all people using them. **ADA Standards: 2010 707 (NEW)**

A6 Locate accessible fare vending machines and gates close to accessible parking, routes, and elevators. ca

B Clear Floor Space

If a self-service machine or depository is installed in an alcove, provide additional clear floor space for maneuvering. Drive-up-only self-service machines and depositories do not need to conform to the requirements for clear floor space.

B1 Locate self-service machines and depositories so that one fully unobstructed side of the clear floor space overlaps or adjoins an accessible route. **ADAAG: 1998 4.1 & ADA Standards: 2010 707, 305**

B2 Provide a minimum clear floor space that
   a. **measures 30in. (760mm) by 48in. (1220mm),**
       36in (915mm) by 54in (1370mm) min preferred, ca and
   b. is positioned to allow either forward or parallel approach. **ADAAG: 1998 4.34, 4.27 & ADA Standards: 2010 707, 305**

See Figure VS.1

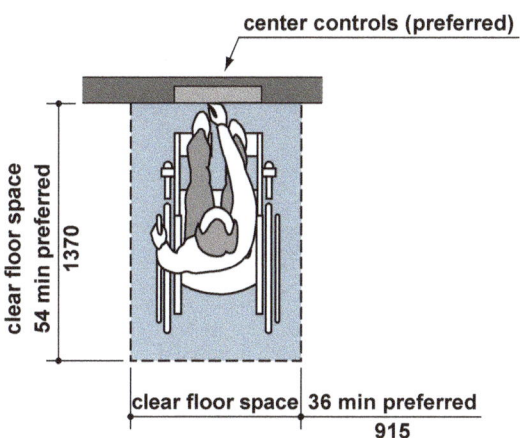

VS.1 **Preferred** minimum clear floor space for a forward approach to reach controls

B3 If a self-service machine or depository is located in an alcove that is 24in. (610mm) or more deep and positioned for a forward approach, provide a minimum clear floor space width of 36in. (915mm) in the alcove. **ADAAG: 1998 4.2 & ADA Standards: 2010 707, 305**

See Figure VS.2

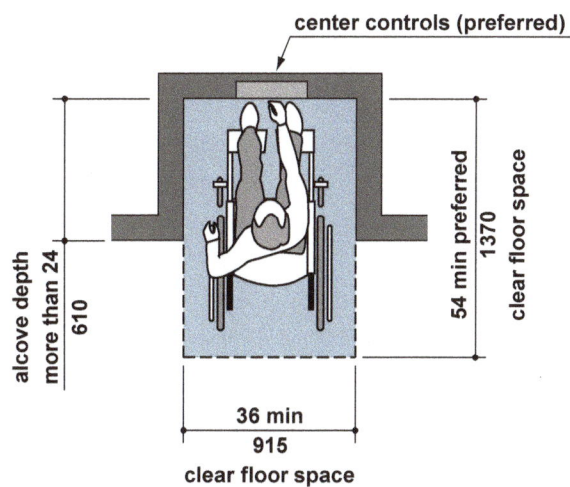

VS.2 **Preferred** minimum clear floor space for a forward approach in a deep alcove to reach controls

B4 If a self-service machine or depository is located in an alcove that is 15in. (380mm) or more deep and is positioned for a parallel approach, provide a minimum clear floor space width of 60in. (1525mm) in the alcove. 67in (1702mm) min preferred ca **ADAAG: 1998 4.2 & ADA Standards: 2010 707, 305**

See Figure VS.3

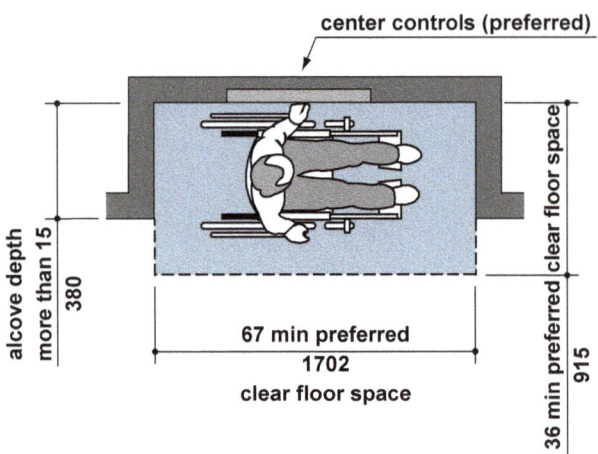

VS.3 **Preferred** minimum clear floor space for a parallel approach in a deep alcove to reach controls

B5 **Provide for a parallel approach and side reach where free-standing or built-in self-service machines or depositories do not have clear space under them.** ca

C Reach Ranges

Determine the appropriate height for operating mechanisms, controls and drop slots based on the type of reach required and any obstructions that may impede the use of self-service machines and depositories.

Requirements for height and reach of controls do not apply where the use of special equipment dictates otherwise, or where electrical and communications systems receptacles are not normally intended for use by building occupants. Drive-up-only self-service machines or depositories do not need to conform to the requirements for height and reach, though controls need to be operable by persons with limited dexterity. **See VS-E.**

C1 For a front reach with no obstructions, locate controls and depository openings 48in. (1220mm) maximum and 15in. (380mm) minimum above the floor. **ADAAG: 1998 4.34, 4.27 & ADA Standards: 2010 308**

See Figure VS.4

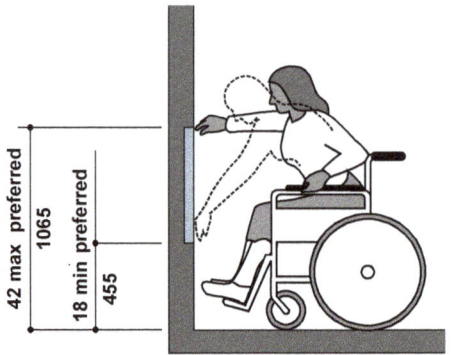

VS.4 **Preferred** unobstructed front reach range

C2 **Wherever possible, locate controls and depository openings between 36in. (915mm) and 42in. (1065mm) above the floor.** ca

C3 For a forward approach where there is an obstruction, locate controls within the following ranges:
  a. where an obstruction is 20in. (510mm) or less, provide controls at a maximum high front reach of 48in. (1220mm);
   A height of 43in. (1090mm) is preferred. ca
   or
Refer to Figure RR.3
  b. where an obstruction is between 20in. (510mm) and 25in. (635mm), provide controls at a maximum high front reach of 44in. (1120mm). **ADAAG: 1998 4.34, 4.27 & ADA Standards: 2010 308**
   A height of 43in. (1090mm) is preferred. ca
Refer to Figure RR.4

C4 For a side reach with no obstructions or an obstruction that is 10in. (255mm) deep maximum, locate controls and mechanisms between 15in. (380mm) minimum and 48in. (1220mm) maximum above the floor. **43in (1090mm) max preferred** ca **ADA Standards: 2010 308 (New)**
See Figure VS.5

C5 For a side reach where there is an obstruction, ensure that the obstruction is less than 34in. (865mm) high and less than 24in. (610mm) deep. **ADA Standards: 2010 308 (New)**
See Figure VS.6

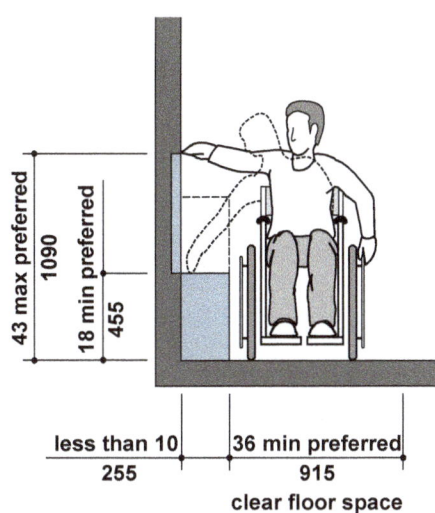

VS.5 Preferred reach range for an unobstructed or minimally obstructed side reach

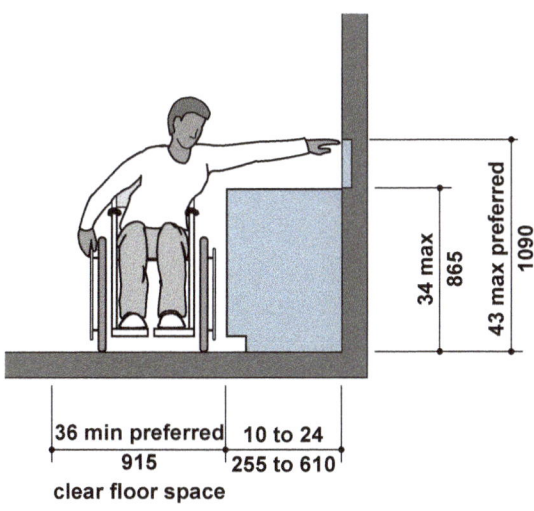

VS.6 Preferred reach range for an obstructed side reach

C6 For a side reach where there is an obstruction that exceeds 10in. (255mm) but is no more than 24in. (610mm) deep, locate controls and objects no higher than 46in. (1170mm). **43in (1090mm) max preferred** ca **ADA Standards: 2010 308 (NEW)**

D Approach and Clearances

Where the approach to a self-service machine or depository is from the front, and people need to pull up to use the equipment, provide adequate legroom.

D1 Provide adequate legroom, including knee and toe clearance, under a self-service machines and depositories. **ADAAG: 1998 4.2 & ADA Standards: 2010 602, 306** See RT Routes and Spaces, RT-Q.

E Controls and Operating Mechanisms

E1 Provide controls and mechanisms that
  a. are operable with one hand;
  b. do not require tight grasping, pinching, or twisting of the wrist; and
  c. can be operated with a force less than or equal to 5 lbs. (22.2N). **ADAAG: 1998 4.27 & ADA Standards: 2010 309, 707**

F Automatic Teller Machines and Fare Vending Machines: Input Controls

Ensure that all keys used to operate an ATM or a fare vending machine have both text and tactile information. The touch areas of video display screens are not required to include tactile elements.

F1 Ensure that
  a. key surfaces not on active areas of display screens are raised above the surrounding surfaces, and
  b. membrane keys are tactilely discernible from surrounding surfaces and adjacent keys. **ADA Standards: 2010 707 (NEW)**

F2 Where numeric keys are used, ensure that
  a. keys are arranged in an ascending or descending 12-key telephone keypad layout, and
  b. the number five key is tactilely distinct. **ADA Standards: 2010 707 (NEW)**

F3 Where function keys are used, ensure that
  a. keys contrast visually from background surfaces, and
  b. characters and symbols on function keys contrast visually from key surfaces

(dark-on-light or light-on-dark). **ADA Standards: 2010 707 (New)**

F4 Mark function keys with tactile characters as follows:
  a. enter or proceed key: raised circle O
  b. clear or correct key: raised left arrow ←
  c. cancel key: raised ✖
  d. add value key: raised plus sign ✚
  e. decrease value key: raised minus sign ▬
  ADA Standards: 2010 707 (New)

G Automatic Teller Machines and Fare Vending Machines: Output

The 1998 ADAAG (section 4.35) requires that all information and operating instructions for ATMs be provided in a form that enables people with visual limitations to use them independently. The 2010 ADA Standards requires ATMs to be speech enabled. The speech utilized by the machine may be recorded or digitized human speech or it may be synthesized. Advertisements are not required to be audible unless they provide information that can be used during a transaction. We provide guidelines for speech-enabled ATMs below.

G1 Provide audible instructions through a standard audio mini-jack, a telephone handset, a wireless transmission system, or another mechanism that is readily available to all customers. **ADA Standards: 2010 707 (New)**

G2 Provide an audible beep to indicate that personal identification numbers have been entered. **ADA Standards: 2010 707 (New)**

G3 Provide speech output for all displayed text and labels, including information that is displayed as a picture or graphic. When speech output is provided, allow for the message to be repeated. **ADA Standards: 2010 707 (New)**

G4 Ensure that machines provide both visual and audible instructions for operation including
  a. all transaction prompts within each operation,
  b. verification of all user inputs,
  c. instructions for experienced users to expedite the transaction after initiation, and
  d. orientation and assistance information for inexperienced users about the physical features of the machine, operational options, and details for each function.
  ADA Standards: 2010 707 (New)

G5 Ensure that speech can be interrupted and that people can request that speech be repeated. **ADA Standards: 2010 707 (New)**

G6 Provide Braille instruction for initiating speech transactions. **ADA Standards: 2010 707 (New) See SN Signs.**

H Automatic Teller Machines and Fare Vending Machines: Display Screen

H1 Ensure that wherever visual screens are provided (such as at ATMs), they are visible from either a sitting or standing position. **ca**

H2 Ensure that any visual display screen provided is visible from a point located 40in. (1015mm) above the center of the clear floor space in front of the machine. **ADA Standards: 2010 707 (New)**

H3 Ensure that characters displayed on the screen meet the following requirements:
  a. sans serif font,
  b. 3/16in. (4.8mm) minimum in height based on the uppercase letter **I**, and
  c. characters contrast with their background (either light-on-dark or dark-on-light).
  ADA Standards: 2010 707 (New)

I Automatic Teller Machines and Fare Vending Machines: Receipts and Verifications

I 1 Where receipts are available, speech output must provide the following:
  a. balance inquiry information,
  b. error messages, and
  c. other information provided on the receipt for confirmation. **ADA Standards: 2010 707 (New)**

Exception: Audible information is not required for

the machine location, date and time of transaction, customer account number, or machine identifier. **ADA Standards: 2010 707 (New)**

I 2 When storage or receptacles for envelopes, waste paper, or other purposes are provided, ensure that they are within appropriate reach ranges and that there is appropriate clear floor space. **ADAAG: 1998 4.1, 4.34 & ADA Standards: 2010 220, 308** See RR Reach Ranges.

J Fare Cards and Tokens

J1 Provide fare cards that have one distinctive corner so that people who rely on tactile cues can position cards properly before inserting them into a machine. ca

J2 Provide perforated tokens that allow people to distinguish more readily between tokens and common coins. ca

K Other Interactive Transaction Machines

As of 2010, interactive transaction machines are not required to include voice output. However, such devices used by the federal government or government agencies may need to meet certain guidelines under Section 508 of the Rehabilitation Act.

In the future, more types of public interactive machines (such as information kiosks) may be required to be accessible. Check with the Access Board for the most current guidelines. **See References.**

K1 Ensure that all interactive transaction machines and devices are accessible to the maximum extent possible. ca

L Washers and Dryers: Number and Location

Where self-service clothes washers and dryers are provided as elements of common areas in transient lodging or residential facilities or as part of a business (such as a laundromat) ensure that washer and dryers meet accessibility requirements.

L1 Provide accessible washers and dryers as follows:
   a. at least one accessible washer where 3 or fewer washers are installed,
   b. at least two accessible washers where more than 3 washers are installed,
   c. at least one accessible dryer where 3 or fewer dryers are installed, and
   d. at least two accessible dryers where more than 3 dryers are installed. **ADA Standards: 2010 214 (New)**

M Washers and Dryers: Clear floor space

Clear floor space must be provided for unobstructed access to washers and dryers.

M1 Provide a minimum clear floor space in front of each accessible washer or dryer that is
   a. 30in. (760mm) by 48in. (1220mm), and
   b. configured for a parallel approach. **ADA Standards: 2010 305, 611 (New)**

M2 Position the clear floor space so that it is centered on the washer or dryer. **ADA Standards: 2010 611 (New)**

M3 Ensure that one fully unobstructed side of the clear floor space overlaps or adjoins an accessible route. **ADA Standards: 2010 305, 611 (New)**

N Washers and Dryers: Doors and Controls

N1 On front loading machines, locate the laundry compartment door 15in. (380mm) minimum and 36in. (915mm) maximum above the floor. **ADA Standards: 2010 611 (New)**

N2 On top loading machines, locate the laundry compartment door 36in. (915mm) maximum above the floor. **ADA Standards: 2010 611 (New)**

N3 Ensure that all operating controls, lint screens, and detergent and bleach compartments
   a. meet the requirements for controls in **VS-E**, and
   b. are within appropriate reach ranges. **See RR Reach Ranges. ADA Standards: 2010 308, 309, 611 (New)**

Chapters in Specific Use Areas

HP	Historic Preservation	204
WA	Work Areas	208
AA	Assembly Areas	210
LB	Libraries	216
RS	Restaurants	219
BU	Businesses	222
DS	Dressing, Fitting, and Locker Rooms	228
TL	Transient Lodging	230
DU	Dwelling Units	235
MC	Medical Care	241
KT	Kitchens	244
SG	Storage	247
AB	ABA Requirements	249

Section 5. Specific Use Areas

The chapters in this section cover the following:
1) buildings and facilities that are designed and used for specific types of activities (such as stores, hotels, and medical care facilities), and
2) areas in buildings that are used for specific purposes (such as storage and dressing rooms)

All establishments that serve the public must provide access to their facilities, goods, and services in a manner that allows equivalent experiences and participation for everyone. This includes restaurants; convenience, specialty and department stores; hotels and motels; and other buildings and spaces that are open to the public.

If it is not possible to ensure that an existing building is fully accessible, consider other alternatives for providing goods and services to people. Title III of the ADA stresses four priority areas in order of importance for removing barriers and improving accessibility:

Priority 1: accessibility of routes, including entrances, doors and vertical access (stairs, ramps, elevators, escalators)

Priority 2: accessibility of goods and services, including alternatives for providing access to goods and services where altering the structure is not possible (for example, when there is no elevator and second floor spaces are not accessible)

Priority 3: accessibility of restrooms

Priority 4: additional accessibility throughout the building and site, such as interior features, furnishings, equipment, floor surfaces, and lighting

The chapters in this section provide specific recommendations for various types of buildings and spaces. The requirements in the other four sections of *Design for All* also apply to all buildings and spaces in Specific Use Areas.

Please note that we do not cover several specific types of facilities and services that are, or may be, covered by ADA Standards, including

- recreation facilities and play areas
- judicial, legislative and regulatory facilities
- detention areas and correctional facilities
- transportation
- HUD housing
- electronic and information technology (Refer to Section 508 of the Rehabilitation Act) See References.

Many of the general accessibility guidelines covered in *Design for All* apply to these types of facilities and services. However the Access Board provides additional, specific guidelines in the ADA Standards and in other publications.

For additional information on these types of facilities and services, call your regional Disability and Business Technical Assistance Center or the Access Board, or visit the Access Board website at www.access-board.gov for information and publications.

HP Historic Preservation

A	Planning and Assessment	204
B	Levels of Compliance	205
C	Exterior Routes	206
D	Public Entrances	206
E	Interior Routes	206
F	Toilet Rooms and Bathrooms	206
G	Services, Displays, and Exhibits	207

Historic buildings and sites that are open to the public must meet accessibility requirements under the ADA. Making historic buildings accessible presents unique challenges because modifications to historic buildings and sites should not compromise historic character. Unfortunately, solutions that compromise the historic character of buildings are commonplace. However, with proper analysis and well-informed decisions, most historic buildings and sites can be brought into compliance with the ADA without negative impacts.

The intent of the ADA requirements is to provide access to historic buildings and sites for people with disabilities while allowing preservationists to maintain, to the greatest extent possible, the historic character of the site. The central issue is not whether the structures should be made accessible, but how they should be made accessible and to what extent.

Since there is a need to balance historic preservation and accessibility requirements, the ADA Standards includes allowances for qualified historic buildings and sites where meeting all of the normal ADA Standards standards would threaten the historic characteristics. It is important to note that any exceptions to ADA Standards requirements that allow a lower level of accessibility (based on the historic importance of a building or site) are limited to qualified historic buildings and sites; See HP-B, Levels of Compliance, for additional information.

This chapter provides a process for assessing historic buildings and sites, discusses the application of ADA Standards to historic buildings and sites, and lists exceptions where full compliance is not required.

A Planning and Assessment

If you are making changes to a historic building or site to provide a greater level of accessibility, or if alterations to a historic building or site require you to meet accessibility standards, a thorough assessment of the existing conditions and proper planning are critical.

A1 Work with consultants who have recognized expertise in both accessible design and historic preservation. It may be necessary to work with more than one consultant to gather the appropriate expertise. ca

A2 Identify, evaluate, and articulate the historic significance of the property. ca

A3 Determine which accessibility requirements apply to your project. For example, a higher level of accessibility is required in alterations to primary function areas in existing buildings than is required for barrier removal in existing buildings. The purpose and use of the building may also be a factor in determining the level of accessibility required under ADA Standards. ca

A4 Conduct a thorough assessment of existing conditions to determine accessibility problems and deficiencies. Focus on priority areas in the following order:
   a. Priority 1: accessibility of routes, including entrances, doors and vertical access (stairs, ramps, elevators, escalators)
   b. Priority 2: accessibility of goods and services, including alternatives for providing access to goods and services where altering the structure is not possible (for example, when there is no elevator and second floor spaces are not accessible)
   c. Priority 3: accessibility of restrooms
   d. Priority 4: additional accessibility throughout the building and site, such as interior features, furnishings, equipment, floor surfaces, and lighting ca

A5 Work with consultants to identify and analyze exemplary solutions that have been implemented in buildings and sites similar to yours.

A6 Solicit representative community input from people with disabilities. Include people who use wheelchairs and people who have mobility, vision, and/or hearing limitations. Contact local disability groups to identify people who may be willing to help with an accessibility review.

A7 Prioritize accessibility goals and establish criteria for evaluating alternatives. Develop a short and long term plan for improving accessibility. Work with a qualified architect to develop and select alternatives for accomplishing accessibility goals. Evaluate each alternative based on
   a. benefits to users with disabilities,
   b. effects of modifications on the historic character of the building,
   c. impact of changes on staff and employees,
   d. initial cost and cost of maintenance, and
   e. safety considerations.

A8 Develop viable options and obtain sketches of proposed design solutions. This is particularly important for changes involving site grading and building entrances.

A9 When appropriate, review options with your State's Historic Preservation Officer.

A10 Select the best solution and choose a qualified contractor to implement the solution. While initial cost is always a factor, obtaining quality workmanship by a contractor familiar with historic preservation and/or accessibility issues may be the most cost effective approach in the long run.

A11 Maintain a high degree of supervision to ensure quality control during construction.

B Levels of Compliance

The ADA Standards requirements for historic buildings and sites are exactly the same as the ADA Standards requirements for existing buildings and sites, unless the historic building or site is approved as qualified to follow the ADA Standards's lower level of requirements for qualified historic buildings and sites.

The ADA Standards states that "Where the State Historic Preservation Officer (SHPO) or Advisory Council on Historic Preservation determines that compliance with the requirements for accessible routes, ramps, entrances, or toilet facilities would threaten or destroy the historic significance of the building or facility, the exceptions for alterations to qualified historic buildings or facilities for that element shall be permitted to apply." **ADA Standards: 2010 202 (also see 1998 4.1)**

B1 The following two conditions must be met for historic buildings and sites to be qualified to follow the ADA Standards's lower level of requirements;
   a. the historic building or site must be listed in, or be eligible for listing in, the National Register of Historic Places (or be designated as historic under an appropriate state or local law), and
   b. the State's Historic Preservation Officer (or Advisory Council on Historic Preservation) must approve the owner's request to follow the ADA Standards's lower level of requirements for historic buildings and sites. **ADAAG: 1998 4.1 & ADA Standards: 2010 202**

B2 Ensure that additions to existing buildings meet the requirements for new construction. **ADAAG: 1998 4.1.7 & ADA Standards: 2010 202**

B3 When alterations affect or could affect the accessibility of (or access to) an area containing a primary function, ensure that areas serving the altered area are accessible to the maximum degree possible, including
   a. the path of travel to the altered area,
   b. restrooms,
   c. telephones, and
   d. drinking fountains. **ADAAG: 1998 4.1 & ADA Standards: 2010 202**

B4 Where existing spaces are altered, follow all requirements for new construction to the maximum extent technically feasible. Where alterations would threaten or destroy the historic significance of the building or site, review options with the State Historic Preservation Officer or Advisory Council on Historic Preservation. **ADAAG: 1998 4.1 & ADA Standards: 2010 202**

B5 Where buildings are altered, ensure that all elements or spaces that are part of the alteration and that can be made accessible are made accessible within the scope of the alteration. **ADA Standards: 2010 202 (NEW)**

B6 Ensure that alterations do not decrease accessibility of a building below the requirements for new construction. **ADA Standards: 2010 202 (NEW)**

See RT Routes and Spaces, RT-C for an explanation of the limits on the cost and scope of alterations required to areas serving altered primary function areas.

C   Exterior Routes

In general, the ADA Standards requires that accessible routes connect site access points (including sidewalks, public transportation stops, and parking lots) to accessible entrances.

C1 In qualified historic buildings or sites, provide at least one accessible route from a site arrival point to an accessible entrance. **ADAAG: 1998 4.1 & ADA Standards: 2010 206**

D   Public Entrances

Typically, 60% of public entrances are required to be accessible. In qualified historic buildings, entrances must meet the following minimum requirements.

D1 In qualified historic buildings or sites, provide at least one public entrance that meets the requirements for accessible entrances in new construction. **ADAAG: 1998 4.1 & ADA Standards: 2010 202**

D2 In qualified historic buildings or sites, where no entrance generally used by the public can be made accessible, provide an alternative accessible entrance. Ensure that the alternative accessible entrance is unlocked or that a locked accessible entrance is monitored for traffic or includes a notification system so that visitors can request access. **ADAAG: 1998 4.1 & ADA Standards: 2010 206**

D3 In qualified historic buildings or sites, where alternative accessible entrances are provided, install directional signs at the primary public entrances notifying people of alternate accessible entrance locations. **ADAAG: 1998 4.1 & ADA Standards: 2010 206**

E   Interior Routes

If possible, accessible routes should be provided to all accessible levels of a building. In qualified historic buildings, interior routes must meet at least the following requirements.

E1 In qualified historic buildings or sites, provide accessible routes from at least one accessible entrance to all publicly used spaces on at least the level of the accessible entrance. **ADAAG: 1998 4.1 & ADA Standards: 2010 206**

F   Toilet Rooms and Bathrooms

If space or other structural constraints limit the possibility of making all restrooms accessible, a single-user restroom is permitted as an alternative to providing separate, fully accessible men's and women's restrooms. However, it is always preferable to make all public restrooms accessible.

In qualified historic buildings, toilet rooms and bathrooms must meet the following minimum requirements.

F1 In qualified historic buildings or sites, where restrooms are provided, ensure that at least one restroom for each sex is accessible to the maximum extent feasible. **ADAAG: 1998 4.1 & ADA Standards: 2010 202, 213 See the Restrooms and Bathrooms section.**

F2 In qualified historic buildings or sites, where a single-user toilet room is provided, ensure that it contains at least the following accessible features:
- a. one toilet,
- b. one lavatory, and
- c. a door with a privacy latch. **ADAAG: 1998 4.1 & ADA Standards: 2010 213**

F3 In qualified historic buildings or sites, where a single-user bathroom is provided, ensure that it contains at least the following accessible features:
- a. one toilet, **ADAAG: 1998 4.1 & ADA Standards: 2010 213**
- b. one lavatory, **ADAAG: 1998 4.1 & ADA Standards: 2010 213**
- c. a door with a privacy latch, **ADAAG: 1998 4.1 & ADA Standards: 2010 213** and
- d. a shower or one shower and one bathtub. **ADA Standards: 2010 213** (New)

G Services, Displays, and Exhibits

If a historic building (such as a museum) includes services or provides information or displays of information, use the following recommendations to make the services, displays, and exhibits as accessible as possible.

G1 Arrange spaces so that services and information provided to the public are located in accessible spaces on accessible levels. Use inaccessible spaces and levels for work areas, storage, and other purposes that do not include the public. ca

G2 Locate displays and written information, documents, and exhibits so they can be viewed by a seated person. ca

G3 Place exhibits and signs displayed horizontally (e.g., open books) no higher than 43in. (1090mm) above the floor. ca

G4 On accessible levels, provide alternative displays of exhibits and information that are available on inaccessible levels. For example, where vertical access to levels above the ground floor is not accessible, provide a 'video tour' of the inaccessible levels. ca

G5 Provide adequate lighting along all accessible routes and in all accessible spaces. ca

G6 Keep circulation paths free of obstacles. ca

G7 Use contrasting floor and wall colors. ca

G8 Eliminate glare from light sources and reflective surfaces. ca

G9 Avoid using highly patterned floor and wall coverings. ca

WA Work Areas

A	Parking	208
B	Routes and Entrances	208
C	Work Areas and Spaces	209
D	Alarms	209
E	Common Areas	209
F	Fixtures and Furnishings	209

Under Title I of the ADA, employers have certain responsibilities to accommodate employees with disabilities. For purposes of complying with ADA Standards, employees include people covered in the definition of employee under Title I of the ADA, other people who perform employee-type duties (such as independent contractors) and volunteers.

Generally, accommodations for employees are handled on an individual basis because the types of accommodations people need vary from person to person. For this reason, the ADA Standards contains only a few requirements that pertain specifically to areas of buildings and sites that are provided strictly for employee work.

We recommend that architects and designers implement universal design principles to create work areas that are inviting to and usable by people with different needs. If accessibility is considered during the planning stages, it will be easier in the long run to meet the needs of employees who have disabilities.

An employee work area is all or any portion of a space used only by employees and used only for work. Employee work areas are not required to meet all ADA Standards requirements. However, many areas that employees use (including corridors, toilet rooms, kitchenettes and break rooms) must be fully accessible. To differentiate these areas it is important to understand who is considered an employee and to distinguish among the types of areas that employees use.

1. Employee work areas (as defined above) are not required to fully accessible. However, routes to these areas and alarms in these areas must be accessible.

2. Work areas also used by public (such as patient exam rooms) must be fully accessible for public use, but the fixtures and controls within such work areas used only by employees are not required to be accessible.

3. Areas used by employees for purposes other than work must be accessible. Restrooms, break rooms, lounges, locker rooms, vending areas, cafeterias, Auditoriums and similar areas used for purposes other than work must be Accessible even if the use of those areas is restricted to employees.

4. Service areas and equipment spaces that are used only by service and maintenance employees (such as elevator pits, elevator penthouses, mechanical, electrical, or communications equipment rooms, piping or equipment catwalks, water or sewage treatment pump rooms and stations, electrical substations and transformer vaults, and highway and tunnel utility spaces) do not hove to be accessible.

A Parking

A1 Parking provided for employees must meet at least the minimum requirements for accessible parking in PA Parking. **Ca**

B Routes and Entrances

Routes and entrances into employee work areas must be accessible. Routes to every individual work station or space within work areas are not required to be accessible.

Building codes and fire and life-safety codes for new construction contain requirements that will often result in accessible routes and spaces within employee work areas being made accessible to the maximum extent feasible.

B1 Design and construct employee work areas and connecting routes so that individuals with disabilities and people who use wheelchairs can approach, enter and exit the areas. **ADA Standards: 2010 203 (New) See RT Routes and Spaces**.

B2 Ensure that entrances, doors, gates and other features of entrances to employee work areas are accessible. **ADA Standards: 2010 203 (New) See EN Entrances, DR Doors, EL Elevators, AR Areas of Refuge,** and other chapters that pertain to routes and entrances.

B3 Ensure that common use circulation paths within employee work areas are accessible. **ADA Standards: 2010 206 (New) See RT Routes and Spaces.**
Exception: Where the circulation path is located in an area that is less than 1000 sq. ft. (92.9 sq. m) and divided by permanently installed partitions, counters, casework, or furnishings, the route is not required to be accessible. ADA Standards: 2010 206 (New)
Exception: Where the circulation path is an integral component of equipment, the route is not required to be accessible. ADA Standards: 2010 206 (New)
Exception: Where the circulation path is an exterior route exposed to the weather, the route is not required to be accessible. ADA Standards: 2010 206 (New)

C Work Areas and Spaces

The ADA Standards does not currently require employee work areas to meet accessibility guidelines. However, prior to 2010, ADA Standards included a recommendation that 5%, but not less than one, of individual work areas (such as laboratory stations, computer stations, service counters, and ticket booths) have adequate maneuvering space. We recommend that you follow this guideline to the maximum extent possible.

C1 Wherever possible, and the extent possible:
   a. provide adequate maneuvering space in the work areas,
   b. locate shelves, receptacles, and other features in work areas at accessible heights,
   c. ensure that mechanisms and controls are accessible, and
   d. design and construct a portion of work areas so that they are accessible. Ca

D Alarms

Prior to 2010, ADA Standards only required audible alarms in employee work areas. The 2010 ADA Standards requires audible and visual alarms in employee work areas.

D1 Where work areas have audible alarm coverage, design the area including the wiring system so that visual alarms can be integrated into the alarm system. **ADA Standards: 2010 215 (New) See AL Alarms.**

E Common Areas

The ADA Standards does not consider areas that employees use for activities other than work to be employee work areas. Therefore, all areas that are used by employees for purposes other than work (break rooms, restrooms, lounges, etc.) must be accessible. This includes access to sinks, microwave ovens and all other self-serve equipment.

E1 Follow the guidelines in the appropriate chapters in *Design for All* to ensure that all areas used by employees for all purposes other than work (including all break rooms) are fully accessible. Ca

E2 Follow the guidelines in the appropriate chapters to ensure that equipment, fixtures, and furnishings in areas used by employees for purposes other than work are accessible. Ca

F Fixtures and Furnishings

The ADA Standards does not require that accessible fixtures and furnishings (such as desks, counters, lab sinks, and computer work-stations) be provided in employee work areas. However, we recommend that you follow accessibility guidelines for counters, desks, and other fixtures to the maximum extent possible.

F1 Include accessible furnishings and features in employee work areas wherever possible. Ca

F2 Select furnishings and fixtures that will work well for everyone, such as adjustable chairs, desks and tables. Ca

AA Assembly Areas

A	Accessible Routes	210
B	Vertical Access	211
C	Egress	211
D	Wheelchair Spaces: Number and Location	211
E	Wheelchair Spaces: Lines of Sight	212
F	Wheelchair Spaces: Dimensions	213
G	Companion Seating at Wheelchair Spaces	214
H	Designated Aisle Seating	214
I	Dispersion of Seating	214
J	Audible Communications: Number and Location	215
K	Teaching Stations, Lecterns, and Presentation Areas	216

Assembly areas are places where people gather for recreational, educational, political, social, or civic purposes.

Assembly areas include movie theaters, other types of theaters, concert halls, stadiums, arenas, auditoriums, convention centers, classrooms, lecture halls, courtrooms, legislative chambers, public meeting rooms, hearing rooms, and other similar facilities.

In addition to assembly areas, other areas serving these spaces must be accessible. For example, theaters, stadiums, and concert halls almost always contain support spaces where goods and services are provided (such as ticket sales areas and concession stands).

When considering the accessibility of assembly areas and support spaces, review the following:

- routes and entrances, including ticket sales areas and ticket-taking areas
- routes to accessible areas and seating, including the features along routes (such as drinking fountains)
- public restrooms
- concession stands and seating, lobbies, reception areas, and event sales areas
- seating throughout main event areas
- focal areas (such as a performance area, stage, speakers' table area)
- egress, signage, and alarms
- communication needs of people with visual and hearing disabilities

Refer to the appropriate chapters in *Design for All* to ensure that all of the above areas and features meet appropriate accessibility requirements.

Equivalent seating for people with disabilities in assembly areas is essential. To be accessible, assembly areas must contain adequate numbers of spaces for wheelchairs, companion seats (that can be removed quickly and easily for people accompanying others who use wheelchairs), and designated aisle seats (for people with limited mobility).

Each type of seating in the assembly area must meet specific accessibility requirements. To ensure that all people have similar choices within the full range of seating, it is important to provide accessible seating (including wheelchair spaces) in all ticket price ranges and from different viewing positions. It is also important to ensure that people who need to remain seated during events have clear lines of sight from wherever they are seated. It is not acceptable to isolate people who use wheelchairs by locating them in separate seating areas or by placing companion seating in front of or behind wheelchair spaces.

In addition, where audible communication is an important part of the activities in an assembly area, an assistive listening system should be provided for people with hearing disabilities.

A Accessible Routes

Routes to and within assembly areas must meet the requirements for accessible routes. Routes to accessible seating within event areas and to stages and other performance areas must also be accessible. **See RT Routes and Spaces.**

A1 Provide accessible routes to all accessible spaces within assembly areas. **ADAAG: 1998 4.1 & ADA Standards: 2010 206**

A2 Provide accessible routes to all accessible seating within assembly areas. **ADAAG: 1998 4.1 & ADA Standards: 2010 206**
Exception: Within assembly areas, routes to seating that do not include wheelchair spaces or designated aisle seats are not required to be accessible.
ADAAG: 1998 4.1 & ADA Standards: 2010 206

A3 Provide accessible routes to lawn seating areas. **ADA Standards: 2010 221** (NEW)

A4 Provide accessible routes where circulation paths directly connect assembly seating areas to performance areas. **ADAAG: 1998 4.1 & ADA Standards: 2010 206**

A5 Provide accessible routes from performance areas to other areas used by performers. **ADAAG: 1998 4.1 & ADA Standards: 2010 206**

A6 Provide accessible routes to press boxes. **ADA Standards: 2010 206** (NEW)

Exception: Press boxes in bleachers are not required to be on an accessible route, provided that their total size is 500sq. ft. (46sq. m) maximum, and they have entrances at only one level. ADA Standards: 2010 206 (NEW)

Exception: Free-standing press boxes that are elevated 12ft. (3660mm) minimum above grade are not required to be on an accessible route, provided that their total size is 500sq. ft. (46sq. m) maximum. ADA Standards: 2010 206 (NEW)

B Vertical Access

Many assembly areas contain seating and other spaces on various levels. Vertical access must be included to all levels, including mezzanines, as outlined in **RT Routes and Spaces.** For areas served by elevators, **see EL Elevators.** In assembly areas, some spaces may also be served by platform lifts. **See PL Platform Lifts.**

B1 In new construction, do not install platform lifts except where permitted and where there is no other viable option. ca

In new construction, platform lifts are permitted to be used to provide accessible routes to performance areas or speakers' platforms, and to ensure appropriate dispersion and lines of sight for wheelchair accessible seating. **ADAAG: 1998 4.1 & ADA Standards: 2010 206**

B2 In new construction, where platform lifts are used to provide access to performance areas or speakers' platforms, or to provide appropriate dispersion and lines of sight for wheelchair seating, ensure that platform lifts meet all accessibility requirements in PL Platform Lifts. **ADAAG: 1998 4.1 & ADA Standards: 2010 206**

B3 Where elevators or platform lifts are used to provide vertical access to wheelchair spaces or designated aisle seats, ensure that the level of service (in terms of number, capacity, and speed) is equivalent to that provided in the same seating area to patrons who can use stairs or other means of vertical access. **ADA Standards: 2010 221** (NEW)

B4 In existing construction, where platform lifts are part of existing accessible routes (including routes to seating and access to performance areas), ensure that platform lifts meet all accessibility requirements in **PL Platform Lifts.** ca

B5 Ensure that all accessibility requirements are followed for all stairs. See **ST Stairs.** ca

B6 To ensure safety, follow all *Design for All* recommendations for all stairs. See **ST Stairs.** ca

C Egress

Most, if not all, assembly areas are required by building and life-safety codes to have multiple exits.

C1 At a minimum, provide accessible egress from assembly areas to exits as outlined in EG Egress. **ADAAG: 1998 4.1 & ADA Standards: 2010 206**

D Wheelchair Spaces: Number and Location

In assembly areas that contain seating, wheelchair spaces must be provided in each type of seating area provided (such as general seating, luxury boxes, tiered box seating, club boxes, suites, and team and player seating areas). Wheelchair spaces must be integrated throughout assembly areas.

D1 Provide wheelchair spaces on every level used for seating, including mezzanines. **ADAAG: 1998 4.33 & ADA Standards: 2010 221**

D2 Provide wheelchair spaces in each type of seating area provided. **ADAAG: 1998 4.33 & ADA Standards: 2010 221**

D3 Provide at least the minimum required number of accessible wheelchair spaces. **ADA Standards: 2010 221 (Modified, Some More Restrictive & Some Less Restrictive)**
See AA-A

Number of seats	Minimum number of wheelchair spaces required
4 to 25	1
26 to 50	2
51 to 150	4 ADASAD: 2010 221 (Modified-More Restrictive)
151 to 300	5 ADASAD: 2010 221 (Modified-More Restrictive)
301 to 500	6
501 to 5000	6, plus 1 for each 150, or fraction thereof, between 501-5000 ADASAD: 2010 221 (Modified-Less Restrictive)
5001 and over	36, plus 1 for each 200, or fraction thereof, over 5001 ADASAD: 2010 221 (Modified-Less Restrictive)

AA-A Minimum number of wheelchair spaces required in assembly areas

D4 Ensure that at least 20% of all boxes provided are accessible. **ADA Standards: 2010 221 (NEW)**

D5 Ensure that lawn seating areas and overflow seating areas (where fixed seats are not provided) are connected to an accessible route. **ADA Standards: 2010 221 (NEW)**

D6 Integrate wheelchair spaces throughout each type and level of seating area provided within the seating plan or the seating area. **ADAAG: 1998 4.33 & ADA Standards: 2010 221, 802** Locating wheelchair spaces in a separate area is not permitted.

E Wheelchair Spaces: Lines of Sight
People using wheelchairs must have clear lines of sight during events.

E1 Where spectators are expected to remain seated during events, locate wheelchair spaces to provide people seated in wheelchairs with lines of sight comparable to the lines of sight of the closest spectators in front of and/or below them. **ADAAG: 1998 4.33 & ADA Standards: 2010 802**
See Figure AA.1

AA.1 Lines of sight over seated spectators

E2 Where people are expected to stand at their seats during events, locate wheelchair spaces to provide people seated in wheelchairs with lines of sight over the closest standing spectators in front of and/or below them. **ADAAG: 1998 4.33 & ADA Standards: 2010 802**
See Figure AA.2

AA.2 Lines of sight over standing spectators

F Wheelchair Spaces: Dimensions

The space needed for wheelchair seating depends on the approach and the number of wheelchair spaces grouped together.

F1 Where a single wheelchair space is provided, ensure that the space is a minimum of 36in. (915mm) wide. **ADA Standards: 2010 602 (Modified-More Restrictive)**
See Figure AA.3

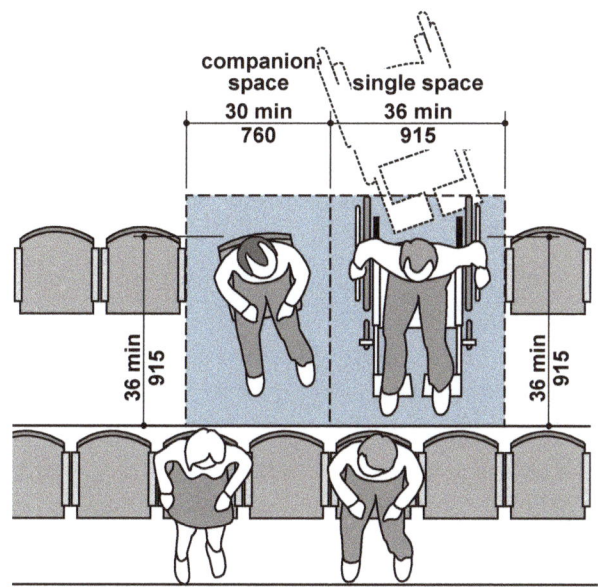

AA.3 Minimum width for a *single* wheelchair space

F2 Where two or more wheelchair spaces are adjacent to each other, ensure that each space is a minimum of 33in. (840mm) wide.
36in (915mm) min preferred Ca
ADAAG: 1998 4.33 & ADA Standards: 2010 802
See Figure AA.4

F3 Where a wheelchair space can be entered from the front or rear, ensure that the wheelchair space is a minimum of 48in. (1220mm) deep.
54in (1370mm) is preferred Ca
ADAAG: 1998 4.33 & ADA Standards: 2010 802

F4 Where a wheelchair space can be entered only from the side, ensure that the wheelchair space is a minimum of 60in. (1525mm) deep. **ADAAG: 1998 4.33 & ADA Standards: 2010 802**

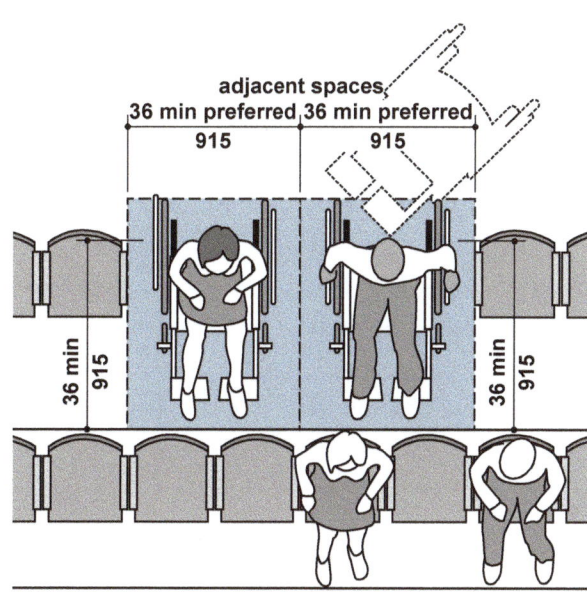

AA.4 **Preferred** minimum width for each of *two or more* **adjacent wheelchair spaces**

F5 Locate wheelchair spaces so that one side adjoins an accessible route or another wheelchair space. **ADAAG: 1998 4.33 & ADA Standards: 2010 802**

F6 Ensure that access to a wheelchair space is not through more than one adjoining wheelchair space. **ADA Standards: 2010 802 (New)**

F7 Ensure that wheelchair spaces do not overlap required exit widths of circulation paths. **ADA Standards: 2010 802 (New)**

F8 Ensure that wheelchair spaces have level floor surfaces with no more than 1:48 (approx. 2%) slope in any direction. **ADA Standards: 2010 602 (Modified-Less Restrictive)**

F9 Ensure that floor surfaces are firm, stable, and slip-resistant. **ADAAG: 1998 4.33 & ADA Standards: 2010 802, 302**

F10 **Ensure that designated wheelchair accessible seating spaces are not used for trash receptacles or as storage areas.** Ca

G   Companion Seating at Wheelchair Spaces

Companion seating must be provided next to wheelchair seating locations. Companion seating is permitted to be moveable.

G1   Provide one companion seat for each wheelchair space. **ADAAG: 1998 4.1 & ADA Standards: 2010 221**

G2   Locate companion seats next to, and in the same row as, each required wheelchair space. **ADA Standards: 2010 802 (New)**

G3   Ensure that each required "readily removable" companion seat provides an additional wheelchair space when removed. **ADAAG: 1998 4.1 & ADA Standards: 2010 221**
Refer to Figure AA.3

G4   In row seating ensure that provisions are made for shoulder alignment by:
   a. allowing enough space so that the shoulders of a person using a companion seat can be aligned with an adjoining person using a wheelchair, and
   b. ensuring that a minimum of 36in. (915mm) is maintained between the shoulder alignment and the front of the clear floor space. **ADA Standards: 2010 802 (New)**
Refer to Figures AA.3 and AA.4

G5   In row seating ensure that the floor surface of the companion seat is at the same elevation as the floor surface of the wheelchair space. **ADA Standards: 2010 802 (New)**

G6   Ensure that companion seats are equivalent in size, quality, comfort, and amenities to the seating in the immediate area. **ADA Standards: 2010 802 (New)**

H   Designated Aisle Seating

Designated aisle seats are required in assembly areas. Designated aisle seats are useful for people who have difficulty walking.

H1   Provide at least one designated aisle seat for every 100 (or fraction of 100) seats. **ADAAG: 1998 4.1 & ADA Standards: 2010 221**

H2   For every four required designated aisle seats, locate at least one on an accessible route. Locate all other required designated aisle seats no more than two rows from an accessible route. **ADA Standards: 2010 221 (New)**

H3   Provide removable or folding armrests, or no armrests, on the aisle side of designated aisle seats. **ADAAG: 1998 4.1 & ADA Standards: 2010 802**

H4   Identify each designated aisle seat by a sign or marker. **ADAAG: 1998 4.1 & ADA Standards: 2010 802**

H5   *Use markers that help people identify the seats in a darkened room (such as light-on-dark or dark-on-light contrast or reflective markers).* Ca

H6   Post signs at the ticket office to notify patrons of the availability of designated aisle seats. **ADAAG: 1998 4.1 & ADA Standards: 2010 802**

I   Dispersion of Seating

All people should have choices of location and price range for seating at performances or events.

I 1   Where the number of seats exceeds 300, disperse wheelchair spaces and designated aisle seats to provide a choice of admission prices and viewing angles comparable to that provided to other spectators. **ADAAG: 1998 4.33 & ADA Standards: 2010 221**

I 2   Where the minimum number of required wheelchair spaces or designated aisle seats is not sufficient to allow for complete dispersion, disperse wheelchair spaces or designated aisle seats according to the following priorities.
   a. **Priority 1:** provide wheelchair spaces and designated aisle seats in each price level of each type of seating area provided
   b. **Priority 2:** locate wheelchair spaces and

in accessible seating with viewing angles generally representative of those available to other spectators

c. **Priority 3:** locate wheelchair spaces and designated aisle seats at varying distances from performance areas on each accessible level and in each balcony or mezzanine that is located along an accessible route **ADA Standards: 2010 802 (New)**

Lecture hall with accessible seating on three levels

J Audible Communications: Number and Location

In areas where audible communications are integral to the use of assembly areas (e.g., concert and lecture halls, playhouses, movie theaters, and meeting rooms), provide assistive listening systems. **ADAAG: 1998 4.1 & ADA Standards: 2010 219**

J1 Provide at least the minimum required number of assistive listening and hearing-aid compatible receivers.

a. Ensure that at least 25%, but not less than two, of the receivers are hearing-aid compatible. **ADA Standards: 2010 219 (New)**

See AA-B

Seating capacity	Assistive listening receivers	Hearing-aid compatible receivers
50 or less	2	2
51–200	2, plus 1 per 25 seats over 50 seats (or fraction thereof)	2
201–500	2, plus 1 per 25 seats over 50 seats (or fraction thereof)	1 per 4 receivers, (or fraction thereof)
501–1000	20, plus 1 per 33 seats over 500 seats (or fraction thereof)	1 per 4 receivers, (or fraction thereof)
1001–2000	35, plus 1 per 50 seats over 1000 seats (or fraction thereof)	1 per 4 receivers, (or fraction thereof)
2001 plus	55, plus 1 per 100 seats over 2000 seats (or fraction thereof)	1 per 4 receivers, (or fraction thereof)

AA-B Required number of assistive listening receivers and hearing-aid compatible receivers per capacity

J2 Provide an assistive listening system in one of the following categories:
   a. induction loop, **ADAAG: 1998 4.33 & ADA Standards: 2010 706**
   b. infrared system, **ADAAG: 1998 4.33 & ADA Standards: 2010 706**
   c. FM radio frequency system, **ADAAG: 1998 4.33 & ADA Standards: 2010 706**
   d. hard-wired earphones, **ADA Standards: 2010 706 (New)** or
   e. other equivalent devices. **ADA Standards: 2010 706 (New)**

J3 Provide receiver jacks that include a 1/8in. (3.2mm) standard mono-jack. **ADA Standards: 2010 706 (New)**
   a. If other receiver jack types are used, provide adapters to fit standard mono-jacks. **ADA Standards: 2010 706 (New)**

J4 Provide neck-loops to ensure that receivers required to be hearing-aid compatible interface with T-coils in hearing aids. **ADA Standards: 2010 706 (New)**

J5 Where an assistive listening system is provided, post signs to inform people of the availability of the system.
   a. Locate signs at ticket offices, counters, or windows.

b. Ensure that the signs include the International Symbol of Assistive Listening Systems and meet all other requirements for accessible signs. **ADAAG: 1998 4.1 & ADA Standards: 2010 219 See SN Signs.**

K   Teaching Stations, Lecterns and Presentation Areas

All teaching stations, lecterns, and presentation areas need to be fully accessible with accessible routes leading to them.

K1   Ensure that all lecterns and teaching stations include accessible counters. ca

K2   Ensure that all lecterns and teaching stations have switches and controls that are accessible and within reach range. ca

LB   Libraries

A	Stacks	216
B	Shelves and Displays	217
C	Tables and Seating	217
D	Circulation & Service Counters	218
E	Security Barriers and Bollards	218
F	Electronic Equipment	218
G	Self-Service Machines and Depositories	219

This chapter covers the accessibility requirements that apply specifically to libraries. General accessibility requirements (such as those for parking, entrances, routes, and restrooms) also apply. **See PA Parking, EN Entrances, RT Routes and Spaces, TB Toilet/Bath Rooms,** and other sections that apply.

A   Stacks

Stacks refer to the shelves and shelving units where books and materials (available to the public for browsing and borrowing) are stored. Because shelf height in stack areas is unrestricted, stacks are often very tall and compact in order to conserve space. However, this often results in extremely narrow and confining aisles, making maneuvering between and within these spaces difficult for everyone. Books that extend beyond bookshelves, step stools in the aisles, and other obstructions make aisles even more difficult to navigate. Providing ample clearances between stacks will make it easier for people to pass through aisles and turn from one aisle into the next.

A1   Where stacks (shelving units) are 48in. (1220mm) or more wide, provide clear aisles between stacks that are 36in. (915mm) wide minimum. **ADAAG: 1998 4.3, 8.5 & ADA Standards: 2010 403**
   A 42in. (1065mm) wide aisle is preferred. ca
Refer to Figures RT.12.

A2   Where stacks (shelving units) are less than 48in. (1220mm) wide, allow sufficient clear floor space for people using mobility aids to make turns between stacks as follows:
   a.   provide clear aisle space between two stacks (or between stacks and walls or between stacks and other obstructions) that is 42in. (1065mm) wide minimum;

b. provide clear space that is 48in. (1220mm) wide minimum between the end of a stack and any wall or obstruction parallel to the end of a stack;
   60in. (1525mm) preferred; Ca
   and
c. provide a clearance of 60in. (1525mm) past any obstruction before narrowing the route to the minimum width required for an unobstructed route.
   ADAAG: 1998 4.3 & ADA Standards: 2010 403 See RT Routes and Spaces.

See Figure LB.1

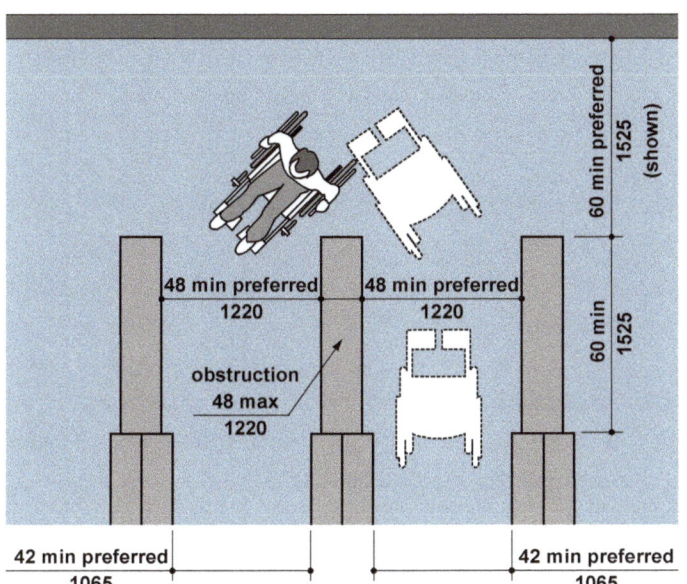

LB.1 Preferred minimum dimensions for a route with turns through library stacks

A3 Provide accessible signs to make identifying aisles easier for people with visual impairments. Ca See SN Signs.

A4 When books in stacks are not within accessible reach ranges, provide alternative services such as having staff available to retrieve items. Ca

B Shelves and Displays

Libraries often have shelves and displays set up to showcase books surrounding a theme or to introduce items or services available. Displays are also used in children's areas and for magazines and literature on local events. For people with disabilities, getting items from shelves and displays is often difficult because aisles and maneuvering spaces adjacent to shelves and displays are too narrow or because reaching items is too difficult. Shelves, displays, and items on shelves and displays can often be rearranged to make them more accessible to people whose reach range is limited.

B1 Locate all accessible shelves and displays on accessible routes. **ADAAG: 1998 4.3 & ADA Standards: 2010 403 See RT Routes and Spaces.**

B2 Provide adequate turning and maneuvering spaces adjacent to shelves and displays. **ADAAG: 1998 4.3 & ADA Standards: 2010 403 See RT Routes and Spaces.**

B3 Provide shelves and displays at accessible heights where possible. **ADAAG: 1998 4.2 & ADA Standards: 2010 308   See RR Reach Ranges.**

B4 Relocate shelves and displays on raised platforms or inaccessible levels and spaces to accessible locations where possible. Ca

B5 Provide accessible signage and labels to make identifying items easier for people with visual impairments. See SN Signs. Ca

B6 Where improving access to shelves and displays is not currently readily achievable, provide alternative services such as having staff available to retrieve items. Also, provide signs to inform the public that such services are available. Ca

C Tables and Seating

People who use wheelchairs and people who have disabilities should have access to all types of work surfaces, tables, and other built-in furnishings that are provided. Ensure that these furnishings meet the requirements in **TA Tables and Seating.**

C1 Ensure that at least 5%, but not less than one, of each type of fixed table, seat, or study carrel is accessible. **ADAAG: 1998 8.2 & ADA Standards: 2010 226**
   Increasing the number to 10% or more is preferred. Ca

C2 Provide a clear route through areas with desks, tables, study carrels, and furniture that is a minimum of 36in. (915mm) wide. **ADAAG: 1998 4.3 & ADA Standards: 2010 403**
A width of 42in. (1065mm) is preferred.

D Circulation & Service Counters

Circulation and service counters in libraries are often at a height that only accommodates standing patrons. These types of counters make an equal experience for people in wheelchairs impossible. To provide counters that work well for both standing and sitting people, (and people of short stature) follow the requirements below.

D1 Where circulation and service counters are provided, ensure that at least one of each type is accessible. **ADA Standards: 2010 904 (New)**

D2 Where circulation and service counters are dispersed throughout a library, ensure that accessible circulation and service counters are also dispersed.

D3 Where counters are configured for a forward approach, provide a counter or portion of a counter that meets the following requirements:
  a. 36in. (915mm) maximum above the floor,
  b. 30in. (760mm) minimum long, and
  c. configured for knee and toe clearance; see RT Routes and Spaces, RT-Q. **ADA Standards: 2010 904 (New)**

D4 Where counters are configured for a parallel approach, provide a counter or portion of a counter that meets the following requirements:
  a. 36in. (915mm) maximum above the floor, and
  b. 36in. (915mm) minimum long. **ADAAG: 1998 7.2 & ADA Standards: 2010 904**

Exception: Where the entire counter is less than 36in. (915mm) long, ensure that the full length of the counter is 36in. (915mm) maximum high. ADA Standards: 2010 904 (New)

D5 In alterations to existing conditions, where installing or altering a counter to meet the guidelines for height and length would reduce the number of workstations available, provide a counter or portion of a counter configured for a parallel approach that meets the following requirements:
  a. 36in. (915mm) maximum above the floor,
  b. 24in. (610mm) minimum long, and
  c. clear floor space at the counter is centered on the accessible section of the counter **ADA Standards: 2010 904 (New)**

D6 Locate all accessible counters on accessible routes. **ADAAG: 1998 7.2 & ADA Standards: 2010 904 See RT Routes and Spaces.**

D7 Ensure that all queues and waiting lines at accessible service counters are on accessible routes. See RT Routes and Spaces.

E Security Barriers and Bollards

Libraries often include bollards and other security devices near entrances to prevent the theft of books or other items.

E1 Eliminate turnstiles and security gates that restrict access for people with disabilities. **ADA Standards: 2010 206 (New)**

E2 Ensure that wheelchair access and egress is not obstructed by bollards or other devices that are intended to prevent the theft of merchandise. **ADAAG: 1998 7.4 & ADA Standards: 2010 206**

Exception: Providing an alternate accessible entrance that is conveniently located near another entrance is acceptable. ADAAG: 1998 7.4 & ADA Standards: 2010 206

F Electronic Equipment

Most libraries now provide card catalog indexes electronically. The ADA Standards does not cover accessibility requirements for software. For information regarding accessible software and electronic equipment, review Section 508 of the Rehabilitation Act or visit the Center for Applied Special Technology (CAST) online at www.cast.org.

F1 **Ensure that computerized card catalog areas and equipment are fully accessible.** Ca

G Self-service Machines and Depositories

G1 Ensure that all book drops, copy machines, and other self-service equipment (such as change machines and Automatic Teller Machines) meet the requirements in **VS Vending/Self-serve.** ADAAG: 1998 4.34 & ADA Standards: 2010 220

RS Restaurants

A	Dining Areas	219
B	Routes and Access Aisles	220
C	Tables and Seating	220
D	Booths	221
E	Dining Counters and Bars	221
F	Raised Platforms	221
G	Food Service Lines	221
H	Vending and Self-service Machines	222

This chapter covers the accessibility requirements that apply specifically to restaurants and cafeterias. General requirements (such as those for businesses, parking, accessible routes, and restrooms) also apply. **See BU Businesses, PA Parking, RT Routes and Spaces, TB Toilet/Bath Rooms,** and other sections that may apply to your establishment.

It is important that all people have the same opportunities and experiences when dining out. This includes having choices in seating location, seating type, reservation time, or other services offered.

ADA Standards imposes strict requirements regarding the accessibility of dining areas, including mezzanines, sunken areas, loggias and outdoor seating areas. **See BU Businesses.**

A Dining Areas

A1 Ensure that all dining areas in new construction are accessible, including sunken areas, loggias, and outdoor seating areas. **ADAAG: 1998 5.4 & ADA Standards: 2010 206**

Exception: In buildings that are not required to provide a means of vertical access (see RT-D2), an accessible means of vertical access to a mezzanine is not required under the following conditions:

   a. if the area of the mezzanine seating measures no more than 25% of the total accessible seating area; **ADA Standards: 2010 206** (MODIFIED-MORE RESTRICTIVE)

   b. if the same services and decor are provided in another accessible space; **ADAAG: 1998 5.4 & ADA Standards: 2010 206** and

c. if the accessible areas are not for the exclusive use of people with disabilities. **ADAAG: 1998 5.4 & ADA Standards: 2010 206**

Exception: In alterations, accessibility to sunken dining areas and to all parts of outdoor seating areas is not required if the same services and decor are provided in an accessible space that is not for the exclusive use of people with disabilities. ADAAG: 1998 5.4 & ADA Standards: 2010 206

B Routes and Access Aisles

Routes within clusters or groups of tables often become a congested maze when tables are occupied. Routes become cluttered with items such as bulky shopping bags, backpacks, baby carriers, strollers, etc. Seated occupants and highchairs also become obstacles, especially when routes are too narrow. Maneuvering between and within these spaces is challenging for everyone. Providing appropriate clearances will help prevent routes and access aisles from being obstructed.

B1 Provide a clear route a minimum of 36in. (915mm) wide around the perimeter of all clusters or areas of tables and seating. **ADAAG: 1998 4.3 & ADA Standards: 2010 403**
   A 42in. (1070mm) wide route is preferred. Ca

B2 Provide a clear route through large clusters or areas of tables and seating a minimum of 36in. (915mm) wide. **ADAAG: 1998 5.4 & ADA Standards: 2010 206**
   42in. (1070mm) is preferred. Ca

B3 Ensure that emergency exits are on accessible routes. **ADAAG: 1998 4.3 & ADA Standards: 2010 206**

B4 Ensure that all queues and waiting lines are on accessible routes. **ADA Standards: 2010 207 (New)**

B5 Eliminate turnstiles, security gates, and queue ropes to ensure that access is not restricted for people with disabilities. **ADA Standards: 2010 206 (New)**

Exception: Providing an alternate accessible entrance that is conveniently located near another entrance is acceptable. ADA Standards: 2010 206 (New)

See **RT Routes and Spaces** for further information regarding accessible routes.

C Tables and Seating

People need adequate legroom under tables and other dining surfaces to approach and use them comfortably.

See **TA Tables and Seating** for additional requirements related to tables and legroom.

C1 In each room, area, or cluster of seating, ensure that at least 5% of tables are accessible. **ADAAG: 1998 5.1 & ADA Standards: 2010 226**
   Increasing the number to 10% or more is preferred. Ca

C2 In each room, area, or cluster of seating, ensure that at least one table is accessible. **ADAAG: 1998 5.1** Ca

C3 Distribute accessible seating proportionally throughout each area or cluster of seating. **ADAAG: 1998 4.1 & ADA Standards: 2010 226**

C4 Distribute accessible seating proportionally throughout each type of seating such as indoor and outdoor. **ADAAG: 1998 4.1 & ADA Standards: 2010 226**

C5 Locate accessible tables and seating on accessible routes. **ADAAG: 1998 4.1 & ADA Standards: 2010 226**

C6 Ensure that the tops of dining surfaces are between 28in. (710mm) minimum and 34in. (865mm) maximum above the floor. **ADAAG: 1998 4.32 & ADA Standards: 2010 902** See **TA Tables and Seating, TA-D.**

D Booths

A traditional dining booth has bench seats along the two long sides of a rectangular dining table surface. Usually only one end of the booth is open to allow people to slide into the seat. This may be difficult for a number of people. An additional problem is that some people may not be able to use booths if they are elevated by one or more steps. Steps into booths are unsafe because people sometimes fall when leaving booths.

To ensure that people can join others at a booth comfortably, access to the open end of the booth's table is necessary.

D1 In each room, area, or cluster of seating, ensure that at least 5% of booths are accessible. **ADA Standards: 2010 226 (New)**
Increasing the number to 10% or more is preferred. ca

D2 In each room, area, or cluster of seating, ensure that at least one booth is accessible. ca

D3 Install accessible booths at floor level and eliminate any level changes or steps up to booths to increase accessibility and safety. ca

D4 Provide a clear floor space configured for a forward approach at the open end of a booth. **ADA Standards: 2010 305, 902 (New)**

D5 Ensure that the space provided for legroom is unobstructed. Legroom under a table must be 27in. (685mm) high minimum. **ADA Standards: 2010 306 (New)**
A height of 30in. (760mm) is preferred. ca

Refer to Figures TA.2.

D6 Provide the required legroom below the dining surface. **ADA Standards: 2010 306 (New)** See **RT Routes and Spaces, RT-Q.**

D7 Ensure that the tops of dining surfaces are between 28in. (710mm) minimum and 34in. (865mm) maximum above the floor. **ADAAG: 1998 4.32 & ADA Standards: 2010 902** See **TA Tables and Seating, TA-D.**

E Dining Counters and Bars

Dining counters and bars (elevated dining surfaces with stools) where food and drink are consumed must be accessible. Counters where food and drink are sold but not consumed are also required to be accessible, but are considered to be sales and service counters. **See BU Businesses, BU-A** for accessibility requirements for sales and service counters.

E1 Ensure that all counters and bars have accessible locations. ca

E2 Where a counter or bar used for serving food or drink is higher than 34in. (865mm), provide an accessible portion
  a. at least 60in. (1525mm) minimum in length, and
  b. 34in. (865mm) maximum in height. **ADAAG: 1998 5.2** ca

F Raised Platforms

People who use wheelchairs or who have difficulty with stairs must be provided access to head tables and speakers' lecterns. Care must be taken to ensure that raised platforms do not pose falling hazards.

F1 Provide platform lifts or ramps to head tables or speakers' lecterns that are located on raised platforms. Ensure that all requirements for platform lifts and ramps are followed. **ADAAG: 1998 4.11 & ADA Standards: 2010 206** See **PL Platform Lifts and RP Ramps.**

F2 Ensure that raised platforms are large enough to provide ample clear floor space around head tables and speakers' lecterns. ca

F3 Protect people from the open edges of raised platforms by appropriate table placement, by painting platform edges, and/or by providing a curb or railing. ca

G Food Service Lines

Food service lines include permanent cafeteria lines with tray slides and permanent and temporary buffet lines. Consider people with limited grasp, strength, and dexterity when specifying food service utensils such as serving spoons and tongs.

G1 Provide a 36in. (915mm) minimum clear width in all food service lines. **ADAAG: 1998 5.5 & ADA Standards: 2010 403**
A clear width of 42in. (1070mm) is preferred to allow passage around other people and wheelchairs. ca

G2 Ensure that the top of tray slides is between 28in. (710mm) minimum and 34in. (865mm) maximum above the floor. **ADAAG: 1998 5.5 & ADA Standards: 2010 904**
A height of 30in. (760mm) is preferred. ca

G3 Ensure that food selections are within a 24in. (610mm) side reach, measuring from the front edge of the tray slide. **ADA Standards: 2010 308 (Modified-More Restrictive)**

G4 Ensure that at least 50% of self-service shelves and dispensing devices (for tableware, dishware, condiments, food and beverages) are within accessible reach ranges. **ADAAG: 1998 5.5 & ADA Standards: 2010 227, 904**

G5 Ensure that accessible food service lines overlap or adjoin accessible routes. **ADAAG: 1998 4.1 & ADA Standards: 2010 226**

H Vending and Self-service Machines

All self serve areas and equipment, including controls and spouts, must be accessible and within reach ranges.

H1 Ensure that the controls and mechanisms of self-service equipment
  a. are operable with one hand;
  b. do not require grasping, pinching, or twisting of the wrist; and
  c. are operable with a force no greater than 5 lbs. (22.2N). **ADAAG: 1998 4.27 & ADA Standards: 2010 309**

For additional accessibility requirements for vending and self-service equipment, **see VS Vending/Self-serve.**

BU Businesses

A	Accessibility of Floor Levels in a Business	223
B	Determining What Constitutes a "Floor Level" in a Business	224
C	Sales and Service Counters	224
D	Checkout Aisles	225
E	Security Glazing	226
F	Shelves and Displays	226
G	Signs	227
H	Security Barriers and Bollards	227
I	Communication	227

All businesses that provide goods or services to the public must be accessible, regardless of their size. The information in this chapter focuses specifically on features in buildings that relate to conducting business. General requirements (such as those for parking, routes, interior spaces, restrooms, safety features, and other amenities) also apply. **See PA Parking, RT Routes and Spaces, TB Toilet/Bath Rooms,** and other chapters that apply to your establishment.

All new businesses must comply with all general ADA requirements. Additionally, all newly constructed buildings and sites that contain businesses need to fully comply with specific ADA Standards requirements for new construction.

The ADA recognizes that existing small businesses may need to accomplish accessibility goals as they have the resources to do so. In businesses that are located in buildings constructed before 1992, readily achievable accessibility improvements are required. Readily achievable improvements are those that are fairly easy to accomplish without much difficulty or expense. For small, independently owned businesses, what is considered to be readily achievable is based on the size and resources of the individual business or store. However, if the business is part of a large national chain with extensive financial resources, a substantially greater level of compliance is expected. Each business needs to decide what constitutes readily achievable. Consult your regional Disability and Business Technical Assistance Center for further information about requirements that apply to your business.

Improving accessibility for exiting buildings and sites is an ongoing obligation under the ADA. Changes that are not readily achievable now may become readily achievable in the future due to changes in financial resources, improvements in technology, or changing customer needs. The owners and managers of businesses need to review their progress toward increasing accessibility periodically, and make additional improvements as appropriate. **ADA Standards: 2010 202 (New)**

Businesses need to prioritize accessibility improvements as follows:

Priority 1: accessibility of routes, including entrances, doors and vertical access (stairs, ramps, elevators, escalators)
Priority 2: accessibility of goods and services, including alternatives for providing access to goods and services where altering the structure is not possible (for example, when there is no elevator and second floor spaces are not accessible)
Priority 3: accessibility of restrooms
Priority 4: additional accessibility throughout the building and site, such as interior features, furnishings, equipment, floor surfaces, and lighting

When modifications to existing conditions are not readily achievable, businesses are required to make alternative methods of accommodation available, such as providing services at an alternate accessible location, offering home delivery, or retrieving merchandise from inaccessible shelves or spaces. No additional fees can be charged for these types of services and accommodations, which must be safe and must maintain the dignity of the customer. If an additional service is made available by a business, employees need to be fully aware of the service. Employees also need to be trained to provide the service to customers with disabilities.

A Accessibility of Floor Levels in a Business

A1 Ensure that all areas in a business (including sunken areas, loggias, raised platforms, mezzanines and outdoor spaces) are accessible. **ADAAG: 1998 7.1** Ca

Exception: A building that has less than three floor levels does not have to comply with this requirement. However, shopping centers, shopping malls, health care providers, and other types of facilities as determined by the U.S. Attorney General, Department of Justice (e.g. transportation buildings and government buildings) are not included in this exception. Therefore all floor levels in all of these types of buildings are required to be accessible. **ADA Standards: 2010 206 (New)**

Example *one*: A building with commercial retail space has two floor levels open to the public, one floor level at grade and one floor level above grade. The floor level at grade is required to be accessible but the floor level above grade is not required to be accessible. It is recommended to make both floor levels accessible where possible. Ca

Example *two*: A building with commercial spaces has three floor levels, one floor level at grade, one floor level above grade, and one floor level below grade. In this example the building is considered to have three floor levels, even though one level is below grade. Therefore the entire building (all three floor levels) are required to be accessible.

Exception: A building that has less than 3000sq. ft. (279sq. m) per floor level does not have to comply with this requirement. However, shopping centers, shopping malls, health care providers, and other types of facilities as determined by the U.S. Attorney General, Department of Justice (e.g. transportation buildings and government buildings) are not included in this exception. Therefore all floor levels in all of these types of buildings are required to be accessible. **ADA Standards: 2010 206 (New)**

Exception: If the occupant load for a floor level is 5 or less and the floor level is not at grade, the floor level is not required to be accessible. **ADA Standards: 2010 206 (New)**

B Determining What Constitutes a *Floor Level* in a Business

Definitions of a *mezzanine* and a *floor level* follow. However, these definitions should be reviewed with state and local building code officials before depending on them as criteria in determining which *levels* in a building are required to be accessible.

ADA Standards requirements for the accessibility of levels in restaurants (including sunken areas, loggias, and outdoor seating areas) are more stringent. **See RS Restaurants.**

Example: If the total floor area of the upper level in a two story space (not counting the area that is open to below) is less than one-third of the total floor area of the floor level below, then the upper level is by definition a "mezzanine". **ADA Standards: 2010 106 (New)**

> If the total floor area of the upper level in a two story space (not counting the area that is open to below) is more than one-third percent of the total floor area of the floor level below, then the upper level is by definition a "floor level" of its own. **ADA Standards: 2010 106 (New)**

B1 Review the definitions of a *mezzanine* and a *floor level* with state and local building code officials before determining which levels in a building are required to be accessible. Ca

B2 Follow all minimum ADA Standards requirements in making levels in a business accessible. Ca

C Sales and Service Counters

Counters that are used for providing sales or services to customers must be accessible. Counters that provide different services in the same business also need to be accessible. This includes order counters, pick-up counters, express counters, return counters, and other types of counters. Sometimes one continuous counter can be used to provide two different types of services, such as ordering and pick-up. In these cases both sections, or the entire counter, must be accessible.

Depending on the purpose and arrangement of the counter, people may approach from the front or side. The ADA Standards requirements are different for each type of approach. Accessible counters, or accessible portions of counters, must have the appropriate clear floor space.

Follow the guidelines below for ticket counters, teller stations in banks, registration counters in hotels and motels, and all counters where goods and services are distributed.

C1 Where sales and service counters are provided, ensure that at least one is accessible. **ADAAG: 1998 7.2 & ADA Standards: 2010 904**

C2 Where sales and service counters are dispersed throughout a building or site, ensure that accessible counters are also dispersed to provide comparable accessible services. **ADAAG: 1998 7.2** Ca

C3 Where sales and service counters are configured for a forward approach, provide counters or portions of counters that meet the following requirements:
  a. 36in. (915mm) maximum above the floor,
  b. 30in. (760mm) minimum long, and
  c. configured for knee and toe clearance; see **RT Routes and Spaces, RT-Q**. **ADA Standards: 2010 904 (New)**

C4 Where sales and service counters are configured for a parallel approach, provide counters or portions of counters that meet the following requirements:
  a. 36in. (915mm) maximum above the floor, and
  b. 36in. (915mm) minimum long. **ADAAG: 1998 7.2 & ADA Standards: 2010 904**

See Figure BU.1

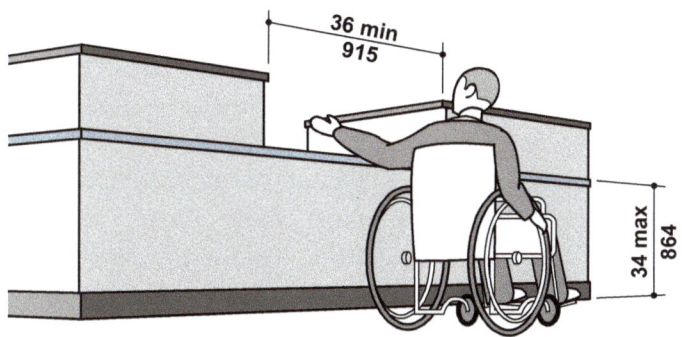

BU.1 An accessible sale and service counter configured for a parallel approach

C5 Where the entire sales and service counter is less than 36in. (915mm) long, ensure that the full length of the counter is 36in. (915mm) maximum high. **ADAAG: 1998 7.2 & ADA Standards: 2010 904**
34in (864mm) preferred.

C6 Ensure that the accessible portions of sales and service counters extend the same depth as adjoining sections of counters. **ADA Standards: 2010 904 (New)**

C7 In alterations to existing conditions, where installing or altering a counter that meets the guidelines for height and length would reduce the number of workstations or mailboxes available, provide a counter or portion of a counter configured for a parallel approach that meets the following requirements:
  a. 36in. (915mm) maximum above the floor, **ADAAG: 1998 7.2 & ADA Standards: 2010 904**
  34in (864mm) preferred.
  b. 24in. (610mm) minimum long, **ADA Standards: 2010 904 (New)** and
  c. clear floor space at the counter is centered on the accessible length of the counter. **ADA Standards: 2010 904 (New)**

C8 Make the entire length of sale or service counters accessible where possible.

C9 Locate all accessible counters on accessible routes. **ADAAG: 1998 7.2 & ADA Standards: 2010 904** See RT Routes and Spaces.

C10 Ensure that all queues and waiting lines at accessible service counters are on accessible routes. **ADA Standards: 2010 904 (New)** See RT Routes and Spaces.

C11 Modify or replace service counters that do not meet or exceed current ADA accessibility requirements.

D Checkout Aisles

Businesses often include multiple types of checkout aisles to serve different functions. A grocery store, for instance, often includes aisles with conveyor belts for moving purchases from the cashier to the person who bags the groceries, and separate aisles that are permanently designated as self-serve or "express" lanes. Each of these various types of checkout aisles needs to meet the following requirements.

D1 In new construction over 5000sq. ft. (1500sq. m), provide at least the minimum number of accessible checkout aisles of each type. **ADAAG: 1998 7.3 & ADA Standards: 2010 227**
See BU-A

Total checkout aisles of each type	Accessible checkout aisles of each type
1 to 4	1
5 to 8	2
9 to 15	3
16 or more	3, plus 20% of additional aisles

BU-A Minimum number of required accessible checkout aisles for new construction over 5000sq. ft. (1500sq. m) **ADAAG: 1998 7.3 & ADASAD: 2010 227**

D2 In new construction under 5000sq. ft. (1500sq. m), provide at least one accessible checkout aisle of each type. **ADAAG: 1998 7.3 & ADA Standards: 2010 227**

D3 When altering existing conditions, ensure that at least one checkout aisle is accessible. **ADAAG: 1998 7.3 & ADA Standards: 2010 227**

D4 When altering existing conditions, continue to increase (over time) the number of accessible aisles of each type or function until the number of accessible checkout aisles equals the number required for new construction. **ADAAG: 1998 7.3 & ADA Standards: 2010 227**
Refer to Table BU-A

D5 Where checkout aisles are dispersed throughout a building, ensure that accessible checkout aisles are also dispersed. ca

D6 Ensure that accessible checkout aisles are a minimum of 36in. (915mm) wide. **ADAAG: 1998 4.3 & ADA Standards: 2010 403**
A 42in. (1065mm) wide aisle (or wider) is preferred. ca
Exception: The clear width of the aisle may be reduced to 32in. (815mm) if the depth of the counter does not exceed 24in. (610mm). ADAAG: 1998 4.3 & ADA Standards: 2010 403

D7 Ensure that accessible checkout aisles meet all other requirements for accessible routes. **ADA Standards: 2010 904 (New)** See RT Routes and Spaces.

D8 Ensure that the height of checkout counters is 38in. (965mm) high maximum. **ADA Standards: 2010 904 (New)**

D9 Where a safety curb or lip is provided between the counter and the checkout aisle, ensure that the maximum height of the top of the safety curb or lip is 40in. (1015mm). **ADA Standards: 2010 904 (New)**

D10 Where check writing counters are provided, ensure that they are 28in. (710mm) minimum to 34in. (865mm) maximum above the floor. **ADA Standards: 2010 904 (New)**

E Security Glazing
People with hearing impairments often have difficulty communicating with sales persons who are behind security glazing at ticket counters and teller windows.

E1 Where increased security is needed at ticket counters and teller windows, provide an accessible method of voice communication by including
   a. talk-through grilles, slates or baffles;
   b. accessible intercoms; or
   c. accessible telephone handset devices with volume controls **See PT Public Telephones. ADA Standards: 2010 904 (New)**

E2 Provide open ticket counters and teller windows (in conjunction with security cameras and other security systems) where possible. ca

F Shelves and Displays
For people with disabilities, getting merchandise from shelves and displays is often difficult because aisles and maneuvering spaces adjacent to shelves and displays are too narrow or because reaching items is too difficult. Merchandise can often be rearranged to increase accessibility to people whose reach range is limited.

F1 Ensure that accessible routes to and through all display areas are maintained at all times and that any temporary displays do not narrow routes below minimum requirements. **ADAAG: 1998 4.1 & ADA Standards: 2010 206 See RT Routes and Spaces.**

F2 Locate all accessible shelves and displays on accessible routes. **ADAAG: 1998 4.1 & ADA Standards: 2010 206 See RT Routes and Spaces**

F3 Provide adequate turning and maneuvering spaces adjacent to shelves and displays. **ADAAG: 1998 4.3 & ADA Standards: 2010 206 See RT Routes and Spaces.**

F4 Provide shelves and displays at accessible heights where possible. **ADAAG: 1998 4.2 & ADA Standards: 2010 308 See RR Reach Ranges.**

F5 Relocate shelves and displays that are in inaccessible locations (or on raised platforms or inaccessible levels) to accessible locations where possible. ca

F6 Where possible, arrange duplicated merchandise on shelves vertically instead of horizontally to make retrieving items possible for people in wheelchairs and people of short stature. Ca

F7 Ensure that all customer use items in concession areas, such as cups, lids, straws, plates, forks, spoons, and knives, are within reach range. Ca

F8 Provide accessible signs and labels to make identifying items easier for people with visual impairments. **ADAAG: 1998 4.30 & ADA Standards: 2010 216** See SN Signs.

F9 Where improving access to shelves and displays is not currently readily achievable, provide alternative services such as having staff available to retrieve items. Ca

G Signs

G1 Provide signs at inaccessible entrances that direct people to other accessible entrances. Ca

G2 Install accessible signs (including those for parking, restrooms, and telephones) throughout the building and site where appropriate. Ca

G3 Identify accessible checkout aisles with the International Symbol of Accessibility. Ca

G4 Mount signs displaying the International Symbol of Accessibility above accessible checkout aisles in the same location where the aisle number or type of checkout aisle is displayed. **ADA Standards: 2010 703 (New)**

See SN Signs

H Security Barriers and Bollards

Stores often include bollards and other security devices near entrances to prevent the theft of merchandise and shopping carts.

H1 Eliminate turnstiles and security gates that restrict access for people with disabilities. **ADAAG: 1998 7.4 & ADA Standards: 2010 206**

H2 Ensure that wheelchair access and egress is not obstructed by bollards or other devices that are intended to prevent the theft of merchandise or shopping carts. **ADAAG: 1998 7.4 & ADA Standards: 2010 206**

Exception: Providing an alternate accessible entrance that is conveniently located near another entrance is acceptable. ADAAG: 1998 7.4 & ADA Standards: 2010 206

I Communication

Effective communication with customers is essential for all businesses. About 10% of the general population, and approximately 60% of people over 65 years of age, have hearing impairments. Additionally, millions of Americans have speech and language impairments. Communication difficulties result when people's ability to send, receive, and/or process information is reduced. Many people also have multiple impairments (for example vision, mobility, speech and hearing) that affect their communication.

I 1 Remove partitions and other obstacles that block or restrict audible and/or visual information between employees and customers. Ca

I 2 Provide auxiliary communication aids and services where appropriate. Ca

I 3 Provide visual and auditory information where appropriate. Ca

I 4 Install sound buffers and panels to reduce noise and reverberation where appropriate. Ca

I 5 Provide accessible signage where required and where appropriate. **ADAAG: 1998 4.30 & ADA Standards: 2010 216** See SN Signs.

I 6 Train and educate staff and employees to communicate effectively with people who have communication difficulties. Ca

DS Dressing Rooms

A New Construction:
   Number and Location 228
B Alterations to Existing Conditions:
   Number and Location 228
C Clear Floor Space 228
D Doors 229
E Benches 229
F Mirrors 229
G Storage 230

Where dressing rooms, fitting rooms, locker rooms, and other areas for similar uses are provided, accessible rooms of each type must also be provided. For instance, where locker rooms are available for use by people of different genders, or where dressing rooms are available in medical care facilities, accessible rooms of each type must be available.

Adequate floor space and bench sizes in dressing, fitting, and locker rooms are important for people who may have to maneuver a wheelchair or stretch out to dress and undress. Accessible benches are required in accessible dressing, fitting, and locker rooms. Where other features are provided (such as lockers, shelves, mirrors, and hooks) they must be accessible.

General requirements (such as those for routes, interior spaces, restrooms, and other amenities) also apply. **See RT Routes and Spaces, TB Toilet/Bath Rooms,** and other chapters that apply.

A New Construction: Number and Location

A1 Ensure that at least 5%, but not less than one, of each cluster of dressing, fitting, or locker rooms is accessible and includes accessible features. **ADAAG: 1998 4.1 & ADA Standards: 2010 222**

B Alterations to Existing Conditions: Number and Location

B1 When altering existing buildings or sites, follow the requirements for dressing rooms in new construction to the maximum extent feasible. Ca

Exception: Where it is technically infeasible to make 5% of each cluster of dressing, fitting, or locker rooms accessible, ensure that at least one of each type of room for each gender on each level is accessible. **ADAAG: 1998 4.1 & ADA Standards: 2010 222**

B2 Where only unisex dressing rooms are provided, ensure that at least one accessible unisex dressing room is provided. **ADAAG: 1998 4.1 & ADA Standards: 2010 222**

C Clear Floor Space

People need clear floor space to comfortably use dressing, fitting, and locker rooms. The clear floor space in a room must be sufficient for a single wheelchair to turn around. Toe clearance under a partition may be used as part of the clear floor space.

C1 Ensure that accessible dressing, fitting, and locker rooms are on accessible routes. **See RT Routes and Spaces. ADAAG: 1998 4.3 & ADA Standards: 2010 206**

C2 Provide unobstructed clear floor space for turning a wheelchair that is at least 60in. (1525mm) by 60in. (1525mm) [or a 60in. (1525mm) diameter circular area] including toe clearance. **ADAAG: 1998 4.35, 4.2 & 2010 803, 304**
A clear floor space of 60in. (1525mm) by 78in. (1980mm) is preferred. Ca
Refer to Figures RT.5 and RT.6

C3 Where space under partitions is used as part of the clear floor space, provide toe clearance under the partition that extends
   a. vertically 9in. (230mm) minimum above the floor, and
   b. horizontally 6in. (150mm) minimum beyond the compartment-side face of the partition. **ADA Standards: 2010 803, 304 (New)**
Refer to Figure TS.12

C4 Where a number of dressing or fitting rooms are provided in a row, locate accessible rooms at the end of the row where possible to provide additional space inside the room. Ca

See **RT Routes and Spaces** for additional information about clear floor space and toe clearance.

D Doors

Doors to dressing, fitting, and locker rooms must be accessible. **See DR Doors.**

D1 Ensure that doors have a clear width of 32in. (815mm) minimum. **ADAAG: 1998 4.35 & ADA Standards: 2010 404**
A width of 36in. (915mm) is preferred. Ca

D2 Ensure that doors do not swing into wheelchair turning spaces. **ADAAG: 1998 4.35 & ADA Standards: 2010 803**

E Benches

Accessible dressing, fitting, and locker rooms must include accessible benches. Accessible benches must be large enough and sturdy enough so that people can safely transfer to them from a wheelchair. Accessible benches should also provide back support.

E1 Configure clear floor space for a parallel approach to the end of the bench seat. **ADAAG: 1998 4.37 & ADA Standards: 2010 305, 903**

E2 Where space permits, position the bench within the clear floor space so that the clear floor space extends 12in. (305mm) minimum behind the back of the bench to make maneuvering and transferring easier. Ca

E3 Ensure that the top of an accessible bench seat is between 17in. (430mm) minimum and 19in. (485mm) maximum above the floor. **ADAAG: 1998 4.37 & ADA Standards: 2010 903**

E4 Ensure that an accessible bench seat is
   a. 20in. (510mm) minimum to 24in. (610mm) maximum deep (from front to back), and
   b. 42in. (1065mm) minimum long. **ADAAG: 1998 4.37 & ADA Standards: 2010 903**

E5 Provide permanently installed back support that is a minimum of 42in. (1065mm) long or attach the bench to a wall that can provide back support. **ADA Standards: 2010 903 (New)**

E6 Ensure that the back support
   a. begins no more than 2in. (51mm) vertically, **ADAAG: 1998 4.37 & ADA Standards: 2010 903**
   b. 2.5in (64mm) maximum horizontally from the seat, **ADA Standards: 2010 903 (New)** and
   c. continues to at least 18in. (455mm) above the seat. **ADAAG: 1998 4.37 & ADA Standards: 2010 903**

E7 Where benches are attached to walls, provide grab bars on walls adjacent to the benches. **ADA Standards: 2010 903 (ADVISORY)** Ca

E8 Do not install grab bars on the walls behind benches where people lean for back support. **ADA Standards: 2010 903 (New)**

E9 Ensure that the materials used for benches can support a vertical or horizontal force of 250 lbs. (1112N) applied at any point on the seat, fastener, mounting device, or supporting structure. **ADAAG: 1998 4.37 & ADA Standards: 2010 903**

E10 Wherever benches are installed in wet locations (such as locker or shower rooms), ensure that the surface of the bench seat is slip resistant and does not accumulate water. **ADAAG: 1998 4.37 & ADA Standards: 2010 903**

F Mirrors

F1 Provide at least one mirror measuring at least 18in. (455mm) by 54in. (1370mm); **ADAAG: 1998 4.35** Ca
Larger full-length mirrors are preferred. Ca

F2 Install mirrors in locations that provide adequate views for both sitting and standing. **ADAAG: 1998 4.35** Ca

G Storage

Storage in dressing, fitting and locker rooms may include coat hooks, shelves, lockers, or other storage elements.

G1 Ensure that single-user and multiple-user rooms contain one of each type of accessible storage element. **ADA Standards: 2010 222 (New)**

G2 Mount accessible coat hooks within the appropriate reach range. **ADA Standards: 2010 803, 308 (New)**
A 43in. (1090mm) height is preferred. Ca

G3 Where shelves are provided, install fold-down shelves mounted between 40in. (1015mm) and 48in. (1220mm) above the floor. **ADA Standards: 2010 803 (New)**
A 40in. (1015mm) height is preferred. Ca

G4 Where lockers are provided, ensure that at least 5%, but not less than one, of each type is accessible. **ADAAG: 1998 4.1 & ADA Standards: 2010 225**
Increasing the number to 10% or more is preferred. Ca

TL Transient Lodging

A	New Construction: Number and Location	231
B	Alterations to Existing Conditions: Number and Location	231
C	Accessible Guest Rooms	231
D	Visual Alarms, Notification Devices and Telephones in Sleeping Rooms	233
E	Common Areas	234

Transient lodging includes buildings that provide sleeping accommodations that are intended to be used primarily for short-term residency. Transient lodgings include, but are not limited to, hotels, boarding houses, motels, resorts, homeless shelters, and halfway houses. Dwelling units and medical care facilities are not considered transient lodging. See DU Dwelling Units and MC Medical Care.

If you are not sure whether your building must meet accessibility requirements for transient lodging, request additional information from the Department of Justice to determine whether particular facilities or portions of them are covered under ADA Standards. See References.

This section does not apply to establishments that contain five or fewer rooms for rent or hire and that are occupied by the proprietor as the proprietor's primary residence.

The information in this section focuses on the accessibility of individual guest rooms and spaces. The common areas of the building must also be accessible at least to the same degree that the public use or common areas of any other building must be accessible.

In addition to following the guidelines in this chapter, review information on accessible routes and spaces, doors, entrances, restrooms, public telephones, and elevators as needed. See RT Routes and Spaces, DR Doors, EN Entrances, TB Toilet/Bath Rooms, PT Public Telephones, and EL Elevators, and all other chapters that apply.

A   New Construction: Number and Location

To meet the needs of all people, a number of guest rooms must be accessible with respect to clear floor space, room type, bathroom type, and emergency alarm type. The information below indicates the numbers of rooms that must be accessible based on the types of features they include.

In providing an equivalent range of options in accessible guest rooms, consider room size, room style, cost, view, bathroom fixtures (such as hot tubs and spas) smoking and non-smoking, the number of beds, and bed size.

A1   Ensure that at least the minimum number of accessible guest rooms are provided. **ADAAG: 1998 9.1 & ADA Standards: 2010 224**
See TL-A

A2   In buildings with 51 or more guest rooms, ensure that accessible guest rooms include roll-in showers with folding seats. **ADAAG: 1998 9.1 & ADA Standards: 2010 224, 608**
See TL-A

A3   Where there are accessible guest rooms, ensure that all features of the guest room and bathroom (including grab bars and tub seats in the shower or bathtub) are accessible. **ADAAG: 1998 9.2 & ADA Standards: 2010 224, 806**

A4   In guest rooms or dormitory-style sleeping areas that contain four or more beds, ensure that the clear floor space meets at least the minimum accessibility requirements around required accessible beds. **ADA Standards: 2010 224 (New)**
See TL-B

A5   Ensure that at least the minimum required number of guest rooms contain communication features. **ADAAG: 1998 9.1 & ADA Standards: 2010 224**
See TL-C

A6   Provide choices of types and styles of accessible guest rooms and sleeping areas comparable to the choices provided in rooms that are not accessible. **ADAAG: 1998 9.1 & ADA Standards: 2010 224**

A7   Disperse accessible guest rooms among the types and styles of guest rooms provided throughout the building. **ADAAG: 1998 9.1 & ADA Standards: 2010 224**
Exception: Where the minimum number of rooms or beds required to be accessible is not sufficient to allow for complete dispersion by room type or style, prioritize dispersion in the following order: room type, bed type, and amenities. ADA Standards: 2010 224 (New)

B   Alterations to Existing Conditions: Number and Location

In alterations, the minimum required number of accessible guest rooms is based on the total number of guest rooms altered or added instead of the total number of guest rooms provided in a building.

B1   Where guest rooms are altered or added, apply the guidelines for type and number of accessible guest rooms until the number of accessible guest rooms complies with the minimum number required for new construction. **ADAAG: 1998 9.1 & ADA Standards: 2010 224**

B2   When accessible guest rooms are added as a result of alterations or additions, ensure that proper dispersion is achieved. **ADA Standards: 2010 224 (New)**

C   Accessible Guest Rooms

The space within an accessible guest room should allow guests to move around and access room features comfortably.

C1   Locate accessible units, sleeping rooms, and suites on accessible routes. **ADAAG: 1998 9.1 & ADA Standards: 2010 806 See RT Routes and Spaces.**

C2   Provide clear floor space within accessible guest rooms that meets the following requirements:
  a.   36in. (915mm) clear width maneuvering space on both sides of a bed where a single bed is provided;
       A clear width of 42in. (1065mm) is preferred. ca

Design for All: The Best Path Forward — Dr. Arvid E. Osterberg

Total guest rooms (accessible and non-accessible)	Accessible guest rooms required	Accessible guest rooms *with* roll-in showers	Accessible guest rooms *without* roll-in showers
1 to 25	1	0	1
26 to 50	2	0	2
51 to 75	4	1	3
76 to 100	5	1	4
101 to 150	7	2	5
151 to 200	8	2	6
201 to 300	10	3	7
301 to 400	12	4	8
401 to 500	13	4	9
501 to 1000	3 percent of total	1 percent of total	2 percent of total
1001 and over	30 plus 2 for each 100, or fraction thereof, over 1000	10 plus 1 for each 100, or fraction thereof, over 1000	30 plus 2 for each 100, or fraction thereof, over 1000

TL-A Minimum required number of accessible guest rooms by type

Number of beds in room/sleeping area	Guest rooms with communication features
4 to 25	1
26 to 50	2
51 to 79	4
76 to 100	5
101 to 150	7
151 to 200	8
201 to 300	10
301 to 400	12
401 to 500	13
501 to 1000	3 percent of total
1001 and over	30 plus 2 for each 100, or fraction thereof, over 1000

TL-B Minimum required number of accessible guest beds in dormitory-style sleeping areas

Total number of guest rooms provided	Guest rooms with communication features
1	1
2 to 25	2
26 to 50	4
51 to 75	7
76 to 100	9
101 to 150	12
151 to 200	14
201 to 300	17
301 to 400	20
401 to 500	22
501 to 1000	5 percent of total
1001 and over	50, plus 3 for each 100 over 1000

TL-C Minimum required number of guest rooms with communication features

    b. 36in. (915mm) clear width maneuvering space between the beds where 2 beds are provided;
    60in. (1525mm) is preferred; Ca
    and
    c. the clear floor space connects to all accessible spaces and features within the unit. **ADAAG: 1998 9.2 & ADA Standards: 2010 806, 403**

Refer to Figure MC.1 in MC Medical Care that shows the preferred clear floor space and unobstructed turning space in an accessible sleeping room.

C3 Ensure that doors and doorways into and within guest rooms and sleeping areas (including doors to bathrooms) are accessible. **ADAAG: 1998 9.2 & ADA Standards: 2010 224 See DR Doors.**

Exception: Shower and sauna doors in non-accessible guest rooms are not required to be accessible. ADA Standards: 2010 224 (New)

C4 Ensure that at least one of each type of fixed or built-in storage units (such as cabinets, shelves, closets, and drawers) is accessible. Additional storage may be provided outside accessible reach ranges. **ADAAG: 1998 9.2 & ADA Standards: 2010 225, 811 See SG Storage.**

C5 Locate controls (such as those for heating and cooling, ventilation, lighting, televisions, and other room features) on accessible routes. **ADAAG: 1998 4.3 & ADA Standards: 2010 206 See RT Routes and Spaces.**

C6 Mount controls within the appropriate reach ranges and ensure that controls
    a. are operable with one hand;
    b. do not require tight grasping, pinching, or twisting of the wrist; and
    c. can be operated with a force less than or equal to 5 lbs.(22.2N). **ADAAG: 1998 4.27 & ADA Standards: 2010 309, 707 See RR Reach Ranges.**

C7 Ensure that all areas connected to an accessible guest room are accessible, including
    a. living area;
    b. dining area;
    c. at least one sleeping area;
    d. patios, terraces, or balconies;
    e. at least one full bathroom (with toilet, lavatory and tub or shower);
    f. at least one half-bath, (where only half-baths are included); and
    g. carports, garages, or parking spaces. **ADAAG: 1998 9.2 & ADA Standards: 2010 806**

C8 Ensure that kitchenettes or wet bars included in accessible guest rooms provide
    a. clear floor space for a front or parallel approach to cabinets and appliances,
    b. countertop and sink heights at 34in. (865mm) maximum above the floor, and
    c. 50% of shelf space in cabinets and refrigerators/freezers within accessible reach ranges. **ADAAG: 1998 9.2 & ADA Standards: 2010 804**

See KT Kitchens for additional requirements.

D Visual Alarms, Notification Devices and Telephones in Sleeping Rooms

Accessible sleeping rooms need to be equivalent to other sleeping rooms with regard to the installation of electrical outlets (including outlets connected to the building's alarm system) and telephone wiring to enable persons with hearing impairments to use portable visual alarms and communication devices. Accessible rooms must also include alarm systems that are usable by people with visual and auditory disabilities.

D1 Ensure that all fire alarm systems in transient lodging comply with the requirements of *NFPA 72*. **ADA Standards: 2010 215, 702 (New)**

D2 Install auxiliary visual alarms. **ADAAG: 1998 4.31 See AL Alarms.** Ca

Design for All: The Best Path Forward — Dr. Arvid E. Osterberg

D3 Provide visual notification devices to alert residents when someone is knocking on the door or ringing the doorbell or when the telephone is ringing. **ADAAG: 1998 9.3 & ADA Standards: 2010 806**

D4 Do not connect notification devices to visual alarm appliances. **ADAAG: 1998 4.31 & ADA Standards: 2010 806**

D5 Provide volume controls on telephones that have
  a. a gain adjustable up to a minimum of 20dB,
  b. at least one intermediate step of 12dB of gain for incremental volume control, and
  c. an automatic reset. **ADA Standards: 2010 704 (MODIFIED-MORE RESTRICTIVE)**

D6 Ensure that accessible telephones have electric outlets that accommodate the use of TTYs. **ADAAG: 1998 4.31 & 2010 217, 806**

E Common Areas

All common areas of the building and site (including exterior and interior routes and spaces, lobbies, registration areas, lounges, restrooms, restaurants, recreation areas, self-service and vending areas, and shops) need to meet all appropriate accessibility requirements. See the chapters in *Design for All* that apply.

Entry lobbies often have sales and service counters for check-in and registration, concierge services, and self-serve beverage areas that must be accessible. Tables and seating, shelves and displays, and other areas used by guests also must be accessible.

E1 Locate accessible common areas on accessible routes. **ADAAG: 1998 9.1 & ADA Standards: 2010 806**
See **RT Routes and Spaces.**

E2 Ensure that at least one of each type of sales and service counter is accessible. **ADAAG: 1998 7.2 & ADA Standards: 2010 904**
See **BU Businesses, BU-A.**

E3 Ensure that at least one of each type of table and seating arrangement is accessible. **ADAAG: 1998 4.32 & ADA Standards: 2010 902**
See **TA Tables and Seating.**

E4 Ensure that at least one of each type of shelves and displays is accessible. **ADAAG: 1998 7.2 & ADA Standards: 2010 904**
See **BU Businesses, BU-F.**

E5 Ensure that at least one of each type of self-serve machine or appliance included in common areas (such as washers, dryers, coffee makers, and newspaper and magazine racks) is accessible. **ADAAG: 1998 4.27 & 2010 707** See **VS Vending/Self-serve.**

DU Dwelling Units

A	Parking	235
B	Common Areas	236
C	Mailboxes	236
D	Entrances and Doors	236
E	Kitchens	237
F	Toilet Rooms and Bathrooms	237
G	Communication and Warning Systems	237

Wheelchair Accessible Units 231
H	New Construction: Number and Location	237
I	Alterations to Existing Conditions: Number & Location	238
J	Routes and Spaces	238

Communication Accessible Units 239
K	New Construction: Number and Location	239
L	Alterations to Existing Conditions: Number & Location	239
M	Notification and Identification Features	240
N	Alarms and Warning Devices in Communication Accessible Units	240

The ADA defines residential dwelling units as units that are intended to be used primarily for *long-term* residency. Residential dwelling units include housing that is rented on a long-term basis, such as units in an apartment building. At college and university campuses, undergraduate and graduate dormitories and residence halls are considered residential dwelling units.

See TL Transient Lodging for the requirements for buildings that contain one or more guest rooms for sleeping that are primarily for *short-term* residency, such as hotels, motels, and shelters.

The information in this chapter focuses on ADA Standards requirements for residential dwelling units. However, accessibility requirements for residential dwelling units are also covered by the Fair Housing Act (FHA), and sometimes two or more standards may apply. For instance, privately owned apartment buildings need to meet the design requirements of the FHA. Refer to FHA or contact the Department of Justice (DOJ) or your regional Disability and Business Technical Assistance Center at 800-949-4232 if you need further information to determine which requirements you need to follow. **See References.** Accessible dwelling units covered by ADA Standards fall into two categories: those that are accessible for people with mobility difficulties, and those that are accessible for people who are deaf or who have hearing limitations. In this chapter we have labeled these types of units as 'wheelchair accessible' and 'communication accessible.'

A portion of dwelling units in *new* residential buildings and complexes must meet the requirements for wheelchair accessible units and another portion must meet the requirements for communication accessible units. A portion of units in *existing* buildings must meet the requirements for each type of unit when units are added to the building or complex and/or when units are altered. Alterations include remodeling, renovation, rehabilitation, or other construction that involves changes in structural elements, for instance removing or reconfiguring permanent partition walls in units. Normal maintenance, redecorating (such as painting or wallpapering), and changes to mechanical or electrical systems are considered alterations only if the changes affect the accessibility of the building.

The requirements of each type of accessible unit must be met independently. In other words, some units must be wheelchair accessible and some units must be communication accessible.

The requirements for the number of each type of unit cannot be satisfied by combining requirements for wheelchair accessible and communication accessible units in the same units. However, we recommend that you go beyond the minimum required number and provide additional units that are both wheelchair accessible and communication accessible to meet the needs of all people.

This chapter is divided into three parts, Common Areas, Wheelchair Accessible Dwelling Units, and Communication Accessible Dwelling Units.

A Parking

Where parking is provided at residential buildings and complexes that are required to include wheelchair accessible units, a portion of parking for residents must be accessible.

A1 Where parking is provided at residential dwelling units for guests and employees, ensure that ADA

Standards requirements for accessible parking are met. To determine the minimum required number of accessible parking spaces for guests and employees. **See PA Parking, PA-A.** **ADA Standards: 2010 208 (NEW)**

A2 Where each unit in a building or complex has one parking space, ensure that one accessible parking space is provided for each accessible dwelling unit. **ADA Standards: 2010 208 (NEW)**

A3 Where at least one parking space is provided for each residential dwelling unit in a building or complex,
- a. provide at least one accessible parking space for each accessible unit in a building or complex, and
- b. locate accessible parking spaces serving accessible units on the shortest possible accessible route to the units they serve. **ADA Standards: 2010 208 (NEW)**

A4 Where additional parking is provided so that the total number of parking spaces for residents exceeds one parking space for each unit,
- a. ensure that at least 2%, but not less than one, of the additional parking spaces is accessible, and
- b. disperse the additional accessible spaces throughout all types of additional parking provided for residents. **ADA Standards: 2010 208**

A5 Where parking is not assigned, provide accessible parking in all lots serving residents as described in **PA Parking. ADA Standards: 2010 208 (NEW)**

A6 Ensure that all accessible parking spaces meet the requirements for accessible parking. See PA Parking. **ADA Standards: 2010 208 (NEW)**
Exception: Signs identifying accessible parking are not required at accessible spaces that are assigned to specific accessible dwelling units. ADA Standards: 2010 216 (NEW)

B Common Areas

Common areas that serve wheelchair accessible units and/or communication accessible units must meet all general accessibility requirements.

All common routes and spaces that serve the public (such as gift shops, book stores, or restaurants) within buildings that contain residential dwelling units must be accessible. **See BU Business.**

Common areas that serve accessible residential dwelling units (such as lobbies, corridors, lounges, laundry rooms, storage areas, and vending areas) must be fully accessible. See all chapters in *Design for All* that apply.

B1 Ensure that common areas that serve accessible residential dwelling units are fully accessible. **ADA Standards: 2010 201 (NEW)**

C Mailboxes

C1 In buildings and complexes where a mailbox is provided for each residential unit,
- a. provide an accessible mailbox for each accessible unit, and
- b. ensure that each accessible mailbox meets all accessibility requirements for mailboxes. **ADA Standards: 2010 228 (NEW) See VS Vending/Self serve and RR Reach Ranges.**

D Entrances and Doors

D1 Ensure that at least one primary entrance to each accessible unit is accessible and meets ADA Standards door and doorway requirements. The primary entrance to a wheelchair accessible unit cannot be to a bedroom. **ADA Standards: 2010 206 (NEW) See EN Entrances and DR Doors.**

D2 Ensure that all doors and doorways within accessible units that provide full user passage meet ADA Standards requirements for accessible doors. **ADA Standards: 2010 206 (NEW)**

D3 Where peepholes are provided as visual identification devices, install two peepholes at the following heights:

a. 48in. (1220mm) above the floor (or the appropriate height for the individual resident); and
   b. 63in. (1600mm) above the floor (for the average standing adult). ca

E Kitchens

E1 Ensure that kitchens within accessible residential dwelling units meet all ADA Standards requirements for kitchens and kitchenettes. **ADA Standards: 2010 809** (New) See KT Kitchens.

F Toilet Rooms and Bathrooms

F1 Ensure that toilet rooms and bathrooms within accessible units meet all of the ADA Standards requirements for toilet rooms and bathrooms. **ADA Standards: 2010 809** (New) See the Restrooms and Bathrooms section.

F2 When transfer shower stalls are provided, ensure that either folding seats are installed or walls are reinforced to permit future installation of folding seats. **ADA Standards: 2010 608** (New)

G Communication and Warning Systems

Where a two-way communication system (including a closed-circuit system) is provided to permit voice communication between visitors in common areas of the building (for instance at the entrance or lobby) and occupants of residential dwelling units, the system must include compatible features that permit communication between the common areas and the communication accessible units. **ADA Standards: 2010 809, 708** (New)

G1 Install communication systems that include
   a. an interface in the common area of the building, site, or floor that is capable of supporting both voice and TTY communication between the common area and communication accessible residential units within the building, and
   b. an interface in each communication accessible unit that includes a telephone jack capable of supporting both voice and TTY communication between the residential unit and the common area. **ADAAG: 2010 708** (New)

G2 Ensure that all fire alarm systems in residential dwelling units comply with the requirements of *NFPA 72*. **ADA Standards: 2010 215, 702** (New)

Wheelchair Accessible Units

A portion of units in every residential building or complex must be accessible to people who have mobility limitations. The total number of units in each building or complex determines the number of wheelchair accessible units. The units should be dispersed to provide choices of location for all residents. Where dwelling units must be wheelchair accessible, many of the requirements for dimensioning and other specifics are the same as those for all accessible buildings and sites. For further information, we refer you to other chapters in *Design for All*.

H New Construction: Number and Location

Where a building or complex contains **15 or fewer** residential dwelling units, ensure that the minimum number of accessible residential dwelling units meets the following requirements. These requirements apply to the total number of residential dwelling units that are constructed under a single contract, or are developed as a whole, whether or not they are located on a common site. **ADA Standards: 2010 233**

H1 In a building that contains five or more residential units, ensure that at least 5%, but not less than one, of the total number of units in the building is wheelchair accessible. **ADA Standards: 2010 233** (New)
   a. Ensure that wheelchair accessible units are dispersed among and integrated with the various types of dwelling units in the building. **ADA Standards: 2010 233** (New)

H2 In projects or complexes where each building contains four or fewer residential dwelling units, ensure that at least 5%, but not less than one, of the total number of units in the project or complex is wheelchair accessible. **ADA Standards: 2010 233 (NEW)**

    a. Ensure that wheelchair accessible units are dispersed among and integrated with the various types of dwelling units in the **project or complex**. **ADA Standards: 2010 233 (NEW)**

Note: To determine or verify the number of residential dwelling units that are required to be wheelchair accessible, call your regional Disability and Business Technical Assistance Center at 800-949-4232.

H3 Ensure that the choice of wheelchair accessible units is comparable to the choice available to other residents. **ADA Standards: 2010 233 (NEW)**
Exception: Where individual dwelling units are multi-story (such as townhouse units) one-story wheelchair accessible units may be provided to meet the required number of wheelchair accessible units, as long as the space and amenities are comparable to the multi-story units. ADA Standards: 2010 233 (NEW)

I Alterations to Existing Conditions: Number and Location

Where a building or complex contains **15 or fewer** residential dwelling units, ensure that the minimum number of accessible residential dwelling units meets the following requirements. These requirements apply to the total number of residential dwelling units that are **altered** under a single contract, or are developed as a whole, whether or not they are located on a common site. **ADA Standards: 2010 233 (NEW)**

I 1 When new units are added to existing buildings or when existing units are altered, provide wheelchair accessible units until the number of wheelchair accessible units complies with at least the minimum required number for new construction. **ADA Standards: 2010 233 (NEW)**

I 2 In alterations where meeting all accessibility requirements for new construction is technically infeasible, alter or construct wheelchair accessible residential dwelling units that have comparable amenities to the other residential dwelling units. **ADA Standards: 2010 233 (NEW)**

I 3 Where a building is vacated for the purposes of alteration include 15 or more residential dwelling units, ensure that at least 5% of the units are wheelchair accessible and that at least 2% of the units have accessible communication features. **ADA Standards: 2010 233 (NEW)**

I 4 Where a building is vacated for the purposes of alteration includes 15 or more residential dwelling units, ensure that at least one unit is wheelchair accessible and has accessible communication features. **ADA Standards: 2010 233 (NEW)**

I 5 Where a residential dwelling unit is substantially altered (a bathroom or kitchen and at least one other room) ensure that the alteration meets all accessibility requirements. Continue to make altered units accessible until the minimum requirement for the number of accessible units required for new construction is met. **ADA Standards: 2010 233 (NEW)**

J Routes and Spaces

Having adequate maneuvering space at entrances and in hallways is important for people who use wheelchairs or other mobility aids.

J1 Ensure that all interior and exterior routes that serve accessible units in residential buildings, complexes, and sites meet all ADA Standards requirements for accessible routes. **ADA Standards: 2010 206 (NEW)** See RT Routes and Spaces.
Exception: Where accessible residential dwelling units and accessible common use and public use areas (that serve the accessible residential dwelling units) are on an accessible route, accessible routes are not required to connect building stories. ADA Standards: 2010 206 (NEW)

J2 Ensure that all spaces and elements within accessible units are connected by at least one accessible route. **ADA Standards: 2010 206 (NEW)** See RT Routes and Spaces.
Exception: Unfinished attics and unfinished basements are not required to be accessible or to

have accessible routes within them. **ADA Standards: 2010 809** (New)

J3 Where there is only one accessible route provided within a residential dwelling unit, ensure that it does not pass through bedrooms, bathrooms, closets, or similar spaces. **ADA Standards: 2010 809** (New)

J4 Provide turning spaces in all rooms within accessible dwelling units that are connected by an accessible route. **ADA Standards: 2010 809** (New) See RT Routes and Spaces.
Exception: Turning spaces are not required in exterior spaces (e.g. patio, balcony, or porch) that have a 30in. (760mm) maximum depth or width. ADA Standards: 2010 809 (New)

J5 Ensure that all elements, amenities, features, and spaces provided for residents' use within accessible units (such as light switches, electrical outlets, shelves, hooks, and other controls and handles) meet requirements for clear floor space and reach ranges. **ADA Standards: 2010 809** (New)
See RT Routes and Spaces, RR Reach Ranges, and SG Storage.

Communication Accessible Units

A portion of units in every residential building or complex must contain communication features that are accessible to people who are deaf or who have hearing limitations. The communication features notify people when visitors arrive and provide warnings in emergency situations. The total number of units in each building or complex determines the number of communication accessible units. These units must be dispersed to provide choices of location for residents.

K   New Construction: Number and Location

K1 In a building that contains five or more residential dwelling units, ensure that at least 2%, but not less than one, of the total number of units in a building is communication accessible. **ADA Standards: 2010 233** (New)
   a. Ensure that communication accessible units are dispersed among and integrated with the various types of dwelling units in the **building**. **ADA Standards: 2010 233** (New)

K2 In projects or complexes where each building contains four or fewer residential units, ensure that at least 2%, but not less than one, of the total number of units in the project or complex is communication accessible. **ADA Standards: 2010 233** (New)
   a. Ensure that communication accessible units are dispersed among and integrated with the various types of dwelling units in the **project or complex**. **ADA Standards: 2010 233** (New)

K3 Ensure that the choice of communication accessible units is comparable to the choice of units available to other residents. **ADA Standards: 2010 233** (New)

L   Alterations to Existing Conditions: Number and Location

Where residential dwelling units are altered or added to existing buildings or complexes, the requirements for communication accessible units apply to the added or altered units. **ADA Standards: 2010 233** (New)

L1 When new units are added to existing buildings or when existing units are altered, provide communication accessible units until the number of communication accessible units complies with at least the minimum required number for new construction. **ADA Standards: 2010 233** (New)

L2 In alterations where meeting all accessibility requirements for new construction is technically infeasible, alter or construct communication accessible residential dwelling units that have comparable amenities to the other residential dwelling units. **ADA Standards: 2010 233** (New)

M Notification and Identification Features

Deaf people and people with limited hearing need communication features that notify them when someone is at the door. Where visual identification devices (such as peepholes, view panels, or side lites) are included at entrances and doors, they must be accessible.

M1 Provide hard-wired electric doorbells in all communication accessible units that include the following features:
   a. a button or switch outside the primary entrance to the unit to activate the doorbell,
   b. both audible tones and visual signals within the unit that are initiated by a button or switch, and
   c. controls to deactivate the doorbell signals where the signals are included in sleeping areas. **ADA Standards: 2010 809 (NEW)**

M2 Install visual identification devices (peepholes, view panels, or side lites) in entrance doors or doorways to accessible dwelling units that provide a minimum of 180° view so that residents can identify visitors without opening the door. **ADA Standards: 2010 809 (NEW)**

N Alarms and Warning Devices in Communication Accessible Units

State and local building codes and other regulations typically require residential dwelling units to be equipped with smoke alarm and fire alarm systems. Where smoke alarm and/or fire alarm systems are included in communication accessible residential dwelling units and in buildings that include communication accessible units, alarms must meet specific ADA Standards requirements. Where building-wide fire alarms are installed, alarms connected to the system must be provided in communication accessible units.

The ADA Standards permits alarm devices in communication accessible units to be used to notify residents of both detection of smoke in individual units and activation of the building-wide fire alarm system. The ADA Standards does not permit the alarm devices to be used for any other purposes apart from smoke and fire warnings.

N1 Install smoke detectors in communication accessible units that include visual warnings and that comply with *NFPA 72*. **ADA Standards: 2010 809 (NEW)**

N2 Where fire alarm appliances are installed within accessible residential dwelling units, ensure that they are permanently installed and have both audible and visual alarms that comply with *NFPA 72*. **ADA Standards: 2010 702 (NEW)**

N3 Ensure that the maximum sound level of audible notification appliances is 110dB at the minimum hearing distance from the audible appliance complying with *NFPA 72*. **ADA Standards: 2010 707 (NEW)**

N4 Where building-wide fire alarm systems are provided in a building that includes communication accessible dwelling units, extend the system wiring into communication accessible units to a point near the individual units' smoke detection systems. **ADA Standards: 2010 809 (NEW)**

N5 Where alarms that are part of the building-wide alarm system are installed in individual communication accessible units, ensure that
   a. alarms in units comply with *NFPA 72*, and
   b. visual alarms in units are activated when the building-wide system is activated in the part of the building where the unit is located. **ADA Standards: 2010 809 (NEW)**

N6 Ensure that all visual alarm devices (including both fire and smoke detection devices) are activated by smoke detection. **ADA Standards: 2010 809 (NEW)**

MC Medical Care

A	Parking and Loading Zones	241
B	Entrances	241
C	Doors	242
D	Vertical Access	242
E	Reception and Service Counters	242
F	Public Telephones	242
G	New Construction: Number and Location	242
H	Alterations to Existing Conditions: Number and Location	242
I	Patient Sleeping Rooms: Clear Floor Space	243
J	Adjoining Toilet Rooms and/or Bathrooms	243

This chapter discusses accessibility requirements for medical care and long-term care facilities. In buildings where patients stay more than twenty-four hours (including physical rehabilitation, psychiatric care, detoxification facilities, and hospitals) specific requirements for patient sleeping rooms and adjoining toilet and bathrooms apply. Public use and common areas (such as parking, restrooms, waiting rooms, telephones, and other spaces and elements in a building) must also be accessible.

All medical buildings, including doctor's offices and clinics that primarily treat people on an outpatient basis, are covered under ADA Standards general requirements for new construction and alterations. Refer to all applicable chapters in *Design for All* for specific accessibility requirements.

Fire alarm systems in medical care facilities (not specified in ADA Standards) must be installed in accordance with current industry practice and state and local codes and requirements.

The items below provide information on the requirements for medical care and long-term care facilities that are different from, or in addition to, the requirements for other types of buildings.

A Parking and Loading Zones

In addition to the requirements for parking and loading zones in **PA Parking,** the following requirements also apply to medical care and long-term care facilities.

The percentage of accessible parking varies depending on the type of medical facility. A higher number of parking spaces for visitors and patients of rehabilitation and physical therapy facilities (both inpatient and outpatient) are required to be accessible. People receiving rehabilitation or physical therapy may use braces, canes, crutches, prosthetic devices, wheelchairs, or other mobility aids; or they may have arthritic, neurological, respiratory, cardiac, or orthopedic conditions that impose significant limitations on their mobility.

A1 Ensure that 10% minimum of the total number of patient and visitor parking spaces serving outpatient facilities are accessible. **ADAAG: 1998 4.1 & ADA Standards: 2010 208**
A higher percentage is preferred. ca

A2 Ensure that 20% minimum of the total number of patient and visitor parking spaces serving facilities that specialize in rehabilitation, physical therapy, and other services for persons with mobility impairments are accessible. **ADAAG: 1998 4.1 & ADA Standards: 2010 208**

A3 At medical care facilities that provide inpatient services (where patients' stay may exceed 24 hours) and at long-term care facilities, provide at least one accessible passenger loading zone at an accessible entrance. **ADA Standards: 2010 209 (New)**

A4 Ensure that curb ramps and routes from loading zones to building entrances are accessible. **ADAAG: 1998 4.7 & ADA Standards: 2010 406 See CR Curb Ramps and EN Entrances.**

B Entrances

In addition to the requirements for entrances in **EN Entrances,** the following requirements also apply to medical care and long-term care facilities.

B1 Ensure that accessible entrances are protected from inclimate weather by a canopy or other type of fixed or removable covering. ca
ADAAG: 1998 6.2

Design for All: The Best Path Forward — Dr. Arvid E. Osterberg

C Doors

C1 Follow the requirements for doors in DR Doors. **ADAAG: 1998 4.13 & ADA Standards: 2010 404**

Exception: Clearance beyond the latch side of doors is not required at doors to critical care and intensive care patient rooms. ADAAG: 1998 6.3 & ADA Standards: 2010 404

D Vertical Access

D1 The ADAAG does not require vertical access (such as elevators) in most private buildings that are less than three stories, or less than 3000sq. ft. (279sq. m) per story. However, all buildings that contain offices of heath care providers must include vertical access between stories. **ADA Standards: 2010 206 (New)**

E Reception and Service Counters

Medical care and long-term care facilities include reception and service counters that need to be accessible to provide patient and visitor information and for other purposes.

E1 Ensure that at least one of each type of reception and service counter is accessible. **ADAAG: 1998 7.2 & ADA Standards: 2010 904 See BU Businesses.**

F Public Telephones

F1 Where public pay telephones are provided in hospital waiting rooms or other public areas, provide at least one accessible TTY at each location. **ADAAG: 1998 4.1 & ADA Standards: 2010 217 See PT Public Telephones.**

Patient Sleeping Rooms

The requirements for patient sleeping rooms in medical care facilities vary by the type of facility because of the different needs of patients who use them. Since the distribution of various types of patient rooms is subject to change based on patient care needs and other considerations, ADA Standards does not require that accessible patient rooms be dispersed throughout medical care facilities or hospitals, except in the case of long-term care facilities. However, it is best to disperse accessible rooms where possible among various types of patient rooms (such as private, semiprivate, and rooms of specialized care units) in all types of health care facilities.

G New Construction: Number and Location

G1 Ensure that all patient or resident sleeping rooms in medical care facilities that do specialize in the treatment of conditions affecting mobility are accessible. **ADAAG: 1998 6.1 & ADA Standards: 2010 223**

G2 Ensure that at least 10%, but no fewer than one, of patient or resident sleeping rooms in all medical care facilities that do not specialize in the treatment of conditions affecting mobility are accessible. **ADAAG: 1998 6.1 & ADA Standards: 2010 223**

A higher percentage is preferred.

G3 Ensure that at least 50% of patient or resident sleeping rooms in all licensed long-term care facilities are accessible. **ADAAG: 1998 6.1 & ADA Standards: 2010 223**

A higher percentage is preferred.

G4 Disperse accessible sleeping rooms among all types of sleeping rooms available to the maximum extent possible.

H Alterations to Existing Conditions: Number and Location

Where patient sleeping rooms are altered or added to existing medical care or long-term care facilities, the requirements for accessible rooms apply to the added or altered units. **ADAAG: 1998 6.1 & ADA Standards: 2010 223**

H1 When new rooms are added to existing buildings or complexes, or when existing rooms are altered, provide accessible rooms until the number of accessible rooms in the building or complex complies with at least the minimum required number of accessible rooms for new construction. **ADAAG: 1998 6.1 & ADA Standards: 2010 223**

I Patient Sleeping Rooms: Clear Floor Space

The requirements pertaining to patient sleeping rooms are listed below. Refer to the appropriate chapters in *Design for All* for information on other features and elements in accessible spaces. **See RT Routes and Spaces, RR Reach Ranges, and DR Doors.**

I 1 Provide a 36in. (915mm) wide minimum accessible route to the bed. **ADAAG: 1998 4.3 & ADA Standards: 2010 403**
A 42in. (1065mm) wide route is preferred.

I 2 Provide a 36in. (915mm) wide clear floor space on each side of the bed. **ADAAG: 1998 6.3 & ADA Standards: 2010 805, 305**
A 42in. (1065mm) wide clear floor space is preferred.
Provide a clear floor space for a parallel approach on at least one side of the bed. **ADA Standards: 2010 805, 305 (MODIFIED-LESS RESTRICTIVE)**

I 3 Provide at least one unobstructed turning space in the room as follows:
  a. circular: 60in. (1525mm) diameter, or
  b. T-shaped: 60in. (1525mm), 67in. (1702mm) preferred square with three 36in. (915mm) legs. 42in. (1065mm) preferred.
  ADA Standards: 1998 6.2, 4.2 & 2010 805, 304
Refer to Figures RT.5, RT.6, and RT.7

I 4 In rooms with 2 beds, locate the turning space between the beds. **ADAAG: 1998 6.3**
See Figure MC.1

J Adjoining Toilet Rooms and/or Bathrooms

Toilet rooms and/or bathrooms adjoining accessible sleeping rooms must meet ADA Standards requirements. **See TB Toilet/Bath Rooms.**

J1 Locate all toilet rooms and/or bathrooms that adjoin accessible sleeping rooms on accessible routes. **ADAAG: 1998 6.4 & ADA Standards: 2010 805 See RT Routes and Spaces.**

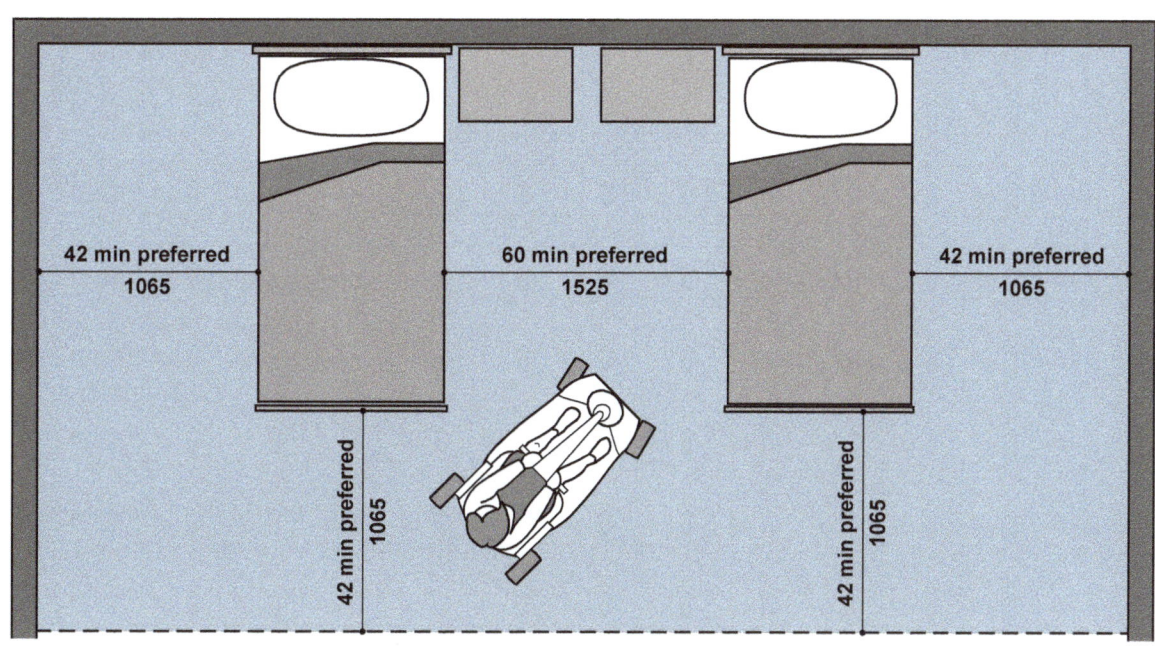

MC.1 Preferred minimum clear floor space and unobstructed turning space in an accessible sleeping room

J2 Where provided, ensure that at least one toilet, one lavatory, and one bathtub or shower is accessible. **ADA Standards: 2010 805, 223 (New)** See the Restrooms and Bathrooms section.

Exception: Toilet rooms in critical care and intensive care patient sleeping rooms are not required to be accessible. ADA Standards: 2010 223 (New)

J3 Ensure that all features and fixtures in accessible toilet rooms and/or bathrooms are accessible. **ADAAG: 1998 6.4 & ADA Standards: 2010 805** See FX Fixtures.

KT Kitchens

A	Clearance: Pass-Through Kitchens	244
B	Clearance: U-Shaped Kitchens	244
C	Clear Floor Space	245
D	Counters	245
E	Sinks	245
F	Faucets and Operable Parts on Fixtures	245
G	Dishwasher	246
H	Range or Cooktop	246
I	Oven	246
J	Refrigerator/Freezer	246
K	Washers and Dryers	246
L	Controls and Operable Parts	247
M	Storage	247

This chapter covers ADA Standards requirements for kitchens and kitchenettes, which are commonly found in break rooms, common areas (such as those in businesses and hotel and motel lobbies), and accessible residential dwelling units. Kitchens and kitchenettes in accessible guest rooms in transient lodging (such as hotels and motels), also need to be accessible.

In kitchens, it is important for people to have sufficient clear floor space for maneuvering. It is also helpful to install at least some of the cabinets and shelves at appropriate levels for people with limited reach ranges.

A Clearance: Pass-Through Kitchens

Pass-through kitchens include two separate entries and have counters, appliances, or cabinets located on two opposing sides (or have counters, appliances, or cabinets located opposite a parallel wall). The following requirement only applies to pass-through kitchens with cooktops or conventional ranges.

A1 In pass-through kitchens, provide 40in. (1015mm) minimum clearance between all opposing base cabinets, counter tops, appliances, or walls. **ADA Standards: 2010 804 (New)**

B Clearance: U-Shaped Kitchens

U-shaped kitchens are enclosed on three contiguous sides. The following requirement applies only to U-shaped kitchens with cooktops or conventional ranges.

B1 In U-shaped kitchens, provide 60in. (1525mm) minimum clearance between all opposing base cabinets, counter tops, appliances, or walls. **ADA Standards: 2010 804 (NEW)**

C Clear Floor Space

Clear floor space must be provided for unobstructed access to kitchen elements including appliances, shelves and sinks. Clear floor spaces are permitted to overlap.

C1 Provide a minimum clear floor space of 30in. (760mm) by 48in. (1220mm).
36in (915mm) by 54in (1390mm) preferred. ca
ADAAG: 1998 4.2 & ADA Standards: 2010 305

C2 Ensure that one completely unobstructed side of the clear floor space overlaps or adjoins an accessible route. **ADAAG: 1998 4.2 & ADA Standards: 2010 305**

D Counters

D1 Position the clear floor space at counters for a forward approach. **ADA Standards: 2010 804 (NEW)**

D2 Provide knee and toe clearance under counters for a forward approach. **ADA Standards: 2010 804 (NEW)** See RT Routes and Spaces, RT-Q.
Exception: Cabinetry under counters is permitted, provided that
  a. the cabinetry under counters can be removed without the removal or replacement of the counter;
  b. the floor extends under the cabinetry; and
  c. the walls behind and surrounding the cabinetry are finished. **ADA Standards: 2010 804 (NEW)**

D3 Ensure that the top of counter is 34in. (865mm) maximum above the floor. **ADA Standards: 2010 804 (NEW)**
Exception: An adjustable counter that provides a work surface at variable heights between 29in. (735mm) minimum and 36in. (915mm) maximum is permitted. ADA Standards: 2010 804 (NEW)

E Sinks

Sinks in kitchens and kitchenettes need to be accessible. Sinks used for custodial purposes (such as mop basins) are not required to be accessible.

E1 Where sinks are provided in a kitchen or kichenette, ensure that at least 5%, but not less than one, is accessible. **ADA Standards: 2010 202 (NEW)**
Exception: Mop or service sinks are not required to be accessible. ADA Standards: 2010 606 (NEW)

E2 Position the clear floor space for a forward approach to sinks. **ADAAG: 1998 4.24 & ADA Standards: 2010 804, 606**
Exception: A parallel approach to sinks and to wet bars is permitted where a cooktop or range is not provided. ADA Standards: 2010 606 (NEW)

E3 Mount accessible sinks so that the highest part in front (either the rim of the sink or the top of a counter) is no higher than 34in. (865mm) above the floor. **ADAAG: 1998 4.24 & ADA Standards: 2010 804, 606**
Note: The depth of a sink basin is not specifically addressed by ADA Standards, but can be determined by the maximum height of the sink or counter and the minimum amount of knee space required below the basin.
Refer to Figure FX.F.

E4 Provide a 36in. (915mm) length of counter to the right of the sink where possible. ca

F Faucets and Operable Parts on Fixtures

Lever-operated, push-type, and electronically controlled mechanisms are examples of acceptable faucet designs.

F1 Install faucets and other fixtures with controls that
  a. are operable with one hand; **ADAAG: 1998 4.18 & ADA Standards: 2010 309**
  b. do not require tight grasping, pinching, or twisting of the wrist; **ADAAG: 1998 4.18 & ADA Standards: 2010 309**
  c. are activated with a force less than or equal to 5 lbs.(22.2N); **ADAAG: 1998 4.18 & ADA Standards: 2010 309** and

    d. include temperature and pressure regulating valves. Ⓒa

F2 If you install a faucet with a self-closing valve, ensure that the faucet valve is set to remain open for at least 10 seconds. **ADAAG: 1998 4.19, 4.27 & ADA Standards: 2010 606, 309**

G **Dishwasher**

G1 Position the clear floor space for a forward or parallel approach to the dishwasher. **ADA Standards: 2010 804 (New)**

G2 Position the clear floor space adjacent to the dishwasher door. **ADA Standards: 2010 804 (New)**

G3 Ensure that when the dishwasher door is open, it does not obstruct the clear floor space for either the dishwasher or the sink. **ADA Standards: 2010 804 (New)**

G4 Provide a 36in. (915mm) length of counter on at least one side of the dishwasher where possible. Ⓒa

H **Range or Cooktop**

H1 Position the clear floor space for a forward or parallel approach to the range or cooktop. **ADA Standards: 2010 804 (New)**

H2 Where legroom is provided underneath the range or cooktop, ensure that the underside is insulated (or otherwise equipped) to protect people from burns, abrasions, or electrical shock. **ADA Standards: 2010 804 (New)**

H3 Locate controls so that people do not reach across burners. **ADA Standards: 2010 804 (New)**

H4 Provide a 24in. (610mm) length of counter on both sides of the range or cooktop where possible. Ⓒa

I **Oven**

I1 Position the clear floor space for a forward or parallel approach to the oven. **ADA Standards: 2010 804 (New)**

I2 Locate controls on front panels. **ADA Standards: 2010 804 (New)**

I3 Locate the counter adjacent to the latch side of a side-hinged oven door or to one side of a bottom-hinged oven door. **ADA Standards: 2010 804 (New)**

I4 Provide a 24in. (610mm) length of counter on at least one side of the oven where possible. Ⓒa

J **Refrigerator/Freezer**

The clear floor space in front of the refrigerator must be configured so that people can approach and open the door.

J1 Ensure that the clear floor space is
    a. positioned for a parallel approach, and
    b. offset no more than 24in. (610mm) from its centerline to the centerline of the refrigerator/freezer. **ADA Standards: 2010 804 (New)**

J2 Ensure that at least 50% of the freezer space is located a maximum of 54in. (1370mm) above the floor. **ADA Standards: 2010 804 (New)** A maximum of 48in. (1220mm) is preferred. Ⓒa

J3 Provide an 18in. (455mm) length of counter adjacent to the opening-side of the refrigerator/freezer where possible. Ⓒa

J4 Ensure that the door(s) can swing 180° to the fully open position where possible. Ⓒa

K **Washers and Dryers**

K1 Ensure that washers and dryers meet accessibility requirements. **ADA Standards: 2010 214 (New)** See VS Vending/Self-service, **VS-L through VS-N** for specific requirements.

L Controls and Operable Parts

L1 Locate all controls within the appropriate reach ranges. **ADAAG: 1998 4.2 & ADA Standards: 2010 308** See RR Reach Ranges.

Exception: Bottom-hinged doors in the open position are not required to comply with reach ranges. ADA Standards: 2010 804 (NEW)

L2 Where electrical outlets are located on either side of a sink, ensure that at least one is within the appropriate reach range. **ADA Standards: 2010 205 (NEW)** See RR Reach Ranges.

L3 Where appliances and/or electrical switches have redundant controls, ensure that at least one control is accessible. **ADA Standards: 2010 205 (NEW)**

L4 Ensure that controls are
  a. operable with one hand;
  b. do not require tight grasping, pinching, or twisting of the wrist; and
  c. are activated with a force less than or equal to 5 lbs. (22.2N). **ADAAG: 1998 4.18 & ADA Standards: 2010 309**

Exception: Appliance doors and door latching devices are not required to comply. ADA Standards: 2010 804 (NEW)

M Storage

M1 Ensure that at least 50% of shelf space is accessible. **ADA Standards: 2010 804 (NEW)** **See SG Storage** for additional storage requirements.

SG Storage

A	Clear Floor Space	247
B	Reach Ranges	247
C	Operable Parts	248
D	Storage Elements:Number and Location	248
E	Self-serve Storage Units:Number and Location	248

All people should be able to use fixed or built-in storage in public spaces. Storage falls into two categories: storage elements (such as shelves and lockers) that are provided for personal use in public spaces, and self-serve storage units that are individual units available for rent in housing projects or commercial warehouses. Some accessibility requirements apply to both types of storage. This chapter is divided into three parts, All Accessible Storage, Storage Elements, and Self-serve Storage Units.

All Accessible Storage

The following requirements pertain to both storage elements (such as shelves and lockers) and self-serve storage units.

A Clear Floor Space

Clear floor space must be provided for unobstructed access to storage.

A1 Provide a level clear floor space a minimum of 30in. (760mm) by 48in. (1220mm) configured for a forward or parallel approach. **ADAAG: 1998 4.25 & ADA Standards: 2010 811, 305** See RT Routes and Spaces.

A2 Ensure that one side of the clear floor space overlaps or adjoins an accessible route. **ADAAG: 1998 4.2 & ADA Standards: 2010 305**

B Reach Ranges

When installing storage features, consider the age and abilities of the users. Use reach ranges for adults and children as appropriate. **See RR Reach Ranges.**

Design for All: The Best Path Forward — Dr. Arvid E. Osterberg

B1 Install accessible lockers, cabinets, and other storage elements within the appropriate reach range. **ADAAG: 1998 4.25 & ADA Standards: 2010 811**

B2 Although ADA Standards does not require self-serve shelving to be within accessible reach ranges, it is recommended that they are made accessible to the maximum extent possible. 🌀

C   Operable Parts
Operable parts (such as latches and handles on lockers) should be easy to reach and use.

C1 Ensure that the heights of operable parts of accessible storage comply with reach range requirements. **ADAAG: 1998 4.25 & ADA Standards: 2010 811** See RR Reach Ranges.

C2 Provide controls and mechanisms that
   a. are operable with one hand;
   b. do not require tight grasping, pinching, or twisting of the wrist; and
   c. do not require force exceeding 5 lbs. (22.2N) to operate. **ADAAG: 1998 4.27 & ADA Standards: 2010 309**

Storage Elements
Storage elements include shelves, folding shelves, hooks, lockers, cubby holes, drawers, closets, and other storage devices for personal or individual use.

For specific information about storage located in toilet rooms and/or bathrooms and dressing, fitting, and locker rooms, **see TB Toilet/Bath Rooms, TB-N and DS Dressing Rooms, DS-G.**

D   Storage Elements: Number and Location
A portion of storage elements provided for public use in buildings must be accessible.

D1 Where lockers are provided, ensure that at least 5%, but not less than one, of each type is accessible. **ADAAG: 1998 4.1 & ADA Standards: 2010 225**

D2 Where storage elements (other than lockers) are provided, ensure that at least one of each type is accessible. **ADA Standards: 2010 225 (New)**

D3 Locate accessible storage on accessible routes. **ADAAG: 1998 4.1 & ADA Standards: 2010 225**

Self-serve Storage Units
Self-serve storage units are individual units available for rent in housing projects or commercial warehouses. In addition to the requirements below, general accessibility requirements also apply, including parking, routes, entrances, and doors. See the appropriate chapters in *Design for All* that apply.

E   Self-Serve Storage Units: Number and Location
A portion of self-serve storage units must be accessible.

E1 Provide at least the minimum required number of accessible self-serve storage units in self-serve storage facilities. **ADA Standards: 2010 225 (New)**
See SG-A

Self-service storage spaces	Accessible self-service storage spaces
1 to 200	5 %, but no fewer than 1
201 and over	10, plus 2 % of number over 200

SG-A   Minimum required number of accessible self-serve storage units

E2 Integrate accessible self-serve storage units throughout the various types and classes of units provided. **ADA Standards: 2010 225 (New)**
Exception: Accessible storage units in a multi-story building are not required to be dispersed. ADA Standards: 2010 225 (New)

AB ABA Requirements

A	Additions to Buildings	249
B	Leased Spaces, Buildings and Sites	249
C	Washing Machines and Clothes Dryers	250
D	Residential Dwelling Units	250
E	Military Residential Dwelling Units	250
F	Employee Work Areas	250

The 2010 ADA Standards contains the requirements of the Architectural Barriers Act (ABA) in addition to the requirements of the ADA. The ABA requirements apply to buildings that are designed, constructed, leased, and altered with federal funds. Examples include post offices, which are federal buildings, and public schools that are built with federal funds. The ABA also applies to buildings and sites that are leased by federal agencies. **ADA Standards: 2010 F101**

The scoping requirements for the ABA and the ADA contain some differences. The basic technical accessibility requirements (such as dimensions and features of routes and spaces, mounting heights and reach ranges of controls and other elements, and technical requirements for devices) are the same for both the ADA and ABA. To determine if the ABA requirements apply to your building or site, or to clarify the differences between the ADA and the ABA requirements, contact your regional Disability and Business Technical Assistance Center at 800-949-4232.

This chapter lists only the ABA scoping requirements that are different from the ADA requirements. The ABA reference number is also provided and is differentiated from the ADA reference by an 'F' preceding the number. For example, **ADA Standards: 2010 F202.**

For information on all areas and features in buildings and facilities covered by the ABA but not listed in this chapter, refer to and follow the requirements in all applicable chapters of *Design for All*.

A Additions to Buildings

Both the ADA and ABA require all additions to existing buildings to comply with the requirements for new construction. However, the ABA has requirements for additions that differ from, or extend beyond, the ADA requirements, as follows.

A1 When an entrance is not provided in an addition, provide at least one accessible entrance to the existing building. **ADA Standards: 2010 F202 (New)**

A2 When the only accessible entrances serving an addition are in the existing building, provide an accessible route to connect at least one existing entrance to all accessible spaces and elements within the addition. **ADA Standards: 2010 F202 (New)**

A3 When toilet rooms and/or bathing rooms are not provided in an addition, ensure that the toilet rooms and/or bathing rooms in the existing building are accessible. Where it is technically infeasible to comply with this requirement, provide an accessible single-user toilet room and/or bathing room. **ADA Standards: 2010 F202 (New)**

A4 When toilet rooms and/or bathing rooms are provided in an existing building, ensure that at least one for men and one for women are accessible. Where there is only one toilet room and/or bathing room in the existing building, it must be accessible. **ADA Standards: 2010 F202 (New)**

A5 When a public telephone is not provided in an addition, ensure that at least one public telephone in the existing building is accessible. **ADA Standards: 2010 F202 (New)**

A6 When a drinking fountain is not provided in an addition, ensure that at least one drinking fountain in the existing building is accessible. **ADA Standards: 2010 F202 (New)**

B Leased Spaces, Buildings and Sites

The ABA requirements apply when federal funds are used to lease buildings and sites, and when buildings and sites are leased by federal agencies. Buildings and sites that are leased on a temporary, emergency basis and those that are leased for twelve months or less do not need to comply with these requirements, provided that the lease may not be extended or renewed. The ABA requirements also apply to joint-use areas serving leased spaces. However, alterations and additions to joint-use areas serving leased spaces do not need to comply with ABA requirements provided that the alterations and additions are not undertaken by, or on behalf of, the federal government. The ABA has requirements for leased spaces, buildings, and sites that differ from the ADA requirements as follows.

B1 In leased spaces, accessible routes to primary function areas are required. Spaces and elements that are required to be accessible must be on accessible routes, except for fire alarm systems and assistive listening systems. **ADA Standards: 2010 F202 (New)**

B2 Where provided, ensure that at least one toilet room and/or bathing room for each sex on each floor is accessible. Where only one toilet room and/or bathing room is provided for each sex on each floor in the building, it must be accessible or an accessible single-user toilet room must be provided. **ADA Standards: 2010 F202 (New)**

B3 Fire alarms are not required to comply with the ADA requirements where existing power sources must be upgraded to meet the requirements. **ADA Standards: 2010 F202, F215 (New)**

C Washing Machines and Clothes Dryers

The ABA does not require washing machines and clothes dryers in employee work areas to be accessible.

C1 Ensure that laundry equipment provided for use by employees as part of their housing, recreation, or other accommodation is accessible (since that equipment is not used by the employee to perform job related duties). **ADA Standards: 2010 F214, 611 (New)**

D Residential Dwelling Units

The following exception to the dispersion requirement applies to the ABA but not to the ADA.

D1 Disperse accessible dwelling units among the various types of units in the building, comparable to and integrated with those available to other residents. **ADA Standards: 2010 F233 (New)**

Exception: Where buildings contain four or fewer residential dwelling units, accessible units must be dispersed among the various types of residential dwelling units in the project, comparable to and integrated with those available to other residents. **ADA Standards: 2010 F233 (New)**

D2 Where residential dwelling units are altered or added, the altered or added units must be accessible until the number of units in a project complies with the minimum number of accessible unit requirements for new construction. **ADA Standards: 2010 F233 (New)**

E Military Residential Dwelling Units

The ADA does not address military residential dwelling units. The following are requirements of the ABA.

E1 Ensure that at least 5%, but not less than one, of the total number of residential units in a military project is accessible. **ADA Standards: 2010 F233 (New)**

E2 Ensure that at least 2%, but not less than one, of the total number of residential units in a military project include accessible communication features. **ADA Standards: 2010 F233 (New)**

E3 Disperse accessible dwelling units in a military project among the various types of units, comparable to and integrated with those available to other residents. **ADA Standards: 2010 F233 (New)**

F Employee Work Areas

The ADA has specific requirements for access within employee work areas, but the ABA does not have those requirements.

Websites

Access Board
access-board.gov

ADA National Network
adata.org

ASLA Universal Design Guide
asla.org

Center for Inclusive Design and Environmental Access (IDEA)
idea.ap.buffalo.edu/

Center for Universal Design at North Carolina State University
design.ncsu.edu/research/center-for-universal-design/

Design Guideline for the Visual Environment, National Institute of Building Sciences,
nibs.org

Fair Housing Act Design Manual
huduser.gov

Inclusive Design Research Center (at OCAD University)
idrc.ocadu.ca

Institute for Human Centered Design
humancentereddesign.org

U.S. Department of Housing and Urban Development (HUD)
hud.gov

U.S. Department of Justice (DOJ)
ADA Information Line, ada.gov

List of Figures

Figure 1	Sample Page	17
Figure 2	How to determine slope	20
RR.1	Dimensions used by ADA Standards in establishing reach ranges for an adult using a wheelchair	21
RR.2	Reach range for an unobstructed front reach	22
RR.3	Reach range for a front reach over a 20in. (510mm) maximum deep obstruction	22
RR.4	Reach range for a front reach over an obstruction between 20in. (510mm) and 25in. (635mm) deep	23
RR-A	ADA Standards reach ranges for adults and children	23
RR.5	Reach range for an unobstructed or minimally obstructed side reach	24
RR.6	Reach range for an obstructed side reach	24
RR.7	Maximum and preferred height to operable parts of fixtures and dispensers	25
PA-A	Minimum required number of accessible parking spaces	27
PA.1	Three parking lots serving a building with one accessible entrance	27
PA.2	Three parking lots serving a building with three accessible entrances	28
PA.3	Three parking lots (including a satellite lot) serving a building	28
PA-B	Minimum required dimensions for accessible parking spaces	29
PA.4	Standard accessible and van accessible parking spaces and access aisles	31
PA.5	Standard accessible and van accessible angled parking spaces and access aisles	31
PA.6	Passenger loading zone design	32
PA.7	International symbol of accessibility	34
CR.1	A 48in (1220mm) wide landing at the top of a curb ramp with preferred side flares slope	37
CR.2	Hazardous side flares at a curb ramp	37
CR.3	Recommended gently sloped side flares at a curb ramp	38
CR.4	Excessive slopes at street and curb ramp intersection	38
CR.5	Maximum slopes at a street and curb ramp intersection	38
CR.6	A landing less than 48in (1220mm) wide at the top of the curb ramp with preferred slope of side flares	39
CR.7	Curb ramps with returned curbs in an urban area	40
CR.8	Curb ramp with returned curbs in a residential area	40
CR.9	Minimum space between a diagonal curb ramp and the intersection of a marked cross walk	40
CR.10	Crossing through island at street level	41
CR.11	Crossing through island with curb ramps	41
CR.12	Truncated domes	43
CR.13	Detectable warning perpendicular to direction of travel	43
RT.1	Preferred minimum route width for a wheelchair	48
RT.2	Preferred minimum route width for a pedestrian to pass a wheelchair	48
RT.3	Preferred minimum dimensions for a route with protrusions less than 24 inches in length	48
RT.4	Preferred minimum route width for two wheelchairs to pass	49
RT.5	Preferred minimum clear space for turning around and passing	50
RT.6	Preferred minimum clear space for turning around and passing	50
RT.7	Preferred minimum space at a T-shaped intersection for turning around	50
RT.8	Preferred minimum space at a T-shaped intersection for passing	50
RT.9	Preferred minimum space needed for maneuvering between display cases in an exhibition area	51
RT.10	Preferred minimum dimensions for maneuvering around a display case that is less than 48 inches wide	51
RT.11	Preferred minimum dimensions for maneuvering around a display case that is more than 48 inches wide	51
RT.13	A wheelchair user struggling to travel straignt on a sidewalk with excessive cross slope	52
RT.12	Preferred minimum dimensions for a route with turns around obstructions	52
RT.15	Level change with a beveled edge	54
RT.16	Grate opening orientation	55
RT.17	Maximum allowable grate opening in the dominant direction of travel	55

RT.18	Minimum headroom in an accessible route	56
RT.19	A warning barrier used to alert people of limited headroom	56
RT.20	Person using a cane to detect obstacles in a route while passing an allowable protrusion	57
RT.21	Objects mounted between posts and required clearances	57
RT.22	Maximum overhangs for objects mounted on a post	57
RT.24	Preferred minimum clear floor space for a forward approach (front reach) into a shallow alcove	58
RT.23	Minimum headroom and protruding tolerances in an accessible route	58
RT.25	Preferred minimum clear floor space for a parallel approach (side reach) into a shallow alcove	59
RT.26	Preferred minimum clear floor space for a forward approach (front reach) in a deep alcove	59
RT.27	Preferred minimum clear floor space for a parallel approach (side reach) in a deep alcove	59
RT.28	Preferred unobstructed legroom	60
RT.29	Preferred minimum legroom width	60
RT.30	Toe clearance and knee clearance	60
RT.31	Legroom with reduced knee clearance	61
RT.32	Preferred maximum height to the bottom of corridor windows	63
RP-A	Maximum ramp run permitted for various slopes	66
RP.1	Ramp with top and bottom landings, handrails, and handrail extensions	67
RP.2	Accessible handrail dimensions and profiles	69
RP.3	Accessible recessed handrail profile	69
RP.4	Preferred minimum landing dimensions for a ramp	70
RP.5	Ramp with extended platform edge protection	71
RP.6	Ramp with edge protection walls and handrails	71
RP.7	Ramp with edge protection curbs and handrails	71
RP.8	Ramp with edge protection rails and handrails	71
DR.1	Door and doorway components	77
DR.2	Preferred space between two hinged doors in a series that swing in the same direction	79
DR.3	Preferred space between two hinged doors in a series that swing in opposite directions	79
DR.4	How to measure the clear opening at a doorway with a hinged door	79
DR.5	How to measure the clear opening at a pocket door or sliding door	80
DR.6	How to measure the clear opening at a folding door	80
DR.8	Minimum clear opening at a door that does not require full passage	81
DR.9	How to measure maneuvering space at a doorway with a hinged door	81
DR.10	Preferred minimum maneuvering space for a front approach to the pull face of a door	82
DR.11	Preferred minimum maneuvering space for a front approach to the pull face of a door recessed 8in.	82
DR.12	Preferred minimum maneuvering space for a front approach to the push face of a door with a closer and latch	82
DR.13	Preferred minimum maneuvering space for a front approach to the push face of a door without a closer and latch	83
DR.14	Preferred minimum maneuvering space for a hinge side approach to the pull face of a door	83
DR.15	Preferred minimum maneuvering space for a handle side approach to the pull face of a door	84
DR.16	Preferred minimum maneuvering space for a hinge side approach to the push face of a door with a closer and latch	84
DR.17	Preferred minimum maneuvering space for a hinge side approach to the push face of a door without a closer and latch	84
DR.18	Preferred minimum maneuvering space for a handle side approach to the pull face of a door with a closer and latch	85
DR.19	Preferred minimum maneuvering space for a handle side approach to the pull face of a door without a closer and latch	85
DR.20	Preferred minimum maneuvering space for a handle side approach to the push face of a door with a closer and latch	85
DR.21	Preferred minimum maneuvering space for a handle side approach to the push face of a door without a closer and latch	86
DR.22	Preferred minimum maneuvering space for 1) a front approach to a folding or sliding door, and 2) at a passageway without a door	86
DR.23	Preferred minimum maneuvering space for 1) a handle side approach at a folding or sliding door, and 2) at a passageway without a door	86

DR.24	*Preferred* minimum maneuvering space for 1) a recess side or fold side approach to a folding or sliding door, and 2) at a passageway without a door	87
DR.25	Headroom and placement of a door closer or stop at a doorway or passageway	87
DR.26	Level changes at a threshold with beveled edges	88
DR.28	Smooth surface or kickplate on a door	90
DR.27	Placement of an auxiliary door handle on a door without a closer	90
DR.29	Vision lite in a door	91
EL.1	Elevator controls and indicators on the hallway side at an elevator entrance	95
EL.2	Elevator with a centered door	97
EL.3	Elevator with a side an off-centered door	98
EL.4	Elongated elevator with a centered or off-centered door	98
EL.5	Square elevator with a centered or off-centered door	98
EL-A	Minimum elevator car dimensions, door placement, and clear door width	99
EL.6	Elevator controls inside an elevator car	101
EL.7	Standard symbols used on elevator car control buttons	102
EL.8	Placement of designations on an elevator car control panel	102
PL.1	Platform lift with end doors	109
PL.2	Platform lift with a side door and an end door	109
ST.1	Stair components	112
ST.2	Accessible stair profiles	112
ST.3	A continuous stair handrail at a switch-back	114
ST.4	Handrail with the required extension at the bottom of a stair flight	115
ST.5	Handrail with the required horizontal extension at the top of a stair flight	115
ST.6	Accessible handrail dimensions and profiles	116
ST.7	Accessible recessed handrail profile	117
AR.1	Area of refuge located in a stairway	126
SN.1	A sign with visual and tactile characters, a pictogram, and Braille	130
SN.2	Placement of a sign at a door	131
SN-A	Required dimensions for Grade 2 Braille	133
SN.3	Minimum required headroom for an overhead sign	134
SN.4	International Symbol of Accessibility	136
SN.5	International Symbol of TTY	136
SN.6	International Symbol of Volume Controlled Telephones	136
SN.7	International Symbol of Assistive Listening Systems	136
TB.1	Minimum and *preferred* clearances for an accessible public restroom entrance without a door	141
TB.2	Ambulatory accessible and wheelchair-accessible stalls in a public bathroom	144
TB.3	*Preferred* minimum clearances for a restroom entrance with a door and closer	146
TB.4	Required legroom dimensions at accessible fixtures or counters	147
TB.5	Permitted reduced knee clearance	148
TB.6	Reach ranges for accessible storage shelves	148
TS.1	*Preferred* minimum maneuvering clearance for a latch side approach to a wheelchair accessible stall	151
TS.2	*Preferred* maneuvering clearance for both hinge side and latch side approaches to a wheelchair accessible toilet stall	151
TS.3	*Preferred* minimum clear door width for both a wheelchair accessible and a ambulatory accessible toilet stall	151
TS.4	*Preferred* placement of the toilet	153
TS.5	Grab bar on a side wall or partition in an accessible toilet stall	154
TS.6	Grab bar on the rear wall in a wheelchair accessible toilet stall	154
TS.7	Toilet paper dispensers in an accessible toilet stall	155
TS.8	End-of-row wheelchair accessible toilet stall	156

TS.9	Wheelchair accessible toilet stall width	156
TS.10	Wheelchair accessible toilet stall depth for a wall-hung toilet	157
TS.11	Wheelchair accessible toilet stall depth for a floor-mounted toilet	157
TS.12	Dimensions for toe clearance under a toilet stall partition	158
TS.13	Ambulatory accessible toilet stall	158
UR.1	Mounting dimensions for a wall-hung urinal	159
FX.1	Maximum and preferred height for operable parts of fixtures and dispensers	162
FX.2	Legroom height under a lavatory	162
FX.3	Minimum required legroom dimensions under a counter	163
FX.4	Permitted reduced knee clearance	163
FX.5	Accessible faucet control	165
FX.6	Mouting heights for a mirror above a lavatory	165
FX.7	Accessible light switch	167
SS.1	Transfer shower stall dimensions	169
SS.2	Grab bar heights in transfer and roll-in shower stalls	170
SS.3	Control heights in transfer and roll-in shower stalls	170
SS.4	Standard roll-in shower stall with a folding seat	171
SS.5	Alternative roll-in shower stall with a folding seat	171
SE.1	Dimensions for bathtub seats	173
SE.2	A rectangular shower stall seat	174
SE.3	An L-shaped shower stall seat	175
BT.1	Preferred clear floor space for a parallel approach to a bathtub with an in-tub or portable seat	176
BT.2	Preferred clear floor space for a forward approach to a bathtub with an in-tub or portable seat	176
BT.3	Preferred clear floor space for a parallel approach to a bathtub with a permanent seat	177
BT.4	Grab bars and controls in a bathtub with a permanent seat	178
BT.5	Grab bars and controls in a bathtub with an in-tub or portable seat	178
GB.1	Grab bar profiles and dimensions	180
DF.1	Preferred minimum clear floor space at a wheelchair accessible drinking fountain	185
DF.2	Preferred minimum clear floor space for a forward approach to a drinking fountain in a deep alcove	185
DF.3	Spout height and location for a wheelchair accessible drinking fountain	186
PT.1	International Symbol of Volume Controlled Telephones	188
PT-A	Minimum required number of wheelchair accessible public telephones	188
PT.2	Parallel approach to a wheelchair accessible telephone with an enclosure or privacy panel	188
PT.3	Forward approach to a wheelchair accessible telephone with a counter	189
PT.4	TTY keypad height	190
PT.5	The International Symbol of TTY	191
TA.1	Height of a wheelchair accessible dining or work surface	193
TA.2	Unobstructed legroom under a table	194
TA.3	Preferred minimum legroom width under a table	194
TA.4	An accessible bench	195
VS.1	Preferred minimum clear floor space for a forward approach to reach controls	197
VS.2	Preferred minimum clear floor space for a forward approach in a deep alcove to reach controls	197
VS.3	Preferred minimum clear floor space for a parallel approach in a deep alcove to reach controls	198
VS.4	Preferred unobstructed front reach range	198
VS.5	Preferred reach range for an unobstructed or minimally obstructed side reach	199
VS.6	Preferred reach range for an obstructed side reach	199
AA.1	Lines of sight over seated spectators	212
AA.2	Lines of sight over standing spectators	212
AA.3	Minimum width for a single wheelchair space	213

AA.4	Preferred minimum width for each of two or more adjacent wheelchair spaces	213
AA-B	Required number of assistive listening receivers and hearing-aid compatible receivers per capacity	215
LB.1	Preferred minimum dimensions for a route with turns through library stacks	217
BU.1	An accessible sale and service counter configured for a parallel approach	225
BU-A	Minimum number of required accessible checkout aisles for new construction over 5000sq. ft. (1500sq. m)	225
MC.1	Preferred minimum clear floor space and unobstructed turning space in an accessible sleeping room	243
SG-A	Minimum required number of accessible self-serve storage units	248

Index

A

Access aisles 15, 26, 29-36, 40, 42, 219-220, 252
Accessible spaces 15-16, 26-27, 29-30, 34-35, 45, 61, 63, 130, 135, 207, 210, 233, 236, 243, 249
Adjacent to parking 34
Alarms 3, 21, 103, 119-122, 140, 208-210, 230, 233, 235, 240, 250
Alterations 6, 8-12, 36, 38, 44, 46-47, 65-66, 72, 74, 76, 78, 106-107, 110-112, 114, 120, 122-123, 126, 140-141, 144, 160-161, 204-206, 218, 220, 225, 228, 230-231, 235, 238-239, 241-242, 250
    At doors 79-80, 87, 91, 128, 242
    At elevators 94, 96
    At entrances 48, 75, 91, 238, 240
    At medical care facilities 241
    At parking 34
    At TTYs 190
Audible 19, 96, 100, 103-104, 119-121, 127, 196, 200, 209-210, 215, 227, 240
Auditoriums 9, 208, 210
Automatic 72-73, 75-77, 88, 91-94, 99, 103, 105, 112, 123-126, 130, 139, 153, 160, 164, 187, 196, 199-200, 219, 234
Automatic Leveling 93-94
Auxiliary 88, 120-122, 177, 227, 233, 254

B

Barriers 8-9, 11, 19, 44, 54, 56, 63, 70, 203, 216, 218, 222, 227, 249
Bars 3, 9, 88, 99, 139, 142-144, 150, 153-155, 158, 160, 167-170, 172, 175, 177, 179-181, 191, 194-195, 219, 221, 229, 231, 233, 245, 255
Bathroom 140-147, 161-162, 173, 207, 231, 233, 238, 254
Bathrooms 3, 139-150, 160-162, 164, 168, 177, 204, 206, 233, 235, 237, 239, 241, 243-244, 248
Benches 45, 106, 191, 194-196, 228-229
Boarding houses 230
Bollards 34, 63, 216, 218, 222, 227
Book drops 219
Booths 106, 191, 209, 219, 221
Braille 75, 97, 101-102, 104, 127, 129-130, 132-134, 200, 254
Built-up 36, 40
Businesses 3, 191, 203, 219, 221-223, 225, 227, 234, 242, 244

C

Cafeterias 208, 219
Children's Reach Ranges 21, 25
Classrooms 5, 90, 164, 210
Clear opening 76, 79-81, 88, 91, 105, 108, 253
Clear opening width 76, 79-80, 108
Clear width 33, 36, 49, 51, 56, 66-69, 76, 78, 80, 91, 97, 99-100, 105, 107, 110, 112, 116, 124, 151, 222, 226, 229, 231, 233
Closers 76-78, 81, 87-89, 131, 150
Coat hooks 21, 140, 148-150, 155, 160, 165, 230
Common areas 120, 140, 160, 164, 201, 208-209, 230, 234-237, 241, 244
Communication accessible 235-237, 239-240
Communication systems 103-104, 127, 237
Concert halls 9, 210
Controls 19, 21-22, 24-25, 28, 44, 61, 63, 66, 92-95, 97, 100-102, 104-105, 107-109, 127, 139-140, 145, 147-148, 150, 153, 159-160, 163-164, 167-179, 181, 183-184, 186-187, 189-190, 194, 196-199, 201, 208-209, 216, 222, 226, 233-234, 239-240, 244-249, 254-255
Correctional facilities 11, 14, 203
Corridors 19, 44-46, 56, 62, 89, 120, 208, 236
Counters 59, 144-147, 160-162, 164, 191, 193, 209, 215-216, 218-219, 221-222, 224-226, 234, 241-242, 244-245, 254
Cross slope 20, 37, 52-53, 65-66, 252
Curb cut 36, 38
Curb ramps 3, 19-20, 33, 35-42, 44, 52-55, 65, 241, 252
Curbs 33, 36, 39-40, 54, 56, 71, 167-168, 252-253
    Definition of 208

D

Department of Justice 6, 10-12, 223, 230, 235, 251
Depositories 183, 196-199, 216, 219
Destination-oriented 93, 104
Detectable warnings 32, 36, 41-42, 44, 54-55
Diagonal 36, 40-41, 252
Dining 191-193, 219-221, 233, 255
Dining areas 219-220
Dining surfaces 191-192, 220-221
Disability 8, 12, 14, 36, 42, 203, 205, 222, 235, 238, 249
Dispensers 21, 24-25, 61, 140, 145, 148-150, 154-155, 161-162, 164, 181, 196, 252, 254-255
Displays 51, 127, 204, 207, 216-217, 222, 226-227, 234
Doorbells 240

Doors 3, 5, 13-14, 16, 19, 45, 48, 62, 65, 69-70, 72-84, 86-93, 97-100, 104-109, 114, 122-124, 126-128, 130-132, 139-142, 145-146, 149-152, 158, 196, 201, 203-204, 209, 223, 228-230, 233, 235-236, 240-243, 247-248, 253-254
Doorway 14, 70, 74, 76-88, 236, 253-254
Double-Leaf 76, 78, 81
Dressing rooms 3, 195, 203, 228, 248
Drinking fountains 3, 10, 21, 46, 64, 66, 183-186, 205, 210
Dryers 24, 139, 161-162, 196, 201, 234, 244, 246, 249-250
Dwelling units 3, 45, 93, 120, 140, 168, 203, 230, 235-240, 244, 249-250

E

Edge protection 40, 53-54, 65, 67, 70-71, 111, 253
Egress 3, 62-63, 72, 78-79, 81, 93-94, 107, 110-112, 116, 119, 122-128, 130, 210-211, 218, 227
Electric carts 12-13, 139
Electronic and information technology 14, 203
Elevator doors 93, 97, 99-100, 105
Elevators 3, 19, 45-47, 62, 65, 93-101, 103-106, 110, 122-124, 127-128, 130, 197, 203-204, 209, 211, 223, 230, 242
Employee 45, 120, 208-209, 249-250
Employee work areas 45, 120, 208-209, 249-250
Enclosures 127, 167-168, 175, 179, 188-190
Entrances 3, 5, 13, 15, 19, 26-28, 30, 33, 44-45, 47-48, 62, 64-65, 69, 72-75, 88, 91, 93, 96, 106-107, 123, 131, 139, 168, 183, 203-206, 208-211, 216, 218, 223, 227, 230, 235-236, 238, 240-241, 248-249, 252
Exhibits 204, 207
Existing buildings 8-9, 11-12, 14, 47, 66, 72, 80, 111, 119, 121, 123, 126, 145, 150, 204-205, 228, 235, 238-239, 242, 249
Fair Housing Act 235, 251
Fare Vending Machines 197, 199-200
Faucets 144, 160-161, 164, 168, 170, 178, 244-245
Fitting rooms 228
Fixtures 3, 16, 21, 24-25, 59, 61, 121, 139-140, 142, 144-150, 155, 159-162, 164, 166, 168-169, 176, 178, 183, 193, 208-209, 231, 244-245, 252, 254-255
Flared sides 36-41
Floor surfaces 19, 55, 64, 93, 100, 106, 109-110, 140, 145-146, 203-204, 213, 223
Flush controls 150, 153, 159-160

Folding 14, 76, 80-81, 86-87, 89, 170-174, 214, 231, 237, 248, 253-255
  For areas of refuge 125, 127
  For Assistive Listening Systems 136
  For businesses 219
  For children 25, 166
  For fixtures 162
  For historic buildings and sites 205
  For parking 33-34, 216, 222, 227, 241
  For ramps 53, 65-66, 130
  For routes 228
  For signs 61, 130, 134
  For stairs 124
  For toilet 141, 237
  For vending 222
Front reach 21-23, 58-59, 61, 198, 252-253, 255

G

Gates 56, 63, 72, 76-78, 91, 99, 106-107, 123, 197, 209, 218, 220, 227
Glazing 46, 222, 226
Grab bars 3, 139, 142-144, 150, 153-155, 158, 167-170, 172, 175, 177, 179-181, 194-195, 229, 231, 255
Grates and Openings 44, 55

H

Halfway houses 230
Hall call buttons 93, 95-96
Hall Signals 93, 96, 104
Hallways 46, 56, 238
Handrails 36, 41, 47, 53, 56, 65-71, 93, 99, 106, 109-116, 124, 253
Hazards 7, 33-36, 38-39, 45, 53-55, 63, 65-66, 69, 78-79, 87-88, 92, 112-113, 119, 146, 169, 221
Headroom 44, 56-58, 76, 87, 106-107, 127, 134, 253-254
Historic Preservation 3, 12, 45, 203-206
Homeless shelters 10, 230
Horizontal exit 94, 112, 122-125, 127
Hospitals 9, 241-242
Hotels 9, 11-12, 203, 224, 230, 235, 244
HUD housing 14, 47, 203
Illumination Levels 93, 100, 129, 136
  In areas of refuge 127
  In assembly areas 62, 67, 106, 114, 130, 210-212, 214
  In bathtubs 173
  In businesses 222, 244

In doorways 87, 89
In dressing, fitting, and locker rooms 228
In elevators 93, 99-101
In kitchens 244-245
In libraries 218
In medical care 140, 142, 168, 228, 241-242
In medical care facilities 140, 142, 228, 241-242
In Platform Lifts 106, 109
In restaurants 224
In roll-in shower stalls 173
In single-user toilet rooms 142, 153-154
In toilet 142, 145-148, 150, 155-157, 164, 248
In toilet stalls 155-157
In transfer shower stalls 173
In transient lodging 140, 174, 201, 233, 244
In work areas 164, 209

J
Judicial facilities 47

K
Kickplates 76, 89-90
Kitchenettes 160, 208, 233, 237, 244-245
Kitchens 3, 203, 233, 235, 237, 244-245
Knee clearance 59-61, 146-148, 163, 193-194, 253-255

L
Landings 36-37, 40-41, 47, 63, 65-67, 69-71, 73, 94, 100, 107, 110, 112-114, 253
Lavatories 144, 147-149, 160-162, 164-166, 169, 171, 176
Lecture halls 5, 9, 90, 210, 215
Legroom 23, 44, 59-61, 140, 146-147, 160-163, 176, 184-186, 191-194, 196, 199, 220-221, 246, 253-255
Legroom under 59-60, 146-147, 162-163, 192-194, 220-221, 255
Level changes 26, 30, 33, 36, 44, 53-55, 59, 65, 69, 87-88, 108, 111, 193, 221, 254
Libraries 3, 10, 191, 203, 216-218
Light levels 100
Limited Use 93, 105
Lines of sight 210-212, 255
Lobby 125, 127, 237
Locker rooms 195, 203, 208, 228-230, 248
Lockers 228, 230, 247-248
Long-term care 168, 241-242

M
Mailbox 236
Mailboxes 196-197, 225, 235-236
Maneuvering space 13, 48, 56, 69-70, 74, 76-78, 81-87, 91-92, 108, 145, 149-150, 168, 191, 209, 231, 233, 238, 253-254
Marking 26, 29, 34, 110
Measuring 20, 29, 37, 52, 76, 79, 162, 222, 229
Measuring slopes 20, 37, 52
Medical care 3, 26, 45, 140, 142, 168, 203, 228, 230, 233, 241-242
Medicine cabinets 160-161, 165
Meters 15, 26, 35
Mezzanines 47, 94, 211, 219, 223
Military 249-250
Mirrors 110, 121, 144, 148, 160-161, 165, 228-229
Motels 9, 12, 191, 203, 224, 230, 235, 244
Movie theaters 210, 215

N
National Fire Protection Association (NFPA) 125
Nosings 110, 113, 115
Notation System 8, 14

O
Obstructions 19, 21, 35, 51-52, 59, 61, 68, 87, 116, 119, 146-147, 149-150, 163, 193-194, 198, 216, 252
Offset hinges 80
On ramps 66, 68
On stairs 110, 112, 115
Opening force 76, 88-89, 92, 100

P
Parking 3, 5, 15-16, 19-20, 26-36, 40, 42, 44, 48, 64, 73, 112, 124, 130, 197, 206, 208, 216, 219, 222, 227, 233, 235-236, 241, 248, 252
Passageway 74, 76, 78, 86-87, 253-254
Passageways 14, 44, 62, 72, 74, 76, 86
Passenger loading zones 15, 20, 26, 29, 32-35, 44
Passing space 49
Patient sleeping rooms 241-244
Peepholes 236, 240
Pictograms 61-62, 101, 104, 129-130, 133-134, 136
Platform lifts 3, 19, 45, 47, 93, 106-109, 123, 211, 221
Platforms 42-43, 55, 100, 211, 217, 219, 221, 223, 226
Play areas 11, 14, 203

Pocket 14, 80, 86, 253
Portable 140, 143, 173, 175-177, 187, 189-190, 233, 255
Power-assist 73
Power-assisted doors 91-92, 107
Primary function area 10, 46, 141
Private use 6, 140-142, 145
Program accessibility 9
Protruding objects 44, 56, 181, 189
Public Accommodations 9, 12
Public areas 63, 120, 140-141, 242
Public telephones 3, 183, 187-190, 226, 230, 241-242, 255

Q
Qualified historic buildings 204-207
Queues 218, 220, 225

R
Raised platforms 217, 219, 221, 223, 226
Ramps 3, 5, 12-13, 19-20, 26, 33, 35-42, 44-47, 52-55, 65-68, 70-71, 73, 99, 106, 109, 130, 203-205, 221, 223, 241, 252
Reach Ranges 3, 19, 21, 23, 25, 61, 63, 78, 92, 101, 107-109, 140, 144, 147-148, 153, 155, 162-163, 165-167, 178-179, 181, 183, 189, 194, 196, 198, 201, 217, 222, 226, 233, 236, 239, 243-244, 247-249, 252, 254
Readily accessible 9-10
Readily achievable 11, 217, 222-223, 227
Recreation facilities 11, 47, 203
Referencing Key 8, 15
Regulatory facilities 11, 14, 203
Residential facilities 120, 201
Restaurants 3, 9, 11, 45, 191, 203, 219, 224, 234, 236
Restrooms 3, 5, 10, 13, 19, 46, 64, 93, 120, 130, 139-145, 149, 155, 158-160, 162, 164, 166, 181, 203-206, 208-210, 216, 219, 222-223, 227-228, 230, 234, 237, 241, 244
Returned curbs 36, 39-40, 252
Revolving 76, 78
Revolving doors 76, 78
Risers 110-114
Roll-in shower stalls 167-168, 170-174, 255

Routes 3, 5, 7, 19-20, 22-23, 26, 29-30, 32-37, 41-42, 44-51, 53-57, 61-66, 68, 72-73, 75, 81, 93, 97-98, 100, 108, 111-113, 115, 117, 120, 122-124, 126, 128-129, 139-140, 145-146, 148, 159, 161-162, 183-185, 188-189, 192-193, 196-197, 199, 203-211, 216-226, 228-231, 233-236, 238-239, 241, 243, 245, 247-250
Routes and Spaces 3, 7, 19, 22-23, 45, 63, 66, 72, 81, 97-98, 108, 112-113, 123, 140, 145-146, 148, 159, 161-162, 185, 189, 199, 206, 208-211, 216-222, 224-226, 228-231, 233-236, 238-239, 243, 245, 247, 249
Route width 44, 48-49, 51, 56, 114, 252
Running slope 20, 37, 52, 65-66

S
Safety 3, 5-8, 13, 15, 19, 33, 35-36, 42, 44, 59, 66, 77-78, 90, 93-94, 106-107, 110-113, 119-120, 122-127, 146, 153-154, 169, 172, 177, 179, 181, 193, 205, 211, 221-222, 226
Sales and service 191, 221-222, 224-225, 234
Seating 3, 45, 49, 67, 114, 139, 149, 183, 191-193, 195, 210-217, 219-221, 224, 234
Security 44, 63, 77, 216, 218, 220, 222, 226-227
Self-serve 3, 183, 196, 209, 219, 222, 225, 234, 247-248, 256
Self-service machines 183, 196-199, 219, 222
Service ramps 65
Shelves 21, 52, 139-140, 148-150, 155, 160-161, 165, 187, 189-190, 209, 216-217, 222-223, 226-228, 230, 233-234, 239, 244-245, 247-248, 254
Shower stalls 3, 139, 142, 145, 167-175, 180, 237, 255
Side lites 76, 90, 240
Side reach 21-22, 24, 59, 61, 198-199, 222, 252-253, 255
Signs 3, 15, 19, 26, 32, 34-35, 44-46, 56, 61-62, 64, 72, 75-76, 92-94, 97, 102-104, 119, 122, 124-125, 127-137, 139-140, 143, 145, 187, 189, 191, 200, 206-207, 214-217, 222, 227, 236
Sinks 139, 145-147, 160-162, 164-166, 176, 209, 244-245
Sliding 14, 76, 80, 86-90, 105, 123, 253-254
Slope 15, 19-20, 26, 33, 36-40, 44, 52-53, 55, 59, 65-66, 68-69, 87, 108, 112-114, 193, 213, 252
Speakers' lecterns 221
Speakers' platforms 211
Spray units 167-168, 170-172, 175, 179
Stacks 51-52, 216-217, 256
Stadiums 9, 210
Stage 210
Stairs 3, 19, 44, 46-48, 110-116, 123-125, 127-128, 203-204, 211, 221, 223

Stairways 56, 62, 73, 93, 110-115, 117, 122-124, 128
Standard 9-10, 12-13, 15, 20, 26-27, 29-31, 54, 56, 93-94, 98, 102, 104, 121, 144-145, 167-168, 170-174, 187, 200, 215, 252, 254-255
Storage 2-3, 148, 201, 203, 207, 213, 228, 230, 233, 236, 239, 244, 247-248, 254, 256
Stores 9, 73, 191, 203, 227, 236
Surfaces 19-20, 26, 32-39, 41-42, 44, 52-55, 59, 63-68, 76, 87, 89-90, 93, 100, 106, 109-110, 112-113, 115-116, 121, 136, 140, 145-146, 160, 164, 180, 191-193, 196, 199, 203-204, 207, 213, 217, 220-221, 223
Symbols 19, 101-102, 129-130, 133, 135-136, 199, 254

T

Tactile 61-62, 70, 97, 101-102, 110, 124, 127-134, 137, 196, 199-201, 254
Technical Assistance 6, 14, 36, 42, 119, 203, 222, 235, 238, 249
Technical infeasibility 10
Telecommunications Act 187
Telephones 3, 10, 19, 46, 136, 183, 187-191, 205, 226-227, 230, 233-234, 241-242, 254-255
Text telephones 187
Theaters 9, 210, 215
Threshold 76, 78, 87-88, 108, 254
Thresholds 76, 78, 87-88, 91, 100, 168
Ticket counters 224, 226
Toe clearance 59-60, 108, 146-147, 150, 156-158, 162-163, 166, 185-186, 193-194, 199, 218, 224, 228-229, 245, 253, 255
Toilet 3, 90, 139-159, 161-162, 164, 166, 180-181, 204-208, 216, 219, 222, 228, 230, 233, 235, 237, 241, 243-244, 248-250, 254-255
Toilet paper 139, 150, 154-155, 181, 254
Toilet stalls 3, 139-140, 142-146, 149-151, 153-158, 166, 180
Transfer Shower Stalls 167, 169-170, 173, 237
Transient lodging 3, 12, 45, 120, 140, 168, 171, 173-174, 201, 203, 230, 233, 235, 244
Transportation 8, 10-11, 14, 19, 32, 36, 42, 44, 47, 203, 206, 223
Traveling surfaces 20, 33, 36-37, 41, 44, 52, 55, 65-66, 76, 87, 113
Treads 110-113
Tread Surfaces 110, 113
Truncated domes 42-43, 252
TTY 136, 187, 189-191, 237, 242, 254-255
Tub 3, 139, 142, 173, 175-179, 231, 233

Turning space 49, 97-98, 145, 150, 176, 233, 243, 256
Turnstiles 76, 78, 218, 220, 227

U

Under drinking fountains 185-186
Under fixtures 147, 164
Under tables 193, 220
Universal design 12, 81, 144, 208, 251
Urinals 3, 139, 143-144, 158-159

V

Valet 26, 28
Valet parking 26, 28
Van 15, 26-27, 29-31, 33, 35, 130, 252
Vending 3, 21, 24, 183, 196-197, 199-200, 208, 219, 222, 234, 236, 246
Vertical access 44, 46-48, 66, 93, 110-111, 203-204, 207, 210-211, 219, 223, 241-242
Vertical clearance 29-30, 33, 56, 107, 190
Vestibules 72, 75, 145
Vision Lites 76, 90
Visual 7, 19, 21, 36, 42, 54, 56, 61-62, 95-96, 101, 103, 105, 110, 113-114, 117, 119-122, 124, 127-132, 134-135, 145, 196-197, 200, 209-210, 217, 227, 230, 233-234, 236, 240, 251, 254
Volume control 187, 234

W

Washers 24, 196, 201, 234, 244, 246
Washers and Dryers 24, 196, 201, 244, 246
Waste receptacles 140, 149, 197
Wheelchair accessible 3, 143-144, 150-151, 153-159, 184-190, 193, 211, 213, 235-238, 254-255
Wheelchair lifts 29, 106
Wheelchairs 8, 12-13, 15-16, 21-22, 36-39, 44, 49, 51-52, 55, 59-60, 65, 70, 79, 83, 87-90, 97, 106-107, 125-127, 130, 139-140, 143, 146-149, 155-156, 162, 167-170, 180, 184, 191, 205, 208, 210, 212, 217-218, 221-222, 227, 238, 241, 252
Windows 19, 44, 62-63, 90, 121, 160, 167, 215, 226, 253
Work areas 3, 45, 120, 164, 203, 207-209, 249-250
Work surfaces 191-193, 217